Antique Trader

FURNITURE

PRICE GUIDE

3rd Edition

Edited by Kyle Husfloen

©2008 Krause Publications

Published by

krause publications

An Imprint of F+W Publications

700 East State Street • Iola, WI 54990-0001
715-445-2214 • 888-457-2873
www.krausebooks.com

Our toll-free number to place an order or obtain
a free catalog is (800) 258-0929.

Library of Congress Control Number: 2007934359

ISBN-13: 978-0-89689-670-3
ISBN-10: 0-89689-670-6

Designed by Wendy Wendt
Edited by Kyle Husfloen

Printed in China

TABLE OF CONTENTS

INTRODUCTION

For the past decade Antique Trader Books has published a series of furniture price guides, and I'm happy to introduce our all-new edition. As in the past, we feature a comprehensive guide to all styles of furniture from the 17th century through the 20th. A majority of the pieces listed here are American-made, but we also provide a good cross section of examples from England, France, Europe and the Orient. There is something here for everyone.

As always, we strive to provide the most accurate and detailed descriptions for each piece as well as provide a number of special features that make this not only a pricing guide but a good reference for anyone interested in furniture. We include here nearly 1,200 individual listings with nearly 1,150 of them illustrated with full-color photographs. Some of the special features we provide include a Furniture Dating Chart, an illustrated guide to American Furniture Terms, a Select Bibliography for books on furniture, an appendix listing a number of Auction Services and a well-illustrated section with Stylistic Guide-

lines to American and English Furniture.

In order to bring you the most comprehensive price guide, I was given great assistance from a number of auction houses who were kind enough to provide me with high-resolution digital images on CDs. These firms include:

Christie's, New York, New York : (212) 636-2000; Web - www.christies.com

James Julia, Fairfield, Maine: (207) 453-7125; Web - www.jamesjulia.net

Neal Auctions, New Orleans, Louisiana: (504) 899-5329; Web - www.nealauctions.com

Skinner, Inc., Bolton, Massachusetts: (978) 779-6241; Web - www.skinnerinc.com

Garth's, Delaware, Ohio: (740) 362-4771; Web - www.garths.com

Other illustrations were provided by the following auction houses: Alderfers, Hatfield, Pennsylvania; Bonhams & Butterfields, San Francisco, California; Brunk Auctions,

Asheville, North Carolina; Charlton Hall Galleries, Columbia, South Carolina; New Orleans Auctions, New Orleans, Louisiana; David Rago Arts & Crafts, Lambertville, New Jersey; Sloans & Kenyon, Chevy Chase, Maryland; and Treadway Gallery, Cincinnati, Ohio.

I sincerely hope that this new *Antique Trader Furniture Price Guide* will provide you with the most useful and comprehensive furniture price guide available. Our coverage all of the major types of American and European furniture should give

collectors, dealers, auctioneers and students or American material culture an invaluable reference to add to their libraries. I always welcome letters from our readers, and I will do my best to reply if you have questions about this volume. Happy collecting!

Kyle Husfloen, Editor

Please note: Though listings have been double-checked and every effort has been made to insure accuracy, neither the editor nor publisher can assume responsibility for any losses that might be incurred as a result of consulting this guide, or of errors, typographical or otherwise.

ON THE COVER: Upper left - Victorian Novelty armchair composed of elk antlers, Germany, late 19th c., **$690**; lower left - Victorian Rococo style chest of drawers, ebonized and painted wood, Philadelphia, ca. 1845, **$2,185**; right - Federal country style step-back wall cupboard, New England, early 19th c., **$4,994**.

Antique Furniture in the 21st Century

By Kyle Husfloen, Editor

Furniture collecting has been a major part of the world of collecting for over 100 years. In recent years, as we enter the 21st century, it is interesting to note how this marketplace has evolved.

Whereas in past decades, 18th century and early 19th century furniture was the mainstay of the American furniture market, in recent years there has been a growing demand for furniture manufactured since the 1920s. Factory-made furniture from the 1920s and 1930s, often featuring Colonial Revival style, has seen a growing appreciation among collectors. It is well-made and features solid wood and fine veneers rather than the cheap compressed wood materials often used since the 1960s. Also much in demand in recent years is furniture in the Modernistic and Mid-Century taste, ranging from Art Deco through quality designer furniture of the 1950s through the 1970s.

These latest trends have offered even the less wheel-healed buyer the opportunity to purchase fine furniture at often reasonable prices. Buying antique and collectible furniture is no longer the domain of millionaires and museums.

Today more and more furniture is showing up on Internet sites and sometimes good buys can be made. However, it is important to deal with honest, well-informed sellers and have a good knowledge of what you want to purchase. Personally, I still prefer to purchase furniture at antiques shows, shops and auctions where I have the opportunity to carefully examine the piece in person to make sure it is "as represented," with no hidden surprises such as major repairs or replacements.

As in the past, it makes sense to purchase the best pieces you can find, whatever the style or era of production. Condition is still very important if you want your example to continue to appreciate in value in the coming years. For 18th century and early 19th century pieces the original finish and hardware are especially important as it is with good furniture of the early 20th century Arts & Crafts era. These features are not quite as important for most manufactured furniture of the Victorian era and furniture from the 1920s and later. However, it is good to be aware that a good finish and original hardware will mean a stronger market when pieces are resold. Of course, whatever style of furniture you buy, you are better off with examples that have not had major repair or replacements. On really early furniture, repairs and replacements will definitely have an impact on the sale value, but they will also be a factor on newer designs from the 20th century.

As with all types of antiques and collectibles, there is often a regional preference for certain furniture types. Although the American market is much more homogenous than it was in past decades, there still tends to be a preference for 18th century and early 19th century furniture along the Eastern Seaboard, whereas Victorian designs tend to have a larger market in the Midwest and South. In the West, country furniture and "western" designs definitely have the edge except in major cities along the West Coast. Even more localized markets can be found. For example, around Palm Springs, California, only "Mid-century Modern" furniture and decorative accessories have much of a market while less than 100 miles away in the San Diego – Los Angeles corridor a wider range of furniture is marketable.

Whatever your favorite style furniture, there are still fine examples to be found. Just study the history of your favorites and the important points of their construction before you invest heavily. A wise shopper will be a happy shopper and have a collection certain to continue to appreciate as time marches along into the 21st century.

Kyle Husfloen

FURNITURE DATING CHART

AMERICAN FURNITURE
Pilgrim Century – 1620-1700
William & Mary – 1685-1720
Queen Anne – 1720-50
Chippendale – 1750-85
Federal – 1785-1820
Hepplewhite – 1785-1800
Sheraton – 1800-20
Classical (American Empire) –
    1815-40
Victorian – 1840-1900
Early Victorian – 1840-50
Gothic Revival – 1840-90
Rococo (Louis XV) – 1845-70
Renaissance Revival – 1860-85
Louis XVI – 1865-75
Eastlake – 1870-95
Jacobean & Turkish Revival –
    1870-90
Aesthetic Movement – 1880-1900
Art Nouveau – 1895-1918
Turn-of-the Century
    (Early 20th Century) – 1895-1910
Mission-style
    (Arts & Crafts movement) –
    1900-15
Colonial Revival – 1890-1930
Art Deco – 1925-40
Modernist or Mid-Century – 1945-70

ENGLISH FURNITURE
Jacobean – Mid-17th Century
William & Mary – 1689-1702
Queen Anne – 1702-14
George I – 1714-27
George II – 1727-60
George III – 1760-1820
Regency – 1811-20
George IV – 1820-30
William IV – 1830-37
Victorian – 1837-1901
Edwardian – 1901-10

FRENCH FURNITURE
Louis XV – 1715-74
Louis XVI – 1774-93
Empire – 1804-15
Louis Philippe – 1830-48
Napoleon III
    (Second Empire) – 1848-70
Art Nouveau – 1895-1910
Art Deco – 1925-35

GERMANIC FURNITURE
Since the country of Germany did not exist before 1870, furniture from the various Germanic states and the Austro-Hungarian Empire is generally termed simply "Germanic." From the 17th century onward, furniture from these regions tended to follow the stylistic trends established in France and England. General terms are used for such early furniture, usually classifying it as "Baroque," "Rococo" or a similar broad stylistic term. Germanic furniture dating from the first half of the 19th century is today usually referred to as Biedermeier, a style closely related to French Empire and English Regency.

AMERICAN FURNITURE TERMS

CHAIRS

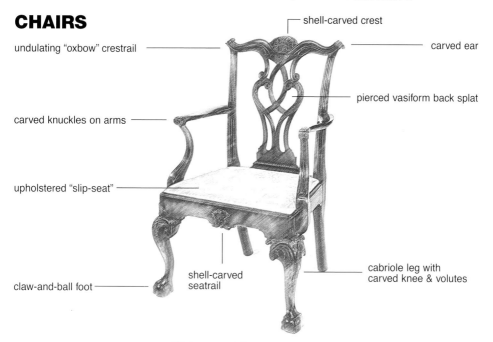

shell-carved crest

undulating "oxbow" crestrail

carved ear

carved knuckles on arms

pierced vasiform back splat

upholstered "slip-seat"

claw-and-ball foot

shell-carved seatrail

cabriole leg with carved knee & volutes

Chippendale Armchair

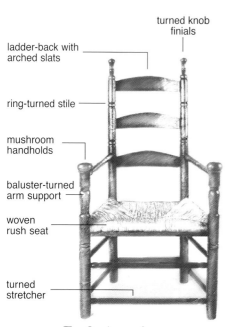

turned knob finials

ladder-back with arched slats

ring-turned stile

mushroom handholds

baluster-turned arm support

woven rush seat

turned stretcher

Early American "Ladder-back" Armchair

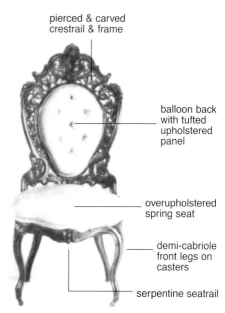

pierced & carved crestrail & frame

balloon back with tufted upholstered panel

overupholstered spring seat

demi-cabriole front legs on casters

serpentine seatrail

Victorian Roccoco Side Chair

CHESTS & TABLES

shaped
molded edge

pierced
brass pull

pierced brass
keyhole
escutcheon

graduated
drawers

beaded drawer
dividers & stiles

straight
bracket feet

serpentine front

Chippendale Chest of Drawers

leather-covered
top with tack trim

corbel

mortise & tenon
through-construction

medial shelf

Mission Oak Library Table

FURNITURE PEDIMENTS & SKIRTS

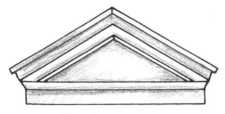

Classic Pediment

Plain Skirt

Broken Arch Pediment

Arched Skirt

**Bonnet Top with
Urn & Flame Finial**

Valanced Skirt

**Bonnet Top with Rosettes &
Three Urn & Flame Finials**

Scalloped Skirt

FURNITURE FEET

Trestle Foot

Pad Foot

Block Foot

Slipper Foot

Spade Foot

Snake Foot

Tapered or Plain Foot

Spanish Foot

FURNITURE FEET

Ball Foot

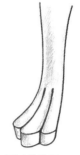

Trifid Foot

Bun Foot

Hoof Foot

Turnip Foot

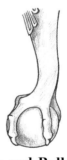

Claw-and-Ball Foot

Arrow or Peg Foot

Paw Foot

FURNITURE
Bedroom Suites

White Art Deco Bedroom Suite

Art Deco: bedstead, two tall two-door cabinets fitted w/drawers, a pair of nightstands, a side table, a shelving unit & a mirrored vanity table & stool; lacquered & painted creamy white, simple rectangular forms, designed by Jules Bouy for Carlos Salzedo, ca. 1931, cabinets 17 1/2 x 20", 4' 6" h., the set (ILLUS., top of page) **$4,780**

Four-Piece Classical Bedroom Suite

Classical style: double sleigh bed, large rectangular ogee-framed mirror, chest-of-drawers & commode: all mahogany & mahogany veneer, the chest w/two small handkerchief drawers w/wooden knobs on the rectangular top above a long ogee-front drawer slightly projecting above the lower case w/three long flat drawers w/turned wood knobs flanked by tall ogee pilasters ending in heavy C-scroll feet, the commode w/a white marble backsplash & rectangular marble top above a long serpentine drawer above a pair of paneled doors over the serpentine apron & casters, ca. 1840, the set (ILLUS.) **$978**

Louis XVI-Style: two twin beds, chifrobe, chest of drawers, nightstand & wall mirror; inlaid mahogany & mahogany veneer, the beds w/a D-shaped headboard w/carved ribbon edge banding & short footposts, the upright chifrobe w/a rectangular red marble top above the tall case w/a pair of tall doors opening to an interior fitted w/a hat box door beside three small drawers above four open pullout shelves, raised on short simple cabriole legs, the chest of drawers w/a rectangular red marble top w/serpentine front atop a conforming case w/a stack of three concave smaller drawers flanking a stack of three bowed long central drawers, thin scalloped apron & simple cabriole legs, the matching nightstand w/a marble top & a case w/three small drawers, the giltwood wall mirror in a high arched design featuring a narrow ribbon banded frame & a ribbon bow crest, produced by Slack Rassnick & Co., New York, New York, first quarter 20th c., chests 20 3/4 x 47 3/4", 37 3/4" h., the set (ILLUS. of most pieces, top next page) **$1,093**

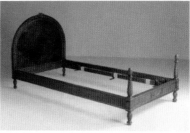

Fine Louis XVI-Style Marble-topped Bedroom Suite

Complete Queen Anne Revival Bedroom Suite

Queen Anne Revival: low-poster double bed, chest of drawers, dressing table & bench, nightstand & side chair; mahogany & mahogany veneer, the bed w/a wide flat-topped headboard flanked by posts w/turned finials & a matching shorter footboard, the case pieces w/arrangements of drawers on cases raised on short cabriole legs, the nightstand, bench & chair all w/cabriole legs ending in pad feet, made by The Thomasville Chair Co., ca. 1920s, the set (ILLUS.) **$690**

Victorian Eastlake substyle: double half-tester bed, a marble-topped chest of drawers w/mirror, a marble-topped washstand w/mirror; walnut & burl walnut, the half-tester on the bed w/a stepped angular cornice w/panels

Eastlake Half-tester Bed from Suite

carved w/stylized flowers between corner blocks, flat serpentine brackets supporting it above the high headboard w/a matching carved cornice, the lower flat-topped footboard w/floral-incised arched & burl panels above rectangular panels, the other pieces w/matching crests, white marble tops & arrangements of drawers w/stamped brass pulls w/angular bails, marble on chest w/old repair & cracks, ca. 1880, bed 63 1/2 x 79 1/2", 8' 3" h., 3 pcs. (ILLUS. of bed only) **$7,188**

Victorian Faux Bamboo Bed from a Suite

Victorian Faux Bamboo: double bed, chest of drawers, octagonal side table & pair of side chairs; turned wood & bird's-eye maple, the high-backed bed w/a tall rectangular headboard w/a top low gallery of bamboo-turned spindles above the bird's-eye maple headboard w/a large oval recessed panel, the bamboo-turned side stiles topped w/large ball finials, the side rails w/bamboo-turned trim & the low footboard matching the highboard, the chest of drawers w/a large oval mirror swiveling between bamboo-turned uprights above the rectangular case w/three long graduated drawers, attributed to R. J. Horner & Co., New York, New York, ca. 1875, bed 60 x 81", 68" h., the set (ILLUS. of the bed).. **$13,800**

Scarce Victorian Faux Bamboo Bedroom Suite

Victorian Faux Bamboo: high-backed bed & chest of drawers; maple & bird's-eye maple, the tall bed head-board w/a stepped crestrail composed of rows of short turned spindles & two small rectangular panels accented w/short turned posts, the tall bamboo-turned headposts w/turned ball finials flank a detailed head-board centered by a large center rectangular panel framed w/a double band of half-round bamboo turnings flanked by two small square pieced panels w/radiating spindles above two small square panels, the shorter footboard w/matching details; the chest of drawers w/a rectangular top above a pair of drawers over two long drawers, all the edges & sides trimmed w/bamboo turnings, attributed to the Horner Furniture Co., ca. 1880s, bed headboard shortened, bed 60" w., 67 1/2" h., chest 21 x 46 1/2", 29 1/2" h., the set (ILLUS.)
.... **$3,450**

Armoire From Fine Renaissance Suite

Fine Renaissance Revival Bed from Set

Victorian Renaissance Revival style: tall back double bed, chest of drawers & armoire; walnut & burl walnut, each piece w/a large pedimented crest w/three small blocks below the blocked flat crestrail mounted in the center w/a cut-out crest w/a pointed top above a wreath & ribbons enclosing a molded roundel centered by a gilt-bronze cast Classical maiden's head. the bed & chest w/turned drop finials, the bed w/a tall arched burl paneled headboard flanked by free-standing short columns w/turned finials & a low matching arched footboard; the tall chest of drawers w/a tall rectangular mirror above a rectangular white marble top fitted w/two hanky drawers above a case w/three long paneled burl drawers; the armoire w/a projecting flat cornice above a blocked frieze over a tall mirrored door flanked by quarter-round reeded colonettes trimmed w/gilt, a single long burl drawer in the base above the deep molded apron, bed 66 x 86", 96" h., the armoire 22 1/2 x 47", 99 1/2" h., the set (ILLUS. of armoire)... **$15,525**

Victorian Renaissance Revival style: tall back double bed, two-door armoire, chest of drawers & washstand; walnut & burl walnut, the bed w/a large triangular molded pediment topped by a scroll-cut crest & enclosing two burl panels above the tall back w/two tall pointed recessed panels framed by various raised burl panels all flanked by tall cylindrical free-standing corner posts w/turned finials, the low matching footboard w/a large double-diamond raised center burl panel flanked by other shaped burl panels w/curved corner posts w/further panels, the wide siderails also w/raised burl panels, bed 63 1/2 x 86", 89" h., the set (ILLUS. of the bed, top next column) **$5,750**

Tall Renaissance Revival Chest from Set

Victorian Renaissance Revival style: tall double bed & chest of drawers; walnut & burl walnut, each piece of matching design, the chest of drawers w/a very tall central section w/an arched pediment centered by a large pointed crest w/a roundel flanked by arched molding over burl panels, on tall flat stiles w/further burl panels flanked by cut-out side sections each mounted w/a small half-round candle shelf above a small burl panels & a carved loop & drop design, the center well base w/a pair of square white marble tops at each side over a stack of four

Two-piece Renaissance Revival Bedroom Suite

small molded drawers each w/a burl panel & pear-shaped black & brass pull flanked by reeded corner columns, the drop-well center w/a rectangular white marble top over a single long molded drawer w/matching pulls, deep molded flat base, ca. 1870, bed 64 x 84", 90" h., chest 20 x 62", 94" h., the set (ILLUS. of chest of drawers).................................... **$5,463**

Canopied French Renaissance Revival Bed

Victorian Renaissance Revival substyle: canopied double bed & mirrored armoire; ebonized beech, the bed headboard w/a broken-scroll crestrail centered by a scroll-carved plaque centered by a classical female mask, low spindled galleries on each side between the blocked stiles w/turned finials, all above an arched frieze band over a solid panel, the low footboard w/a flat top rail above two large rectangular raised panels centered by large roundels & flanked on each side by slender columns, the bed w/an appropriate giltwood canopy frame centered w/a scroll & palmette finial, Napoleon II Era, France, ca. 1860, bed 60 x 82", 72" h. (ILLUS. of bed).................................... **$11,213**

Victorian Renaissance Revival substyle: queen-sized bed & chest of drawers; walnut & flame-grained cherry veneer, both pieces w/matching crestrails centered by a long rectangular flaring block-form crest above scroll cutouts over a small arched cherry burl panel flanked by a broken-arch pediment, the headboard w/shaped scroll-carved sides centering a large burl cherry panel, a matching low footboard & deep side boards; the chest crest above a large rectangular mirror flanked by shaped supports w/small rounded shelves over the rectangular white marble top & a case of three long burl-paneled drawers, all on flattened bun feet, original finish, ca. 1880, chest overall 8' 7" h., 2 pcs. (ILLUS., top of page) **$4,500**

Beds

Majorelle Art Nouveau Inlaid Bed

Art Nouveau bed, carved & inlaid mahogany, "Aux Pavots," the high rectangular headboard w/an upper band inlaid w/poppy seed heads above a wide veneered panel topped by a band of scallops accents inlaid mother-of-pearl & copper stylized blossoms, matching lower footrail w/rounded top corners, on small swelled square feet, designed by Louis Majorelle, France, ca. 1898, 63 3/8 x 83 3/4", 60 1/4" h. (ILLUS.) **$9,560**

Classical Country-Style Low-Poster Bed

Classical country-style low-poster bed, maple, four rod- and ring-turned low posts, the paneled & scroll-cut headboard w/a turned horizontal rod crest, simple narrow arched footboard, heavy turned tapering legs, ca. 1825-40, side rails extended, 54 5/8 x 84 5/8", 46 3/4" h. (ILLUS.) **$1,265**

Classical country-style tall-poster canopy bed, cherry & walnut, the rectangular canopy frame w/a stepped flaring cornice & line w/pleated fabric raised on four matching tall slender ring-, rod- and knob-turned posts each ending in ring- and baluster-turned legs ending in ball feet, the footrail mounted w/a narrow rail above a row of eight short baluster- and knob-turned spindles, ca. 1840-50, 53 x 77", 109" h. (ILLUS., top next column) **$4,600**

Classical Country Tall-Poster Bed

One of Two Classical Low-Poster Beds

Classical low-poster beds, twin-sized, each w/a headboard topped w/a round crest bar ending in leafy scrolls raised above serpentine sides flanked by ring-, knob- and baluster-turned headposts topped by carved pineapple finials, matching footboard w/the posts joined by an baluster-, ring- & knob-turned blanket rail & a flat lower rail, first half 19th c., 39 x 75", 49" h., pr. (ILLUS. of one) **$1,006**

Fine Classical Revival Mahogany Bed

French Classical "Sleigh" Bed

Classical Revival double bed, mahogany, the headboard w/an arched crestrail over a wide panels flanked by square side posts w/narrow recessed panels & flat tops, the low footboard w/a concave crestrail between matching shorter posts, wide concave siderails, made by Michael Craig, Columbia, South Carolina, "Railroad Baron's" style, 20th c., 68 3/4 x 90", 58 1/2" h. (ILLUS., previous page) **$8,050**

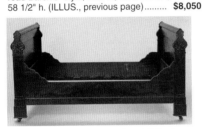

American Classical "Sleigh" Bed

Classical "sleigh" bed, carved mahogany, twin-sized, the head- and footboards of the same height, each w/trefoil carvings atop the side stiles joined by figured veneer panels, the ends w/applied carving & molding, joined by highly figured veneered siderails, ca. 1840, 37 x 82", 43 1/2" h. (ILLUS.) **$920**

Mahogany Classical "Sleigh" Bed

Classical "sleigh" bed mahogany & mahogany veneer, the matching head- and footboards w/outscrolled stiles flanking plain veneered panels, wide flat legs w/curved bases, original simple turned round rope rails, second quarter 19th c., 48 x 80", 42 1/2" h. (ILLUS.) **$1,725**

Classical "sleigh" bed, mahogany, matching head- and footboards w/outscrolled sides w/delicate carved scrolls flanking plain panels, deep molded siderails & long block feet on casters, France, first half 19th c., 45 x 80", 43" h. (ILLUS., top of page) **$1,610**

Fine Classical Tall-Poster Bed

Classical tall-poster bed, mahogany, four matching tall tapering octagonal posts w/high baluster- and ring-turned finials, the headboard w/a rolled crest bar w/turned finials above cut-out scrolls over two raised panels, heavy corner blocks joining the heavy siderails & raised on heavy ring-turned tapering feet, fitted w/a half-lapped slatted tester, some alternations to posts, ca. 1850, 65 3/4 x 84", 94" h. (ILLUS. without tester) **$8,625**

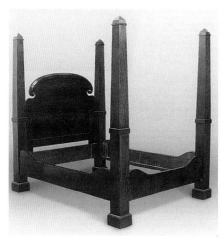

Fine Classical Tall-Poster Bed

Classical tall-poster bed, mahogany & mahogany veneer, the headboard w/tall square obelisk-style posts flanking a high arched & scroll-trimmed burled headboard, matching foot posts, deep shaped rails, ca. 1840-50, 68 x 86", 82" h. (ILLUS.) **$5,060**

Fine Carved Classical Tall-Poster Bed

Classical tall-poster canopy bed, carved mahogany, the headboard w/a pair of scroll-carved crests w/a small bobbin-turned top bar above a narrow reeded panel over a plain panel flanked by headposts spiral-carved w/ribbons & acanthus leaves & ending in large blocks above the baluster-form leaf-carved legs, matching footposts, all supporting the canopy frame, square side rails, restoration & alterations, ca. 1830, 62 x 84", 94" h. (ILLUS.) **$13,800**

Outstanding Classical Canopy Bed

Classical tall-poster canopy bed, mahogany, a large rectangular canopy w/a deep frame & wide flaring cornice supported on four matching slender spiral-twist turned posts topped by pineapple carving & ending in a ring-turned section w/an acanthus leaf-carved section, all supported on short ring- and, rod-turned legs ending in ball feet, the high headboard w/scroll-cut top ending in rosettes, early 19th c., 62 x 82", 122" h. (ILLUS.) **$51,750**

Mahogany Louisiana Tall-Poster Bed

Classical tall-poster canopy bed, mahogany, a large rectangular canopy w/a deep frame & wide stepped & flaring cornice supported on four matching slender ring- and baluster-turned posts, all supported on ring- and baluster-turned legs ending in ball feet, the headboard w/flat rolled crest, made in Louisiana, ca. 1825, excellent surface, 60 x 81", 104" h. (ILLUS., previous page) **$14,950**

Mahogany Classical Canopy Bed

Classical tall-poster canopy bed, mahogany, the rectangular canopy frame w/rounded corners & deep ogee sides & lined w/fabric, raised atop heavy columns w/a tapering ring-turned top sections above heavy paneled posts above tall square corner blocks raised on heavy turned legs on disk & peg feet, the headboard w/a simple arched molded crestrail above a plain panel, the siderails & footboard w/shaped corner brackets, Mississippi Valley, ca. 1840, 67 x 86", 97" h. (ILLUS.) **$6,325**

Classical tall-poster canopy bed, mahogany, the rectangular full canopy w/rounded corners & deep ogee rails & lined w/radiating fabric, resting atop tall tapering clustered-column posts w/plain round lower sections on disk feet, the headboard w/a flat molded crest flanked by scroll-carved sides over a large plain rectangular panel, the deep siderails & footboard w/scrolling leaf-carved corner brackets, probably New Orleans, ca. 1840, 69 x 90", 120" h. (ILLUS., top next column) **$16,675**

Fine Southern Classical Canopy Bed

Classical Maple & Mahogany Canopy Bed

Classical tall-poster canopy bed, tiger stripe maple & mahogany, a large rectangular canopy w/a deep frame & flaring cornice supported on four matching slender ring- and rod-turned posts, all supported on ring- and rod-turned legs, the high headboard w/scrolled crest, ca. 1825, fitted w/later rails but original rope rails available, associated canopy w/mosquito netting, 60 x 80", 98" h. (ILLUS.) **$6,038**

Classical Tall-Poster Canopy Bed

Classical tall-poster canopy bed, walnut, a large rectangular canopy w/a deep frame & wide flaring corners supported on four matching slender paneled posts w/ring-turned sections & a tapering top section all supported on short ring-, rail- and knob-turned legs, the two-paneled headboard w/scroll-cut top w/a blanket roll w/turned acorn end finials, second quarter 19th c., 65 x 86", 109" h. (ILLUS.)........... **$4,370**

Louisiana Classical Tall-Poster Bed

Classical tall-poster canopy bed, walnut, a large rectangular canopy w/a deep frame & wide flaring cornice w/rounded corners added later; supported on four matching slender ring- and baluster-turned posts, all supported on ring- and baluster-turned legs, the headboard w/scroll-cut crest, made in Louisiana, ca. 1825, 56 x 81", 100" h. (ILLUS.) **$19,550**

Scroll-cut Low-poster "Cannon Ball" Bed

Country-style low-poster "cannon ball" bed, curly maple, each post w/detailed ring-, rod- and baluster turning topped by a large ball, raised on turned tapering plain legs, the headboard & matching lower footboard w/an elaborate repeating scroll-cut decoration, mellow golden brown finish, some glued splits in scrolls, first half 19th c., 51 1/2 x 71 1/2", 50" h. (ILLUS.)... **$920**

Louisiana Low-Poster "Cannon Ball" Bed

Country-style low-poster "cannon ball" bed, cypress, the matching rod-turned posts each topped by a turned large ball, the heavy rod-turned legs ending in cushion feet, the scroll-cut headboard w/a flat crest, old red stain, made in Louisiana, early 19th c., 56 x 78", 45" h. (ILLUS.)... **$3,450**

Country-style settle-bed, painted pine, the low two-board back flanked by wide single-board ends curving down to form low arms flanking the wide plank seat & deep apron that fold out to form a bed, worn red paint w/traces of black, some rose head nails, replaced bottom boards & hinges, edge wear & some damage, first half 19th c., 21 3/4 x 53", 31" h. (ILLUS., top next page).. **$1,610**

Unusual Painted Pine Country Settle-Bed

French Directoire-Style "Sleigh" Bed

Directoire-Style "sleigh" bed, painted & decorated wood, the matching head- and footboards w/out-scrolled crestrails decorated w/a band of dark green diamonds enclosing small classical motifs on a deep cream ground, simple turned columns flank the plain head- and footboard panels in deep cream w/dark green trim, narrow siderails, short turned disk & peg feet, France, mid-19th c., 50 x 82 1/2", 45" h. (ILLUS., middle of page) **$2,155**

Maple Country Federal Tall-Poster Bed

Federal country-style tall-poster bed, maple & pine, four ring-, rod- and baluster-turned posts w/acorn finials, the flat-topped scroll-cut headboard & matching lower footboard, simple turned tapering legs, early 19th c., 59 3/4 x 83", 92" h. (ILLUS.)... **$2,185**

Nice New York Federal Mahogany Sleigh Bed

Federal "sleigh" bed, carved mahogany, the matching outswept head- and foot-board w/a rolled crestrail above a paneled section flanked by reeded stiles, original square rails raised on baluster- and ring-turned legs tapering to short cylindrical feet, New York City, ca. 1800-20, 86" l. (ILLUS.)... **$2,400**

Federal tall-poster bed, carved mahogany, four turned tapering reeded & carved posts topped by urn-turned finials joined by tester rails, fitted w/a simple arched

Mahogany Federal Tall-Poster Bed

headboard w/incurved sides, baluster- and peg-turned legs, one finial broken, headboard finish flaking, early 19th c., 58 3/4 x 83", 82" h. (ILLUS.).................. **$2,300**

Fine New Hampshire Federal Bed

Federal tall-poster bed, carved & painted mahogany, the baluster- and ring-turned leaf-carved & reeded footposts continuing to square molded legs joined to the red-painted tapering headposts & blue-painted arched headboard, Portsmouth, New Hampshire, ca. 1805, old surface, 51 x 72", 87 1/2" h. (ILLUS.).................. **$6,463**

Federal Tiger Stripe Maple Tall Post Bed

Federal tall-poster bed, tiger stripe maple, the four baluster- and ring-turned octagonal chamfered posts continuing to ring-turned tapering legs joined by the peaked recessed paneled headboard, Middle Atlantic States, ca. 1820, refinished, imperfections, 54 x 75", 86" h. (ILLUS.) **$3,819**

Simple American Federal Canopy Bed

Federal tall-poster canopy bed, maple & pine, simple arched headboard between simple turned & tapering headposts w/urn-turned finials, matching low arched footboard & footposts, swelled tapering turned legs, full arched canopy frame, old repairs, first half 19th c., 49 1/2 x 78 1/8", 82" h. (ILLUS.) **$1,000**

Fine American Federal Canopy Bed

Federal tall-poster canopy bed, mahogany, a low arched headboard joining simple square tapering headposts, the footposts turned tapering shape w/reeding above tall square tapering legs, square siderails, full arched canopy frame, ca. 1800, 60 x 80", 67 1/2" h. (ILLUS.) **$7,170**

Fine Federal Maple Tall-Poster Bed

Federal tall-poster canopy bed, maple, the slender ring-turned & tapering posts joined by a rectangular canopy frame, the headposts joined by a simple arched headboard w/incurved sides, original rope rails, raised on tall ring- and baluster-turned legs w/knob feet, possibly Connecticut, 1790-1810, 55 1/4 x 78 3/4", 84 1/2" h. (ILLUS.) **$3,840**

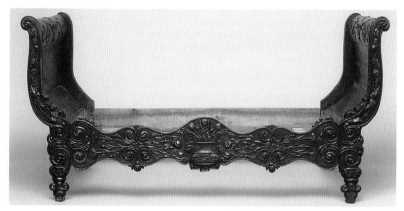

Ornately Carved French Provincial Fruitwood "Sleigh" Bed

French Provincial "sleigh" bed, carved fruitwood, the matching S-scroll head- and footboards each w/an ornate scroll-carved crestrail & fruiting vine-carved sides joined by wide siderails w/serpentine top & bottom & carved overall w/ornate leafy scrolls centered by a large flower-filled vase, raised on scroll-carved short legs, France, mid-19th c., 43 x 84", 42" h. (ILLUS.) **$4,830**

Simple Late Victorian Brass Bed

Late Victorian brass bed, the high headboard w/a flat tubular top rail above seven vertical brass tubes joined to a lower brass rail, a matching lower footboard, ca. 1900, 56" w., 4' 10" h. (ILLUS.)..................... **$200-300**

Louis XVI-Style bed, painted & decorated, twin-size, a high arched headboard w/a gilt intricate-carved crestrail above an upper panel carved w/a thin raised arched rectangular panel framing leafy swags centered by a bow suspending crossed quivers all on a pale green ground & flanked by ring-and-knob-turned & reeded posts w/ball finials, the slightly lower matching footboard decorated w/a large arched panel enclosing ornate gilt leafy scrolls centered by a ribbon bow suspending a large oval figural medallions,

Green & Gold Louis XVI-Style Twin Bed

toupie   feet,   France,   ca.   1900, 40 1/2 x 79", 60 1/2" h. (ILLUS.) **$3,220**

Unusual Signed Louis XVI-Style Bed

Fancy Rococo Style Tall-Poster Canopy Bed

Louis XVI-Style bed, painted & upholstered, a half-round carved molded canopy resting on curved metal supports extending from one side of the matching head- and footboards, each w/an arched crest above an upholstered panel, the square front stile w/a small ball finial, front rail w/a ring-turned band above molded rail, turned tapering & fluted legs on casters, signed by the maker Courtois, Paris, France, first half 19th c., wear, paint chips, back rail chipped, 45 x 75", 92" h. (ILLUS., previous page) **$4,600**

Elaborate Renaissance-Style Canopy Bed

Renaissance-Style canopy bed, carved mahogany, the large rectangular canopy frame w/a flaring molded cornice above scroll-carved sides w/florette-carved cor-

ner blocks, raised on tall heavy spiral twist-turned posts, the high headboard w/an arched crestrail w/ornate floral carving above three square panels carved w/shaped panels & roundels above two plain panels, the lower footboard w/a long rectangular upper panel incised w/delicate scrolls above a midmolding & a long lower panel boldly carved w/leafy scrolls centered by a large roundel, the deep siderails w/matching scroll carving, a narrow flaring gadroon-carved base molding above the large flattened bun feet, Portugal, mid-19th c., 58 1/2 x 85 1/2", 117" h. (ILLUS.) **$8,625**

Rococo style tall-poster canopy bed, carved hardwood, the rectangular canopy frame w/covered sides raised on four spiral- and foliate-carved posts joined by scrolling floral-carved rails flanking an arched headboard centering a rampant lion & unicorn supporting an oval mirror w/pierce-carved foliate panels to each side, raised on baluster- and beaded turned legs, Portuguese colonial or Anglo-Indian, 19th c., 63 x 88", 8' 1" h. (ILLUS., top of page) **$6,463**

Unusual Victorian Bamboo-turned Bed

Victorian bamboo-turned bed, maple w/blackened rings, the tall headboard composed of an intricate lattice design of bamboo-turned spindles flanked by heavy bamboo-turned posts w/large turned ball finials, a matching lower footboard, raised curly maple panels in the lower head- and footboard, original side rails, late 19th c., 39 1/2 x 77 1/4", headboard 63 1/2" h. (ILLUS.) **$1,208**

Simple Renaissance Revival High Bed

Victorian Renaissance Revival bed, walnut & burl walnut, the high headboard w/a molded arched crestrail supporting an arched broken-scroll crest centered by an arched crest w/raised cartouche, small raised burl panel trim, all above a large recessed oval panel flanked by flat shaped stiles w/bobbin-carved trim, the low footboard w/an arched center above a raised cut-out cartouche & roundel, curved corner posts, ca. 1875, 62 x 72", 82" h. (ILLUS.) **$431**

Simple Renaissance Revival Walnut Bed

Victorian Renaissance Revival substyle bed, carved walnut, the low headboard w/an arched crestrail w/a broken-scroll crest above a cartouche flanked by leafy scrolls & tapering raised panels all over a plain panel, tapering shaped stiles, a slightly shorter matching footboard, original siderails, ca. 1875, 54 x 68", 53" h. (ILLUS.) **$405**

Nice Renaissance Revival Walnut Bed

Victorian Renaissance Revival substyle bed, walnut & burl walnut, the very high headboard w/an arched & scroll-carved crestrail centered by a blocked flaring crest w/a turned urn finial above curved raised burl panels & rondels above a large arched central burl panel flanked by projecting side brackets & shorter stiles w/turned urn finials above raised burl blocked panels flanking three tall vertical panels, the low footboard w/a flat molded crestrail above rectangular burl panels & a central sunburst rondel all flanked by heavy blocked & carved stiles, original paneled side rails w/scroll-carved brackets, ca. 1875, 56" w., 8' 8" h. (ILLUS.) **$823**

Fine Renaissance Half-Tester Bed

Victorian Renaissance Revival substyle half-tester bed, carved walnut, the half-tester w/a serpentine frame mounted at the front w/an arched pierced scroll-carved crest & large turned bulbous finials, raised on angled serpentine brackets above the tall square tapering headposts & tall square legs w/block feet, the tall headboard w/an arched broken-scroll crest center w/a carved cartouche finial & carved scrolls & raised panels above an arched rail over a pair of tall arched oblong burl panels below a cluster of scroll carving, the low footboard w/a raised arched central panel over a large molded roundel flanked by raised asymmetrical panels, curved corner panels w/scroll-carved finials & feet, ca. 1875, 67 x 82 1/2", 112" h. (ILLUS.) **$3,680**

Very Fine Carved Renaissance Revival Half-tester Bed

Victorian Renaissance Revival substyle half-tester bed, walnut & burl walnut, the large rectangular half-tester frame w/a bowed front rail centered by a large blocked panel topped w/a carved palmette crest, small corner palmette finials, the flaring top molding above narrow raised burl panels, the tester supported by large pierced & carved curved panels decorated w/raised burl panels, joined to the tall square tapering headposts trimmed w/raised burl panels & roundels, the very high headboard w/a large blocked & arched crestrail topped by a carved palmette finial & small end finials above small raised burl panels all above a large rectangular molded burl panel flanked by narrow vertical raised burl panels, a large bottom rectangular burl panel, the low arched footboard w/the crestrail centered by a carved palmette & small burl panels above a pair of small rectangular burl panels, heavy square footposts w/paneled caps, raised

burl panels & heavy block feet, the wide siderails w/narrow raised burl panels & quarter-round corner brackets, ca. 1865, 72 x 88", 129" h. (ILLUS.) **$8,625**

High-backed Renaissance Revival Walnut & Burl Walnut Bed

Victorian Renaissance Revival substyle high-backed bed, walnut & burl walnut, the high headboard w/an arched & molded crestrail centered w/a large blocked panel topped by a large carved palmette finial, all above narrow raised burl panels & small blocks over a large rectangular burl panel, the square sideposts w/a blocked & banded design w/a roundel, the lower footboard w/a simple stepped crestrail above blocks & raised burl panels over two smaller rectangular burl panels, capped square footposts w/raised burl panels, heavy block feet, the wide siderails w/long raised burl panels & corner brackets w/burl panels, ca. 1875, 67 1/2 x 89", 86" h. (ILLUS.) **$1,840**

Renaissance Revival Tall-Poster Bed

Victorian Renaissance Revival tall-poster bed, walnut & burl walnut, the headboard w/a pair of tall slender square posts w/turned finials flank the very tall double-panel arched headboard w/an ornately carved scroll & leaf crest above an arched burl panel & raised burl trefoil panel, the footboard w/matching posts flanking a low serpentine footboard panel centered by an incised oval panel above a row of very short spindles, ring-turned feet on casters, ca. 1875, 55 x 76", 98" h. (ILLUS.).. **$1,840**

Fine Rococo Revival Mahogany Bed

disk-turned finials, the low footboard w/a low arched top above raised panels flanked by rounded corners w/floral carving, original side rails, old surface, posts now shortened, mid-19th c., 70 x 83", 87 1/2" h. (ILLUS.) **$4,600**

Extraordinary Victorian Rococo Mahogany Half-Tester Bed

Victorian Rococo half-tester bed, carved mahogany, the tall tapering columnar head posts support a half-tester w/a deep serpentine-sided frame w/gadrooned bands, an ornate arched & pierced scroll-carved crest & double-knob turned corner finials, the high headboard panel w/a tall arched & scroll-carved top centered by a leafy scroll finial above a carved grape cluster, two triangular raised panels above a long molded rectangular recessed panel w/a carved rosette at each corner, a short columnar foot posts carved w/Moorish arch panels below the heavy ring- and knob-turned tops flank the serpentine leafy scroll & shell-carved footboard, matching fancy siderails, ca. 1850s, 65 x 84", 110" h. (ILLUS.)......... **$26,450**

Victorian Rococo Revival substyle bed, carved mahogany, the high arched headboard topped by a large carved shell crest above a large knob & floral swags & scroll-carved edging above a long rectangular burl panel w/cut-corners, the ring- and rod-turned head posts topped by

Black Lacquer Victorian Rococo Bed

Victorian Rococo Revival substyle bed, gilt-decorated black lacquer, double-size, the arched serpentine headboard w/a molded edge decorated w/gilt trim above the smooth panel decorated under the arch w/a band of delicate gold florals & chinoiserie designs including birds & arabesques, simple serpentine stiles above the blocked legs w/block feet, the low footboard w/a heavy flat molded crestrail & tapering blocked corner posts w/half-round spindles above the stepped block feet, probably Philadelphia, ca. 1850-60, 66 x 78", 4' 9" h. (ILLUS.) **$1,380**

Very Elaborate Rococo Rosewood Full-tester Bed

Victorian Rococo Revival substyle tall-poster full-tester bed, carved rosewood, the large tester frame decorated on each side w/an ornate arched & scroll-carved crestrail centered by a shell cartouche above a flared cornice band over a paneled frieze band w/a central roundel, raised on four heavy paneled knob- and ring-turned posts above heavy paneled legs ending in heavy paneled feet, the fairly low headboard w/a simple central arched crest above a plain panel, the paneled side rails centered by a florette & trimmed on top w/scroll-carved corner brackets & a central serpentine-carved crest, America or France, ca. 1850, 84 x 89", 10' h. (ILLUS., top of page)... **$13,800**

headboard w/a high crest composed of three high pointed arches outlined w/ornately carved scrolls around the bird's-eye maple panels, the central panel w/a carved floral sprig, the lower headboard composed of three tall bird's-eye maple panels, all suspended by side latches to the heavy turned headposts w/tall ring-turned finials, a simple low footboard w/matching shorter posts, heavy ball feet, original side rails, ca. 1850, 54 x 78 3/4", 73" h. (ILLUS.) **$4,313**

Fine Rococo Substyle Bed Attributed to Prudent Mallard

Victorian Rococo substyle high-backed bed, carved rosewood, the headboard w/a high arched broken-scroll pediment w/pierced scrolls below the large floral-carved cartouche over a simple arched

Rare Victorian Rococo Tall-Poster Bed

Victorian Rococo style tall-poster bed, walnut & bird's-eye maple, the very tall crestrail & panel, the square sideposts topped by tall paneled posts w/large ring- and knop-turned finials, the simple arched footboard w/simple molded pan- els & curved corners w/scrolls & curved panels, the deep siderails w/molded rect- angular panels, scroll-carved end feet, formerly a half-tester bed now reduced in height, probably from New Orleans & the shop of Prudent Mallard, ca. 1855, 69 1/2 x 87", 84 1/2" h. (ILLUS.) **$19,550**

Benches

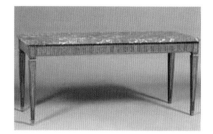

Adams-Style Marble-topped Bench

Adams-Style bench, mahogany marque- try, the long rectangular grey marble top above a narrow marquetry apron raised on inlaid square tapering legs, 20th c., 45 1/2" l., 20" h. (ILLUS.) **$264**

Bucket (or water) bench, painted pine, a long narrow rectangular top board above single-board ends w/arched cut- out feet & sloping at the front above two open shelves, two back braces, mor- tised construction, crusty old reddish brown paint, mid-19th c., 12 x 37 1/4", 34 1/2" h. (ILLUS., top next column) **$2,013**

Early Painted Bucket or Water Bench

Simple Country Pine Bucket Bench

Bucket (or water) bench, pine, the rectan- gular top above a closed lower shelf flanked by single-board bootjack ends, 19th c., 36" l., 23" h. (ILLUS.) **$104**

Fine Pair of Classical Benches

Classical benches, carved mahogany, the long deep upholstered top raised on four heavy tapering ring- turned & gadrooned legs w/knob feet, American or English, ca. 1815-25, 20 x 35", 18" h., pr. (ILLUS.) **$7,200**

Fine American Classical Window Bench

Classical window bench, carved mahogany, the long rectangular upholstered
seat flanked by open end arms w/balus-
ter- and ring-turned spiral-carved crestrails on scrolled spiral-carved stiles
continuing to form the sabre legs, each
back w/a lower horizontal splat w/a central shaped tablet flanked by scrolls, old
refinish, possibly Pennsylvania, ca.
1820-25, minor imperfections, 16 x 41",
33" h. (ILLUS.) **$5,875**

Large Victorian Oak Hall Bench

mirror 50 x 52 1/4", bench 20 x 55", 43" h.,
the pair (ILLUS. of bench)....................... **$2,070**

Simple Painted Kneeling Bench

Kneeling bench, painted wood, long narrow
rectangular top w/narrow side aprons,
short bootjack legs, original worn green
paint, possibly Shaker-made, 19th c.,
7 x 30" lo., 8 1/2" h. (ILLUS.) **$403**

Simple Country-Style Hardwood Bench

Country-style bench, hardwood, a long flat
crestrail above a spindled back flanked
by square stiles continuing to the rear
legs, shaped open arms on low turned
supports flanking the long plank seat,
ring- and rod-turned tapering front legs,
19th c., 71" l. (ILLUS.)............................ **$1,016**

Hall bench & mirror, late Victorian style,
oak, the bench w/a tall rectangular back
w/a flat crestrail ending in rosette ends
above a large central beveled square panel
flanked by pairs of smaller panels all
flanked by heavy reeded & scrolled end
arms on large reeded ball arm supports
above the rectangular seat w/a lift-top
above the deep apron w/double front panels & single end panels, heavy flaring molded base on large bun feet, together w/a
matching wall mirror w/a flaring flat cornice
w/a dentil-carved crestrail above a frieze
band centered by a scroll-carved panel
panel above a large rectangular mirror
w/heavy molding, late 19th - early 20th c.,

Louis XV-Style Decorative Bench

Louis XV-Style bench, inlaid mahogany,
the rectangular padded upholstered lift-
top seat flanked by low scrolled arms
joined by turned rails, the base w/an
arched front panel marquetry & ivory inlaid w/an urn & ornate leafy scrolls,
raised on cabriole legs w/leaf-carved
knees & ending in pad feet, France, late
19th c., 21" w., 23" h. (ILLUS.)................. **$558**

Fine Louis XVI-Style Giltwood Window Bench

Louis XVI-Style window bench, giltwood, the padded rectangular top w/padded & outscrolled upholstered low ends, above a narrow apron centered by a cornucopia-carved pendant, raised on eight tapering fluted legs ending in peg feet, France, mid-19th c., 22 x 48", 18 1/2" h. (ILLUS.).. **$4,830**

Mammy's bench (rocking settee w/removable cradle rail on seat), painted & decorated wood, a long flat crestrail above numerous simple turned spindles flanked by tapering stiles & S-scroll arms over spindles & bamboo-turned canted arm support, the long shaped plank seat fitted w/an S-scroll arm & removable baby guard rail w/eight spindles, heavy baluster-, knob- and ring-turned front legs joined by a long flat stretcher & inset into rockers, old black paint over red graining & gold stenciled designs on the crestrail including pineapples, cherries & leaves, yellow line borders, a few splits & some added later nails, mid-19th c., 18 x 52/2", 30 1/2" h............................. **$1,783**

Leather-covered Regency-Style Bench

Regency-Style window bench, upholstered mahogany, the long U-shaped top w/inscrolled ends & raised on arched flat legs covered overall w/ tufted & tack-trimmed brown leather, England, late 19th - early 20th c., 18 x 36", 24" h. (ILLUS.).. **$1,495**

French Neoclassical Cross-Sword Benches

Neoclassical benches, parcel-ebonized & gilt beech, 'crossed-sword' design, a rectangular upholstered seat on a narrow carved seatrail raised on realistically-carved cross-sword supports on each side, France, 19th c., 17 x 40", 26 1/2" h., pr. (ILLUS.)... **$1,035**

Pair of Fine Regency-Style Window Benches

Regency-Style window benches, faux bois & giltwood, the long U-shaped seats w/inscrolled ends upholstered on the interior & exterior, the seatrails w/mahogany-grained panels trimmed w/giltwood & centered by a rosette & leaf-carved panel, the scrolling outswept legs headed by large gilt leaf clusters & ending in scroll feet w/a gilt rosette, England, late 19th - early 20th c., 18 x 46 1/2" h., 24 1/2" h., pr. (ILLUS.) **$2,530**

School bench, country-style, oak & pine, the back composed of a single long rectangular rail between wide rectangular stiles continuing to form the back legs, long rectangular seat above a shallow set-back shelf, heavy square legs joined by a heavy H-stretcher, old mellow brown finish, mortise & peg construction w/various nails in the seat, minor split on stretcher, late 19th - early 20th c., 14 x 99", 33 1/2" h. **$546**

Bookcases

Simple Art Deco Style Bookcase

Art Deco bookcase, walnut veneer, the rectangular top curved down at the ends & continuing into the sides, above a patterned veneer frieze band above the tall geometrically-glazed cupboard door opening to three wooden shelves, raised on stepped bracket front feet, refinished, 23" w., 44" h. (ILLUS.)............................. **$264**

Arts & Crafts Revolving Bookcase

Arts & Crafts bookcase, oak, revolving-style, the square top w/a narrow molded edge over three open graduated shelves separated by cut-out inner panels & three-rail corners, revolving on a four flat cast-iron cabriole legs on a X-form platform, two small chips, repair to base & rails, signed by John Danner, Canton, Ohio, ca. 1890, 23" sq., 51 1/4" h. (ILLUS.) **$633**

Rare Roycroft Mission Oak Bookcase

Arts & Crafts (Mission-style) bookcase, glazed oak, the rectangular top w/blocked ends above a frieze band w/blocked corners & incised w/the word "Roycroft," above a tall glazed cupboard door opening to three wooden shelves, a single deep drawer at the bottom w/a small metal knob & two incised Roycroft logos, simple bracketed front apron, Roycrofters, East Aurora, New York, ca. 1908, 16 1/4 x 33 1/4", 67 7/8" h. (ILLUS.)................................. **$16,730**

Handsome Biedermeier-Style Bookcase

Biedermeier-Style bookcase, blonde wood, a plain rectangular top above an open compartment w/three adjustable wood shelves flanked by free-standing ebonized columns above the lower case w/a pair of large plain cupboard doors each centered by a small lion mask & ring pull, narrow molded base on low bracket feet, Europe, late 19th - early 20th c., 13 x 49", 63" h. (ILLUS., previous page) **$2,070**

Simple Large Classical Bookcase

Classical bookcase, mahogany & mahogany veneer, a high arched & scroll-carved crest on the rectangular top w/a deep flaring cornice above a case w/a pair of tall doors w/large glazed panes above recessed panels opening to wooden shelves, the stepped-out base w/a pair of deep drawers w/simple turned wood knobs above a deep platform base w/thin block feet, shrinkage cracks in side panels, veneer chips, ca. 1850, 18 3/4 x 48 1/4", 74" h. (ILLUS.)................. **$633**

Classical bookcase, mahogany & mahogany veneer, in the Louis Philippe taste, the rectangular top w/a deep flaring ogee cornice above a pair of tall four-pane glazed doors framed by ogee molding & opening to three wooden shelves above a pair of shorter paneled doors, deep flat apron w/low bracket feet, second quarter 19th c., 19 x 58", 98 1/2" h. (ILLUS., top next column).. **$8,050**

Classical Bookcase in Louis Philippe Taste

American Classical Mahogany Bookcase

Classical bookcase, mahogany & mahogany veneer, the rectangular top w/a flat flaring cornice above a projecting arch above a pair of tall glazed cupboard doors flanked by disengaged columns w/leaf-carved capitals, a mid-molding above a long deep bottom drawer flanked by plinths faced w/carved paterae, raised on tall leaf-carved paw front feet & plain back feet, small veneer chips & repairs, ca. 1850, 18 1/4 x 48 1/4", 67 1/4" h. (ILLUS.) **$1,840**

Large Classical Revival Mahogany Veneer Bookcase

Classical Revival bookcase, mahogany & mahogany veneer, the long rectangular top above a pair of tall front end columns carved w/sections of spiral acanthus leaves, reeded baluster & a leaf-carved base all atop a large paw foot, the front fitted w/three tall glazed doors opening to wooden shelves, flat base, some veneer chipping, old dark finish, ca. 1900, 20 x 77", 4' 10" h. (ILLUS.)..................... **$1,116**

Nice Classical-Style Mahogany Bookcase

Classical-Style bookcase, carved mahogany & mahogany veneer, the rectangular top w/blocked ends & a narrow flaring cornice above a wide frieze band & a pair of tall geometrically-glazed doors opening to wooden shelves, all flanked by free-standing ring- and leaf-carved columns resting on paw-carved front feet, ca. 1890, 21 1/4 x 48", 72 1/4" h. (ILLUS.)... **$1,840**

South Carolina Old Heart Pine Bookcase

Country-style bookcase, heart pine, the rectangular top w/a deep flaring cornice above a wide frieze above an open case of five adjustable wooden shelves, flaring molded flat base, South Carolina, ca. 1900, 13 x 56", 84 3/8" h. (ILLUS.) **$1,380**

Pair Early Country-Style Grain-painted Bookcases

Country-style bookcases, painted & decorated pine, a rectangular top w/narrow molded cornice above a tall case w/a very tall 28-pane glazed door opening to five wooden shelves, a mid-molding above a long deep drawer w/two turned wood knobs, flat molded base, original reddish brown grain painting, central Massachusetts, ca. 1830, minor imperfections, 14 x 33", 82 3/4" h., pr. (ILLUS.)
.... **$10,575**

Three-part Stacking Lawyer's Bookcase

Early 20th century bookcase, oak, lawyer's stacking-type, three-section, the rectangular top w/rounded front edge above the three sections each w/a glazed lift-front door, raised on a base section w/a single long ogee-front drawer w/a pair of turned wood knobs, ca. 1910, some water damage, 25" w., 47" h. (ILLUS.)................. **$881**

Two-part Lawyer's Stacking Bookcase

Early 20th century bookcase, oak, lawyer's stacking-type, two-section, a rectangular top w/rounded front crest above the top sections w/lift-front glazed door shelves raised on a platform w/square legs, original finish, Globe-Wernike, 34" w., 40" h. (ILLUS.)................................ **$411**

English Edwardian Revolving Bookcase

Edwardian bookcase, mahogany, revolving-style, the square top above a cornice w/line-incised decoration above four slender turned & reeded corner columns framing the two shelf inner revolving bookcase w/angled corner panels, a narrow apron & small tapering corner block legs on casters, minor veneer chip, England, ca. 1900, 20" sq., 31 1/4" h. (ILLUS.) **$1,265**

Fine French Empire-Style Bookcase

Empire-Style bookcase, gilt-mounted mahogany, the molded breakfront crown over a conforming frieze w/gilt-metal mounts, above a tall central door w/a tall glazed pane above a recessed lower panel trimmed w/gilt-metal ribbons, opening to wooden shelves, tall narrow side doors each flanked by a pair of columns & mounted w/a large gilt-metal torch & wreath mount & smaller corner mounts, conforming breakfront flat base molding, France, late 19th - early 20th c., 15 1/2 x 68", 87" h. (ILLUS.) **$2,415**

Fine George III Hanging Bookcase

George III bookcase, mahogany, hanging-type, composed of five graduated open shelves supported by a flat back rail & joined at the sides w/ornate pierce-carved rails, England, ca. 1810, 6 3/4 x 37 1/4", 45 1/2" h. (ILLUS.) **$3,105**

Golden Oak bookcase, rectangular top w/thin flared cornice above serpentine corner brackets flanking a tall glazed door w/angled carved top corner brackets, opening to three adjustable shelves, glass sides, molded apron on simple cabriole legs, ca. 1900, 30" w. 5' 3" h. **$604**

Simple Late Victorian Mahogany Bookcase

Late Victorian bookcase, mahogany, two-part construction: the upper section w/a rectangular top w/a deep flaring cornice above a banded frieze band over a pair of tall glazed doors opening to four wooden shelves & double-paneled sides; the low-

er section w/a mid-molding over a pair of drawers w/simple bail pulls over the deep platform base, last quarter 19th c., 19 x 67 1/2", 93" h. (ILLUS.) **$1,438**

Victorian Country-style Bookcase

Victorian country-style bookcase, pine & walnut, the long rectangular top w/a shaped three-quarters gallery above a pair of tall glazed doors each w/a short rectangular pane over a tall rectangular pane, a long deep drawer w/carved leaf pulls across the flat bottom, 34" w., 4' 5" h. (ILLUS.) **$470**

Country Victorian Walnut Bookcase

Victorian country-style bookcase, walnut, a rectangular top above a wide flat frieze band above a pair of tall single-pane glazed doors opening to five wooden shelves, a pair of drawers w/black teardrop pulls at the bottom above the flat apron, ca. 1880, 43" w., 6' 7" h. (ILLUS.).. **$764**

Victorian Country-Style Bookcase

Victorian country-style bookcase, walnut, the rectangular top w/a stepped flaring cornice above a pair of tall two-pane glazed cabinet doors opening to six adjustable wooden shelves, a pair of drawers w/turned wood knobs at the bottom, raised on a later base frame w/simple bracket feet, second half 19th c., 14 x 45", 80" h. (ILLUS.) **$1,610**

Victorian Eastlake Revolving Bookcase

Victorian Eastlake substyle bookcase, inlaid mahogany, revolving-style, the square top w/a line-incised molding above two open shelves separated on each side w/cut-out panels & trimmed w/three narrow rails at each corner, satin wood inlay trim, rotating atop a cross-form base on casters, late 19th c., 21" sq., 32" h. (ILLUS.)................................. **$1,610**

Victorian Golden Oak Open Bookcase

Victorian Golden Oak style bookcase, oak, the rectangular top w/a low three-quarters gallery w/a central leaf-carved swag above a tall open case fitted w/four adjustable wooden shelves & a paneled back, line-incised decoration down the sides & across the wide flat apron, on wheels, ca. 1890-1900, some finish wear, 14 x 49 1/2", 62" h. (ILLUS.) **$633**

Bureaux Plat

Simple French Directoire Bureau Plat

Directoire bureau plat, brass-mounted fruitwood, the rectangular top overhanging an apron fitted w/two small drawers, raised on square tapering fluted legs, Southern France, early 19th c., 27 1/2" h. (ILLUS.)... **$1,380**

Directoire-Style bureau plat, gilt bronze-mounted parquetry, the rectangular top w/inset leather writing surface over a recessed frieze drawer flanked by pairs of short drawers & faux drawers on the reverse, raised on square tapering legs ending in brass cuffed feet, overall inlaid w/chevron & herringbone banding & mounted on each side w/gilt-bronze ribbon-tied foliate swags, France, late 19th c., 23 1/2 x 51", 29" h. (ILLUS., next page)
.... **$3,819**

Original French Empire Bureau Plat

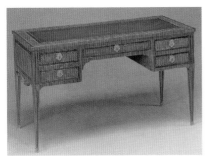

Empire bureau plat, gilt-bronze mounted mahogany, the rectangular top w/inset leather writing surface & stepped gilt banded edges over a leaf tip-banded frieze drawer & a pair of lion mask-mounted short drawers, raised on square tapering legs headed w/ribbon-tied swags ending in anthemia mounted on compressed ball feet, France, early 19th c., 28 x 47 1/2", 30" h. (ILLUS., top of page) **$3,819**

Fine French Directoire-Style Bureau Plat

French Empire Revival Bureau Plat

Empire Revival bureau plat, gilt bronze-mounted mahogany, the rectangular top inset w/gilt-tooled green leather within a wooden frame above the case w/a pair of small cross-banded drawers flanking a single long drawer, each mounted w/a long pierced scrolling brass, the square tapering legs headed by gilt carved Egyptian masks & palmettes & ending in a gilt paw foot, France, ca. 1900, 30 x 55", 30 1/2" h. (ILLUS.)
.... **$1,380**

Original French Louis XV Bureau Plat

Louis XV bureau plat, gilt bronze-mounted kingwood & rosewood, the rectangular top w/inset leather writing surface over a scalloped frieze w/a conforming drawer, raised on cabriole legs headed w/warrior masks & ending in animal hoof foot mounts, France, mid-19th c., 33 x 70", 29" h. (ILLUS.) **$8,225**

Small Louis XV-Style Bureaux Plat

Louis XV-Style, ebonized ormolu-mounted wood, the rectangular top inset w/a tooled brown leather writing surface framed by a molded ormolu rim, the apron mounted on one side w/two drawers flanking a large ormolu mask w/entwined hair & foliage, the back apron & sides w/matching decoration, raised on cabriole legs w/fancy ormolu chutes & sabots, stains on writing surface, some nicks, France, late 19th c., 24 1/2 x 39 1/2", 28 1/2" h. (ILLUS.) **$1,380**

Very Fine English Louis XV-Style Bureau Plat

Louis XV-Style bureau plat, gilt bronze & porcelain-mounted kingwood, the gilt-banded rectangular top w/serpentine sides centered by an inset leather writing surface within inlaid herringbone banding, three frieze drawers w/gilt-banded porcelain panels each decorated in polychrome w/birds & foliate plaques, the simple cabriole legs decorated w/gilt-bronze mounts & ending in gilt-bronze sabots, England, late 19th - early 20th c., 25 1/2 x 51", 30" h. (ILLUS.) **$15,275**

Very Fine Louis XV-Style Bureau Plat

Louis XV-Style bureau plat, ormolu-mounted kingwood & marquetry, the rectangular top w/serpentine ormolu-mounted edges set w/a leather writing surface, above a conforming frieze, the front w/three drawers fronted w/foliate srigs within scrolling frames, the sides & back similarly decorated, the C-scrolled ormolu long leg mounts trailing foliage down the cabriole legs tapering & ending in scrolled sabots, after the model by Jacques Dubois, France, last quarter 19th c., 31 x 53", 31" h. (ILLUS.) **$12,000**

Restrained Louis XVI-Style Bureau Plat

Louis XVI-Style bureau plat, burlwood & mahogany, the rectangular top w/a large leather inset above a simple apron w/a long diamond panel inlay flanked on each side by pairs of matching smaller drawers, gilt-metal & carved ebonized wood panels atop the square tapering legs ending in brass caps, France, ca. 1900, 32 x 55 1/2", 29 1/2" h. (ILLUS.) **$1,725**

Very Fine Louis XVI-Style Bureau Plat

Louis XVI-Style bureau plat, ormolu-mounted kingwood, the rectangular top w/serpentine ormolu edging around an inset leather writing surface, the serpentine apron w/fine banded veneering, two narrow drawers w/an ormolu escutcheon or pull separated by a long pierced scroll mount from the single long central drawer, the reverse apron fitted w/matching faux drawers, raised on simple cabriole legs w/ornate scroll & floral mounts at the knees & ending in leaf & scroll metal sabots, France, late 19th c., 31 1/2 x 56 1/2", 30" h. (ILLUS.) **$5,060**

Cabinets

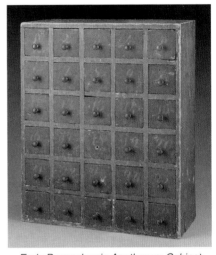

Early Pennsylvania Apothecary Cabinet

Apothecary cabinet, country-style, painted wood, a narrow rectangular top & sides enclosing an arrangement of 30 small square drawers w/simple turned wood knobs, flat base, original dark painted decoration, Pennsylvania, first half 19th c., 6 1/2 x 15 1/2", 18 1/2" h. (ILLUS.) **$4,200**

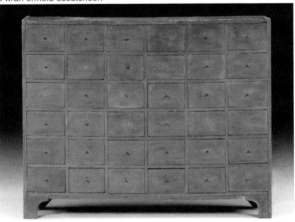

Rare Blue-Painted Country Apothecary Cabinet

Apothecary cabinet, country-style, the narrow long rectangular top above a case fitted w/six rows of six small drawers each, on simple bracket feet, old powder blue paint, 19th c., 9 3/4 x 58 1/2", 45 3/4" h. (ILLUS.)
.... **$10,800**

Fine Victorian Oak & Glass Cane Cabinet

Cane cabinet, oak & glass, tall upright rectangular form, the oak framework topped w/a hinged curved glass top & glass sides opening to a mirrored back & a stick-band-ball grid w/78 square cane holes, the tall lower case w/a mirrored back & glass front & sides, raised on a deep stepped oak base on metal casters, ca. 1880, 18 1/4 x 36", 48" h. (ILLUS.)... **$1,840**

Tall Rectangular Victorian Cane Cabinet

Cane cabinet, oak & glass, the tall rectangular cabinet w/an oak framework & rectangular oak hinged top opening to a removable grate w/a decorative metal center section for holding 65 canes, all four sides composed of two large glass panes, ca. 1880, 14 1/2 x 30", 44 3/4" h. (ILLUS.)... **$1,265**

Rare Early Mahogany Cellarette

Cellarette (wine cabinet), early American style, mahogany, the hexagonal hinged top w/an inlaid holly edge opening to a tin-lined sectioned interior for wine bottles & w/a drainage hole, the hexagonal case trimmed w/three wide brass straps & brass carrying handles, sitting on a conforming mahogany stand w/three square splayed & reeded legs w/arched returns, old surface, Boston, late 18th c., family provenance provided, minor surface imperfections, 19 x 19 1/8", 28 3/4" h. (ILLUS.) **$5,875**

Fine Federal Inlaid Walnut Cellarette

Cellarette (wine cabinet), Federal style, inlaid walnut, two-part construction: the upper section w/a nearly square hinged top opening to a deep well above a single flush drawer below, the front decorated w/a line-inlaid panel w/inlaid fans in each corner & centered by an inlaid rayed paterae below the inlaid diamond keyhole escutcheon; the lower section w/a molded edge above an apron w/two small square drawers flanking a wider central drawer w/an oval brass, raised on slender square tapering legs, late 18th - early 19th c., 20 x 22", 41 1/2" h. (ILLUS.)...... **$4,560**

Inlaid Mahogany Federal-Style Cellarette

Cellarette (wine cabinet), Federal-Style, inlaid mahogany, two-part construction: the upper section w/a rectangular hinged top opening to a divided interior, the front w/a line-inlaid large panel centered by a small oval enclosing a spread-winged eagle; the later lower section w/a single drawer w/oval brass raised on square tapering legs w/inlaid accents, late 19th c., top w/old repair, 16 x 22", 41 3/4" h. (ILLUS.) **$1,035**

Large Chippendale-Style China Cabinet

China cabinet, Chippendale-Style, mahogany & mahogany veneer, breakfront-style, the rectangular top w/a projecting central section, the narrow flaring bead-carved cornice above a conforming blind fret-carved frieze band above a wide tall glazed central door opening to three long wood shelves & flanked by tall narrow geometrically-glazed doors & glazed side panels above the slightly stepped-out base cabinet w/a gadrooned band above a blind fret-carved frieze band above a pair of center doors decorated w/veneered panels framing a large oval reserve carved in relief w/Chinese figures & a small temple, flat side doors decorated w/veneered panels & a diamond-shaped burl center panel, narrow molded base raised on four carved ogee bracket feet, England, early 20th c., 19 1/2 x 60 1/2", 81" h. (ILLUS.) **$5,750**

Fine Federal-Style China Cabinet

China cabinet, Federal-Style, inlaid mahogany & mahogany veneer, two-part construction: the rectangular breakfront top w/a narrow cornice above a dentil-carved band over a conforming case w/two tall narrow glazed side doors flanking the wider center glazed door, all w/semi-circular & diamond-shaped panes; the stepped out lower section w/a bowed center section above a stack of three deep drawers w/veneer banding & round brass pulls flanked by tall narrow veneer-banded cabinet doors, flat conforming base, one pane missing, minor edge damage, 20th c., 19 x 50", 80 1/2" h. (ILLUS.) **$575**

Fine Louis XVI-Style China Cabinet

China cabinet, Louis XVI-Style, mahogany & mahogany veneer, the wide half-round top w/a projecting center section above a conforming frieze band carved w/a repeating design of ormolu swags above tall curved glass sides flanking a pair of slender reeded pilasters on either side of the tall central door w/a flat glazed panel above a mahogany veneer lower panel outlined w/ormolu banding, the lower curved side panels w/matching banding, raised on four sharply tapering funnel legs w/oromlu bands & tips, probably France, mid-20th c., 16 x 48", 5'9" h. (ILLUS.) **$3,525**

Mission Oak China Cabinet with Crest

China cabinet, Mission-style (Arts & Crafts movement), oak, the rectangular top w/a low arched carved crest above the case w/a tall rectangular glazed center door flanked by tall narrow arched glass panels, glass sides, door opens to three wooden

shelves, flat apron w/beaded band, square stile legs w/curved & pierced front corner brackets, legs joined by an H-stretcher, branded number on the back, early 20th c., 19 x 44", 63 1/2" h. (ILLUS.) **$345**

Oak Classical Revival China Cabinet

China cabinet, Victorian Classical Revival style, oak, half-round top w/a low flat back crest & front blocks above a conforming case w/tall curved glass sides & a curved glass center door flanked at the top by a pair of heavy S-scroll brackets, opens to four wooden shelves, a narrow molded base band raised on four heavy C-scroll feet, ca. 1900, 36" w., 5' h. (ILLUS.) **$500**

Unusual Oak Curved Glass China Cabinet

China cabinet, Victorian Classical Revival style, oak, the rectangular top w/a long low crestrail above the tall curved-front cabinet & supported at the projecting front corners by slender free-standing columns, the cabinet w/curved glass sides & a tall curved glass center door opening to four wooden shelves, the rectangular lower case w/a gently serpentine front over a long serpentine drawer w/wooden knobs, simple blocky serpentine front legs, original finish, ca. 1900, 37" w., 5' 7" h. (ILLUS.) **$999**

Simple Golden Oak China Cabinet

China cabinet, Victorian Gold Oak style, the half-round top mounted by a long low flat back rail centered by a small pierced arch scroll crest, the flat-centered conforming case w/a tall glass door opening to four wooden shelves & flanked by curved glass side panels, molded base raised on four simple flattened cabriole legs on casters, ca. 1900, 35" w., 69" h. (ILLUS.) **$863**

Ornate Golden Oak Side-by-Side China Cabinet

China cabinet, Victorian Golden Oak substyle, side-by-side type, the top w/a wide broken-scroll crest centered by a carved fruit finial above small open shelf w/upturned ends supported on a scroll-carved bracket & slender turned spindle, above the two-section case w/the wider left side topped by a large shaped rectangular beveled mirror above a stepped top w/a shaped side panel carved w/an animal head & a serpentine front above two long serpentine drawers w/fancy pierced-brass pulls & keyhole escutcheons above a pair of wide paneled cupboard doors w/ornately scroll-carved panels & projecting flat cabriole legs, the right side of the case w/a tall glazed door w/a scroll-carved top & base opening to adjustable wooden shelves, original finish, late 19th c., 52" w., 5' 7" h. (ILLUS.) **$1,645**

Unusual Ebonized Rococo Cabinet

China cabinet, Victorian Rococo substyle, ebonized oak, the top w/a very tall arched & ornately carved crest in a broken-scroll design centered by a shell finial above a large cartouche flanked by ornate ribbon & flower carving, the small projecting round top corners fitted w/squatty turned finials, the long chamfered front cabinet sides w/carved details flanking the tall glazed door w/a large oval of glass surrounded by a twig-carved molding & opening to three glass shelves & an oval mirrored back, the flat molded base rail w/a scroll-carved center drop, all raised on cabriole legs ending in pad feet, original black finish, by G.W. Horrix Company, Gravenhage, mid-19th c., 16 x 42", overall 82 1/2" h. (ILLUS.) **$1,610**

Extremely Ornate Japanese Collector's Cabinet on Stand

Collector's cabinet on stand, Oriental style, parcel-gilt black lacquer, two-part construction: the upper cabinet w/a rectangular top, sides & pair of doors richly decorated w/scenes of flowers & birds, the doors w/molded panels decorated w/landscapes in heavy gold enamel & mounted w/brass fitting, opening to an interior composed of 12 drawers of varying sizes each w/ornate flower & insect decoration; the lower stand section made in Europe & features similar decoration, the cabinet made in Japan, ca. 1850, some brass loose, minor wear, 21 x 40 1/4", 62" h. (ILLUS.) **$12,650**

Unusual Classical Country Commode Cabinet

Commade cabinet, Classical country-style, painted pine, rectangular hinged top & hinged fall-front w/two turned wood knobs open to reveal a seat w/hole flanked by arm rests, the lower cabinet flanked by simple turned columns continuing into ring-turned front feet, original black & red grain painting w/wear, age crack in scrubbed top, some minor edge damage, first half 19th c., 19 x 25", 29" h. (ILLUS.)... **$374**

Fine Louis XV-Style Curio Cabinet

Curio cabinet, giltwood, Louis XV-style, the wide molded arched crestrail centered by a high crest carved w/scrolls & cherub heads above a large glass-paned door w/an ornately leaf-carved lower panel, bowed glass side panels above matching carved lower panels, raised on simple cabriole legs, open to two glass shelves, France, last half 19th c., original finish, 19 x 33 1/2", 69 3/4" h. (ILLUS.) **$1,265**

Late Victorian Rococo Revival Cabinet

Curio cabinet, mahogany & mahogany veneer, late Victorian Rococo Revival style, a tall half-round case topped by a very high back crest w/rounded sides & a pointed center finial, fitted w/two small round projecting shelves w/spindled galleries raised on a slender spindle support, the case composed of two tall curved glass panels, one half forming the hinged door opening to the mirrored interior, molded base raised on three very slender simple cabriole legs, ca. 1890s, 15 x 26", 70 1/2" h. (ILLUS.) **$863**

Ornately Carved Chinese Curio Cabinet

Curio cabinet, Oriental style, carved hardwood, the tall case w/a high peaked & or-

nately pierce-carved cornice of scrolling foliage centering a cartouche of carved birds & animals, above a three-part open gallery w/pierced border trim & floral-pierced back panels above an arrangement of four staggered open shelves all w/pierce-carved aprons & a continuous ornately pierce-carved back, a lower shelf over a pair of small drawers above four small open shelves beside a small cupboard w/a pair of carved panel doors, a gadrooned base molding over a pierce-carved scrolling apron raised on claw-and-ball feet, some shrinkage separation to backs & joints, China, late 19th c., 14 x 46 3/4", 83 1/2" h. (ILLUS.) **$1,150**

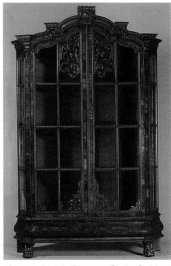

Ornate Dutch Rococo Curio Cabinet

Curio cabinet, Rococo style, walnut & burl walnut, an ornate arched & stepped deep front crestrail centered by shell-carved crest flanked by small stepped platforms on each side, all above a pair of tall arched 8-pane glazed doors w/delicate ornate pierced carving over the top two center panes & lower two center panes, the sides composed of four glass panels, the deep ogee apron fitted w/a pair of drawers w/fancy brass pulls in the front, a molded base raised on heavy paw-carved front feet, Holland, ca. 1880, 17 x 63", 99" h. (ILLUS.) **$4,600**

Curio cabinet, Victorian Aesthetic Movement style, walnut, table-top model, the small upright hexagonal cabinet w/a low pierced gallery along each side of the top separated by shaped blocks w/small turned finials above frieze bands over six arched glazed doors finely inlaid w/geometric & floral designs, fitted w/two glass shelves, raised on a deep cross-form base w/short bobbin-turned stiles & out-scrolled feet each w/a outer stick-and-ball spindle, third quarter 19th c., 23" w., 36" h. (ILLUS., next page) **$2,070**

Victorian Aesthetic Curio Cabinet

Ornate Tall Japanese Curio Cabinet

Curio cabinet on stand, carved & decorated handwood, Oriental, the tall upper cabinet w/a rectangular top w/a narrow scroll-carved cornice above a pair of small projecting cupboard doors decorated w/panels in dark blue applied w/carved bone figures of people, birds, flowers & trees, each trimmed w/pierce-carved bands & flanking a pair of similar smaller recessed doors, the projecting narrow side sections each w/two open compartments w/decorative figural panels or pierce-carved panels above another pair of decorated doors at the bottom, the wider central section below the upper doors composed of two long rectangular open compartments backed by figural panels & another pair of small cupboard doors over an open backless compartment, three small drawers across the bottom; the high platform base w/a pierce-carved narrow frieze above a leaf-carved apron continuing into flat scrolling front legs

joined by a long delicate scroll-carved bracket, Japan, Meiji period, ca. 1880, some repairs & missing applied pieces, 15 1/2 x 59 1/4", 86" h. (ILLUS.) **$3,910**

Chinese Chippendale-Style Curio Cabinet

Curio cabinet on stand, carved & lacquered wood, Chinese Chippendale-Style, two-part construction: the upper section w/a rectangular top above a pair of tall flat doors opening to shelves, decorated overall w/green lacquer panels painted in gold & black w/stylized Chinese landscape & trimmed w/fancy pierced & chased metal strapwork hinges & keyhole escutcheons; the lower section w/a shell-carved mid-molding above a serpentine scroll-carved narrow apron raised on leaf-carved cabriole legs ending in scroll & peg feet, England, late 19th - early 20th c., 19 x 38", 62" h. (ILLUS.) **$1,610**

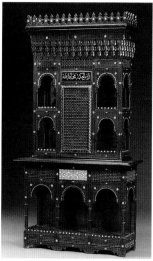

Elaborate Tall Moorish-Style Cabinet

Curio cabinet on stand, mother-of-pearl inlaid hardwood, Moorish-Style, two-part
construction: the upper section w/a very
tall pierced spearpoint-carved crestrail inlaid w/small stars above the very deep
cornice frieze composed of carved tiered
spearpoints above a cabinet w/a pair of
small carved & star-inlaid panels flanking
a pierced lattice-carved rectangular panel above a raised panel inlaid w/Arabic
script above a pair of tall latticework
doors framed by an inlaid leafy vine,
flanked on each side by two open compartments w/Moorish arches carved w/in-
cised designs & decorative inlay, the
sides w/matching Moorish arch compartments; the stepped-out lower cabinet w/a
rectangular top overhanging a case w/a
pair of rectangular pierced lattice panels
flanking a single geometrically-inlaid
drawer above three tall Moorish arches
raised on simple turned columns, the
sides w/matching pierced panels & arches, the deep platform base w/a scalloped
top band w/button inlay above three
carved & lattice-pierced rectangular panels, scroll-cut bracket feet, ca. 1890,
17 1/2 x 47 1/4", 88 1/4" h. (ILLUS., pre-
vious page)... **$7,768**

Very Ornate Italian Display Cabinet

Display cabinet, Baroque-Style, ebonized
rosewood w/ivory inlay, the very tall upper section w/an architectural pointed
pediment above an arched inlaid frieze
surmounted by urn-form finials, the tall
paneled doors decorated w/allegorical
figures & flanked by columns, the upper
stage interior containing thirteen drawers
centered by a niche & above a long drawer; the projecting lower section w/a rectangular top above a pair of paneled
doors w/ornate oval inlaid panels & borders flanked by tall narrow side panels a
spiral-twist carved front corners, on a
deep widely stepped & blocked plinth
base, Italy, mid-19th c., 21 x 52", 110" h.
(ILLUS.)... **$16,675**

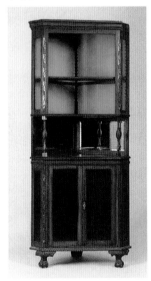

Colonial Revival Curio Corner Cabinet

Curio corner cabinet, Colonial Revival
style, oak, the flat top w/a molded cornice
above a tall open one-shelf cabinet w/two
narrow beveled glass side windows &
carved front stiles, above an open section w/two knob-turned front spindles &
backed by two rectangular mirrors, the
lower section w/a pair of tall glazed doors
flanked by narrow beveled side windows,
all resting on two front ball-and-claw feet,
second half 19th c, 20 x 34", 79 1/2" h.
(ILLUS.)... **$460**

Unusual Old Oak File Cabinet

File cabinet, oak, early 20th c., stacking-
type, the rectangular top section w/a
rounded front rail above a row of seven

vertical pull-out file drawers w/brass loop handles & brass name tag holders, the center section w/a row of three large pull-out file drawers w/matching pulls & tag holders, the short bottom section composed of four short drawers w/name tag holders & metal finger-grip pulls, ca. 1920, 41" w., 36" h. (ILLUS.).................... **$999**

Tall Late Victorian Music Cabinet

Music cabinet, mahogany-finished hardwood, tall upright form w/an arched crestrail carved w/a rondel & pierced scrolls above a narrow open shelf raised on pairs of slender spiral-turned spindles above a back panel fitted w/a rectangular beveled mirror, the projecting case w/a rectangular top flanked by simple end galleries above a narrow carved front edge over a pair of tall narrow paneled doors each carved w/stylized leaves & berries centered by a carved harp, narrow half-round spiral-carved pilasters down the sides above an open bottom compartment above the flat reeded legs ending in scallop-cut feet, doors open to six birch or maple pull-out drawers, patent-dated tag in the lower drawer dated 1892, some wear to finish, 14 1/2 x 19 1/2", 62" h. (ILLUS.) **$1,080**

Music cabinet, oak, Mission-style (Arts & Crafts movement), the rectangular top w/a low three-quarters mortised gallery above a single tall 12-pane glazed door w/hammered amber glass panes, stamped copper door pull, opening to shelves, flat base w/simple cut-out sides, mint original finish, one replaced glass pane, branded mark of Gustav Stickley & evidence of a paper label, 16 x 20", 54 1/2" h. (ILLUS., top next column) **$16,100**

Rare Gustav Stickley Music Cabinet

Early French Empire Boulle Cabinet

Side cabinet, French Empire style, boullework, the rectangular top decorated w/elaborate pierced & inlaid gilt-bronze boulle florals & scrolls, the case w/a single tall arched glazed door bordered w/further fancy boullework, the deep plinth base w/a serpentine apron, France, early 19th c., 12 x 21", 40" h. (ILLUS.).......................... **$2,415**

Fancy Louis XV-Style Side Cabinet

Unusual Early Jacobean Style Cabinet

Side cabinet, hardwood, Jacobean style, the flat two-board trapezoidal top tapers toward the front above a wide frieze band w/the sides finely carved w/scrolls & scallops, the front w/a single drawer w/a metal teardrop pull & decorated w/a repeating scroll band, flanked by small scrolled leaf-carved panels, the case above open sides w/arched top brackets at each side, the front supported by two heavy knob- and baluster-turned supports above the plain trapezoidal lower shelf, the solid back divided into four recessed panels, the flat base apron w/shallow leafy scroll carving & resting on two small bun feet, Europe, probably 18th c. or possibly 17 th c., dark finish, 19 1/2 x 33", 32" h. (ILLUS.) **$1,035**

Side cabinet, Louis XV-Style, boullework, oak & mahogany veneer, the rectangular white marble top w/a narrow ormolu gadrooned border band above rounded corners w/openwork ormolu mounts flanking a long drawer w/fine brass boullework w/dark red & black tortoiseshell, a thin ormolu band above the tall lower cabinet w/the angled front corners topped by ornate Minerva head ormolu mounts above a narrow boullework panel & a scroll-cast bottom ormolu mount, a single wide door centered by a large boullework oval panel bordered by an ormolu band & four oblong leafy scroll ormolu mounts dividing the boullework borders, the slightly stepped-out plinth base w/a narrow ormolu band above the serpentine apron w/rounded front corners w/pierced rectangular ormolu mounts & a long pierced leafy scroll center ormolu mount, France, second half 19th c., 15 1/2 x 33", 44" h. (ILLUS.).......... **$978**

Elaborately Carved, Inlaid & Painted Early Spanish Side Cabinet

Side cabinet, polychromed & bone-inlaid walnut, Renaissance-Style, a long rectangular top above a case w/a central arch-paneled door opening to three drawers & above a bottom drawer, the door flanked by a stack of three drawers on either side, the outer frame inlaid w/a zig-zag band, the arched door panel w/carved & inlaid stylized columns, each drawer centered by an inlaid six-point star flanked by small inlaid panels, raised on ring-turned bun feet, Spain, late 18th - early 19th c., 13 x 35", 22" h. (ILLUS.) **$3,450**

Fine Victorian Aesthetic Side Cabinet

Side cabinet, Victorian Aesthetic Movement style, mahogany, in the Renaissance taste, the tall superstructure w/an ornate arched crestrail pierce-carved w/a pair of birds & leafy scrolls flanking a medallion above a cornice molding over a long low rectangular mirror flanked by large scroll-carved ends all raised on stepped gadroon-carved rails, the rectangular top w/molded edges overhanging the case w/end doors w/rectangular beveled glass doors flanking reeded & carved pilasters flanking the large central solid door carved w/ornate scrolls & a central urn, the end stiles carved w/bold caryatids, beveled glass end panels, all above a long narrow scroll-carved central drawer flanked by carved masks above a serpentine scroll-carved apron raised on heavy baluster- and ring-turned posts resting on an large open shelf w/a paneled board back & flaring stepped & carved apron raised on squatty bun feet, late 19th c., 14 x 46", 72" h. (ILLUS.)..... **$2,070**

Fine Signed Renaissance Revival Cabinet

Side cabinet, Victorian Renaissance Revival style, brass & mother-of-pearl-inlaid ebonized wood, the rectangular top w/molded edge above a tall molded panel door w/faux drawers decorated w/fine inlaid design, the top panel w/an elaborate scene of a fountain & two birds issuing ornate leafy flowering vines, tall slender fluted columns down each side w/gilt-metal capitals & ring-turned bases resting on a molded base w/disk-turned feet, stamped "Elzentum," Europe, ca. 1875, top missing string inlay, some scuffs & scratches, 25 x 31", 38" h. (ILLUS.)....... **$1,610**

Rare Elaborate Renaissance Revival Side Cabinet

Side cabinet, Victorian Renaissance Revival style, bronze-mounted rosewood, ebonized cherry & maple, the long top w/a raised rectangular central section supported by carved palmettes & a panel of gilt-trimmed carved wheat centering an upright arch-topped bronze panel featuring the figure of a classical maiden, the lower side section w/wide incurved sides above a conforming apron w/a narrow inlaid frieze band over a gilt-bronze narrow applied band, the case w/tall incurved end doors & three doors across the front, the outer matching doors flanked by inlaid pilasters w/gilt capitals & decorated w/a raised narrow rectangular burl molding w/a small round bronze disk at the top & bottom center, surrounding a black panel centered by a large fruit-filled gilt-bronze urn, the taller central arched door w/a recessed panel bordered by gilt & ebonized band, the panel ornately inlaid w/delicate leafy scrolls & flowers centered by a large oval porcelain plaque h.p. w/a colorful romantic garden landscape, the heavy blocked black w/bronze band trim & gilt-bronze accents, attributed to Alexander Roux, New York, New York, ca. 1866, 21 x 91 1/2", 55" h. (ILLUS., bottom previous page) **$31,200**

Ornate French Renaissance Side Cabinet

Side cabinet, Victorian Renaissance Revival substyle, parcel giltwood & bronze-mounted ebonized wood, the rectangular top w/incurved sides & a blocked front trimmed w/stepped brass banding above a fluted cornice & egg-and-dart frieze, the wide cabinet door w/a large double-band gold-outlined panel centered by an arched bronze relief plaque of the toilette of Venus framed by boldly carved arched scrolls & columns, fancy gilt-bronze latch, projecting spiral-carved columns at each corner flanking the concave side panels w/a thin rectangular metal panel enclosing long beribboned floral gilt-bronze pendants, the wide conforming molded base banded w/gilt-bronze gadrooning & a shell & leaf central panel, raised on short disk- and knob-turned feet, France,

Napoleon III era, ca. 1860-70, 20 x 40", 44" h. (ILLUS.) **$8,050**

Charles II-Style Side Cabinet

Side cabinet on stand, Charles II-Style, the upper black-lacquered cabinet w/a rectangular top over two doors decorated w/polychrome Japanese landscape scenes & fitted w/brass strap hinges & ornate lock mounts, the doors opening to an arrangement of ten drawers, composed of mid-19th century elements, raised on a late 19th century rectangular stand w/a paneled apron & square paneled legs joined by a flat X-stretcher & ending in square tapering feet, England, late 19th c., 18 1/2 x 35 1/2", overall 4' 10" h. (ILLUS.) **$2,070**

Victorian Upright Store Spool Cabinet

Spool cabinet, cherry, upright revolving store-type, the square top w/a notched pediment above the molded cornice, the front fitted w/a stack of narrow spool drawers w/pull-down glass fronts over two narrow bottom drawers, the sides & back fitted w/mirrors, revolving on a short base, late 19th c., 18" sq., 38" h. (ILLUS., previous page) **$1,093**

Victorian Two-Drawer Spool Cabinet

Spool cabinet, walnut, store counter-type style, the square top w/an inset panel overhanging the short case fitted w/two shallow drawers w/turned pulls flanking an inset oval glass panel, one printed in gold on black "Goff's," the other "Braid," narrow molded flat base, late 19th c., 17 1/4" sq., 7 1/2" h. (ILLUS.) **$173**

Chinese Decorated Lacquer Cabinet

Storage cabinet, Oriental-style, decorated black lacquer, the rectangular top above a pair of tall flat cupboard doors decorated w/a continuous gold & red Chinese landscape scene filled w/people, trees & temples, three small drawers below the doors each w/red & gold floral designs, four heavy square stile legs, old worn fin-

ish, opens to three shelves w/some remains of the old wallpaper lining, old restorations w/areas of touch-up, Shanxi, China, 22 x 43", 79" h. (ILLUS.)............... **$345**

Early Biedermeier Vitrine Cabinet

Vitrine cabinet, Biedermeier style, inlaid rosewood, the stepped rectangular top over an arched glazed door opening to a shelved & mirrored interior flanked by three-quarter round columns above a foliate-inlaid long drawer, raised on ring- and baluster-turned legs ending in compressed ball feet, Europe, early 19th c., 19 x 33 1/2", 5' 8" h. (ILLUS.) **$4,113**

French Charles X Vitrine Cabinet

Vitrine cabinet, Charles X style, rosewood & inlaid boxwood, the rectangular stopped top w/a wide flaring stepped cornice w/rounded corners above a frieze panel inlaid w/a line-inlaid long rectangle above a single tall door w/a large glazed panel above a cross-grain veneered lower panel, a single long line-inlaid drawer across the bottom, deep molded base w/further line inlay, raised on low bracket feet, France, second quarter 19th c., 18 1/2 x 42", 86" h. (ILLUS., previous page) **$3,738**

Fine Louis XV-Style Vitrine Cabinet

Vitrine cabinet giltwood, Louis XV-Style, the half-round paneled top mounted by a high central arched broken-scroll crest decorated w/leaves above the triple-arched molded cornice, the front w/a tall flat glazed door w/an arched top opening to two half-round wooden shelves, the angled sides w/arched glazed panels, the stiles each carved w/floral pendants & narrow raised panels, the lower section w/a gadrooned mid-molding over the conforming apron decorated w/bold shell & leaf carvings, raised on four tapering square legs topped by large leafy scroll & rosette sections & ending in pointed block feet, the legs joined by a flattened cross-stretcher centered by a small bulbous turned finial, France, late 19th c., 14 x 36 1/2", 84" h. (ILLUS.) **$4,600**

Vitrine cabinet, Louis XVI-Style, ormolu-mounted mahogany, the rectangular variegated rouge marble top w/canted corners above a conforming frieze applied w/Bacchic putti, masks & garlands, over a pair of tall beveled glass doors w/curved bases & matching glazed sides, opening to a green velvet-lined interior w/three ad-

Very Fine Louis XVI-Style Vitrine Cabinet

justable glass shelves, on foliate-hipped cabriole legs & scrolled ormolu sabots, marked on the lock, by Francois Linke, Paris, France, first quarter 20th c., 16 1/4 x 41 3/4", 65" h. (ILLUS.) **$14,400**

Chairs

Rustic Bentwood Tall Rocking Chair

Adirondack rustic bentwood rocker, the tall rounded back & arms composed of long bentwood hickory branches forming bands, the back w/long criss-crossed branches forming a lattice design, the seat composed of narrow slats, on rockers, old mellow brown finish, a couple of old putty restorations, late 19th - early 20th c., 41 1/2" h. (ILLUS.) **$288**

Art Deco Tubular Steel Upholstered Armchairs Attributed to Thonet

Art Deco Bent Bamboo Armchair

Art Deco armchair, bamboo, the back w/a squared bent bamboo frame fitted w/a large cushion, the large five-layered bent bamboo pretzel-style arms enclosing further bamboo rails, the deep oblong seat frame made of five-layered bent bamboo, deep cushion seat, after a design by Paul Frank, 30" h. (ILLUS.) **$150-300**

Art Deco armchairs, chrome-plated tubular steel & upholstery, each w/a high, wide upholstered back, one back framed by tubular steel, open tubular steel arms above the deep slightly angled upholstered seat, one w/a flat rectangular tubular steel frame & legs, the other w/an angled seat frame, short front legs & tubular flat side stretchers, attributed to Thonet, Austria, ca. 1935, 31" h. & 30" h., the set (ILLUS., top of page) **$8,963**

Pair of Fine Art Deco Armchairs

Art Deco armchairs, mahogany, a slightly flaring rectangular back panel w/bone white linen upholstery raised above the over-upholstered seat flanked by curved open wood arms, raised on slender square tapering slightly shaped front legs, in the style of Emile-Jacques Ruhlmann, ca. 1930, 32" h., pr. (ILLUS.)
.... **$2,990**

Luxurious Brown Leather Art Deco Club Chairs

Art Deco club armchairs, leather & walnut, overstuffed design w/serpentine crestrails & thick outcurved arms, cushion seat, ca. 1930, 30 x 36", 31" h., pr. (ILLUS.) **$3,450**

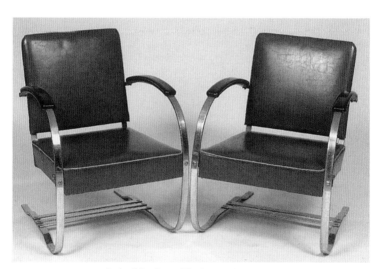

Pair of Art Deco "Springer" Armchairs

Art Deco "Springer" armchairs, chrome & leatherette upholstery, the square upholstered back joined to curved chrome rails mounted w/black pads & curving down & back to form the supports joined under the upholstered seat by three flat chrome bars, signed "Howell," ca. 1935, 31" h., pr. (ILLUS.) **$259**

Ornately Carved Art Nouveau Armchair

Art Nouveau armchair, ornately carved mahogany, the tall back topped by pierced & solid butterfly wings centered by the head of an Art Nouveau maiden above a tall flaring cluster for flower stems topped by lily-like blossoms, fluted curved open arms continuing into serpentine arm suports above the upholstered spring seat, the gently peaked front seatrail carved w/crossed stick clusters & a pendent flower cluster supported by long ribbons, fluted cabriole front legs, France, ca. 1905, 46" h. (ILLUS.) **$7,768**

Art Nouveau dining chair, carved walnut & tooled leather, the tall arched open back carved w/pierced Art Nouveau loops above the original leather seat w/tooled design, the pierced & loop-carved apron raised on four stem-like legs joined by slender angled side stretchers, designed by Hector Guimard, France, for the dining room of the Maison Coillot, Lille, France, ca. 1898-1900, 38 1/2" h. (ILLUS.) **$31,070**

Unusual Spindled Gustav Stickley Chair

Arts & Crafts style side chair, oak, the tall slightly canted band w/square stiles joined by two rails centered by a tight grouping of slender square spindles, raised above the leather-upholstered slip seat above square legs joined by high flat front & rear stretchers & low side stretchers joined by a tight grouping of slender square spindles to the bottom of the seatrail, Model No. 384, red decal mark of Gustav Stickley, ca. 1907, 46" h. (ILLUS.) **$3,585**

Very Rare French Art Nouveau Chair

Large Flemish Baroque-Style Armchair

Baroque-Style armchair, carved walnut, the large squared & arched back upholstered in a needlepoint tapestry material above the serpentine open arms on incurved arm supports above the wide tapestry-upholstered seat, serpentine front legs & square rear legs joined by an H-stretcher, Flemish, mid-19th c., 48" h. (ILLUS., previous page).. **$1,495**

Fine French Baroque-Style Armchair

Baroque-Style armchair, carved walnut, the tall arched back upholstered in tapestry trimmed w/roundhead nails, long scrolling open arms w/incurved arm supports above the wide tapestry-upholstered seat, the front cabriole legs headed by finely carved cherub heads w/wings & ending in claw-and-ball feet, cabriole rear legs w/paw feet, all joined by a scroll-carved X-stretcher, France, late 19th c., wear to upholstery, 48" h. (ILLUS.)... **$2,300**

Baroque-Style armchairs, carved walnut & marquetry, Black Forest-style, the large ballon-shaped back boldly carved overall w/naturalistically carved branches, clusters of grapes & leaves amid scrolls & centered by a small oval panel inlaid w/floral designs in light wood, the long scroll-carved open arms on C-scroll supports above the wide shaped seat w/gadroon-carved edges, heavy cabriole front legs carved w/leaf designs & leaf-carved serpentine rear legs, Switzerland, late 19th c., 43" h., pr. (ILLUS., bottom of page)... **$3,738**

Wonderfully Carved Swiss Armchairs

Spanish Baroque-Style Hall Chairs

Baroque-Style hall chairs, carved oak, the high flat balloon-form backs carved w/a large lion mask framed by ornate scrolls , rectangular board seats w/cut-corners, raised on fancy shaped front & rear supports, the front one centered by a large oval medallion framed by carved scrolls & swags, scroll feet, Spain, ca. 1900, 41" h., pr. (ILLUS.) **$920**

English Charles II Walnut Armchair

Charles II armchair, walnut, the tall rectangular base w/a blossom- and foliate-carved frame around a caned panel flanked by block- and spiral-twist stiles topped by small ball finials, shaped open arms w/scroll grip raised on spiral-turned supports above the carved & caned trapezoidal seat above a wide flat foliate-carved front stretcher, raised on block- and spiral-turned legs joined by a spiral-

turned H-stretcher & raised on ball feet, England, late 17th c., 47" h. (ILLUS.) **$1,763**

Rare Chippendale Mahogany Armchair

Chippendale armchair, carved mahogany, the ox-yoke crestrail w/scrolled ear centered by a carved shell above the pierced vasiform splat, serpentine open arms ending in scroll-carved hand grips above incurved arm supports, wide upholstered slip seat w/a flat seatrail centered at the front by a carved shell, cabriole front legs w/shell-carved knees ending in claw-and-ball feet, canted turned rear legs, descended in the Stevenson Family, Philadelphia, ca. 1770, 40 7/8" h. (ILLUS.) **$36,000**

One of Two Country Chippendale Chairs

Chippendale country-style side chairs, mahogany, the serpentine crest above the pierced vasiform splat above the upholstered slip seat, square Marlborough front legs & square canted rear legs joined by box stretchers, refinished, minor imperfections, possibly Virginia, late 18th c., 37 1/2" h., pr. (ILLUS. of one) ... **$2,938**

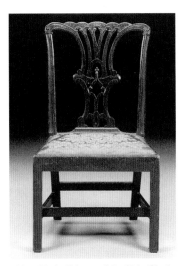

New York Chippendale Side Chair

Chippendale side chair, carved mahogany, scalloped & scroll-carved crestrail above a wide slit-carved splat centered by scroll carving above the upholstered slip seat, square legs joined by flat box stretchers, retains old & possibly original finish, New York City, 1765-85, 38 1/2" h. (ILLUS.) ... **$6,573**

Chippendale side chair, carved mahogany, the serpentine crestrail ending in carved ears above an ornately carved Gothic style splat above the upholstered slip seat, double-arched front seatrail & cabriole

front legs w/leaf-carved knees & ending in claw-and-ball feet, simple turned rear legs, Philadelphia, 1760-80, descended in the family of Governor John Lambert, New Jersey, 38 1/4" h. (ILLUS., bottom of page) **$14,430**

Carved Walnut Chippendale Side Chair

Chippendale side chair, carved walnut, the oxbow crestrail w/fluted ears above a fancy pierce-carved splat w/scroll-carved accents, the upholstered slip seat w/flat rails raised on cabriole front legs w/carved knees ending in claw-and-ball feet, square canted rear legs, possibly Maryland, ca. 1760-80, 30 3/8" h. (ILLUS.) **$2,400**

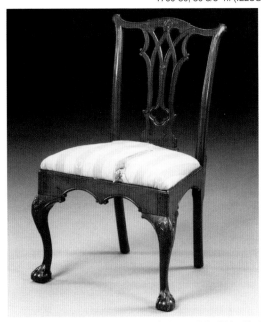

Rare Finely Carved Philadelphia Chippendale Side Chair

Set of Philadelphia Chippendale Side Chairs

Chippendale side chairs, carved mahogany, the back composed of four arched & pierced slats above the upholstered slip seat, square tapering legs joined by box stretchers, Philadelphia, 1770-90, 37" h., set of 4 (ILLUS.)...................................... **$2,390**

Fine Pair of Newport Chippendale Chairs

Chippendale side chairs, carved mahogany, the serpentine crestrail ending in fluted ears above a loop-pierced vasiform splat above the upholstered slip seat, square legs joined by flat H-stretchers, Newport, Rhode Island, 1780-1800, 38" h., pr. (ILLUS.)................................ **$7,800**

One of Two Chippendale Side Chairs

Chippendale side chairs, carved mahogany, the serpentine crest centered by a carved shell above the pierced scroll-carved splat, upholstered slip seat, square Marlborough front legs & canted square rear legs, joined by box stretchers, old refinish, minor imperfections, Boston or Salem, Massachusetts, 1755-85, 38" h., pr. (ILLUS. of one) **$4,113**

Pair Philadelphia Chippendale Chairs

Chippendale side chairs, mahogany, a serpentine crestrail w/rounded ears above a pierced vasiform splat over a trapezoidal slip seat, raised on cabriole legs ending in ball-and-claw feet, Philadelphia, second half 18th c., 31 1/2" h., pr. (ILLUS.).. **$6,463**

Chippendale "Wingback" Armchair

Chippendale "wingback" armchair, cherry, the wide arched upholstered back flanked by wide shaped & outswept upholstered wings above rolled arms, the cushion seat raised on square tapering & fluted front legs & canted square rear legs joined by box stretchers, New England, 1780-1800, 45 1/2" h. (ILLUS.) ... **$7,200**

Finely Carved Chippendale-Style Chair

Chippendale-Style armchair, carved mahogany, the shaped crestrail centered by a high arched scroll-carved crest w/a central shell above the pierce-carved Gothic-style back splat flanked by the molded & gently outswept stiles, shaped open arms ending in scroll grip raised on incurved arm supports above the over-upholstered wide seat, square front legs carved w/Gothic panels, square canted

rear legs, all joined by an H-stretcher, ca. 1890, 54" h. (ILLUS.) **$920**

One of a Set of Chippendale-Style Chairs

Chippendale-Style dining chairs, carved mahogany, the serpentine eared & acanthus leaf-carved crestrail above a vasiform pierced splat of interlacing serpentine bands, shaped open arms w/incurved arm support above the wide padded seat, flat seatrail raised on cabriole front legs w/leafy scroll-carved knees & ending in claw-and-ball feet, late 19th - early 20th c., 38" h., set of 12 (ILLUS. of one)... **$2,875**

Chippendale-Style Chair from a Set

Chippendale-Style dining chairs, mahogany, the back composed of four pierce-carved ribbon slats between molded gently outswept stiles above the over-upholstered seat, molded square front legs & canted rear legs joined by box stretchers, old dark finish, two armchairs w/re-attached arms & a glued split, one loose crest & split in one ribbon, one side stretcher replaced, late 19th - early 20th c., set of 8 (ILLUS. of one)............ **$1,150**

Fine American Early Classical Carved Armchairs

Set of Oak Chippendale-Style Chairs

Chippendale-Style dining chairs, oak, a
serpentine crest w/eared corners above
a scroll- and bar-pierced splat flanked by
stiles above an over-upholstered seat,
square legs on casters joined by an H-
stetcher, late 19th - early 20th c., 38" h.,
five side chairs & one armchair, set of 6
(ILLUS.)... **$920**

Fine Chippendale-Style "Wingback"

Chippendale-Style "wingback" armchair,
the high upholstered back w/an arched

crest flanked by outswept serpentine
wings over the out-scrolled upholstered
arms flanking the seat cushion, raised
on square molded legs joined by an H-
stretcher, linen upholstery w/overall
hand-stitched crewelwork, first half
20th c., 44" h. (ILLUS.)........................ **$3,105**

Chippendale-Style "Wingback" Armchair

Chippendale-Style "wingback" armchair,
the high wide upholstered back flanked
by serpentine flared wings above the upholstered rolled arms, deep upholstered
seat raised on cabriole front legs w/claw-
and-ball feet, refinished, 20th c.,
43 3/4" h. (ILLUS.) **$345**
Classical armchairs, carved mahogany,
the high rectangular upholstered back
w/shaped stiles & rolled flat crestrail
above shaped open arms ending in
heavy carved scrolls & resting on S-scroll
scroll-carved arm supports, the wide upholstered seat w/a gently carved front seatrail raised on scroll-carved front sabre
legs, probably Philadelphia, ca. 1815-30,
37 7/8" h., pr. (ILLUS., top of page) **$20,315**

A Classical and Country-Style Windsor Child's Chairs

Classical child's side chair, mahogany & mahogany veneer, the back stiles & rails forming a pointed arch above a vasiform splat above the horsehair-upholstered slip seat, flat serpentine front legs & plain canted rear legs, ca. 1830-40, 21" h. (ILLUS. left with country-style low-back child's Windsor) **$1,840**

Set of Bird's-Eye Maple Classical Side Chairs

Classical country-style side chairs, bird's-eye maple, the crestrail w/a rolled center & rounded ends above the vasiform splat & curved back stiles, caned seat above sabre-style front legs & outswept rear legs, curved flat front rung & turned side & back stretchers, ca. 1830, three w/no seat caning, one w/a back repair, 33" h., set of 4 (ILLUS.) **$518**

Classical country-style side chairs, painted & decorated, the wide gently curved crestrail h.p. w/a stylized rustic landscape over a narrow pierced knob band & raised above a smaller knob band slat between the decorated stiles, round-fronted caned seat raised on ring- and baluster-turned front legs joined by a flat front stretcher centered by a large flat rosette in gold, simple turned side & back stretchers, each crestrail w/a different landscape, probably New York State, ca. 1820-30, 35" h., set of 4 (ILLUS., bottom of page) **$9,560**

Unusual Landscape-decorated Classical Side Chairs

American Classical Grecian Rocker

Classical rocking chair w/arms, mahogany, Grecian-style, the tall serpentine-shaped upholstered back flanked by padded open arms on large open-scroll arm supports flanking the over-upholstered seat, the carved flat seatrail on flat curved front legs joined to the shorter rear legs by the long rocker, ca. 1830-40, 41" h. (ILLUS.) **$920**

Boston Classical Mahogany Side Chair

Classical side chair, mahogany & mahogany veneer, the curved flat-topped crest rail w/rounded corners & incised carving above the vasiform splat & curved stiles, upholstered slip-seat, flat serpentine front legs & backswept rear legs, Boston, ca. 1830, 34" h. (ILLUS.) **$748**

New York Classical Side Chair

Classical side chair, carved mahogany, the gently curved & rolled crestrail w/fluted end panels above a lower openwork arched rail centered by a roundel, both flanked by fluted backswept styles continuing down to flank the caned seat, front sabre legs ending in leaf-carved front paw feet, New York City, early 19th, 32" h. (ILLUS.) **$960**

Duncan Phyfe Classical Chair

Classical side chairs, carved mahogany, a narrow curved flat crestrail above a large pierced harp-shaped splat raised on a narrow lower rail, flanked by the scrolled & reeded stiles continuing down to flank the upholstered slip seat, incurved acanthus-carved front legs ending in hairy paw feet, canted square rear legs, attributed to Duncan Phyfe, New York, New York, ca. 1815-25, 32 3/4" h., pr. (ILLUS., of one) **$19,120**

Set of Eight Captain's Chairs

One of Two Boston Classical Side Chairs

early 20th c., 30" h., set of 8 (ILLUS., top of page) **$2,588**

Unusual Child's Wingback Rocker

Classical side chairs, carved mahogany, a narrow rectangular crestrail carved w/incised bands & flanked above & below by narrow gadroon-carved bands, raised above a lower pierce-carved slat between the reeded stiles continuing down to frame the upholstered slip seat & form the incurved front legs, square canted rear legs, Boston, ca. 1815-20, 33 1/2" h., pr. (ILLUS. of one) **$1,175**

Country style child's rocking chair, mahogany, the high wingback form w/an arched crest w/a cut-out hand grip, the rounded side wings curve down to solid sides & board seat above a deep front apron w/serpentine base, canted solid sides forming rockers, minor split above handle, 19th c., 27" h. (ILLUS., top next column) **$575**

Country-style "captain's" chairs, oak & mixed wood, a curved & stepped crest atop the curved crestrail curving around & down to form the front arms above a row of slender ring- and rod-turned spindles, wide plank seat raised on ring- and rod-turned front legs joined by a turned stretcher & plain turned rear legs all joined by plain box stretchers, late 19th -

Delaware Valley "Ladder-back" Armchair

Country-style "ladder-back" armchair, painted maple, the tall back w/five arched concave splats flanked by tall tapering turned stiles w/bulbous finials, shaped open arms on baluster- and ring-turned arm supports continuing to turned legs w/bulbous feet incorporating wooden wheel, all joined by double baluster- and ring-turned front stretchers & swelled side stretchers, early black paint over salmon & green, Delaware River Valley, late 18th c., minor imperfections, 50" h. (ILLUS., previous page) **$2,703**

Country-style "low-back" Windsor child's armchair, painted wood, the wide curved crestrail continuing around to form the short arms above a row of seven knob- and rod-turned spindles, wide plank seat raised on rod- and knob-turned front legs joined by a knob-turned stretcher, plain box stretchers to the turned rear legs, old grey paint, second half 19th c., 17 1/2" h. (ILLUS. right with Classical child's side chair, page 68) **$1,380**

Early Painted "Banister-back" Side Chair

Early American "banister-back" side chair, painted hardwood, the arched & scroll-cut crestrail above four tall split balusters flanked by tall baluster- and block-turned stiles topped w/turned finials & raised above the woven rush seat, baluster-, ring- and rod-turned front legs joined by two swelled turned front stretchers, double side & a single back stretcher, old dark brown paint w/gilt stencil & color floral designs, New England, second half 18th c. (ILLUS.)............................ **$1,058**

Early American "ladder-back" armchair, painted hardwood, the tall back composed of four arched slats between the tall ring-turned stiles topped by small turned urn finials & extending down to form the rear legs, shaped open arms ending turned medallion hand rests above baluster-turned arm supports continuing to form the ring-turned front legs, old replaced paper rush seat, old worn

black paint, once used as a rocker w/legs now ended out, 18th c., 47" h. **$575**

Fine Early "Ladder-back" Armchair

Early American "ladder-back" armchair, painted wood, the back w/three arched slats between the knob- and rod-turned stiles continuing down to form the back legs & topped by large ball finials, simple turned open arms joining knob- and rod-turned front supports continuing down to form the front legs joined by two swelled & ring-turned front stretchers, woven rush seat, double side & single rear stretchers, worn old black paint, second half 18th c., 44 3/4" h. (ILLUS.).............. **$2,415**

Early Painted "Ladder-back" Highchair

Early American "ladder-back" highchair, painted wood, three arched slats flanked by the heavy turned stiles forming the rear legs & topped by knob-turned finials, shaped open arms on baluster-turned supports continuing down to form the front legs, old woven rush seat, two worn front stretchers, turned plain side stretchers & one back stretcher, old & possibly original black paint, late 18th c., 41 1/2" h. (ILLUS.) **$1,035**

Delaware Valley "Ladder-back" Highchair

Early American "ladder-back" highchair, turned wood, the back w/four narrow arched slats between heavy turned stiles continuing to form the back legs & topped by knob-turned finials, shaped open arms raised on baluster-turned arm supports continuing into the front legs, woven rush seat, a flattened upper front stretcher above a plain turned lower stretcher, double side stretchers & a single back stretcher, Delaware River-style, natural finish, late 18th - early 19th c., 38" h. (ILLUS.) **$575**

One of Two Edwardian Club Chairs

Edwardian club chairs, leather-upholstered, the wide curved & tufted back joined to the out-scrolled arms flanking the cushion seat & deep upholstered apron, on casters, England, ca. 1900, 38 1/2" h., pr. (ILLUS. of one) **$4,140**

New York Federal Shield-back Armchair

Federal armchair, carved mahogany, the fine shield-back centered by a pierced oval splat enclosing a pierced urn-form design framing Prince-of-Wales feathers, the shaped open arms w/incurved reeded supports above the wide overupholstered seat, square tapering legs, New York City, ca. 1790-1810, 36" h. (ILLUS.) **$6,000**

Federal armchairs, carved mahogany, the flat curved crestrail above three slender carved slats flanked by downswept open arms above the upholstered seat w/a gently bowed seatrail, carved, turned & tapering front legs & canted square tapering rear legs, Philadelphia, 1800-10, 33 1/4" h., pr. (ILLUS., top next page)
.... **$17,925**

One of Six Country Federal Side Chairs

Fine Pair of Carved Mahogany Federal Armchairs

Federal country-style side chairs, painted & decorated, a wide curved & arched crestrail above a narrow medial rail above four short knob-turned spindles all flanked by flaring tapering stiles, wide shaped plank seat, canted ring-turned front legs & plain turned rear legs joined by box stretchers, old dark brown paint w/white floral decoration of the rails & black & white line detail, two w/minor restoration, first half 19th c., 32 1/4" h., set of 6 (ILLUS. of one, previous page) **$690**

One of a Set of Fine Federal Dining Chairs

Federal dining chairs, carved mahogany, the gently arched & molded crestrail & stiles frame four slender carved slats w/flared tops raised above the over-upholstered seat, square tapering fluted front legs & canted rear legs joined by box stretchers, possibly Salem, Massachusetts, 1790-1810, set of 8 (ILLUS. of one) **$15,600**

Federal fancy "Hitchcock" side chairs, painted & decorated, a ring-turned crestrail w/head rest above a wide lower rail all joining the backswept stiles, woven rush seat, half-round ring-turned seatrail raised on ring-, rod- and knob-turned front legs joined by a ring- and knob-turned front stretcher, simple turned side & rear stretchers, original black paint w/gilt stenciled floral & cornucopia designs on the crestrails, overall gilt trim, Hitchcock Company, Connecticut, ca. 1830s, 34" h., set of 4 (ILLUS., top next page).. **$480**

One of a Rare Set of Decorated Chairs

Federal "fancy" klismos side chairs, painted & decorated, the wide curved crestrail decorated w/a fancy gilt design of a fruit-filled urn flanked by long leafy scrolls, the turned & angled stiles joined by a lower rail w/further gilt scroll decoration, square caned seat w/a rounded

Set of Four Early Hitchcock Side Chairs

front edge raised on ring-, knob- and rod-turned front legs w/knob feet joined by a simple turned rung, simple box stretchers & simple canted turned rear legs, stamped w/the mark of John Hodgkinson, Baltimore, Maryland, ca. 1820-40, 30 1/2" h., set of 4 (ILLUS. of one)......... **$5,975**

Finely Decorated Federal "Fancy" Chair

Federal "fancy" side chair, painted & decorated, the flat crestrail w/a pair of low center arches decorated w/a painted urn & drapery swag design continuing down into a pair of slender spindles flanking a slightly wider urn-decorated center spindle, the flat stiles further painted w/leafy swags on a cream ground, a delicate woven rush seat raised on knob- and rod-turned front legs decorated w/further leafy swags above the flute-painted peg feet, a turned front stretcher w/a narrow

central panel painted w/an urn & leaves, simple turned side & rear stretchers, decorated in shades of dark green, gold & creamy white, probably Salem, Massachusetts, 1800-10, 34" h. (ILLUS.)......... **$2,880**

Fine Federal Lolling Armchair

Federal lolling armchair, mahogany, the tall rectangular upholstered back w/an arched crestrail, shaped slender open arms on incurved reeded arm supports flanking the inside upholstered seat, square tapering front legs & canted square rear legs joined by box stretchers, Massachusetts, ca. 1790, old refinish, minor imperfections, 43 1/2" h. (ILLUS.)... **$3,878**

Delicate Carved Federal Side Chair

Federal side chair, carved mahogany, the delicate rectangular back w/slender reeded columnar stiles w/small corner black, the flat crestrail centered by a domed & fluted central crest above a panel carved w/drapery swags continuing into five slender carved spindles to a lower rail, broad over-upholstered seat, turned tapering & reeded front legs ending in simple turned feet, square canted rear legs, 1810-15, 37" h. (ILLUS.) **$3,800**

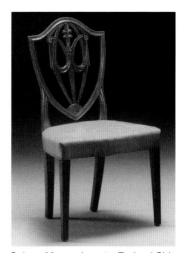

Rare Salem, Massachusetts Federal Side Chair

Federal side chair, carved mahogany, the shield-back centered by a pierced oval splat trimmed w/carved drapery swags, over-upholstered seat on square tapering front legs & canted square rear legs, Salem, Massachusetts, 1790-1810, 38 3/8" h., pr. (ILLUS., one shown) **$13,145**

Delicate Philadelphia Federal Side Chair

Federal side chair, carved mahogany, the delicate rectangular back centered by a tall rectangular frame centered by a slender pierced, urn-form splat, over-upholstered seat on turned tapering front legs & canted square tapering rear legs, Philadelphia, 1800-10, 36" h., pr. (ILLUS., one shown).. **$1,793**

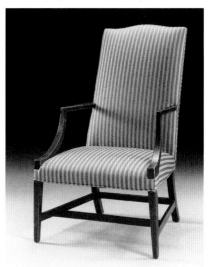

Rare Federal Mahogany Lolling Armchair

Federal style lolling armchair, inlaid mahogany, the tall upholstered back w/a serpentine crest flanked by open arms w/incurved supports above the wide upholstered seat, raised on square tapering front legs & square canted rear legs, joined by flat box stretchers, Massachusetts, 1780-1800, 45 1/2" h. (ILLUS.) **$9,000**

Fine George III-Style Set of Dining Chairs

Pair of French Provincial Slipper Chairs

French Provincial slipper chairs, carved oak, the tall back w/an arched crestrail above a lyre-form splat flanked by square tapering stiles w/turned finial, the rush seat above rod-turned front legs joined by a narrow flat upper stretcher & turned & tapering lower stretcher, simple double stretchers at the sides & back, France, late 19th c., 34" h., pr. (ILLUS.).................................. **$978**

George III-Style dining chairs, carved mahogany, a serpentine crestrail centered by a small carved leaf sprig above a pierce-carved Gothic style splat, two armchairs w/shaped open arms on incurved arm supports, over-upholstered seats on square molded legs joined by H-stretchers, England, late 19th - early 20th c., 38" h., four side chairs, two armchairs, the set (ILLUS., top of page) **$8,970**

Set of Eight George III-Style Dining Chairs

George III-Style dining chairs, mahogany & burled elm, tall back w/arched scroll-carved crestrail curving down to serpentine stiles flanking the solid scroll-cut splat, two w/padded curved open arms, wide upholstered balloon seat on shell-carved seatrail raised on cabriole front legs w/shell-carved knees & ending in hairy paw feet, England, late 19th c., 42" h., set of 8 (ILLUS., bottom previous page) **$2,875**

English George III-Style Wingback Armchair

George III-Style "wingback" armchair, the tall arched upholstered back flanked by tall tapering & rolled upholstered wings above rolled upholstered arms w/incurved scroll-carved arm supports, a cushion seat above the egg-and-dart-carved seatrail raised on heavy cabriole legs w/leaf-and-cartouche-carved knees & compressed ball-and-claw feet, England, mid-19th c., 4' 4" h. (ILLUS.) **$3,450**

Pair of Irish Georgian Hall Chairs

Georgian hall chairs, carved mahogany, the wide balloon-form back carved as a large shell centered by leafy scrolls over adorsed C-scrolls, the solid seat raised on ring-, knob- and reeded turned legs front legs w/outswept peg feet, square canted rear legs, Ireland, second quarter 19th c., 31 1/2" h., pr. (ILLUS.) **$2,070**

Georgian Upholstered Side Chair

Georgian side chair, mahogany, a tall rounded upholstered back above the squared over-upholstered seat, on carved cabriole legs w/leaf-carved knees & ending in pad front feet, gross point & petite point fabric w/floral panels, England, probably late 18th c., small patches & repairs to upholstery, 23 x 24 1/2", 43" h. (ILLUS.) **$1,430**

Fine Carved Georgian-Style Armchair

Georgian-Style armchair, a serpentine leafy scroll-carved crestrail centered by a shell finial & rosette corners above outswept carved stiles enclosing the needlepoint upholstered back, padded open arms on incurved leaf-carved arm supports, wide needlepoint upholstered seat w/a serpentine front above a conforming deep apron carved on the front & sides w/flowering leafy scrolls centered by a shell, on cabriole legs w/shell-carved knees above leaf & ribbon-carved legs ending in paw feet, in the manner of Robert Adams, England, ca. 1900 (ILLUS., previous page) **$2,645**

Nice Gothic Revival Tall Side Chair

Gothic Revival side chair, carved rosewood, the tall back w/a very tall pointed & pierce-carved Gothic arch crest w/a quatrefoil flanked by trefoils over the arched upholstered back panel flanked by block-and rod-turned stiles w/small turned finials, the over-upholstered seat raised on ring- and rod-turned paneled front legs on casters, second quarter 19th c., 48" h. (ILLUS.).. **$863**

Louis XIV-Style Armchair

Louis XIV-Style fauteuils à la reine (open-arm armchairs), carved beech, the tall rectangular upholstered back w/an arched crestrail above heavy serpentine open arms w/scroll-carved grips raised on incurved leaf-carved supports, the wide over-upholstered seat on shaped & carved front legs & simple rear legs joined by arched H-stretchers, France, late 19th c., 29 1/4" h., pr. (ILLUS. of one).. **$1,840**

Unusual 18th Century Sedan Chair

Louis XV sedan chair, giltwood-mounted leather & polychromed leather, squared upright form w/domed top, tall hinged door at front, rectangular rounded windows in the door & on each side, retains period sliding leather window panels, the interior lined in modern black & gold damask w/gold tassellated detailing, the period exterior rear panel painted w/a scene of nude female bathers above a floral panel, floral-decorated side panels, France, last quarter 18th c., 30 1/2 x 37 1/2", 62" h. (ILLUS.) **$4,370**

American Louis XV-Style Armchair

Louis XV-Style armchair, carved mahogany, the wide openwork arched back w/shell- and scroll-carved crestrail over a scroll-carved & oval wreath splat, shaped open arms w/scrolled grips above incurved arm supports, wide upholstered seat w/a serpentine front above a conforming scroll-carved seatrail & carved cabriole front legs ending in scroll feet on casters, square canted rear legs on casters, ca. 1880, minor wear & losses, 37 1/4" h. (ILLUS.) **$350**

One of Two Louis XV-Style Fauteuils

Louis XV-Style fauteuils (open-arm armchairs), fruitwood, the wide upholstered back w/an arched serpentine crestrail centered by a floral-carved crest & continuing down to form the shaped back frame, open padded arms on incurved arm supports above the wide upholstered seat, serpentine molded seatrail centered by a floral-carved reserve, cabriole front legs w/floral-carved knees & ending in simple peg feet, France, ca. 1900, 38 1/2" h., pr. (ILLUS. of one) **$1,840**

Louis XV-Style side chairs, hardwood, the oval back frame enclosing a leather panel raised above leather seats w/brass tack decoration, cabriole front legs w/scroll feet, France, late 19th c., minor stains, wear to leather seats, 36 1/2" h., set of 6 .... **$3,080**

Louis XVI-Style Upholstered Armchair

Louis XVI-Style armchair, painted wood, a wide arched upholstered back w/the frame decorated w/narrow ribbon carving & a top central pierced ribbon & flower-carved crest, closed padded & upholstered arms w/carved & incurved arm supports flanking the wide upholstered seat w/a narrow ribbon-carved bowed seatrail, ring- and rod-turned tapering front legs w/knob & peg feet, light brown w/dark brown highlights, splits on the legs, France, early 20th c., 44" h. (ILLUS.) **$259**

Louis XVI-Style bergères (closed-arm armchairs), beechwood, gently arched & carved crestrail w/ribbon & floral decoration continuing down to frame shallow wings & closed padded arms w/acanthus carving & incurved arm supports, the cushion seat above a carved seatrail raised on tapered & fluted legs, striped upholstery, early 20th c., one leg repaired, separations, small losses, 43" & 46" h., set of two similar chairs **$1,650**

Fine Pair of Louix XVI-Style Fauteuils à la Reine

Louis XVI-Style fauteuils à la reine (open-arm armchairs), giltwood, the arched ornately carved crestrail w/rocailles, C-scrolls & foliage swags continuing down around the wide upholstered back, padded open arms w/incurved arm supports above the wide upholstered cushion seat w/an ornately carved serpentine seatrail continuing to the carved cabriole legs ending in scroll & peg feet, France, first half 20th c., 42" h., pr. (ILLUS., bottom of previous page) **$3,525**

Louis XVI-Style Beech Armchair

Louis XVI-Style open-arm armchair, carved beech, the wide squared upholstered back w/an arched crestrail, padded open arms on incurved arm supports, the wide upholstered seat w/curved front seatrail, tapering fluted front legs, original gilding removed, natural waxed finish, France, mid-19th c., 39" h. (ILLUS.) **$1,150**

Louis XVI-Style Open-arm Armchair

Louis XVI-Style open-arm armchair, fruitwood, the squared upholstered back w/an arched crestrail above padded upholstered arms w/scroll-carved grips raised on incurved leaf-carved arm supports, the wide upholstered seat w/a curved front seatrail, knob- and tapering rod-turned front legs ending in peg feet, France, late 19th c., 36" h. (ILLUS.) **$403**

Giltwood Louis XVI-Style Side Chair

Louis XVI-Style side chair, giltwood, the arched & stepped crestrail above a large pierced lyre splat flanked by canted fluted stiles w/a floral finial, the upholstered seat on a molded seatrail above the turned, tapering & fluted front legs ending in peg feet, simple turned stretchers, France, late 19th c., 33 1/2" h. (ILLUS.) ... **$489**

Unusual Large Mission Oak Armchair

Mission-style (Arts & Crafts movement) armchair, oak, the angled slated back fitted w/a large black leather cushion & flanked by wide flat arms raised on flat supports w/corbels, the deep frame w/heavy square front legs, a long black leather spring cushion seat, cleaned original finish, Charles Limbert Furniture Co., unmarked, early 20th c., 32 x 37", 33" h. (ILLUS.)... **$4,888**

Set of Simple Mission Oak Dining Chairs

Mission-style (Arts & Crafts movement) dining chairs, a wide slightly curved crest above a pair of flat slats joined to a lower back rail, replaced seat w/an upholstered cushion, simple slender square tapering legs joined by an H-stretcher, ca. 1910, 38" h., set of 6 (ILLUS.).................. **$264**

Rare Modern Danish "Ox" Armchair

Modern style armchair, leather & tubular steel, "Ox" design, the wide curved & rolled black leather crestrail resembling ox horns above the wide upholstered back &

wide seat flanked by low rolled leather arms, the curved steel tubular frame w/short outswept rear legs & taller angled front legs, designed by Hans Wegner, manufactured by Johannes Hansen, Model No. EJ 100, Denmark, ca. 1960, 35" h. (ILLUS.)... **$15,534**

Fine Modern Bronze & Leather Set

Modern style armchair & footstool, bronze & leather, the low-backed armchair w/a leather bolster top rail flanked by bronze stiles topped by shell-form devices & continuing down to form the rear legs, the shaped open bronze arms arch to form the front legs, a square upholstered leather seat, the stool w/a thick square leather top supported in a bronze frame w/a shell-like device at each corner of the seat, designed by Philippe Anthonioz, ca. 1999, chair, 30 1/2" h., stool 15 1/2" w., 17 3/4" h., the set (ILLUS.) **$9,560**

Modern style Barcelona chair & ottoman, steel & leather upholstery, the V-form seat composed of two rectangular tufted leather pads in a steel frame w/cross-form legs, the ottoman w/a single pad on a cross-form base, designed by Mies van der Rohe for the 1929 Exposition International in Barcelona, Spain, made by Knoll International, third quarter 20th c., 29 1/2" h., the set (ILLUS. right with other Barcelona chair set, bottom of page)..... **$3,220**

Two Sets of the Barcelona Chair & Ottoman

Pair of Modern "Wassily" Pattern Armchairs

Modern style Barcelona chair & ottoman, steel & leather upholstery, the V-form seat composed of two rectangular tufted leather pads in a steel frame w/cross-form legs, the ottoman w/a single pad on a cross-form base, designed by Mies van der Rohe for the 1929 Exposition International in Barcelona, Spain, made by Knoll International, third quarter 20th c., 29 1/2" h., the set (ILLUS. left with other Barcelona chair set, bottom previous page) **$3,450**

Plycraft 1970s Lounge Chair & Ottoman

Modern-style armchair & ottoman, lounge-style, laminated & bent walnut & black vinyl upholstery, the tall rectangular tufted upholstered back & seat flanked by out-scrolled wood arms, raised & swiveling on a low cross-form base, matching upholstered ottoman, designed by George Mulhauer for Plycraft, ca. 1970, 34" h. (ILLUS.) **$288**

Modern-style armchairs, chromed steel & leather, "Wassily" patt., the rectangular back frame composed of tubular steel fitted w/brown leather straps & suspended in a tubular steel frame w/squared side supports w/narrow brown leather straps & a wide leather seat panel, designed in 1925 by Marcel Breuer for use at the Bauhaus, these made by Knoll International, late 20th c., one w/Knoll paper label, 29" h., pr. (ILLUS., top of page) **$1,955**

1950s Bamboo "Pretzel" Armchair

Modern-style "Pretzel" armchair, bent bamboo, the angled bamboo-framed back & seat flanked by high rounded & looping sides forming the arms & legs, bamboo stretchers, later upholstered cushions, ca. 1955, 26" w., 31" h. (ILLUS.) **$200-300**

Rare Early Bugatti Modernist Side Chair

Pair of Nicely Carved Chinese Armchairs

Modernist side chair, vellum-covered, applied & inlaid ebonized wood, the tall curved back stiles continue down to form the front legs, short block- and rod-turned rear legs, the vellum back painted w/a bamboo spray & a group of fowl & bordered by square & round beaten copper bosses, matching vellum flat seat w/long fring front border, the wood inlaid w/bone, pewter & brass, designed by Carlo Bugatti, Italy, ca. 1902, 43 1/2" h. (ILLUS., previous page).. **$8,963**

Oriental armchairs, carved elm, a narrow shaped crestrail above the open squared backframe w/a curved central three-panel splat w/pierce-carved designs, the simple turned stiles w/small pierced top corner brackets, low open arms w/a single bent spindle, wide paneled square seat above a narrow serpentine apron continuing down along the slender front legs joined at the bottom by a square stretcher, simple turned side & rear stretchers, China, late 19th c., pr.(ILLUS., top of page).............. **$3,105**

Wallace Nutting Reproduction Windsor

Nutting-signed Windsor "fan-back" brace-back side chair, the flat serpentine crestrail w/scroll-carved ends above a back w/nine swelled spindles & two back brace spindles between the slender baluster- and rod-turned stiles above the shaped saddle seat, on four canted baluster-turned legs joined by a swelled H-stretcher, old dark finish, unsigned but branded "326," ca. 1930s, 41" h. (ILLUS.).. **$978**

Pilgrim Century "Great Chair"

Pilgrim Century "Great Chair," turned maple & ash, the tall back w/three shaped splats between turned stiles w/knob- and flame-turned finials, thin straight open arms to the front posts w/a turned knob continuing down to form the front legs, woven rush seat, double sets of turned stretchers, old surface, probably Essex, Massachusetts, 1690s, imperfections, loss to height, 42 5/8" h. (ILLUS.) **$3,819**

Long Island, 1730-50, descended in the family of Rev. Samuel Buell, 45 1/2" h. (ILLUS.).. **$4,080**

Fine Walnut Queen Anne Armchair

Queen Anne armchair, walnut, the oxbow crestrail above a vasiform splat flanked by S-shaped outcurved open arms above a trapezoidal seat raised on cabriole legs joined by turned stretchers & ending in pad feet, Massachusetts, late 18th c., 42" h. (ILLUS.) **$3,525**

Rare Pilgrim Century Oak "Great Chair"

Pilgrim Century "Great Chair," turned oak, the tall back w/heavy ring- and knob-turned stiles continuing down to form the rear legs & topped by turned pointed bulbous finials, fitted w/three wide shaped slats above the woven rush seat, open turned rod arms joined to the tall knob-turned front legs w/knob finials, simple turned double front & side stretchers & a single rear stretcher, Massachusetts, 1690-1710, 43" h. (ILLUS.) **$15,600**

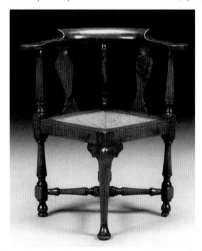

Rare New England Queen Anne Corner Chair

Queen Anne corner chair, maple & walnut, the curved low backrail w/a raised center section & forming flat scroll arms raised on three columnar-turned spindles & two vasi-form splats, wovan rush seet, cabriole front legs ending in a pad foot, three column-, block- and knob-turned side & rear legs all joined by a turned, tapering cross-stretcher, New England, 1730-50, 31" h. (ILLUS.) **$21,510**

Fine Early Queen Anne Armchair

Queen Anne armchair, hardwood, the simple oxyoke crestrail above a very tall slender vasiform splat flanked by tall flat stiles, simple downswept open arms raised on turned tapering arm supports flanked by woven rush seat, knob- and block-turned front legs joined by a baluster-turned front stretcher & swelled side stretchers, Connecticut or East Hampton,

Fine Country Queen Anne Armchair

Queen Anne country-style armchair, hardwood, the tall back w/an oxyoke crest above the vasiform splat flanked by gently backswept stiles & long slender shaped arms w/rounded hand grips, baluster-, ring- and block-turned arm supports continue down to form the front legs, woven rush seat, a three-knob turned front stretcher, Spanish front feet, swelled & turned side & back stretchers, New England, first half 18th c., 42 1/2" h. (ILLUS.).. **$2,300**

Early Queen Anne Country-style Chair

Queen Anne country-style side chair, maple, the ox yoke crestrail above a solid vasiform splat flanked by flat stiles & a lower rail above the woven rush seat, baluster-, knob- and block-turned front legs ending in Spanish feet & joined by a knob-turned stretcher, simple turned side & back stretchers, old finish, some origi-

nal rush in seat, some joints loose, ca. 1730-40 (ILLUS.) **$1,035**

Queen Anne Country-Style Side Chair

Queen Anne country-style side chair, maple, the ox-bow crestrail w/ears above a tall vasiform splat flanked by tall flat stiles, woven rush seat w/a narrow serpentine front seatrail, raised on cabriole front legs ending in pad feet & joined by a knob-turned front stretcher, pairs of simple turned side stretchers, Fussel-Savery School, Philadelphia, 1750-70, 39 3/4" h. (ILLUS.)... **$3,600**

Nice Country Queen Anne Side Chair

Queen Anne country-style side chair, maple, the shaped crestrail w/an incurved crest flanked by small scroll ears above the tall flat stiles flanking the pierced rail splat above the balloon slip seat, conforming seatrail raised on cabriole front legs w/shaped returns & ending in pad feet, a flattened serpentine H-stretcher & a swelled turned back stretcher, refinished, imperfections, Rhode Island, 1740-60, 38 7/8" h. (ILLUS.) **$2,350**

Early Queen Anne Side Chair

Queen Anne side chair, carved birch & maple, the tall back w/a bold arched & scroll-carved crestrail above a tall vasiform splat flanked by gently backswept molded stiles, woven rush seat, cabriole front legs ending in pad feet, square rear legs, all joined by slender turned stretchers, early 18th c., 47" h. (ILLUS.) **$2,032**

Walnut Queen Anne Side Chair

Queen Anne side chair, carved walnut, the arched crestrail w/rounded corners continuing to shaped stiles flanking the tall scroll-carved splat, upholstered compass-seat w/cabriole front legs ending in pad feet & turned, canted rear legs, Philadelphia, 1735-50, 42 1/2" h. (ILLUS.)... **$7,170**

Rare Early Boston Queen Anne Side Chair

Queen Anne side chair, inlaid walnut, the very tall back w/a yoke crest above a tall narrow curved inlaid splat flanked by rounded stiles over a trapezoidal seat, cabriole front legs ending in stocking pad feet, canted square rear legs, boldly shaped H-stretcher, missing slip seat, Boston, ca. 1720-40, 41 1/2" h. (ILLUS.) .... **$10,000+**

Fine Philadelphia Queen Anne Side Chair

Queen Anne side chair, maple, the serpentine crestrail w/flared ears above the vasiform solid splat flanked by the flat stiles & raised above the upholstered slip seat, a narrow serpentine front seatrail raised on tall cabriole front legs ending in simple claw-and-ball feet joined by a swelled front stretcher, canted rear legs, simple turned side & rear stretchers, Fussel-Savery School, Philadelphia, 18th c., 40 1/2" h. (ILLUS.) **$5,019**

Rare Pair of New England Walnut Queen Anne Side Chairs

Fine Massachusetts Queen Anne Chair

Queen Anne side chair, the simple oxyoke crest continuing to the flat backswept stiles flanking a tall vasiform solid splat, ballooned upholstered drop seat w/the conforming seatrail raised on cabriole front legs w/scroll-carved returns & ending in pad feet, square canted rear legs, legs joined by baluster- and block-turned box stretchers, refinished, minor restoration, Massachusetts, ca. 1740-60, 39 3/4" h. (ILLUS.) **$4,406**

Queen Anne side chair, walnut, the spooned crestrail above a vasiform splat & raked chamfered stiles over the upholstered ballon slip seat, cabriole front legs ending in pad feet joined to the chamfered raking rear legs by block-, baluster- and ring-turned stretchers, Boston, ca. 1740-60, refinished, minor imperfections, 40" h. (ILLUS., top next column) **$6,463**

Fine Boston Queen Anne Side Chair

Queen Anne side chairs, carved walnut, the shaped crestrail centered by a carved shell above the tall vasiform splat flanked by the shaped stiles above the balloon slip seat in a conforming seatrail raised on cabriole front legs w/scroll-carved returns & ending in pad feet, canted rear legs, baluster- and block-turned stretchers, probably Boston, 1750-1770, 39 1/4" h., pr. (ILLUS., top of page) **$41,825**

Queen Anne-Style dining chairs, mahogany & mahogany veneer, the arched crestrail curving down to the shaped stiles flanking the scroll-cut vasiform splat, the armchairs w/blocks & incurved arm supports above the upholstered slip seat w/a curved front seatrail, cabriole front legs w/shell-carved knees & ending in snake feet, old dark finish, early to mid-20th c., two armchairs & six side chairs, 39 1/2" h., the set (ILLUS. of one armchair, next page) **$2,760**

Queen Anne-Style Chair from a Set

Queen Anne-Style side chairs, mahogany, a simple shaped crestrail continuing
into the tall gently curved stiles flanking
the vasiform splat, trapezoidal slip seat
raised on cabriole front legs ending in
pad feet, turned swelled H-stretchers, old
dark finish, late 19th - early 20th c.,
One Queen Anne-Style Chair from Set   40 3/4" h., set of 4 (ILLUS. of one) **$575**

Set of Six Simple 1920s Queen Anne-Style Side Chairs

Queen Anne-Style side chairs, oak, the arched crestrail above a plain rectangular splat above the upholstered slip seat, raised on simple tapering cabriole front legs w/pad feet, slender square canted rear legs,
simple box stretchers, ca. 1920s, 41" h., set of 6 (ILLUS.) **$288**

Nice Regency-Style Mahogany & Leather Chairs

Queen Anne-Style "Wingback" Chairs

Queen Anne-Style "wingback" chairs, tall arched upholstered back flanked by tall flared rounded side wings above the out-scrolled upholstered arms flanking the over-upholstered seat, cabriole front legs w/acanthus leaf-carved knees, square canted rear legs, early 20th c., 52" h., pr. (ILLUS.) **$1,100**

Regency-Style armchair & rocker, mahogany & leather, each w/a tall back-swept back upholstered in red tufted leather & continuing down to form deep curved seats flanked by padded scrolled open arms, flattened arched legs joined by simple turned stretchers, England, early 20th c., armchair 38 1/2" h., the set (ILLUS., top of page) **$1,265**

Shaker rocking chair w/arms, the tall "ladderback" w/four graduated slats between turned stiles w/acorn finials, shaped open arms w/mushroom caps, replaced woven tape seat, turned legs on stretchers joined by box stretchers, wear to dark finish, impressed "6," stenciled label "Shaker's Trademark, No. 6, Mt. Lebanon, N.Y.," late 19th - early 20th c., 42" h. (ILLUS., top next column) **$633**

Shaker No. 6 Rocking Chair with Arms

Small Shaker Rocking Chair with Arms

Extremely Rare Herter Bros. Aesthetic Movement Side Chairs

Shaker rocking chair w/arms, the tall "ladderback" w/three graduated slats between turned stiles w/acorn finials, shaped open arms w/mushroom caps, replaced woven tape seat, turned legs on stretchers joined by box stretchers, wear to dark finish, unmarked, Mt. Lebanon, New York, late 19th - early 20th c., 34" h. (ILLUS., previous page) **$403**

Victorian Aesthetic Movement side chairs, giltwood & marquetry, the wide curved & upswept crestrail decorated overall w/fine marquetry inlay & centered by a butterfly-shaped pierced hand grip above a rectangular upholstered panel & thin lower rail all flanked by outswept stiles, the spring-upholstered seat w/a flat seatrail raised on ring-turned tapering front legs w/cuffed flaring peg feet & simple turned rear legs all joined by very slender turned high box stretchers, attributed to Herter Brothers, New York City, 1880-83, original gilt surface, 34 1/4" h., pr. (ILLUS., top of page).................... **$204,000**

chairs w/a shaped back panel upholstered in black leather & raised on a rail above the over-upholstered leather seat, the armchair w/padded open arms w/incurved supports, molded & scroll-carved seatrails, the side chairs w/square tapering legs joined by an H-stretcher & on casters, the armchair w/urn-turned front legs joined to the rear legs w/a curved X-stretcher all on casters, ca. 1880s, seven side chairs & one armchair, armchair 48" h., the set (ILLUS.) **$1,725**

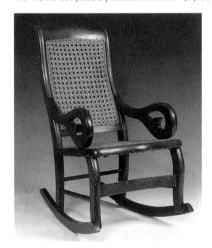

Victorian Caned Grecian Rocker

Victorian country-style Grecian rocker, walnut, the tall caned back w/a gently arched crestrail, looping scroll-carved open arms above the caned seat, simple shaped front legs joined by a flat curved stretcher, simple turned side & back stretchers, ca. 1880s, 27" h. (ILLUS.)
.... **$127**

Set of Victorian Baroque Revival Dining Chairs

Victorian Baroque Revival dining chairs, oak, each w/a high arched crestrail carved w/fancy scrolls & neoclassical designs between columnar stiles, the side

Late Victorian Country Style Highchair

Victorian country-style highchair, oak, the bowed backrail above four slender spindles, hinged side arms supporting the serving tray, shaped plank seat raised on four tall canted simple turned legs joined by simple box stretchers & w/a foot rest at the upper front, late 19th - early 20th c., 39" h. (ILLUS.)................... **$127**

Rare Egyptian Revival Carved Armchairs

Victorian Egyptian Revival style armchairs, carved & gilt-trimmed walnut, each w/a high rectangular back frame enclosing tufted upholstery, the stepped crestrail centered by a raised block panel w/arched top above an inset oval porcelain plaque h.p. w/flowers, the bolding carved stiles continue to the padded open arms ending in large carved Egyptian heads atop curved leaf & carved arm supports w/gilt trim continuing down to form the front legs ending on paw feet on casters, the spring-upholstered seat w/a line-incised & gilt-trimmed seatrail, square gently curved rear legs, New York City or New Jersey, ca. 1850-70, 40 5/8" h., pr. (ILLUS.) **$24,000**

Victorian Gothic Revival Hall Chair

Victorian Gothic Revival hall chair, carved walnut, the tall pointed crest pierced w/Gothic trefoils & quatrefoils & topped by three small turned finials, the tall spiral-turned stiles w/turned pointed finials flank a tall rectangular central upholstered panel w/scroll-carving down the frame & above the raised stretcher above the over-upholstered seat, spiral-turned front legs w/knob feet, square rear legs, third quarter 19th c., 44" h. (ILLUS.).......................... **$460**

Unusual Late Victorian Novelty Chair

Victorian novelty folding chair, carved & painted, the tall back w/slender stiles joined by a crestrail centered by a small pediment above the carved name "Cora" flanked by spearpoint & leaf devices all above the fabric panel back, hinged at the fabric seat w/curved hinged legs joined by ring-turned stretchers, painted black w/color trim on the crestrail, late 19th - early 20th c., 32 3/4" h. (ILLUS.)..... **$120**

Victorian Novelty Horn Armchair

Victorian novelty "horn" armchair, the low arched back & arms composed of interlocking steer horns w/smaller spiral horn spindles, a wide padded black leather seat raised on four tall curved horns & horn corner brackets, from a set made for Alfred Sampson of the Boston, Massachusetts area, late 19th - early 20th c., 30" w., 35" h. (ILLUS.)............................. **$2,300**

Fine Renaissance Revival Armchair

Victorian Renaissance Revival armchair, carved walnut & burl walnut, the ornate oval back framed w/the arche crestrail centered by a ornate pierce-carved crest centered by the carved face of a classical lady above burl panels to the scroll-carved corners & block-carved lower frame enclosing an oval upholstered panel, curved at the front w/the head of a classical lady, wide rounded upholstered seat on a con-

forming burl-trimmed seatrail, turned & tapering trumpet-form front legs, attributed to John Jelliff, Newark, New Jersey, ca. 1875, 42" h. (ILLUS.)............................. **$2,000**

Pair of Renaissance Revival Hall Chairs

Victorian Renaissance Revival hall chairs, carved walnut, a very tall solid back w/a pedimented molded crest w/a scroll-carved cartouche finial, the center of the back w/a raised rectangular molded panel enclosing a large oblong cartouche, wide slip seat above a narrow paneled apron & vase- and baluster-turned front legs w/peg feet, square canted rear legs, ca. 1870, 46 1/2" h., pr. (ILLUS.)... **$1,035**

Renaissance Revival Child's Rocker

Victorian Renaissance Revival style child's rocking chair, walnut, the shield-shaped caned back w/a notched crestrail centered by a small pedimented crest, curved serpentine skirt guards on the shield-shaped caned seat, ring-turned front legs joined by a ring-turned stretcher, simple turned rear legs & plain side & back stretchers, on simple curved rockers, ca. 1875, minor breaks in cane, 18" w., 26" h. (ILLUS.) **$230**

Very Ornately Carved European Victorian Rococo Armchairs

Fine Belter-type Rococo Armchair

Victorian Rococo Revival armchair, pierced & carved laminated rosewood, the high balloon back w/a floral-carved crest above the serpentine pierced scroll-carved side panels flanking the large serpentine oblong tufted upholstered back panel, open padded arms w/scroll-carved incurved arm supports flanking the over-upholstered tufted upholstery seat w/the serpentine scroll-carved seatrail centered by a floral-carved drop, front cabriole legs w/carved grapes at the knees & ending in scroll feet on casters, canted square rear legs on casters, attributed to John H. Belter, New York, New York, ca. 1855, 44" h. (ILLUS.) **$5,520**

Victorian Rococo Walnut Armchair

Victorian Rococo style armchair, walnut, the large oval upholstered back w/a thumbmolded walnut frame, flanked by padded open arms w/incurved arm supports & raised above the over-upholstered wide seat w/a serpentine molded front seatrail, demi-cabriole front legs & canted rear legs, ca. 1870 (ILLUS.) **$200-300**

Victorian Rococo style armchairs, carved walnut, the high back w/large oval upholstered panels framed by wide ornate scroll-carved frames w/a cartouche crest flanked by upholstered open arms w/ornately carved arm supports, raised above the wide over-upholstered seat, ornate scroll- and cartouche-carved front seatrail on outswept carved legs on casters, canted carved rear legs on casters, Europe, mid-19th c., 47 1/2" h., pr. (ILLUS., top of page) **$3,450**

Victorian Rococo "Barrel-back" Armchairs

Victorian Rococo style "barrel-back" armchairs, mahogany, a narrow arched crestrail centered by a pierced carved scroll crest above the high rounded & gently curved upholstered back & rolled upholstered arms w/incurved & rolled arm supports, spring cushion seat w/a scroll-carved apron raised on cabriole front legs ending in scrolls & raised on caster, backswept rear legs on casters, ca. 1850-60, 40 1/2" h., pr. (ILLUS., top of page)......... **$3,450**

Decorative Rococo Papier-mâché Chair

Victorian Rococo style side chair, black-lacquered inlaid papier-mâché, the balloon back w/a wide scrolling center splat above a small lower splat, wide caned seat w/a serpentine seatrail above simple cabriole front legs, the back decorated w/inlaid mother-of-pearl florals & ornate gilt trim, ca. 1860-70, 33" h. (ILLUS.)........ **$920**

Unusual Rosewood Rococo Armchair

Victorian Rococo substyle armchair, carved laminated rosewood, the high back w/a simple arched crestrail enclosing a long shaped upholstered panel flanked by pierce-carved leafy scroll panels continuing into the padded arms w/incurved arm supports, the wide over-upholstered seat w/a serpentine seatrail carved w/a center scroll reserve, carved details at the top of the demi-cabriole front legs ending in scroll feet, on casters, attributed to John Henry Belter, New York, New York, ca. 1855, one back leg repaired, veneer chip, some cracks in the back, 39" h. (ILLUS.).............................. **$1,265**

Victorian Armchair with Horsehair

Belter-Style Carved Rosewood Armchair

Victorian Rococo substyle armchair, carved & laminated rosewood, the tall upholstered balloon back w/a frame composed of long S- and C-scrolls, shaped open arms on incurved arm supports, wide upholstered seat w/a serpentine seatrail & demi-cabriole front legs on casters, attributed to John H. Belter, New York City, ca. 1855, 40" h. (ILLUS.) **$1,380**

Victorian Rococo substyle armchair, walnut, the large oval back frame w/a carved crest enclosing a tufted black horsehair upholstered panel, padded open arms above the wide horsehair-upholstered seat w/a serpentine seatrail above demi-cabriole legs on casters, ca. 1870, 45" h. (ILLUS.) **$288**

"Henry Ford" Pattern Side Chair by Meeks

Victorian Rococo Philadelphia Armchair

Victorian Rococo substyle armchair, carved walnut, the large walnut-framed oval upholstered back w/a cartouche-carved crest above the padded open arms on incurved arm supports, wide upholstered seat w/a serpentine front above a conforming carved apron & demi-cabriole front legs on casters, Philadelphia, ca. 1860, 44" h. (ILLUS.) **$690**

Victorian Rococo substyle side chair, carved & laminated rosewood, the tall balloon-form back w/a central upholstered section framed by an ornate pierce-carved frame w/a very high crestrail w/a bold central cartouche, raised above the rounded over-upholstered seat on a serpentine carved seatrail, slender cabriole front legs on casters, the "Henry Ford" patt., attributed to J. & J. Meeks, New York City, ca. 1855, 42 3/4" h. (ILLUS.) **$1,898**

Pair of "Henry Ford" Rococo Side Chairs

Victorian Rococo substyle side chairs, carved & laminated rosewood, the very high balloon back w/an upholstered panel framed by a wide frame pierce-carved w/scrolls & florals w/a large arched gadrooned crestrail centered by a bold floral cluster-carved crest, raised above a rounded over-upholstered seat w/a carved serpentine seatrail on demi-cabriole front legs on casters, the "Henry Ford" patt. attributed to J. & J.W. Meeks, New York City, ca. 1855, 43 1/2" h., pr. (ILLUS.).. **$4,600**

Two Victorian Rococo Side Chairs

Victorian Rococo substyle side chairs, walnut, balloon-back style, the rounded open back rails carved w/roses & scrolls at the top center above a handgrip hole, a matching shorter lower back rail, serpentine-front over-upholstered seat w/a scroll-carved apron raised on simple cabriole front legs w/leaf-carved knees & scroll feet, ca. 1860, pr. (ILLUS.) **$118**

Victorian Rococo-Style Armchair

Victorian Rococo-Style armchair, carved walnut, the tall balloon-back w/a long scrolled framework & a rose-carved crest above the tufted upholstered back continuing down to rolled upholstered arms w/serpentine front arm supports above the upholstered seat w/a serpentine seatrail and demi-cabriole front legs, pink floral silk upholstery, ca. 1950s, 45" h. (ILLUS.)... **$345**

Victorian Rococo-Style Side Chair

Victorian Rococo-Style side chair, walnut, the oval molded back frame w/a rose-carved crest enclosing a tufted red velvet panel, raised above the tufted seat upholstered in matching velvet, simple cabriole front legs, ca. 1950s (ILLUS.)...... **$201**

Unusual Victorian Horn Armchair

Victorian rustic-style horn armchair, oak & horn, the balloon-shaped open back composed of a pair of large elk horns, the open arms formed by deer antlers, all joined to the squared oak seat frame w/cane insert, the front & rear legs formed by interlocked pairs of antlers, original paper label reading "Weidlich Dresden N6 Schlessinger Plate 2," Germany, late 19th c., 39 1/2" h. (ILLUS.) **$690**

Wicker armchairs, a tightly woven pointed arched crestrail continuing down & around to form the flat arms, a lattice-woven back w/tight weaving under the arms, a tightly woven apron w/a lower arched panel w/loose lattice & tight weaving, added back & seat cushions, labeled by Heywood-Wakefield, several breaks & minor damages, ca. 1915-30, 42 3/4" h., pr. (ILLUS., bottom of page)............... **$1,035**

Rare Early William & Mary Armchair

William & Mary armchair, painted soft maple & birch, the very tall narrow back w/a high ornate scroll-carved crestrail above a tall narrow caned back panel, the ring- and block-turned stiles w/small knob-turned finials, shaped open arms w/scroll-carved grips raised on columnar-turned arm supports above the wide caned seat, knob- and block-turned front legs ending in knob feet & joined by a ball- and rod-turned front stretcher, matching turned rear stretcher & turned H-stretcher joining the legs, old black paint, Massachusetts or Europe, 1690-1730, 55" h. (ILLUS.) **$31,200**

Nice Heywood-Wakefield Wicker Armchairs

William & Mary Child's "Great Chair"

William & Mary child's "Great Chair," turned walnut, the tall back w/baluster- and rod-turned stiles joined by two simple turned rails connected by three slender ring-turned spindles, simple open rod arms joined to the rod- and baluster-turned front legs above the woven rush seat, base w/simple box stretchers, probably Boston, early 18th c., 22 3/4" h. (ILLUS.) **$2,160**

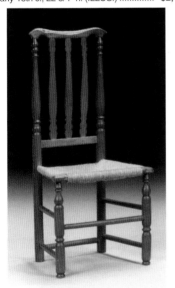

Early William & Mary "Bannister-back" Chair

William & Mary country-style "bannister-back" side chair, cherry, the narrow serpentine crestrail above three slender split-balusters flanked by slender ring- and rod-turned stiles raised above the woven rush seat, knob-, rod- and ring-turned front legs & simple turned rear legs all joined by simple turned stretchers, New England, early 18th c., 39 1/8" h. (ILLUS.)...................... **$1,554**

William & Mary Country-style Armchair

William & Mary country-style "ladder-back" armchair, painted wood, the back w/three double-arch slats between the block- and baluster-turned stiles w/small ring-turned finials, slender shaped open arms on canted ring- and baluster-turned arm supports above the wide woven rush seat, block- and knob-turned legs on button feet w/double turned stretchers at the front & sides, worn bluish paint, probably Canadian, 18th c. (ILLUS.) **$4,541**

William & Mary "Ladder-Back" Armchair

William & Mary country-style "ladder-back" armchair, the tall rod- and button-turned stiles topped by double-knob finials flanking five arched slats, serpentine open arms on baluster-turned arm supports continuing down to form the rod- and button-turned front legs, woven rush seat, double-knob turned front stretcher

& simple turned side stretchers, painted black, first half 18th c. (ILLUS.) **$1,434**

Ornate William & Mary-Style Armchairs

William & Mary-Style armchairs, carved walnut, a very tall back w/the arched wide framework ornately pierce-carved w/leafy scrolls enclosing a long narrow oval upholstered panel & flanked by spiral-turned stiles, long serpentine open arms w/scrolled hand grips raised on incurved arm supports above the wide upholstered seat, the serpentine scroll-carved front seatrail continuing into front cabriole legs ending in scroll feet, late 19th c., 51 1/4" h., pr. (ILLUS.) **$604**

Windsor "arrow-back" side chairs, painted & decorated, original yellowish brown background paint, the wide slightly arched crestrail painted w/an oval panel enclosing a leafy grape cluster, above three arrow slats flanked by curved stiles w/rabbit ear

One of Four Windsor Arrow-Back Chairs

finials, shaped saddle seat on canted bamboo-turned legs joined by bamboo-turned box stretchers, all stamped w/the signature "C. Benjamin," first half 19th c., wear, three seats w/splits, small restoration on crest, 36" h., set of four (ILLUS. of one)...... **$748**

Windsor "bamboo-turned" side chairs, a wide flat crestrail painted w/a cluster of melons & grapes on a yellow ground, between tapering stiles & above four slender tapering bamboo-turned spindles, the shaped saddle seat on canted bamboo-turned legs joined by turned box stretchers, overall old yellow paint w/black & red line trim, first half 19th c., 35" h., set of 6 .... **$1,495**

Yellow-painted & Decorated Windsor Bamboo-turned Side Chairs

Windsor bamboo-turned side chairs, yellow-painted & decorated, each w/a long gently arched crestrail decorated w/a stenciled design of purple fruits & green leaves flanked by dark gold banding, the tapering backswept stiles flanking simple turned spindles above the shaped plank seat w/dark banding, canted bamboo-turned legs joined by box stretchers, probably from Maine, first half 19th c., some touch-up or repaint, some old repairs, 32 1/2" h., set of 8 (ILLUS.) **$2,013**

Set of Five Windsor "Birdcage" Side Chairs

Windsor "birdcage" rod-back side chairs, each w/two narrow bamboo-turned crestrails flanking a row of short spindles alternating w/almond-shaped spindles above seven slender curved bamboo-turned spindles, shaped saddle seat on canted bamboo-turned legs joined by turned box stretchers, New England, early 19th c., 36" h., set of 5 (ILLUS., top of page) **$2,040**

One of a Pair of Fine Bow-Back Windsors

Windsor "bow-back" armchairs, the arched crestrail continuing down to form the narrow arms all above eleven simple turned spindles, canted ring-and-baluster-turned arm supports above the shaped saddle seat, raised on four canted baluster- and ring-turned legs joined by a shaped H-stretcher, probably Rhode Island, old grain-painted finish, late 18th - early 19th c., 37" h., pr. (ILLUS. of one) **$3,450**

Windsor "bow-back" writing-arm armchair, painted wood, the bowed crestrail above seven turned spindles extending through the medial rail that curves to form

Rare New England Writing-arm Windsor

a shaped arm on one side & a wide oblong writing surface on the other side, each arm above a spindle & ring- and baluster-turned arm support w/the writing arm supported by two additional spindles, the wide saddle seat above a single small drawer, raised on canted baluster- and ring-turned legs joined by a swelled H-stretcher, old worn white paint w/green trim, New England, possibly Vermont, 1790-1810, 37" h. (ILLUS.) **$18,000**

Windsor "bow-back" armchairs, elm & oak, the bowed crestrail above a central pierced vasiform splat flanked on each side by four slender spindles, resting on a medial rail curving around to form the arms & above another pierced vasiform splat flanked by spindles, turned incurved arm supports above the wide oblong shaped saddle seat, slender cabriole front legs ending in raised pad feet joined by incurved stretchers joined by simple turned box stretchers to the canted rear legs, England, late 18th c., 36" h., pr. (ILLUS., top of next page) **$2,645**

Pair of English Windsor "Bow-back" Armchairs

Fine New York "Bow-back" Windsor

Fine Windsor "Bow-back" Highchair

Windsor "bow-back continuous arm" armchair, the high arched crestrail curving down to form the narrow flattened arms, nine tall slender back spindles & a pair of rear brace-back spindles, a single short spindle under each arm & a canted baluster- and ring-turned arm support, shaped saddle seat raised on canted baluster-, ring- and rod-turned legs joined by a swelled H-stretcher, old black paint, signed "Samler N York," New York, late 18th c., 36 1/2 h. (ILLUS.) **$4,780**

Windsor "bow-back" highchair, the bowed crestrail above five bamboo-turned spindles, shaped arms above a bamboo-turned spindle & a canted bamboo-turned arm support, thick shaped plank seat, tall canted bamboo-turned legs joined at the front by a footrest & at the base by a bamboo-turned H-stretchers, old red over blue paint w/black highlights, attributed to the Delaware Valley, late 18th - early 19th c., 37 1/2" h. (ILLUS.) **$9,488**

Windsor "brace-back" side chair, the bowed crestrail above seven bamboo-turned spindles backed by two angled brace spindles, deeply shaped saddle seat on canted baluster-, ring- and rod-turned legs joined by a swelled H-stretcher, Rhode Island, late 18th c., old refinish, minor imperfections, 36" h. (ILLUS. right with two Windsor armchairs, top of next page) **$264**

Three Different Early Windsor Chairs

Very Fine "Comb-back" Windsor Armchair

Windsor "comb-back" armchair, painted hardwood, the slender serpentine crestrail above seven tall turned spindles continuing through the U-shaped medial rail, the flat narrow shaped arms raised on two more spindles & a canted baluster-turned arm support, the oval shaped seat on widely canted baluster- and ring-turned legs joined by a swelled H-stretcher, old worn red paint over yellow & early paints, overall 41 1/4" h. (ILLUS.) **$20,700**

Windsor "comb-back" armchair, painted wood, a short curved & arched crestrail atop seven tall slender spindles above the U-form medial rail over nine short spindles & canted baluster-turned arm supports, rounded saddle seat raised on canted baluster-turned legs joined by a swelled H-stretcher, old dark red paint w/dry surface, a few breaks in spindles, restored area on arm rails, 43 1/2" h...... **$1,495**

Windsor "comb-back" armchair, the deeply shaped serpentine crestrail above seven tall spindles continuing through the medial rail that curves to form the flat arms raised on a short spindle & a canted baluster-, ring- and rod-turned arm supports, deeply shaped saddle seat on canted baluster-, ring- and rod-turned legs joined by a swelled H-stretcher, New England, late 18th c., refinished, 37" h. (ILLUS. left with brace-back side chair & comb-back writing-arm armchair, top of page)............... **$1,763**

Fine Philadelphia "Comb-back" Windsor

Windsor "comb-back" armchair, the narrow serpentine crestrail w/scroll-carved ends above eleven tall spindles continuing through the medial rail that curves to form the arms w/carved knuckle grips & raised on short spindles & a canted baluster- and ring-turned arm supports, wide shaped saddle seat on canted baluster-, ring- and rod-turned legs joined by a swelled H-stretcher, old black paint over earlier colors, attributed to Philadelphia, a couple of splits on the armrail, second half 18th c., 45" h. (ILLUS.).................. **$11,500**

Nice Windsor "Comb-back" Armchair

Windsor "comb-back" armchair, the narrow serpentine & curved crestrail above eight tall simple turned spindles continuing through a medial rail extending to form the shaped arms raised on two short spindles & a baluster-turned canted arm support, wide shaped saddle seat, canted baluster-, ring- and rod-turned legs joined by a swelled H-stretcher, old refinish w/traces of old paint, old label w/provenance, late 18th c., 43" h. (ILLUS.) **$1,725**

Rare Philadelphia "Comb-back" Windsor

Windsor "comb-back" armchair, the tall back w/a curved serpentine crestrail end-ing in carved scrolls above nine tall slender spindles continuing through the U-form medial rail curving to form the shaped arms on three short spindles & a baluster- and ring-turned arm support, wide shaped saddle seat raised on widely canted baluster-, ring- and rod-turned legs ending in knob feet, old worn black paint, Philadelphia, 1760-90, 44 1/4" h. (ILLUS.)... **$14,400**

Nice Windsor "Comb-back" Rocker

Windsor "comb-back" rocking chair w/arms, painted wood, the shaped comb on six spindles continuing through the bowed center rail ending in shaped arms on baluster- and ring-turned supports, a wide shaped saddle seat on canted baluster- and knob-turned legs fitted into rockers & joined by a swelled H-stretcher, light brown over earlier green paint, probably Connecticut, ca. 1780, minor imperfections, 41 1/4" h. (ILLUS.)........................ **$1,293**

Windsor "comb-back" writing-arm armchair, a short serpentine crestrail w/curled ends above four slender spindles continuing down through the heavy medial rail that curves to form a wide writing surface on one side & a curled hand grip on the other side, each arm supported on short spindles & baluster- and ring-turned canted supports, wide half-round seat raised on canted baluster-, ring- and rod-turned legs joined by a swelled H-stretcher, New England, late 18th c., refinished, imperfections, 37 1/2" h. (ILLUS. center with brace-back side chair & comb-back armchair, top of page 102) **$3,525**

Windsor country-style side chairs, painted & decorated, a wide gently arched crestrail between canted tapering stiles & a lower narrow rail above four short turned spindles, shaped plank seat on slightly canted ring- and rod-turned front legs & box stretchers, dark green painted

Set of 6 Decorated Late Windsor Chairs

ground, the crestrail h.p. w/large red roses bordered in mustard yellow w/further yellow banding on the stiles, narrow rail, spindles, seat & legs, three chairs signed in pencil under the seat "L. Wheeler Pine Grove, PA," ca. 1830-50, 32 1/2" h., set of 6 (ILLUS.).................. **$1,610**

Fine New England "Fan-Back" Windsor

Windsor "fan-back" side chair, a long serpentine crestrail w/curled ends above seven simple spindles flanked by canted baluster- and ring-turned stiles above the finely shaped saddle seat, canted baluster-, ring- and rod-turned legs joined by a swelled H-stretcher, old black paint over earlier green & red paints, New England, late 18th c., 36" h. (ILLUS.).................. **$7,638**

One of Four Country Windsor Chairs

Windsor country-style side chairs, painted & decorated, the wide flat curved crestrail stenciled w/fruits above four tall slender bamboo-turned spindles flanked by tapering backswept styles, a shaped plank seat raised on canted bamboo-turned front legs & plain turned rear legs all joined by bamboo-turned box stretchers, original yellow paint, a few age splits, one glued stretcher, one repaired leg, first half 19th c., 33 12/" h., set of 4 (ILLUS. of one) **$719**

Nice Painted Windsor "Fan-back" Chair

Windsor "fan-back" side chair, painted hardwood, the narrow serpentine crestrail above seven turned spindles flanked by baluster- and ring-turned canted stiles above the shaped saddle seat, canted baluster- and ring-turned legs joined by a swelled "H" stretcher, old red paint over earlier green, good patina, late 18th - early 19th c., 35 1/2" h. (ILLUS.).................................. **$1,438**

Fine Philadelphia "Fan-back" Side Chair

Windsor "fan-back" side chair, painted wood, narrow serpentine crestrail w/scroll-carved ears above eight slender spindles & tall baluster-turned stiles over the shaped saddle seat, raised on canted baluster-, ring- and rod-turned legs joined by a swelled H-stretcher, old dark green paint over original lighter green, Philadelphia origin, late 18th c., 36 1/2" h. (ILLUS.)..... **$2,875**

Rare Rhode Island "Low-back" Windsor

Windsor "low-back" armchair, the low back w/a U-form crestrail w/a raised top bracket & curving to form the arms, raised on eight baluster-turned spindles above the wide rounded shaped saddle seat, on canted baluster-turned legs

joined by a baluster-turned X-stretcher, old black paint over earlier red, painted inscription under the seat "Found by S.E. Meigs, Madison," Rhode Island, late 18th c., rare form, 31" h. (ILLUS.).. **$9,775**

Fine Windsor Writing Arm Armchair

Windsor "low-back" writing arm armchair, painted, the thick curved crestrail ending in a scrolled arm at one side & a wide rounded writing surface at the other side w/a small drawer below, the back composed of numerous turned spindles w/baluster- and ring-turned arm supports above the wide shaped oblong seat, raised on widely canted ring-, baluster- and rod-turned legs joined by a swelled H-stretcher, old grey-green paint, imperfections, New England, ca. 1780, 28" h. (ILLUS.).. **$3,525**

Fine Windsor "Sack-back" Armchair

Windsor "sack-back" armchair, painted, the high bowed crestrail above seven spindles continuing down through the medial rail extending to scrolled hand grips above spindles & canted baluster- and ring-turned arm supports, wide shaped saddle seat, canted baluster-, ring- and rod-turned legs joined by a swelled H-stretcher, old finely crazed black paint over earlier coats of green & red, bow re-pegged on one side, a couple of later nails added to seat, late 18th c., 35" h. (ILLUS.) **$2,875**

Chests & Chests of Drawers

Unusual Old Pine Apothecary Chest

Apothecary chest, country-style, pine, hanging or table-type, the scroll-carved three-quarters gallery top above two rows of four square drawers w/white porcelain knobs above a pair of rectangular doors fitted on the interior w/bottle racks, flat bottom, complete w/eleven apothecary jars & spices, 19th c., 7 3/4 x 21 1/2", 23" h. (ILLUS.) **$863**

Blanket chest, Chippendale country-style, painted poplar, rectangular hinged top w/molded edges opening to a deep well & covered till, dovetailed sides & peg-construction molded base w/scroll-cut bracket feet, old red paint, original lock removed & old brass escutcheon low-

ered, wrought-iron hinges, attributed to Pennsylvania, minor repair, late 18th - early 19th c., 21 x 46 1/2", 25 1/2" h. **$690**

Simple Cherry Country Blanket Chest

Blanket chest, country-style, cherry, the rectangular top w/a molded edge opening to a deep well, paneled sides raised on turned bun feet, original finish, mid-19th c., 37 1/2" l., 22" h. (ILLUS.) **$345**

Fine Grain-painted Blanket Chest

Blanket chest, country-style, painted & decorated, the hinged rectangular lid w/molded edges opening to a deep well, a molded base raised on shaped bracket feet, decorated overall w/grain painting w/a yellow ground covered w/red burl-style graining, Maine, 1820-40, 21 1/2 x 51 1/2", 27" h. (ILLUS.) **$5,975**

Early Grain-painted Blanket Chest with Unusual Design

Early Grain-painted Blanket Chest

Blanket chest, country-style, painted & decorated, the rectangular top w/molded edges opening to a deep well, a molded base on simple tall bracket feet, original overall bold grain painting forming an eye-like design on the front & sides, New England, early 19th c., 19 x 40", 22 1/2" h. (ILLUS., bottom previous page) **$4,800**

Blanket chest, grain-painted wood, six-board construction w/a rectangular top opening to an interior fitted w/one lidded till & eight drawers w/small turned knobs, original locks, raised on four short turned feet, all original mustard yellow-outlined panels w/simulated mahogany graining, probably from Maryland, early 19th c., 20 1/2 x 41 1/2", 21 3/4" h. (ILLUS., top of page) **$1,150**

Blanket chest, immigrant-type, painted pine, rectangular w/hinged low domed top w/wrought-iron hinges opening to an interior w/a till w/cover, the dovetailed case decorated w/h.p. rosemaling in salmon red highlighted by gold & dark blue scrolls & stylized flowers, front panels painted in white w/"Aar" & "1815," some rosehead nails, iron bail end han-

dles, some repairs, edge damage on base, Scandinavia, probably Norway, 15 1/4 x 17 1/4", 34 1/2" (ILLUS., bottom of page) **$250-500**

Flame-grained Early Blanket Chest

Blanket chest, painted & decorated, the rectangular hinged top w/a molded edge opening to a well & a lidded till, deep sides decorated w/a striped pattern of mustard yellow & light brown flamed grain painting, on short double-knob turned legs, first half 19th c., 20 x 42", 26" h. (ILLUS.) **$2,128**

Decorative Immigrant Blanket Chest

Walnut Chippendale Blanket Chest

Fine Grain-Painted Early Blanket Chest

Rare Massachusetts Block-front Chest

Blanket chest, painted & decorated, the rectangular hinged top w/a thick edge opening to a deep well, the front decorated w/a large rectangular panel of fine wood-grain painting, high arched aprons & tall tapering bracket feet, overall grain painting on the lid & all sides, first half 19th c., 18 x 37 1/2", 24" h. (ILLUS.)...... **$7,170**

Chippendale blanket chest, walnut, the rectangular top w/molded edges opening w/original strap hinges to reveal an interior fitted w/a till, the dovetailed case w/a row of two large & one small drawer w/simple bail pulls along the bottom, molded base on scroll-cut bracket feet, good color, worn surface, age crack on the top, glue blocks & on scroll missing, one back foot renailed, late 18th - early 20th c., 23 x 50", 28" h. (ILLUS., top of page).. **$1,380**

Chippendale "block-front" chest of drawers, mahogany, the rectangular top w/a blocked front above a conforming case of four long graduated drawers w/butterfly brasses & keyhole escutcheons, molded blocked base on tall bracket feet, Massachusetts, 1760-80, original brasses, 18 x 31", 31 1/2" h. (ILLUS., top next column).. **$28,800**

Fine Small Chippendale Chest of Drawers

Chippendale chest of drawers, mahogany, the rectangular top w/molded edges above a case w/four long thumb-molded graduated drawers w/butterfly brasses & keyhole escutcheons, molded base raised on heavy scroll-carved ogee bracket feet, late 18th c., 20 x 29 1/2", 33" h. (ILLUS., previous page) **$7,188**

Southern Chippendale Chest of Drawers

Chippendale chest of drawers, walnut, the rectangular two-board top w/variegated fan inlays at each corner & a double star in the center above a case w/a pair of drawers w/simple bail pulls above three long graduated drawers w/matching pulls & all w/banded inlay borders, flanked by chamfered front corners w/line inlay & small urns, molded base on scroll-cut ogee bracket feet, replaced pulls, small areas of veneer damage & inlay restorations, feet are old replacements, Southern U.S., late 18th c., 21 1/4 x 39", 38 1/8" h. (ILLUS.) **$2,645**

New York Chippendale Chest-on-Chest

Chippendale chest-on-chest, carved mahogany, two-part construction: the upper section w/a rectangular top w/angled front corners & a deep coved cornice abive a pair of drawers over a stack of three long graduated drawers each w/pierced butterfly brasses & keyhole escutcheons, beveled & fluted front edges; the lower section w/a mid-molding over a case w/a pair of drawers over a stack of three long graduated drawers w/pierced butterfly brasses, molded base raised on scroll-carved short cabriole legs ending in claw-and-ball feet, New York City, 1760-90, 22 x 47 1/2", 81" h. (ILLUS.)...................................... **$7,800**

Fine Chippendale Walnut Chest-on-Chest

Chippendale chest-on-chest, figured walnut, two-part construction: the upper section w/a high broken-scroll pediment w/the high molded scrolls above pierced latticework panels & ending in a large carved flower head, centered by a tall ornate pierced & scroll-carved finial, corner blocks w/urn-turned & flame-carved finials all above a deep flaring dentil-carved cornice over a row of three drawers above a pair of drawers above three long graduated drawers each w/butterfly brasses & keyhole escutcheons, fluted quarter-round columns down the sides; the lower section w/a mid-molding above three long graduated drawers flanked by quarter-round fluted columns, molded base on tall scroll-cut ogee bracket feet, Pennsylvania, 1760-80, cornice replaced (ILLUS.) **$13,200**

Country Chippendale Tall Chest

Chippendale country-style tall chest of drawers, pine, the rectangular top w/a flaring stepped cornice above a tall case w/five long graduated drawers w/butterfly brasses, molded base raised on tall shaped bracket feet, old reddish brown colored refinishing, replaced brasses, minor restorations, late 18th - early 19th c., 20 x 39", 51 1/4" h. (ILLUS.) **$1,495**

Country Chippendale Tall Chest

Chippendale country-style tall chest of drawers, pine, the rectangular top w/narrow molded corner hinged & opening above a deep well, the front of the case w/three long false drawer fronts w/simple bail pulls & oval keyhole escutcheons above three long deeper graduated work-

ing drawer w/matching pulls, molded base w/scroll-cut bracket feet, fine alligator brown surface over original red wash, two pulls original, the other replacements, old black writing on the back w/name of owner in Indiana, some edge chips w/glued restorations, three foot facing partially replaced, good patina, late 18th c., 19 x 37 1/2" h., 54" h. (ILLUS.) . **$4,485**

Chippendale "Reverse-Serpentine" Chest

Chippendale "reverse-serpentine" chest of drawers, carved mahogany & mahogany veneer, the rectangular top w/a serpentine front overhanging a conforming case w/four long graduated drawers w/butterfly brasses & keyhole escutcheons, molded base on four short cabriole legs w/claw-and-ball feet & scroll-cut brackets, Boston area, 1770-80, old refinish, veneer losses, 20 3/4 x 41", 34 1/4" h. (ILLUS.) **$3,525**

Chippendale "Reverse-Serpentine" Chest

Chippendale "reverse-serpentine" chest of drawers, mahogany & mahogany veneer, the rectangular top w/a string-inlaid serpentine front edge above a conforming case w/four long graduated drawers w/butterfly brasses & keyhole escutcheons, molded base on boldly carved claw-and-ball feet, Massachusetts, ca. 1780, old replaced brasses, refinished, minor imperfections, 19 1/2 x 35", 33 1/4" h. (ILLUS.) **$9,988**

Mahogany "Reverse-Serpentine" Chest

Chippendale "reverse-serpentine" chest of drawers, mahogany, the rectangular top w/molded edges & a double serpentine top overhanging a conforming case w/four long graduated drawers w/butterfly brasses & keyhole escutcheons, molded base on scroll-cut ogee bracket feet, Massachusetts, 1760-90, appears to have original brasses, 20 1/4 x 41 3/4", 33" h. (ILLUS.) **$9,600**

Chippendale Revival Tall Chest of Drawers

carved ball-and-claw feet, some cockbeading missing on one drawer, minor veneer cracks, probably mid-19th c., 24 x 47 1/2", 5' 4" h. (ILLUS.) **$2,185**

Rare "Reverse-Serpentine" Chippendale Chest

Chippendale "reverse-serpentine" chest of drawers, mahogany, the rectangular top w/molded edges & a reverse-serpentined front edge projecting over a conforming case w/four long graduated drawers w/butterfly brasses & keyhole escutcheons & blocked ends, the conforming base molding over fancy scroll-cut returns & a central drop raised on short claw-and-ball front feet, Salem, Massachusetts, 1760-80, 22 3/4 x 41 3/4", 22 3/4" h. (ILLUS.) **$27,485**

Chippendale Revival tall chest of drawers, mahogany & mahogany veneer, rectangular top w/a wide covered cornice above a frieze band over a case w/a row of three small drawers above five long graduated drawers all w/butterfly pulls, narrow molded case on heavy foliate-

Fine Chippendale Serpentine-front Chest

Chippendale "serpentine-front" chest of drawers, carved birch, the rectangular top w/molded edges & a serpentine front overhanging a conforming case w/four long graduated drawers w/simple bail pulls & small brass keyhole escutcheons, molded apron centered by a small fan-carved pendant & raised on scroll-cut short claw-and-ball front feet, replaced brasses, refinished, probably Newburyport, Massachusetts, ca. 1760-80, minor imperfections, 21 x 35 1/2", 34 1/2" h. (ILLUS.) **$7,638**

Maple Chippendale Tall Chest of Drawers

Chippendale tall chest of drawers, maple, a rectangular top w/a molded edge above a case w/a row of three small drawers above four long graduated thumb-molded drawers, all w/oval brasses, molded base w/scroll-cut bracket feet, old brasses, refinished, some restoration, New England, late 18th c., 17 3/4 x 39", 4' h. (ILLUS.)....... **$2,233**

Fine Pennsylvania Chippendale Tall Chest

Chippendale tall chest of drawers, walnut, the rectangular top above a deep flaring cornice over a row of three drawers above a stack of five long graduated drawers each w/butterfly brasses & keyhole escutcheons, quarter-round fluted colonettes down the sides, molded base on tall scroll-cut ogee bracket feet, Penn-

sylvania, 1760-90, 23 3/4 x 44 1/2", 67" h. (ILLUS.) **$11,400**

Fine Chippendale-Style Block-front Desk

Chippendale-Style "block-front" chest of drawers, mahogany, the rectangular top w/molded edges & a double-blocked front above a conforming blocked case w/four long graduated drawers w/brass butterfly pulls & shield-shaped brass keyhole escutcheons, molded base w/scroll-cut corner blocks & short cabriole legs w/ball-and-claw feet, unsigned, fine quality, early 20th c., 18 x 32", 32" h. (ILLUS.)... **$1,150**

Fine Reproduction Chest-on-Chest

Chippendale-Style chest-on-chest, walnut, two-part construction: the upper section w/a high broken-scroll crest w/carved rosettes & three urn-turned & flame finials above a pair of small drawers flanking a deep shell-carved drawer above four long graduated drawers all w/butterfly brasses & keyhole escutcheons; the lower section w/a mid-molding above a case of four long graduated drawers, molded base on ogee scroll-cut legs, minor hairlines on one drawer, reproduction by the Virginia Crafters w/their branded mark, 20th c., 22 1/4 x 40 1/4", 90 1/2" h. (ILLUS.)....... **$1,610**

Classical Mahogany "Bowfront" Chest

Classical "bowfront" chest of drawers, carved mahogany & mahogany veneer, the scrolled backboard above the rectangular bowfront top w/oval corners above a conforming case of four long graduated beaded drawers w/rosette & ring pulls & brass keyhole escutcheons, flanked by quarter-engaged ring- and spiral-turned posts carved w/flowers & acanthus leaves on punchwork continuing down to ring- and baluster-turned legs w/peg feet, scalloped apron, old replaced brasses, Massachusetts, ca. 1825, imperfections, 20 1/2 x 45", 41 1/2" h. (ILLUS.) **$2,938**

Fine Classical State of Maine Chest

Classical chest of drawers, mahogany grain painting & mahogany veneer, the top w/a very high scroll-carved arched crest w/brass florettes at the scroll tips, above a two-tier section w/a pair of very narrow drawers above a pair of slightly deeper drawers all on the rectangular top slightly overhanging the case w/a project-

ing long curve-fronted top drawer above three set-back long graduated mahogany-veneered drawers, all drawers w/old pressed lacy glass pulls, the lower drawers flanked by turned black columns, molded base raised on tall heavy ring- and baluster-turned legs w/large ball feet, tiered drawers & case sides decorated w/red & black mahogany graining, State of Maine, first half 19th c., 20 1/2 x 44", overall 64" h. (ILLUS.)........................... **$4,313**

Simple Classical Mahogany Chest of Drawers

Classical chest of drawers, mahogany & mahogany veneer, the rectangular top above a case fitted w/a pair of very narrow round-fronted drawers each w/a pair of turned wood knobs above a long deep drawer w/wood knobs slightly projecting above the lower case fitted w/three long graduated drawers w/wood knobs, square tapering legs, ca. 1840-1850, 19 1/2 x 42", 49" h. (ILLUS.) **$1,840**

Fine Classical Mahogany Chest of Drawers

Classical chest of drawers, mahogany & mahogany veneer, the rectangular top above a case w/a pair of long, narrow round-front drawers w/small turned wood knobs above a single long deep drawer w/raised molded & turned wood knobs all projecting over a stack of three long flat graduated drawers w/turned wood knobs flanked by acanthus leaf-carved side columns w/ring-turned tops, the flat base raised on heavy leaf-carved paw front feet & ring- and knob-turned rear feet, ca. 1840, 22 1/2 x 45 1/2", 50 1/2" h. (ILLUS.) **$1,035**

Classical Mahogany Veneer Chest

Classical chest of drawers, mahogany & mahogany veneer, the rectangular top w/a long scroll-cut crestrail above a case w/four long reverse-graduated drawers w/turned wood knobs, ring- and tapering knob-turned legs w/peg feet, ca. 1830, 19 1/2 x 44", 43" h. (ILLUS.) **$1,380**

Classical Chest with Octagonal Mirror

Classical chest of drawers, mahogany & mahogany veneer, the rectangular white marble top fitted w/a large horizontal octagonal mirror within an ogee molded

frame & swiveling between a conforming U-form support, the case w/a long narrow ogee-fronted top drawer above two long drawers each w/two turned wood knobs, another long ogee-fronted drawer across the bottom, raised on scroll-cut bracket feet, ca. 1840-50, 21 x 43", overall 62" h. (ILLUS.) **$2,070**

Simple Classical Cherry Chest of Drawers

Classical country-style chest of drawers, cherry, a rectangular top above a deep long drawer w/turned wood knobs projecting over a stack of three long graduated drawers w/wood knobs flanked by bobbin- and spiral-twist-carved columns, tapering heavy turned front legs, ca. 1830, pulls replaced, 41" w., 44" h. (ILLUS.) **$323**

Cherry & Bird's-Eye Maple Chest

Classical country-style chest of drawers, cherry & bird's-eye- maple, rectangular top w/veneer edging above a single long deep drawer w/a bird's-eye maple front & two turned wood knobs, projecting above the long graduated matching drawers flanked by ring-turned columns, raised on ring- and rod-turned legs, ca. 1830-40, 20 3/8 x 39", 40 1/2" h. (ILLUS) **$1,380**

Classical Country-Style Chest of Drawers

Classical country-style chest of drawers,
cherry, the rectangular top mounted w/a
three-quarters gallery w/a high arched &
scroll-cut back rail & low shaped side
rails over a row of tiny spindles, the case
w/a long deep top drawer projecting
above three long graduated drawers
flanked by free-standing turned columns,
drawers w/old pressed glass knobs, ring-
turned tapering short legs w/peg feet, ca.
1830, 24 x 45", 58" h. (ILLUS.) **$920**

Nice Dated Classical Chest of Drawers

Classical country-style chest of drawers,
curly maple, the rectangular top above a
long deep beaded drawer w/two round
brass pulls projecting above a stack of
three long graduated beaded drawers
w/round brasses flanked by black-paint-
ed bobbin- and knob-turned half columns, raised on turned double-ring &
knob black feet, inlaid diamond-shaped
keyhole escutcheons, replaced pulls,
second drawer opens to a unusual open
till dated in pencil "September 1829," veneering on top edge an old replacement,
21 x 42", 46" h. (ILLUS.) **$1,150**
Classical country-style chest of drawers,
curly maple & walnut, the rectangular top
w/a flat backsplash w/taller blocked ends,
above the base w/a row of three small
curly maple drawers w/early pressed

opalescent pulls above a deep long false-
front drawer w/hinged front & matching
pulls slightly projecting above a stack of
three long graduated matching drawers
flanked by full-round baluster- and spiral-
turned columns resting on projecting
blocks above the tapering turned double-
knob front feet, fold-down compartment
enclosing six pigeonholes & a central
door opening to a compartment & hidden
drawer, first half 19th c., 23 1/4 x 47 1/2",
4' 10" h. (interior hinge needs screws)... **$1,870**

Classical Country Two-tone Chest

Classical country-style chest of drawers,
mahogany & bird's-eye maple, the rectangular cherry top w/a flat maple crestboard above a case of mahogany fitted
w/a pair of ogee-front maple drawers
flanking a small flat-fronted drawer above
a stack of four long graduated maple
drawers w/later brass bail pulls, simple
front bracket feet, ca. 1830, 42" w., 4'
2" h. (ILLUS.) **$353**

Classical Revival Chest of Drawers

Classical Revival chest of drawers, mahogany & mahogany veneer, the superstructure w/a peaked crestrail joined by tall flat uprights flanking a large rectangular swiveling mirror, raised above the rectangular top over a long deep top drawer overhanging two long drawers all w/stamped brass pulls, the lower drawers flanked by ring-turned columns all raised on heavy carved front paw feet, original dark finish, late 19th c., 45" w., 6' 4" h. (ILLUS., previous page) **$529**

Fine New York Classical Silver Chest

Classical silver chest, mahogany & mahogany veneer, a thin rectangular top above a case w/three long graduated drawers w/round brass pulls, raised on four rope twist-turned legs w/ring-turned sections & ending in brass caps w/casters, New York, New York, ca. 1800-20, 20 1/2 x 29 1/2", 36 1/2" h. (ILLUS.) **$3,585**

Early Classical Mahogany Storage Chest

Classical storage chest, mahogany & mahogany veneer, a rectangular top above an upper case w/a row of three narrow drawers w/small turned wood knobs above a single long deep drawer w/wood knobs projecting above the lower cabinet w/a pair of paneled cupboard doors flanked by columns w/carved capitals, on turned knob front feet, shrinkage crack in top, other minor cracks & veneer loss, ca. 1840, 22 3/4 x 47 1/4", 47" h. (ILLUS.) **$920**

Fine Country-style Paneled & Painted Blanket Chest

Country-style blanket chest, painted pine, six-board construction, the rectangular hinged top w/molded edges opening to an interior w/lidded till, vertical pegged corner supports above a row of three recessed panels trimmed w/applied moldings, flat base raised on ring-turned tapering legs, original red paint, Ohio or Kentucky, ca. 1830, minor surface wear, 20 5/8 x 48 3/4", 26" h. (ILLUS.) **$3,760**

Fine Painted & Decorated Chest of Drawers

Country-style chest of drawers, painted & stencilled cherry & pine, the rectangular top above a case w/a pair of drawers h.p w/flower-filled compotes against the red ground above three long graduated drawers w/simple brass knobs, the top long drawer centered by a painted panel around the name "Eve Summey," the lower drawers w/further h.p. potted flower & related designs on the red ground, short ring-turned feet, made by Jacob

Knagy, Myersdale, Somerset County, Pennsylvania, dated 1863, 20 x 40", 45 1/2" h. (ILLUS.) **$6,000**

Scarce Early Tennessee Sugar Chest

Country-style sugar chest, cherry, the rectangular hinged top opening to a deep divided well, above a lower section w/a single drawer w/two small turned pulls, raised on ring- and knob-turned legs, Tennessee, mid-19th c., 18 x 24 1/2", 32 1/2" h. (ILLUS.) **$3,800**

Brightly Painted Pennsylvania Dower Chest

Dower chest, painted & decorated pine, the rectangular hinged top opening to a well w/a till above dove-tailed sides w/a medial rail over two bottom drawers w/turned wood knobs, molded base on bulbous tapering feet, original surface decorated w/pinwheels & quarter-fans against a dotted ground in green, salmon & mustard yellow, Pennsylvania, early 19th c., minor imperfections, 22 x 44", 27" h. (ILLUS.)
.... **$7,638**

Very Rare Decorated Pennsylvania Dower Chest

Dower chest, painted & decorated, the rectangular hinged top w/a molded edge opening to a well, the front elaborately decorated w/brightly painted Pennsylvania Dutch designs, a large central twelve-point star in red & yellow below a facing pair of birds & w/tulips & starflowers below, a rearing unicorn at each side below a large parrot & a cluster of a star, tulip blossoms & starflowers at each end, a German inscription across the top front, all on a dark blue ground, a dark red base molding on dark blue scroll-cut ogee bracket feet, attributed to John Flory (1754-after 1824), Rapho Township, Lancaster County, Pennsylvania, dated 1794, 22 x 51 3/4", 22 1/2" h. (ILLUS., top of page) **$45,410**

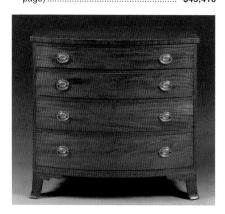

Fine Federal "Bow-front" Chest of Drawers

Federal "bow-front" chest of drawers, mahogany & mahogany veneer, the rectangular top w/a gently bowed front above a conforming case of four long graduated drawers each w/oval brasses, scroll-cut front French feet, Middle Atlantic States, 1790-1810, original brasses, 24 5/8 x 41 1/2", 38" h. (ILLUS.)... **$4,560**

Fine New Hampshire Federal Chest

Federal "bow-front" chest of drawers, cherry & burled birch, rectangular top w/a projecting oval corners & bowed front above a conforming case w/four long graduated drawers each w/banded & paneled veneer & oval brasses, ring-turned & reeded side stiles continue into the ring- and baluster-turned legs w/peg feet, New Hampshire, early 19th c., 19 1/2 x 43 1/2", 38" h. (ILLUS.) **$7,475**

Nicely Inlaid Federal "Bow-front" Chest

Federal "bow-front" chest of drawers, inlaid cherry & maple, the rectangular top w/a gently bowed front & oval corners projecting above a ring-turned segment over a tall reeded corner column flanking the case w/four gently curved long graduated drawers, each w/a long narrow oval central panel & oval brasses, a scroll-cut serpentine apron, turned tapering legs w/peg feet, probably Massachusetts, ca. 1815, replaced brasses, old refinish, minor imperfections, 21 3/4 x 44", 42" h. (ILLUS., previous page) **$5,581**

Southern Federal "Bow-front" Chest

Federal "bow-front" chest of drawers, inlaid mahogany & mahogany veneer, the rectangular top w/a bowed front & oval corners above a conforming case w/four long graduated cross-banded drawers each w/a pair of large turned wood knobs, flanked by projectings ring- and spiral-turned columns, raised on turned tapering legs on tiny casters, possibly South Carolina, ca. 1815-20, pulls replaced, 20 x 40 3/4", 37 1/4" h. (ILLUS.) **$3,200**

Rare New Hampshire "Bow-front" Chest

Federal "bow-front" chest of drawers, mahogany, rosewood & flame birch veneer, the mahogany rectangular top w/bowed front edge w/inlay overhangs the conforming case of four long graduated drawers w/flame birch panels & mahogany veneers interspersed w/rosewood-ve-

neered escutcheons, round turned wood pulls, molded base & flaring front French feet w/contrasting crossbanded mahogany veneers, shaped sides, refinished, Portsmouth, New Hampshire, ca. 1800, imperfections, 22 1/2 x 41 1/4", 36 1/2" h. (ILLUS.) **$14,100**

Cherry & Mahogany Federal Chest

Federal chest of drawers, cherry & inlaid mahogany veneer, the rectangular top w/applied rounded edge & oval corners above a case of four long beaded graduated drawers w/oval brasses & keyhole escutcheons, the inlaid shaped skirt joining the quarter-engaged baluster- and ring-turned reeded corner posts continuing to turned legs, original brasses, old surface, probably Massachusetts, ca. 1815-20, imperfections, 21 1/2 x 42 1/2", 45" h. (ILLUS.) **$2,703**

Federal Inlaid Cherry Chest of Drawers

Federal chest of drawers, inlaid cherry, the rectangular top above a case of four long drawers w/long rectangular line-inlaid panels & a diamond-shaped inlaid ivory keyhole escutcheon, oval brass pulls, simple turned legs w/knob feet, minor restorations, early 19th c., 21 1/4 x 41", 44 1/2" h. (ILLUS.) **$1,035**

Fine New York Federal Chest of Drawers

Federal chest of drawers, inlaid mahogany, rectangular line-inlaid top above a case w/a deep top "bonnet" drawer inlaid w/two large oval reserves each w/an oval brass pulls above three long graduated shorter drawers w/matching pulls, scallop-cut apron & slender long French feet, New York City, ca. 1800-1810, 22 1/4 x 45", 44" h. (ILLUS.) **$2,390**

Inlaid Walnut Southern Federal Chest

Federal chest of drawers, inlaid walnut, the rectangular top w/the narrow front edge decorated w/small inlaid oblong panels above a case w/four long graduated line-inlaid drawers w/inlaid shield-form keyhole escutcheons, the deep serpentine front apron centered by an inlaid design, raised on tall French feet, probably Southern States, early 19th c., restorations to feet, 17 3/4 x 39 1/2", 43" h. (ILLUS.)...................................... **$2,640**

Federal Inlaid Mahogany Chest of Drawers

Federal chest of drawers, inlaid mahogany, the rectangular top above a case w/a pair of drawers w/rectangular banded inlay & two round brass pulls above four matching long graduated drawers, the serpentine apron w/a central fan-carved inlay, raised on high outswept French feet, probably English, replaced brasses, minor pieced repair, 21 x 42", 42" h. (ILLUS.) **$1,265**

Fine Early Federal Chest of Drawers

Federal chest of drawers, mahogany & satin birch veneer, rectangular top w/projecting blocked corners above reeded square stiles flanking the case w/four long drawers each w/two round brass pulls & oval keyhole escutcheons & decorated w/double rectangular panels of satin birch veneer, scroll-cut apron, raised on baluster- and ring-turned legs w/peg feet, original hardware, early 19th c., 19 1/2 x 44 3/4", 39" h. (ILLUS.) **$4,025**

Fine Labeled Pennsylvania Chest

Federal chest of drawers, tiger stripe maple & cherry, the rectangular top above a case w/four long graduated tiger stripe maple drawers w/round brass pulls flanked by fluted pilasters, on ring- and knob-turned legs, two drawer w/interior label reading "Wm. Frick - Cabinet Makers - Two...North - From the court house - Lancaster," Lancaster, Pennsylvania, ca. 1810-25, 21 x 43", 22 1/2" h. (ILLUS.)..... **$3,346**

Federal chest-on-frame, tiger stripe maple, a rectangular top w/a narrow covered cornice above a case w/five long graduated thumb-molded drawers w/brass batwing pulls & keyhole escutcheons, molded base raised on a gently shaped apron w/bracket feet, old refinish, probably Rhode Island, late 18th - early 19th c., 19 x 38 1/4", 47 1/4" h. (replaced brasses, surface imperfections) **$2,350**

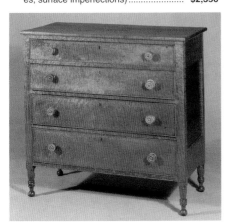

Federal Country Chest of Drawers

Federal country-style chest of drawers, bird's-eye maple, the rectangular top

above a case of four long graduated cock-beaded drawers w/round brass pulls, paneled sides, on tapering ring-turned legs w/knob feet, ca. 1800, old veneer repairs, 21 x 41 1/4", 41 1/2" h. (ILLUS.) **$3,400**

Connecticut Inlaid Cherry Chest

Federal country-style chest of drawers, inlaid cherry, rectangular top w/a central oval inlay above a conforming case w/four long graduated drawers each w/fine line inlay & rounded brass pulls flanked by chamfered & inlaid corners, deep serpentine & scroll-cut apron & simple bracket feet, Connecticut, 1790-1810, 20 x 43 1/2", 37 1/2" h. (ILLUS.) **$4,541**

Painted Country Federal Chest

Federal country-style chest of drawers, painted & decorated walnut & pine, rectangular top above a case w/a pair of drawers over two long drawers all w/beaded edges & old turned wood pulls, scalloped apron, bootjack sides, old red over mustard yellow flame graining, some edge chips & areas of paint wear, early 19th c., 20 x 44", 35 1/2" h. (ILLUS.) **$1,035**

Nice Federal Tiger Maple Chest of Drawers

Federal country-style chest of drawers, tiger stripe maple, rectangular top above a case w/a deep long top drawer above three long graduated drawers all w/oval brass pulls, serpentine apron & French feet, damage to one area of base, some old glue blocks missing, old refinishing, 20 x 45", 43 3/4" h. (ILLUS.) **$3,220**

Rare Federal Southern Sugar Chest

Federal sugar chest, walnut, the rectangular flat lift-lid w/brass knob opening to a deep storage compartment, the molded base w/a single narrow long drawer w/a brass knob, raised on chamfered Marlborough legs, original hardware, yellow pine secondary wood, Southern U.S., late 18th c., 20 x 27", 38" h. (ILLUS.)..... **$6,325**

Rare Federal Inlaid Sugar Chest

Federal sugar chest, inlaid cherry, a hinged rectangular top w/molded edges opening to a deep interior w/a single (missing) divider, dovetailed corners & the front w/fine line inlay w/tiny fans at each corner, a central inlaid oval & a diamond-shaped keyhole escutcheon, fitted in a separate stand w/molded edges above a single long drawer w/matching inlay & inlaid corners raised on four square tapering legs w/further line inlay, restoration, Mid-Atlantic States, early 19th c., 16 1/2 x 32 1/4", 34 3/4" h. (ILLUS.) **$12,925**

Fine Cherry & Mahogany Federal Chest

Federal tall chest of drawers, cherry & mahogany veneer, the rectangular top w/a widely flaring covered cornice above a wide frieze band decorated w/a band of mahogany veneer, above a row of three small drawers, two w/oval brasses, above a stack of five long graduated drawers w/oval brasses all flanked by fluted pilasters, a flat molded base raised on four slender turned legs w/tiny knob feet, small pieced restoration on back left cornice, early 19th c., 22 1/2 x 47 1/2", 65 1/2" h. (ILLUS.) **$3,738**

Fine Federal Inlaid Walnut Tall Chest

Federal tall chest of drawers, inlaid walnut, the rectangular top w/a flat-molded cornice above a row of three thumb-molded drawers over a pair of drawers over a stack of four long graduated drawers all w/simple bail handles, string inlay & escutcheons flanked by meandering vines continuing to vases, on cut-out feet & a shaped skirt centered by an inlaid fan, old pulls, old refinish, probably Pennsylvania, ca. 1800, imperfections, 20 1/2 x 40", 71" h. (ILLUS.) **$5,825**

Fine French Provincial Chest of Drawers

French Provincial chest of drawers, walnut, the rectangular top w/molded edges & a serpentine front overhanging a case w/a pair of top drawers w/molded oblong panels & scrolling brass pulls w/a keyhole escutcheon flanking a center block w/a carved quatrefoil, two long matching lower drawers, w/centered by a quatrefoil, the other a circle, the narrow serpen-

tine apron above high bracket feet, France, early 19th c., 22 1/2 x 50 1/2", 33 1/2" h. (ILLUS.) **$3,738**

Tall French Provincial Chest of Drawers

French Provincial tall chest of drawers, mahogany, a rectangular grey variegated marble top above a tall case w/seven long paneled drawers w/simple bail pulls & brass keyhole escutcheons, flat apron raised on square tapering feet, France, late 19th c., 16 x 32", 5' 5" h. (ILLUS.)... **$2,645**

Quality George III Chest-on-Bureau

Early English Jacobean Oak Chest

George III chest-on-bureau, mahogany, two-part construction: the upper section w/a rectangular top w/a deep flaring cornice w/a dentil band & beveled corners above a case w/a row of three small drawers over three long graduated drawers all flanked by beveled & reeded front corners; the lower section w/a deep fold-down drawer w/a false two-drawer front opening to an interior fitted w/small drawers & cubbyholes, all above three long graduated drawers, molded base on large bracket feet, simple bail pulls & pierced brass keyhole escutcheons, England, ca. 1800, 23 x 45 1/2", 6' 4 1/4" h. (ILLUS., previous page) **$3,680**

Fine Rosemaled Immigrant Chest

Immigrant chest, painted & decorated pine, high domed lid opening to a deep well w/an open till w/one drawer & large decorative iron strap hinges, the front exterior w/five metal straps, painted overall in bluish green highlighted by colorful rosemaling & inscribed "AO - DS 1789," decorative iron end handles, Scandinavian, 27 x 51 1/2", 33 3/4" h. (ILLUS.).... **$1,080**

Jacobean chest, carved oak, long rectangular hinged top opening to a deep well, the front divided into three panels, a narrow carved dart panel across the top, the matching end panels carved w/two small crosses in the center within a molded rectangle w/projecting corners, the center section w/an upper rectangular panel carved w/"AT," the lower panel carved w/rectangular bands & two elongated crosses, thin beaded bands down each front edge, flat base, on bun feet, shrinkage cracks, refinished, normal wear, England, late 17th - early 18th c., 26 1/4 x 63 3/4", 34 1/2" h. (ILLUS., top of page) **$690**

Fancy Louis XV-Style Side Chest

Louis XV-Style side chest, marquetry inlay, the rectangular red marble top w/tapering serpentine sides & a bowed serpentine front above a conforming case fitted w/three bowed drawers fitted w/leafy scroll loop pulls & keyhole escutcheons & decorated w/long dark inlaid panels w/light serpentine inlaid borders, the wide dark side panels inlaid w/large leaf & flower bouquets, square back legs & simple squared front legs tapering at the base & mounted w/gilt-brass mounts, further gilt-brass mounts at the top front case corners, France, late 19th - early 20th c., 17 1/2 x 26 3/4", 32" h. (ILLUS.) **$575**

Fine Louis XVI-Style Two-Drawer Chest

Louis XVI-Style chest of drawers, ormolu-mounted painted & decorated wood, a rectangular mottled white, grey & lavender marble top above a case w/the background painted dark green, a wide upper frieze band decorated w/entwined bands of ormolu laurel leaves, the chamfered front corners & flat rear corners headed by leaf-cast oblong ormolu mounts above a long ormolu swagged torch-like mount above a painted grisaille long panel w/a caduceus, the case w/two long deep drawers w/simple ormolu brass ring pulls & a continuous rectangular ormolu-bordered panels w/a large en grisaille painted scene of the Triumph of Venus w/Venus in a low chariot & additional figures & cherubs, each recessed side panel painted w/a scene of putti around a pyre, on angled square tapering legs each w/a long bordered panel also painted en grisaille, France, second half 19th c., 17 1/2 x 35", 35 1/2" h. (ILLUS.) **$11,950**

Mule chest (box chest w/one or more drawers below a storage compartment), country Queen Anne style, painted pine, the top forming a rectangular hinged lid w/original staple hinges opening to a well w/three false drawer fronts w/small batwing brasses above a stack of three long working drawers w/matching brasses, molded base on scroll-cut bracket feet, old dry red surface, single board sides, New England, first half 18th c., five brasses replaced, chips on feet, 18 1/2 x 39 3/4", 49 3/4" h. (ILLUS., top next column) **$1,380**

Mule chest (box chest w/one or more drawers below a storage compartment), early American country-style, pine, rectangular one-board top w/edge molding opening to a deep well above a long bottom drawer w/edge molding, board ends w/bootjack cut-outs, constructed w/mostly early T-head nails, old refinish, New England, 18th c.,

18 1/4 x 48", 32 1/2" h. (minor age splits, iron batwing keyhole escutcheon replacement) **$770**

Early Country Queen Anne Mule Chest

Mule chest (box chest w/one or more drawers below a storage compartment), pine, rectangular top w/molded edges above two long false drawer fronts fitted w/butterfly brasses & keyhole escutcheon above two long working drawers w/matching hardware, base molding above simple shaped bracket feet, top opening to a well w/a till, wrought-iron hinge pins, refinished, probably late 18th c., New England, 17 1/2 x 37 1/2" (replaced brasses, edge wear, bottom drawer damaged & w/replaced bottom board, lower backboard replaced) **$1,595**

Carved Oriental Storage Chest

Oriental storage chest, carved hardwood, the hinged rectangular dovetailed lid centered w/a large carved oval panel centered by a round Mon design framed by scroll designs, carved stylized bats in quarter-round corner panels, the dovetailed case carved on the front w/designs matching the lid, low bracket feet, carved end handles, probably China, late 19th - early 20th c., 42" l., 22" h. (ILLUS.)........... **$173**

Rare Early Dated Pilgrim Century Blanket Chest

Pilgrim Century blanket chest, carved oak, the rectangular hinged lid opening to a deep well, the front fluted stiles frame three panels carved w/stylized leafy scrolls, brass keyhole escutcheon, attributed to John Houghton, Dedham, Massachusetts, marked w/owner's initials "TB" & dated 1669, lid replaced, 18 3/4 x 42 1/2", 26 1/2" h. (ILLUS.) **$20,400**

Rare Pilgrim Century Connecticut River Valley Chest

Pilgrim Century six-board chest, painted & carved pine, the rectangular top w/molded edges & original cleats overhangs the nailed case crease-molded on the front & sides that continue down to form the cut-out scalloped feet, the front corners chip-carved, original red surface, Connecticut River Valley, 1675-1725, original snipe hinges not holding, missing till, 18 1/4 x 49", 24 1/2" h. (ILLUS., middle of page) **$22,325**

Pilgrim Century-Style chest with drawers, carved oak "Sunflower" style, the hinged rectangular top opening to a deep well fitted w/a candle box, the front decorated w/three shallow-carved panels, two w/stylized florals flanking the central one carved w/three stylized sunflowers, half-round turned spindles separate & flank these panels, a mid-molding above a pair

Pilgrim Century-Style Carved Chest

of paneled bottom drawers w/applied oval bosses & separated & flanked by three pairs of short half-round turned spindles base molding & tall square stile legs, American, probably 19th c., 21 1/4 x 47 1/2", 36" h. (ILLUS.) **$1,912**

Fine Queen Anne Chest-on-Frame

Queen Annue chest-on-frame, tiger stripe maple, two-part construction: the upper section w/a rectangular top w/a deep widely flaring & stepped cornice above a case of five long graduated drawers w/scrolling butterfly brasses & keyhole escutcheons; the lower section w/a mid-molding over a deep arched & scroll-cut apron raised on four simple cabriole legs ending in slender slipper feet, original brasses, old refinish, Newport, Rhode Island, ca. 1750-65, imperfections, 17 3/4 x 39", 59 3/4" h. (ILLUS.) **$7,638**

Fancy Italian Rococo-Style Painted Chest

Rococo-Style chest of drawers, painted & decorated, the rectangular top painted w/a brown central panel highlighted w/white, tan & grey scrolls bordered in light green & overhanging a case w/three long drawers w/fancy wrought-iron escutcheons, each w/matching scroll-painted designs above the lower serpentined apron w/worn green paint, the sides painted w/a symmetrical brown panels w/flowers & scrolls on a pale green ground, Italy, late 19th c., 26 x 52", 32" h. (ILLUS.) **$2,990**

Rare Tramp Art Hanging Chest

Tramp Art hanging chest, painted & decorated pine, a tall peaked top section enclosing a stepped design of thirteen small drawers each brightly painted w/various floral sprigs on the brown ground, a large & small square niche in the center above the two larger base drawers, small pointed reeded front crest, narrow stepped sides, small back section at top is loose, 19th c., 11 x 26", 39" h. (ILLUS.) **$11,788**

Fine Victorian Aesthetic Movement Chest

Victorian Aesthetic Movement chest of drawers, walnut, lowboy-style, the tall superstructure w/a narrow top pierced crestrail above a frieze of shallow carved panels above a large squared mirror swiveling between tall bead-carved uprights supported by curved brackets on the long rectangular mottled chocolate brown marble top, the case w/three long, narrow graduated drawers w/burl panels & geometric brass bail pulls, flat molded base w/blocked front feet on casters, ca. 1880, 45" w., 7' 3" h. (ILLUS., previous page)....................... **$500-700**

Eastlake Marble-top Chest of Drawers

Victorian Eastlake substyle chest of drawers, walnut & burl walnut, the long rectangular white marble top above a case w/three long drawers w/geometric brass pulls, incised line banding & a long narrow raised burl panel, molded base w/simple bracket feet on casters, ca. 1880, 40" w., 28" h. (ILLUS.)............. **$325-425**

Simple Golden Oak Chest of Drawers

Victorian Golden Oak chest of drawers, the superstructure w/a large upright rectangular mirror w/an arched top molding swiveling between tall slender S-scroll uprights, the rectangular top w/molded edges & a double-serpentine front above

a pair of serpentine-front drawers w/round brass pulls above two long flat drawers w/pierced brass pulls, simple curved apron & bracket feet on casters, ca. 1900, 5' 10" h.(ILLUS.) **$206**

Unusual Golden Oak Chest of Drawers

Victorian Golden Oak chest of drawers, the top w/a tall rectangular mirror swiveling within a simple scroll-carved frame at the left w/a lower right section w/a square top above a small rectangular paneled door over two small drawers w/pierced brass bail pulls, two long drawers w/matching pulls across the bottom, deep molded apron & simple block feet on casters, ca. 1895, 46" w., 6' 6" h. (ILLUS.).................... **$323**

Unusual Tall Golden Oak Chest of Drawers

Victorian Golden Oak tall chest of drawers, the superstructure w/a high triple-arched crestrail w/the central shell-carved arch flanked at the corners by scroll-trimmed arches above a long narrow shelf supported on simple brackets above a long rectangular beveled mirror above the rectangular top fitted w/two small hanky drawers, the tall case w/a long deep projecting top drawer w/a facing pair of C-shaped feathery scrolls & stamped brass & bail pulls all flanked by short reeded side pilasters, the lower case w/three additional long drawers each w/pairs of long serpentine carved scrolls & stamped brasses w/long reeded pilasters down the side stiles, deep molded base on casters, some pulls replaced, ca. 1900, 40" w., 6' 2" h. (ILLUS., previous page) **$353**

Renaissance Revival Chest with Mirror

Victorian Renaissance Revival chest of drawers, walnut, a tall oval mirror in a molded frame swiveling between serpentine-shaped wishbone support above a rectangular white marble top panel flanked by small handkerchief drawers w/raised oval bands, quarter-round turned corners & black teardrop pulls, the case w/three long drawers each w/a raised oval panel, pairs of leaf-and-fruit-carved pulls & small scroll-carved keyhole escutcheons, the narrow chamfered front corners w/quarter-round short turned spindles at the top & base corners, serpentine narrow apron on simple bracket feet, ca. 1870s, 17 x 37 1/2", overall 65" h. (ILLUS.) **$403**

Small Victorian Renaissance Chest

Victorian Renaissance Revival chest of drawers, walnut & burl walnut, the rectangular top w/molded edges & a high arched & serpentine back crest above a case of three long drawers, each w/a center rondel flanked by long raised burl panels w/round drop-bail pulls, scroll-carved front bracket feet, ca. 1875, 33" w., 38" h. (ILLUS.) **$176**

Simple Renaissance Revival Chest

Victorian Renaissance Revival style chest of drawers, walnut & burl walnut, the rectangular white marble top w/molded edges & rounded front corners above a conforming case w/four long graduated molded burl drawers w/simple turned wood knobs & keyhole escutcheons, deep apron on thick disk feet on casters, ca. 1870, 20 x 40 3/4", 36 1/2" h. (ILLUS.) **$538**

Fancy Renaissance Revival Chest

Victorian Renaissance Revival style chest of drawers, walnut & burl walnut, the superstructure w/a wide arched pediment w/a projecting blocked crest w/carved sunburst finial over a pair of curved narrow burl panels & roundels, raised on tall carved stiles flanked by flat side pilasters w/pointed finials above half-round candle shelves & raised on wide scroll-carved brackets above a pair of small handkerchief drawers, all atop the inset rectangular white marble top w/projecting rounded corners on the frame above a case w/a narrow long top drawer w/narrow raised burl panels, cutout brass bail pulls & a raised panel rectangular center panel, above a pair of long deeper drawers w/raised burl panels & matching hardware & centered by a raised blocked panel continuing over both drawer fronts, all flanked by projecting corner columns, deep molded & blocked flat base, ca. 1875, 54" w., 92" h. (ILLUS.)... **$1,725**

Victorian Rococo style chest of drawers, ebonized & painted wood, the top fitted w/a tall oblong mirror in a serpentine conforming frame in black decorated w/ornate gilt scrolls & floral details swiveling between a pair of two serpentine uprights w/matching decor, resting atop a rectangular white marble top w/molded serpentine edges, the case w/a single long serpentine drawer w/simple turned knobs above a pair of paneled cupboard doors, a deep ogee apron w/a blind drawer on bun feet, the case painted in black w/an overall ornate decoration of gilt scroll banding & floral reserves, attributed to Hart, Ware and Co., Philadelphia, ca. 1845, overall 72" h. (ILLUS., top next column).. **$2,185**

Fancy Early Victorian Chest of Drawers

Fine Cincinnati Rococo Chest of Drawers

Victorian Rococo style chest of drawers, walnut & burl walnut, the top mounted w/a tall oval mirror within a fancy molded & scroll-carved frame w/a large pierced fleur-de-lis crest, swiveling between tall double C-scroll uprights w/pierced leaf carving & small round candle shelves, all atop the rectangular white marble top w/molded edges, the case w/three long burled drawers w/scroll-carved pulls flanking long scroll-carved escutcheons, narrow angled front corners w/narrow panels & half-round ring-turned mounts, the deep flat apron w/a hidden drawer w/a long scroll-carved pulls, Cincinnati, ca. 1855-60, 44" w., 73" h. (ILLUS.)... **$1,265**

Fine Early William & Mary Chest

William & Mary chest-of-drawers, joined maple, oak & pine, the rectangular top w/applied molded edge over a single arch-molded case of two short drawers over three long graduated drawers w/decorative panel molding, turned bun front feet & rear stile feet, replaced brass teardrop pulls, old refinish, probably Massachusetts, ca. 1690-1710, restoration to top, 20 x 36", 33 3/4" h. (ILLUS.) **$5,875**

Scarce Early William & Mary Chest

William & Mary country-style chest of drawers, maple, oak & pine, the rectangular top above narrow ogee molding above a stack of four reverse-graduated flat drawers w/small turned wood knobs, paneled sides, narrow ogee molded base band, on tall knob- and rod-turned feet, pulls appear early, old Spanish brown paint, Hatfield/Hadley, Massachusetts, ca. 1730, imperfections, 21 x 43", 45" h. (ILLUS.).............. **$5,875**

Cradles

Old Southern Yellow Pine Cradle

Country-style cradle with tester on rockers, yellow pine, mortise & peg construction, the rectangular tester frame supported on heavy paneled posts continuing to form the corner posts & square legs ending in inset one-board rockers, the deep cradle sides w/a zigzag open bar design, simple half-round headboard, tester & cover have age but not original, from a Mississippi collection, reputedly slave-made, old refinishing, 19th c., 22 x 42", 51 1/2" h. (ILLUS.) **$575**

Late Victorian Walnut Swinging Cradle

Swinging cradle on frame, walnut, a tall S-curved drapery bracket on a turned support extending to a yoke from which swings a cradle w/curved & turned side spindles, swinging on a trestle base w/arched end legs, w/lace-trimmed drapery & bedding, old repairs, late 19th c., 23 1/2 x 48", 74" h. (ILLUS.) **$1,035**

Victorian Renaissance Revival Cradle

Victorian Renaissance Revival "trestle-style" cradle, carved walnut, the cradle w/eight pierced slats on each side decorated w/circle carvings, the ends w/pierced scroll carving & applied decorative molding, supported by an iron hanger at each end & hanging between turned posts above the trestle-style framed w/flattened serpentine legs joined by a flat cross stretcher, ca. 1870, one leg w/repaired split, 19 1/4 x 41", 38 1/2" h. (ILLUS.) **$300-500**

Early Painted Windsor Cradle

Windsor cradle on rockers, painted wood, an oval bentwood crestrail above twenty-four ring-turned slanted canted side spindles above the oval base, raised on canted baluster-, ring- and rod-turned legs w/inset rockers & jointed by box stretchers, old white paint over earlier colors, early 19th c.,17 1/2 x 39 3/4", 22" h. (ILLUS.) **$518**

Cupboards

Old Painted Pine Chimney Cupboard

Chimney cupboard, painted pine, a rectangular top w/narrow flared molding across the front above a case bordered by molding framing a tall single paneled cupboard door opening to four shelves, a small brass pull & wooden thumb latch, built-in from the right side, old bluish grey paint, age splits, early 19th c., 12 1/2 x 29", 55 1/4" h. (ILLUS.) **$575**

Small Country Chippendale Corner Cupboard

Corner cupboard, Chippendale country-style, walnut, one-piece construction: the flat top w/a deep covered cornice above a single tall two-panel door opening to a scrubbed interior w/three shelves above a shorter two-panel bottom drawer opening to a scrubbed interior w/two shelves, simple curved apron & bracket feet, exterior hinges, old replaced small brass pulls, cornice, foot facings & hinges old replacements, late 18th - early 19th c., 20 x 35 1/2", 75 1/2" h. (ILLUS., previous page) **$3,738**

Fine Early Cherry Corner Cupboard

Late Classical-Style Corner Cupboard

Corner cupboard, Classical-Style corner cupboard, mahogany, one-piece construction: the flat top w/a very deep & blocked cornice above a single tall 9-pane cupboard door opening to two shelves above a single drawer over a single two-panel door, all flanked by bold half-round columns w/ring- and knob-carving & long section w/a pointed notched carving, short serpentine apron & bracket feet, last quarter 19th c., 22 x 37", 87" h. (ILLUS.) **$850**

Corner cupboard, country-style, cherry, two-piece construction: the upper section w/a flat top & wide canted cornice above a pair of tall six-panel glazed doors opening to a white-painted interior w/two shelves; the lower section w/a medial rail above a row of three drawers w/round brass pulls above a pair of double-panel cupboard doors w/small knobs, thin molded base raised on small knob-turned legs, some pieced restorations to molding & hinge rail, two backboards w/insect damage, attributed to Pennsylvania, first half 19th c., 20 x 54", 89 1/8" h. (ILLUS., top next column) **$2,875**

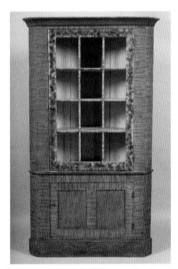

Rare Grain-painted Corner Cupboard

Corner cupboard, country-style, painted & decorated, two-part construction: the upper section w/a deep covered cornice above a single tall 12-pane glazed door opening to three shelves; the lower section w/a mid-molding above a single long two-panel cupboard door above a deep molded flat base, original faux tiger stripe maple graining w/smoke-painted frame around the upper door, possibly Pennsylvania or Ohio, early 19th c., minor imperfections, 25 x 47", 88" h. (ILLUS.) **$11,750**

opening to three shelves above a very narrow drawer w/tiny pulls above a single large two-panel cupboard door, chamfered front corners, deep apron w/serpentine shaping, England, late 19th c., shrinkage cracks in back, some alterations, 19 1/2 x 33 1/2"., 80 3/4" h. (ILLUS.)....... **$1,610**

Painted Pine Corner Cupboard

Corner cupboard, country-style, painted pine, one-piece construction, the rectangular top overhanging a case w/a pair of tall raised panel cupboard doors w/cast-iron latches opening to two shelves above a matching pair of cupboard doors, angled front stiles, flat base & simple angled bracket feet, cleaned down to worn thin grey paint, traces of white on the interior, some edge damage, 20 x 35", 73" h. (ILLUS.) **$1,725**

Country Victorian Corner Cupboard

Corner cupboard, country-style, pine, two-piece construction: the upper section w/a flat top & deep covered cornice above a single wide 9-pane glazed cupboard door opening to two shelves; the lower section w/a mid-molding above a wide single two-panel cupboard door, simple bracket feet, constructed w/square wrought nails, refinished exterior, painted interior, mid-19th c., 43" w., 82" h. (ILLUS.).................. **$690**

English Country Pine Corner Cupboard

Corner cupboard, country-style, pine, one-piece construction, the flat top w/a deep flaring stepped cornice above a single tall geometrically-glazed cupboard door

Nice Early Walnut Corner Cupboard

Corner cupboard, country-style, walnut, two-part construction: the upper section w/a flat top & covered cornice above a pair of tall 8-pane cupboard doors opening to three shelves; the slightly stepped-out lower section w/a pair of double-panel cupboard doors, simple low bracket feet, first half 19th c., 28 1/2 x 56 1/4", 85 1/4" h. (ILLUS., previous page) **$5,290**

Rare Early Louisiana Corner Cupboard

Fine Country Federal Corner Cupboard

Corner cupboard, Federal country-style, cherry, one-piece construction, the flat top w/a deep covered cornice above a pair of tall 8-pane glazed cupboard doors opening to three shelves, a mid-molding above a pair of paneled cupboard doors w/a small brass pull, molded base w/a deep serpentine apron & bracket feet, glued split on one foot facing, apron reshaped, a back foot replaced, first half 19th c., 24 1/2 x 48 3/4", 80" h. (ILLUS.) **$4,025**

Corner cupboard, Federal country-style, cherry, the flat top w/a narrow molding above a pair of full-length two-panel cupboard doors w/diamond inlays in the center of the inner rails, scroll-carved apron on high bracket feet, later robin's-egg blue interior paint, made in Louisiana, early 19th c., 23 x 42", 68" h. (ILLUS., top next column) **$79,500**

Corner cupboard, Federal country-style, inlaid cherry, one-piece construction: the flat top w/a deep stepped cornice above a pair of tall 8-pane glazed doors opening to three shelves above a pair of drawers w/line-inlaid banding & turned wood knobs above a pair of paneled lower doors w/further band inlay & fan-inlaid corners, molded base w/serpentine

Fine Federal Country Corner Cupboard

apron & bracket feet, apron a well done replacement, replaced hinges, minor pieced restorations, mellow refinishing, 21 x 53 1/4" (ILLUS.) **$3,335**

Country Federal Painted Corner Cupboard

Corner cupboard, Federal country-style, painted chestnut, two-part construction: the upper section w/a flat top w/a deep cornice w/a dentil-carved band above a very large arched opening w/a half-dome top over three shaped open shelves; the slightly stepped-out lower section w/a pair of paneled doors above a deep molded flat base, old shrinkage cracks, restoration & alterations, base of later date, ca. 1800, 21 x 49", 87 1/4" h. (ILLUS.) **$1,725**

Nice Federal Country Corner Cupboard

Corner cupboard, Federal country-style, pine, two-part construction: the upper section w/a flat top & blocked covered cornice above stepped reeded pilasters down the front flanking an arched frieze band of small ovals centered by a keystone all above the wide arched door w/geometric glazing opening to three shelves; the lower section w/a mid-molding above a pair of shorter paneled cupboard doors flanked by the continued reeded pilasters, flat base raised on knob-turned front legs, old refinish, Pennsylvania, early 19th c., 24 x 47", 7' 7" h. (ILLUS.) **$6,463**

Pennsylvania Walnut Corner Cupboard

Corner cupboard, Federal country-style, walnut, one-piece construction, the flat top w/a covered cornice above a pair of two-panel cupboard doors opening to three shaped shelves above a mid-molding & a pair of shorter paneled cupboard doors, molded base on scroll-cut bracket feet, Pennsylvania, first half 19th c., 26 x 39", 6' 4 1/2" h. (ILLUS.) **$3,025**

Corner cupboard, Federal country-style, walnut, two-part construction: the upper section w/a flat top & narrow dentil-carved cornice above a pair of tall 8-pane glazed cupboard doors opening to three shelves; the lower section w/a mid-molding above a pair of tall paneled cupboard doors, raised on scroll-cut bracket feet, probably Virginia, first half 19th c., one glass pane cracked, 21 1/2 x 47", 86" h. (ILLUS., next page) **$3,450**

Federal Virginia Country Corner Cupboard

Large Federal Painted Corner Cupboard

Corner cupboard, Federal, painted pine, architectural-type, one-piece construction: the flat top w/a very deep stepped triple-blocked cornice w/two dentil-carved bands above a frieze w/three fluted wide pilasters over a large molded arch w/center keystone above a pair of curved-top three-panel doors opening to butterfly shelves, a mid-molding above molded narrow pilasters flanking a pair of paneled lower doors, square nail construction, cream paint over earlier colors, old brown paint on interior, replacements at cornice & base moldings, late 18th - early 19th c., 26 1/2 x 48", 100 1/2" h. (ILLUS.)... **$1,840**

Early Federal Cherry Corner Cupboard

Corner cupboard, Federal style, cherry, two-part construction: the upper section w/a flat top & narrow cornice above a single tall 12-pane glazed door opening to three shelves; the lower section w/a mid-molding above a pair of tall paneled cupboard doors opening to shelves, simple low bracket feet, Pennsylvania, early 19th c., 21 x 42", 7' 1" h. (ILLUS.).......... **$1,175**

Federal Pennsylvania Corner Cupboard

Corner cupboard, Federal style, inlaid cherry, two-part construction: the upper section w/a flat top over a covered cornice over a band of ribboned inlay above a single 12-pane glazed cupboard door w/the top panes arched, opening to three shelves; the lower section w/a mid-molding over a row of two short drawers flanking one long drawer above a pair of paneled cupboard doors opening to shelves, a serpentine apron centered by an inlaid fan, raised on simple bracket feet, Pennsylvania, early 19th c., 21 x 43 1/2", 7' 2" h. (ILLUS.) **$2,938**

Federal Inlaid Walnut Corner Cupboard

Corner cupboard, Federal style, inlaid walnut, one-piece construction, the flat top w/a deep covered cornice above a narrow dentil-carved band over a pair of tall two-paneled doors, the smaller upper panel centered by a starburst inlay, a single small drawer in the center above a pair of shorter paneled doors, molded base w/scroll-cut ogee bracket feet, restoration & alterations, first half 19th c., 20 x 48", 88 1/2" h. (ILLUS.) **$1,150**

Fine Walnut Federal Corner Cupboard

Corner cupboard, Federal style, inlaid walnut, two-part construction: the upper section w/a broken-scroll pediment centered by a raised panel w/a turned urn finial, above an arched frieze inlaid w/delicate leafy vines above a pair of tall arched 10-pane glazed cupboard doors opening to three shelves & flanked by entwined vining inlay down the front rails; the lower section w/a pair of paneled cupboard doors each centered by an inlaid oval, scalloped apron & simple bracket feet, fitted w/exterior H-hinges, probably Pennsylvania, ca. 1800, imperfections, restorations, 22 x 51", 96 1/4" h. (ILLUS.).................................. **$8,225**

Very Fine Federal Open Corner Cupboard

Corner cupboard, Federal style, painted pine, barrel-back architectural style, two-part construction: the upper section w/a flat top & deep covered cornice w/wide blocked ends above a corning dentil-carved band over a wider lattice-carved band, projecting lattice-carved side blocks flank the arched & molded top to the wide open display compartment fitted w/three shelves flanked by fluted pilasters; a conforming mid-molding above the lower case w/a pair of paneled cupboard doors opening to one shelf, deep molded base w/scroll-cut brackets at the front, remnants of old blue & red paint, Mid-Atlantic region, late 18th - early 19th c., 17 3/4 x 52", 84" h. (ILLUS.) **$8,050**

Corner cupboard, Federal style, poplar, one-piece construction, the flat top w/a wide angled cornice above a single tall 12-pane glazed door opening to three shelves above a pair of small drawers w/oval brasses over a pair of raised panel cupboard doors, molded base w/serpentine apron & shaped bracket feet, refin-

Federal Country-style Corner Cupboard

ished w/dark red stain, restorations including reset backboards & some replacements, early 19th c., 22 x 43", 86" h. (ILLUS.) **$1,150**

Fine Federal Corner Cupboard

Corner cupboard, Federal style, walnut, two-part construction: the upper section w/a cove-molded cornice above two 8-pane glazed doors opening to three shelves; the lower section w/a medial astragal molding above a pair of two-panel cupboard doors, molded base on scroll-cut bracket feet w/reeded faces, original "H" hinges, vertical yellow pine back-

boards w/original hand-wrought nails, Piedmont, North Carolina, late 18th or early 19th c., wear on hinges, one side front of skirt off but present, missing other side, missing several pieces of door molding, 21 x 54", 7' 11" h. (ILLUS.) **$5,280**

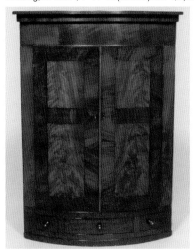

English "Bow-front" Corner Cupboard

Corner cupboard, George III "bow-front" style, mahogany & mahogany veneer, the flat top w/a curved cornice above a conforming base w/a pair of two double-panel curved cupboard doors w/flame mahogany veneer above a curved long central drawer w/small turned wood knob flanked by small square drawers w/matching knobs, flat base, ebonized banding, England, late 18th c., 24 3/4 x 41 1/2", 56" h. (ILLUS.) **$1,495**

Very Fine Nutting-Made Corner Cupboard

Corner cupboard, Nutting-signed Federal-Style, inlaid mahogany, two-part construction: the upper section w/a high molded broken-scroll crest w/rosettes flanking a tall center urn-turned finial, the frieze band inlaid w/an oval paterae above the tall arched 14-pane glazed door w/a fine light inlaid border band & opening to three shelves, the angled sides also inlaid w/long panels; the lower section w/a medial band above a case w/a single long rectangular door opening to a single shelf & w/light inlaid banding & a central paterae, the angled sides also inlaid w/short double panels, molded base w/scroll-cut bracket feet, w/original key, back branded "Wallace Nutting," early 20th c., 15 1/4 x 32 1/2", overall 85 1/2" h. (ILLUS., previous page) **$5,750**

Early New England Blue Corner Cupboard

Corner cupboard, painted pine w/rose head nail construction, one-piece construction, architectural-type; the flat top w/a deep ogee cornice centered by a keystone above a molded arch above the conforming open display section w/three shaped shelves, the lower cabinet w/a single raised panel door w/original wrought-iron "H" hinges, old blue paint, from a 1748 home in Richmond, Massachusetts, cornice replaced, age splits & edge damage, 18th c., 20 1/4 x 42 1/2", 90 3/8" h. (ILLUS.) **$2,875**

Country Victorian Corner Cupboard

Corner cupboard, walnut, country-style, two-part construction: the upper section w/a flat flaring cornice above a pair of tall glazed doors opening to two wooden shelves; the slightly stepped-out lower section w/a long central drawer flanked by small square doors all w/turned wood knobs above a pair of tall paneled cupboard doors, low serpentine apron, mid-19th c., original finish, 48" w., 7' 4" h. (ILLUS.) **$764**

Unusual Long Yellow-painted Counter-Cupboard

Counter-cupboard, painted basswood & poplar, a very long narrow rectangular top above a case w/a stack of three long drawers w/turned wood knobs at each end flanking a single central paneled door, single board ends w/bootjack cutouts, old yellow paint, top board bowed in center & w/front edge split, door panel w/old split, possibly from a Shaker workroom, 19th c., 15 1/2 x 83", 31 1/4" h. (ILLUS., bottom previous page) **$2,415**

Fine Cherry Hanging Corner Cupboard

Hanging corner cupboard, cherry, the flat top w/a deep angled cornice above a single large square raised panel door projecting above shaped tapering base boards joined by a small curved open shelf, old refinishing, two interior shelves, small pieced restoration to left of door, first half 19th c., 19 1/4 x 37", 43 1/2" h. (ILLUS.)... **$2,185**

Unusual Folk Art Hanging Corner Cupboard

Hanging corner cupboard, painted & decorated pine, folk art style, the arched crest applied w/a carved eagle figure flanked by stars within circles, over a hinged door opening to two interior shelves & decorated w/applied & painted carved designs including stars, crescent moons, hearts, clovers, diamonds, doves & a horseshoe, two small open shelves at the bottom, all painted in muted shades of red, white, blue & gold, name "Jake Patterson" inscribed in pencil on the back, late 19th - early 20th c., 10 x 16", 30 3/4" h. (ILLUS.) **$3,173**

Painted Hanging Corner Cupboard

Hanging corner cupboard, painted pine, the flat top w/a deep stepped cornice above a tall single paneled door opening to three shelves w/remnants of whitewash, mortised construction, old red paint, 19th c., 18 x 29", 43" h. (ILLUS.)............ **$2,358**

Hanging cupboard, country-style, painted & decorated pine, rectangular top above an upright dovetailed case w/wrought nails in the backboard & a single tall frame-paneled door w/original hardware, old red & black wood graining, minor damage, 19th c., 12 x 16 1/2", 27" h. (ILLUS. left with large hanging cupboard, top next page) **$431**

Hanging cupboard, country-style, painted pine, rectangular top w/a widely flaring covered cornice above a case w/a single large paneled door w/original hardware, square cut nails in case, two interior shelves, red paint under crazed varnish, edge wear, 19th c., 12 1/2 x 38", 38" h. (ILLUS. right with small hanging cupboard, top next page)................................. **$690**

Two Country-style Hanging Cupboards

Early New England Hanging Wall Cupboard

Hanging cupboard, country-style, painted pine, the arched crestboard pierced w/a hanging hole flanked by shaped sides on the rectangular top above a single flat door attached w/early butterfly hinges, opening to two interior shelves, original greyish blue paint, New England, 18th c., 6 1/4 x 10", 14 1/2" h. (ILLUS.) **$9,988**

Late Victorian Hanging Cupboard

Hanging cupboard, country-style, pine, the flat top w/a deep flaring stepped cornice above a single tall paneled door opening to three shelves, wire nail construction, refinished, 9 1/2 x 18", 22 1/2" h. (ILLUS.) **$604**

Hanging cupboard, painted wood, rectangular top above a pair of large plain single-board doors w/one original brass pull, opening to two shelves, old grey paint over earlier red, square cut-nail construction, late 18th - early 19th c., 8 1/2 x 36", 28 1/2" h **$1,265**

Old One-door Poplar Hanging Cupboard

Hanging cupboard, poplar, rectangular top w/thick angled cornice above a single large 4-pane glazed door opening to two shelves w/plate moldings added later, square cut nail construction, flat base, attributed to New England, early 19th c., 16 3/4 x 25 7/8", 28 1/2" h. (ILLUS.) **$863**

Classical Country-style Jelly Cupboard

Jelly cupboard, Classical country-style, cherry, the thin rectangular top above a pair of drawers each w/a turned wood knob & projecting above a pair of tall two-panel cupboard doors flanked by free-standing ring-turned columns, thick flat base molding supported on ring-turned knob feet, ca. 1830, 21 3/8 x 45", 60" h. (ILLUS.).. **$1,150**

Canadian Country Jelly Cupboard

Jelly cupboard, country-style, painted pine, the thick rectangular top w/a high scroll-cut back crest above a case w/a pair of tall narrow chamfer-paneled cupboard doors w/a cast-iron latch opening to three shelves, scalloped apron & simple bracket feet, old dark red paint, some loss of height, attributed to Canada, 19th c., 19 1/2 x 39 1/2", 50 1/2" h. (ILLUS.).......... **$345**

Painted Poplar Jelly Cupboard

Jelly cupboard, country-style, painted poplar, the rectangular top w/a three-quarters gallery above a case w/a pair of tall paneled cupboard doors w/a cast-iron latch opening to three shelves, square nail construction, old salmon paint, central Pennsylvania, wear, minor chips, first half 19th c., 18 1/2 x 43 3/4", 54" h. (ILLUS.)...................................... **$1,380**

Fine Old Red-Painted Jelly Cupboard

Jelly cupboard, country-style, painted wood, a narrow rectangular top above an open compartment w/shaped sides over a tall flat single door w/wooden thumb latch opening to three shelves, simple bracket feet, old red paint, 19th c., 13 3/4 x 38", 59 3/4" h. (ILLUS.) **$5,400**

Country Pine Jelly Cupboard

Jelly cupboard, country-style, pine, the rectangular top w/molded edges above a pair of narrow paneled drawers w/white porcelain knobs above a pair of tall paneled cupboard doors, paneled sides, deep flat base molding, mid-19th c., 47" l., 42" h. (ILLUS.) **$316**

Old Painted Poplar Jelly Cupboard

Jelly cupboard, painted poplar, a rectangular top above a large single double-paneled door w/an old replaced cast-iron latch, opening to three shelves, old red paint, attributed to Pennsylvania, mid-19th c., a thin strip added to top of door, 16 1/2 x 34 1/2", 42" h. (ILLUS.) **$2,070**

Linen press, Chippendale country-style, cherry, two-piece construction: the upper section w/a rectangular top & flaring stepped cornice above a pair of large paneled doors opening to a divided interior; the stepped-out lower section w/a stack of four long graduated drawers w/simple brass bail pulls & oval keyhole escutcheons, molded base on scroll-cut bracket feet, old replaced drawer pulls, restorations to hinge rails & feet, ends of cornice replaced, old mellow refinishing, late 18th - early 19th c., 21 1/2 x 43", 72 1/2" h. (ILLUS., top next column) **$5,463**

Cherry Country Chippendale Linen Press

Rare Virginia Chippendale Linen Press

Linen press, Chippendale style, mahogany, two-part construction: the upper section w/a rectangular top w/a narrow flaring cornice above a pair of molded panel cupboard doors opening to three linen slides; the lower section w/a hinged slant top w/two simple bail pulls opening to a desk fitted interior w/small drawers above a lower case w/a pair of drawers over two long drawers, all w/simple bail pulls, narrow base molding on scroll-cut bracket feet, one desk drawer signed "J. McCormick" in pencil, Virginia, 1787-1791, 21 x 49", 81" h. (ILLUS.) **$9,560**

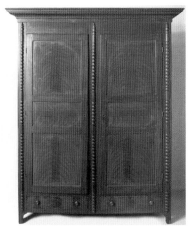

Fine Decorated Classical Linen Press

Linen press, Classical country style, painted & decorated cherry & poplar, the rectangular top w/a widely flaring molded lift-off cornice above a pair of tall three-panel cupboard doors opening to a wardrobe on one side & five shelves & a drawer on the other, doors flanked & divided by tall half-round bobbin-turned pilasters, two drawers at the bottom, original red flame-graining, attributed to Claude Paquelet, Louisville, Kentucky, first half 19th c., 20 1/2 x 70 3/4", 84 3/4" h. (ILLUS.) **$4,313**

Fine Dutch Neo-Classical Linen Press

Linen press, Neo-Classical style, mahogany & mahogany veneer, two-part construction: the upper section w/a rectangular top w/a recessed stepped cornice above a plain frieze band above a pair of large paneled cupboard doors flanked by colonettes w/engine-turned gilt bronze capitals & bases; the lower section w/a

mid-molding over a pair of shorter paneled doors opening to a series of half drawers & flanked by blocked pilasters, molded base w/projecting block feet, Holland, early 19th, 25 x 62 1/2", 94" h. (ILLUS.) **$9,200**

William IV English Linen Press

Linen press, William IV style, mahogany & mahogany veneer, two-part construction: the upper section w/a flat top w/a narrow curved cornice above a pair of tall Gothic arch-paneled mahogany veneer doors opening to shelves; the lower section w/a mid-molding above a stack of four long graduated drawers w/lion head & ring brass pulls, scroll-cut bracket feet, England, mid-19th c., 21 x 47", 80" h. (ILLUS.) **$2,530**

William IV English Linen Press

Linen press, William IV style, mahogany & mahogany veneer, two-part construction: the upper section w/a rectangular top w/a stepped flaring cornice above a pair of tall paneled cupboard doors w/rounded panel corners, the lower section w/a mid-molding over a pair of drawers above two long drawers all w/small round brass pulls, molded base on scroll-cut bracket feet, England, second quarter 19th c., 22 x 48", 84" h. (ILLUS.) **$3,220**

Rare Child-sized Painted Pewter Cupboard

Pewter cupboard, child-sized country-style, painted pine, the rectangular top w/a molded cornice above a serpentine border over the tall open cupboard w/shaped sides flanking two open shelves w/front braces above a deep pie shelf on the stepped-out lower cabinet w/a single square paneled door, molded flat base, old red & black paint, wooden peg construction, wear & three upright spindles missing from a shelf, 19th c., 12 1/2 x 36", 48" h. (ILLUS.) **$4,026**

Country Chippendale Pewter Cupboard

Pewter cupboard, Chippendale country-style, painted pine, two-part construction: the upper section w/a rectangular top w/a deep flaring stepped cornice above a scallop-cut frieze over the tall open compartment w/two long shelves flanked by serpentine-cut sides; the stepped-out lower section w/a pair of drawers w/small old brass knob pulls above a pair of raised-panel cupboard doors, flat molded base on bun feet, old red paint over earlier salmon & black paint, some edge wear & splits, feet old replacements, early 19th c., 23 1/2 x 56", 79 1/4" h. (ILLUS.) **$6,038**

Painted Two-Part Pewter Cupboard

Pewter cupboard, country-style, painted wood, two-part construction: the upper section w/a narrow rectangular top above a tall open compartment fitted w/three shelves w/plate racks; the projecting lower section w/a pair of large paneled cupboard doors opening to two shelves, old red paint, scrubbed surface on lower section, probably a married piece, first half 19th c., 21 1/4 x 47", 68" h. (ILLUS.) **$1,208**

Large Early Blue Pewter Cupboard

Rare Virginia Cherry Pie Safe

Pewter cupboard, painted pine, one-piece construction: the rectangular top w/a deep stepped flaring cornice above an open top section w/four shelves w/front rails above a projecting lower cabinet w/two long drawers flanking a small central drawer all above a pair of long double-paneled cupboard doors, all w/turned wood knobs, shaped shoe feet at the base, old blue paint, found in New York, late 18th - early 19th c., glue splits on right end of cornice, 21 1/2 x 65 1/2", 74 1/2" h. (ILLUS., previous page) **$4,025**

Pie safe, cherry, a rectangular top above a pair of drawers w/pairs of simple turned wood knobs above a pair of wide cupboard doors each mounted w/four pierced tin panels w/pinwheel medallions & floral spandrels, flat apron, raised on baluster- and ring-turned legs w/peg feet, two matching punched tins in each side, opens to three interior shelves, original dark finish, old walnut pulls, Virginia, mid-19th c., restored splits on one door, 18 3/4 x 53", 49" h. (ILLUS., top of page) **$10,350**

Old Pie Safe with Twelve Tin Panels

Pie safe, pine, the rectangular top w/a narrow cornice above a pair of drawers w/turned wood knobs over a pair of tall doors each mounted w/three pierced tin panels decorated w/a pinwheel & corner fan design, three matching tin panels down each side, raised on knob-turned tapering legs, doweled construction, some tin oxidation, first half 19th c., 18 5/8 x 41", 60 3/8" h. (ILLUS., top next column) **$2,070**

Pie safe, pine, the rectangular top w/a widely flaring flat cornice above a pair of cupboard doors mounted w/punched tin panels in a pinwheel & circle design, matching tin panels on the sides, a pair of lower paneled doors, square legs, Southern U.S., first half 19th c., old repairs & alterations, 17 x 46", 77" h. (ILLUS., bottom next column) **$1,610**

Large Early Southern Pine Pie Safe

Fine Walnut Pie Safe

Pie safe, walnut, the rectangular top above a single long drawer w/turned wood knobs above a pair of two-panel doors each fitted w/two punched tin panels decorated w/a design of rings & arches, tall square & slightly tapering legs, two matching tins in each side, one shelf on the interior, original hardware, refinished, age cracks, 19th c., 17 x 41 1/2", 49 1/2" h. (ILLUS.) **$1,610**

Side cupboard, painted & decorated poplar, rectangular top w/a shaped three-quarter gallery above a wide single board-and-batten door w/cast-iron thumb latch, one-board ends, curved bracket front feet, old brown graining, interior shelves, found near Richmond, Indiana, second half 19th c. 19 1/4 x 27 3/4", overall 32 1/2" h. (strip added to door) **$715**

Step-back wall cupboard, cherry, two-part construction: the upper section w/a rectangular top & deep covered cornice above a pair of 6-pane glazed cupboard doors opening to two shelves above an open pie shelf w/shaped sides; the lower stepped-out section w/a pair of drawers above a pair of paneled cupboard doors, molded base w/scroll-cut bracket feet, refinished, brasses & feet old replacements, pieced restorations to doors, 19th c., 19 3/4 x 52", 85 1/2" h. (ILLUS., top next column).. **$2,070**

Step-back wall cupboard, child-sized, country-style, stained pine, one-piece construction, the rectangular top w/a wide flaring & stepped cornice above a pair of single-pane cupboard doors opening to two shelves, iron thumb-latch & small porcelain knobs, the slightly stepped-out lower section w/a pair of paneled doors opening to two shelves, matching latch & knobs, low scroll-carved apron, original

Fine Cherry Stepback Wall Cupboard

Child-Sized Step-back Wall Cupboard

dark red wash, mid-19th c., 14 x 37", 53 1/2" h. (ILLUS.) **$748**

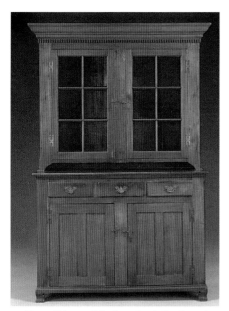

Rare Chippendale Step-back Cupboard

Step-back wall cupboard, Chippendale, cherry, two-part construction: the upper section w/a rectangular top over a very deep stepped & flaring cornice w/a lower dentil-carved band above a pair of large six-pane glazed cupboard doors w/brass H-hinges & latches above a low pie shelf; the lower stepped-out section w/a row of three drawers w/butterfly pulls above a pair of double-paneled cupboard doors w/brass H-hinges & latches, narrow molded base on small ogee bracket feet, Pennsylvania, 1760-80, 20 x 59", 7' 2" h. (ILLUS.) **$5,736**

Fine Chippendale Step-Back Cupboard

Step-back wall cupboard, Chippendale, walnut, two-part construction: the upper section w/a rectangular two w/a deep flaring cornice w/a wide central block & matching corner blocks above a pair of tall 12-pane glazed cupboard doors opening to shelves & flanked by wide fluted pilasters; the stepped-out lower section w/a molded edge above a row of three long, narrow drawers w/butterfly pulls above a mid-molding over a pair of square raised panel doors & three fluted pilasters, molded base w/scroll-cut center drop & scroll-cut ogee bracket feet, late 18th c., 21 x 68", 92" h. (ILLUS.) **$9,560**

Ohio Walnut Step-back Wall Cupboard

Step-back wall cupboard, Classical country-style, walnut, two-piece construction: the upper section w/a rectangular top w/a shallow flaring cornice above a pair of tall 6-pane glazed cupboard doors w/the upper panes arched, opening to two shelves above a deep pie shelf; the lower section w/a pair of drawers w/turned wood knobs slightly projecting over the lower case w/a pair of paneled cupboard doors w/cast-iron latches flanked by half-round knob- and rod-turned pilasters, flat base on small knob feet, attributed to Trumbull County, Ohio, first half 19th c., some age splits & edge damage w/old replaced door latches, 22 x 52", 84 1/2" h. (ILLUS.) **$2,300**

Ohio Two-Part Step-back Wall Cupboard

Step-back wall cupboard, country-style, cherry & curly maple, two-part construction: the upper section w/a rectangular top w/a flaring stepped cornice above a pair of tall 6-pane glazed cupboard doors opening to two shelves above a pie shelf; the stepped-out lower section w/a pair of curly maple drawers above a pair of paneled cupboard doors w/brass latches, old mellow surface, attributed to Wayne County, Ohio, few age splits & glued spits on pie shelf, mid-19th c., 18 1/4 x 55 1/2", 85 1/2" h. (ILLUS.) **$3,795**

English Elm Step-back Wall Cupboard

Step-back wall cupboard, country-style, elm, two-part construction: the upper section w/a rectangular top & flaring stepped cornice above a pair of large double-panel cupboard doors opening to two shelves; the lower section w/molded edges above a case w/a row of three

deep drawer w/butterfly pulls over a row of three square paneled cupboard doors, molded base w/worn down bracket feet, England, mid-19th c., 21 1/2 x 67", 92" h. (ILLUS.)... **$2,645**

Early Tennessee Jackson Press Cupboard

Step-back wall cupboard, country-style Jackson press type, walnut, two-part construction: the upper section w/a rectangular top w/a wide flat flaring cornice above a pair of very tall 8-pane glazed doors opening to three shelves; the stepped out lower section w a single long drawer w/two wooden knobs above a pair of paneled cupboard doors, short ring-turned feet, refinished, Eastern Tennessee, first half 19th c., small putty restoration above the drawer & atop one door, 20 1/2 x 41 3/4", 85 7/8" h. (ILLUS.) **$1,150**

Old Painted Step-back Wall Cupboard

Step-back wall cupboard, country-style, painted pine, one-piece construction, the rectangular top w/a deep flaring covered cornice above a pair of tall solid raised panel cupboard doors w/cast-iron latches opening to three shelves above an arched pie shelf, the stepped-out lower case w/a pair of drawers w/oval brasses above a pair of raised panel cupboard doors opening to two shelves, flat apron & simple bracket feet, old red paint, interior old light blue paint, one iron latch missing, mid-19th c., 19 1/2 x 48 1/2", 84" h. (ILLUS., previous page)..... **$4,000-8,000**

Old Green-painted Wall Cupboard

Step-back wall cupboard, country-style, painted pine, one-piece construction: the rectangular top w/a widely flaring low cornice above a pair of tall cupboard doors composed of beaded boards w/tongue & groove construction & turned wood knobs, the stepped-out lower section w/a matching pair of tall doors, three shelves in the top & three in the base, square nail construction, thin green wash, base cut at one time on underside, 19th c., 20 1/2 x 41 1/2", 75 1/4" h. (ILLUS.) **$1,115**

Step-back wall cupboard, country-style, pine, one-piece construction, the rectangular top board above a pair of tall narrow raised panel cupboard doors w/small wood knobs opening to four shelves, the projecting lower section w/a tall narrow raised panel cupboard door opening to two shelves on the right side & a one-shelf open compartment on the left side, flat base, old mellow refinishing & areas of earlier red wash, square cut nail construction, originally built-in w/the back & top old replacements, top door loose, 19th c., 18 1/4 x 41", 82" h. (ILLUS., top next column)... **$1,150**

Country Pine Step-back Wall Cupboard

Simple Old Pine Step-back Cupboard

Step-back wall cupboard, country-style, pine, one-piece construction: the upper case w/a rectangular top w/a molded cornice above a pair of tall two-panel cupboard doors opening to shelves above a pair of narrow drawers above a stepped-out shelf above a pair of shorter two-panel cupboard doors w/cast-iron latches, refinished, couple of later supports added to base, second half 19th c., 19 3/4 x 51", 6' 9 1/4" h. (ILLUS.)................................. **$1,035**

Early Pennsylvania Step-back Cupboard

Step-back wall cupboard, country-style, softwood, two-part construction: the upper section w/a rectangular top & widely stepped flaring cornice above a pair of large six-pane glazed cupboard doors w/brass latches above an open pie shelf; the stepped-out lower section w/a row of three drawers w/wooden knobs slightly projecting above a pair of paneled cupboard doors w/brass hardware flanked by half-round columns, on short heavy turned feet, replaced hardware & top board, Pennsylvania, mid-19th c., 19 x 52", 7' 1" h. (ILLUS.) **$3,850**

Rare Country New York Stepback Cupboard

Step-back wall cupboard, country-style, stained poplar, two-part construction: the upper section w/a rectangular top w/a flared ogee cornice above a pair of tall paneled cupboard doors w/thumb latches opening to three shelves; the slightly stepped-out lower section w/a shorter pair of cupboard doors, cut-out base w/angled feet, old red-stained surface, original hardware, Watervliet, New York, ca. 1860, minor imperfections, 19 x 25", 78" h. (ILLUS.) **$9,988**

Fine Kentucky Stepback Wall Cupboard

Step-back wall cupboard, Federal country style, cherry, two-part construction: the upper section w/a rectangular top & covered cornice above a pair of tall 6-pane glazed cupboard doors opening to two shelves; the lower stepped-out section w/a pair of drawers w/turned wood knobs overhanging a pair of tall paneled doors flanked by slender ring-, rod- and rope twist-turned columns, on knob feet, attributed to Kentucky, refinished, one back foot re-attached, glued split near one hinge, first half 19th c., 23 1/2 x 43", 87" h. (ILLUS.) **$4,945**

Country Federal Step-back Cupboard

Step-back wall cupboard, Federal country-style, painted wood, two-part construction: the upper section w/a rectangular top w/a deep flaring molded cornice above a pair of 6-pane glazed cupboard doors opening to two shelves above an arched pie shelf; the projecting lower section w/a row of three drawers w/small turned wood knobs over a mid-molding above a pair of two-panel cupboard doors w/small turned knobs, original red surface, pulls probably original, New England, first half 19th c., some repairs, 23 1/2 x 57 1/2", 85" h. (ILLUS., previous page) **$4,994**

Rare Pennsylvania Painted Wall Cupboard

panels & flanked by roundels & shaped reeded panels w/cockbeaded surrounds at the sides above the low arched pie shelf; the stepped-out lower section w/a row of three small drawers flanking two longer drawers all w/simple bail pulls above a pair of raised panel cupboard doors w/exterior hinges flanking a long center reeded panel w/a roundel, molded base w/simple bracket feeet, overall old red paint w/white borders & free-hand black designs, the lower doors w/yellow painted hearts w/scallop & line borders, Pennsylvania, early 19th c., imperfections, restoration, 23 1/2 x 66", 91 1/2" h. (ILLUS.)................................. **$16,450**

Very Fine Federal Step-back Cupboard

Step-back wall cupboard, Federal style, carved mahogany & mahogany veneer, two-part construction: the upper section w/a molded broken-scroll pediment w/brass rosettes at the end of each scroll flanking a raised section decorated w/a gilt-carved pineapple & acanthus leaf design all flanked by spherical brass corner finials, the flat molded & reeded cornice above a pair of 6-pane glazed cupboard doors opening to two shaped shelves; the lower stepped-out section w/a long thin pull-out tray drawer above a row of three narrow drawers above a pair of cupboard doors w/recessed crossbanded panels opening to shelves, all flanked by narrow reeded pilasters ending in carved acanthus leaves, raised on acanthus leaf-carved front hairy paw feet & square rear feet, replaced round brasses, possibly Bergen County, New Jersey, ca. 1825-35, refinished, restorations, 21 1/2 x 48", 103 1/2" h. (ILLUS.).............................. **$7,638**

Step-back wall cupboard, painted & carved wood, two-part construction: the upper section w/a rectangular top w/a deep flaring stepped cornice above a pair of hinged 6-pane glazed doors centered by three glass

Victorian Country Step-back Cupboard

Step-back wall cupboard, Victorian country-style, pine, two-piece construction: the upper section w/a rectangular top above a deep stepped & flaring cornice over a pair of tall single-pane glazed cupboard doors opening to two shelves above a pair of drawers w/white porcelain knobs; the stepped-out lower section w/a single long narrow drawer w/cast-iron pulls above a pair of paneled cupboard doors w/cast-iron latches w/porcelain knobs, low apron & simple bracket feet, second half 19th c., 44" w., 83" h. (ILLUS., previous page) **$978**

Rare Wall Cupboard/Dry Sink

Step-back wall cupboard-dry sink, poplar & pine w/old red wash, two-part construction: the upper section w/a rectangular top & deep flaring cornice above a pair of tall 9-pane glazed doors opening to two shelves above a row of three small drawers over a high pie shelf w/curved side moldings; the lower section w/a shallow stepped-out dry sink well above a pair of paneled doors, original brass latches, another one missing, thin replaced moldings at top of base, pieced restorations, 19th c., 25 x 61", 89" h. (ILLUS.) **$5,463**

Stepback hutch wall cupboard, country-style, painted pine, the flat rectangular top above a tall open compartment w/three shelves, the stepped-out lower case w/a single tall narrow paneled door w/wooden thumb latch, flat base, opens to shelves, layers of green & yellow paint, square nail construction, wear & damage, 19th c., 18 1/2 x 37 1/2", 75" h. (ILLUS., top next column) **$1,150**

Country Stepback Hutch Cupboard

Child's Country-style Wall Cupboard

Wall cupboard, child's size, country-style, pine & poplar, the rectangular top w/a molded flaring cornice above a pair of tall two-panel doors opening to two fixed shelves missing original dividers, scalloped apron & simple cut-out feet, original hardware, square nail construction, old refinishing, 19th c., 13 x 27", 30" h. (ILLUS.) **$546**

Small Early Painted Wall Cupboard

Small Painted Country Wall Cupboard

Wall cupboard, country-style, painted pine, the rectangular top above a single tall cupboard door w/a small recessed panel over a tall rectangular panel, small wooden knob, flat apron & small bracket feet, old red paint, mid-19th c., 20 1/2 x 34 1/4", 57" h. (ILLUS.) **$4,541**

Wall cupboard, country-style, painted walnut, the flat rectangular top above a tall case w/cut-nail construction & a single tall flat walnut one-board door w/small wooden knob & thumb latch, opening to three shelves, on simple angled bracket feet, old red paint, replaced rear foot & breadboard ends on door possibly old replacements, 19th c., 12 x 25 1/2", 42" h. (ILLUS., top next column) **$575**

Wall cupboard, heart pine, the rectangular top w/a narrow stepped cornice above a pair of tall flat cupboard doors w/HL hinges & an iron latch above a shorter pair of flat doors w/matching hardware, Southern U.S., mid-19th c., restorations, alterations, 22 x 48 1/2", 81 1/4" h. (ILLUS., bottom of next column) **$2,530**

Early Southern Heart Pine Cupboard

Large Painted Pine Wall Cupboard

Wall cupboard, painted pine, one-piece construction, the rectangular top above a stepped cornice over a pair of tall raised panel cupboard doors w/small turned wood knobs opening to shelves above another shorter pair of matching doors opening to shelves, flat apron & simple bracket feet, cleaned down to the original salmon paint on exterior & pumpkin paint on interior, pieced repairs, areas of repaint, replaced knobs & fastener, 19th c., 18 x 54", 84" h. (ILLUS.) **$633**

Rare & Unique Plantation Wall Cupboard

Wall cupboard, wood-grained cypress & pine, the wide rectangular top overhanging a case w/a wide frieze band above a pair of tall two-panel doors w/elaborate wood-grained decoration, raised on simple bracket feet, original paint in rouge, yellow, ochre & rich brown, shelved interior, made in Louisiana, probably for the Houmas Plantation, backboard w/old black ink inscription "Houmas Plantat(ion) This side up... with care...Preston," John S. Preston built Houmas House, ca. 1830-50, 22 1/2 x 67", 84" h. (ILLUS.)... **$55,200**

Fine English Inlaid Oak Welsh Cupboard

Welsh cupboard, inlaid oak, two-part construction: the upper section w/a long rectangular top w/a narrow dentil-carved cornice over a deep scallop-cut frieze above a wide deep central open compartment w/three shelves flanked by side sections w/an upper open compartment w/a single arched & shaped shelf above a tall narrow cupboard door w/banded inlay over a very small inlaid drawer; the lower section w/molded edges above a case w/two banded inlay drawers flanking a pair of central paneled cupboard doors w/a central inlaid design, the long scroll-cut apron raised on cabriole front legs ending in pad feet & square rear legs, England, ca. 1900, 19 1/4 x 72", 82" (ILLUS.) **$3,105**

Desks

Art Deco desk, horn-mounted applewood & parquetry, the rectangular top above a case w/a pair of small drawers w/round brass pulls flanking a long center drawer w/two angled brass bar pulls over the kneehole opening flanked by parquetry doors opening to reveal three parquetry-front drawers w/horn tadpole-shaped mounts, one replaced, France, ca. 1930, 30 x 55 1/2", 30 1/4" h. (ILLUS., top next page).. **$3,650**

Fine French Art Deco Applewood & Parquetry Desk

Rare Chippendale "Block-Front" Desk

Chippendale Country Slant-Front Desk

Chippendale "block-front" slant-front desk, carved mahogany, a narrow rectangular top above a hinged slant-lid w/a pair of large blocked panels flanking a central recessed panel & opening to a fitted interior above a case of four long graduated blocked & recessed drawers all w/large butterfly brasss, molded conforming above w/an arched central drop & scroll-carved bracket feet, Boston or Salem, Massachusetts, 1760-80, 24 1/4 x 40", 44 1/4" h. (ILLUS.) **$42,000**

Chippendale country-style slant-front desk, maple, a narrow rectangular top above a wide hinged slant front opening to an interior w/nine pigeonholes over five small drawers, the case w/a pair of pull-out supports flanking a narrow long drawer above three long graduated drawers each w/butterfly brasses & keyhole escutcheons, molded base w/cut-out bracket feet, old dark brown finish, old replaced brasses, nailed split on back foot, New England, late 18th c., 17 1/2 x 36", 41 1/4" h. (ILLUS., top next column) **$4,888**

Chippendale "Oxbow-Front" Desk

Fine Chippendale Revival Mahogany Partner's Desk

Chippendale "oxbow-front" slant-front desk, cherry, a narrow top above a wide hinged slant front opening to an interior fitted w/eight small drawers over eight pigeonholes & a center door, the case w/a long serpentine-blocked top drawer over three long serpentine lower drawers all w/butterfly brasses & keyhole escutcheons, conforming molded base & scroll-cut ogree bracket feet, old refinishing, one small drawer w/a penciled inscription, age splits in end panels, feet w/glued spits, late 18th c., 25 x 42 3/4", 43 3/4" h. (ILLUS., previous page) **$3,738**

Fine Chippendale "Oxbow-Front" Desk

Chippendale "oxbow-front" slant-front desk, mahogany, the narrow rectangular top above a wide hinged fall-front opening to an interior fitted w/a central blocked fan-carved prospect door flanked by valanced compartments & small drawers, the case w/ four long serpentine drawers w/simple bail pulls & oval brass keyhole escutcheons, serpentine molded apron w/a central carved fan drop, raised on short cabriole legs ending in claw-and-ball feet, re-

placed brasses, refinished, imperfections, North Shore, Massachusetts, late 18th c., 23 x 41", 44" h. (ILLUS.) **$5,875**

Chippendale Revival partner's desk, carved mahogany, the wide rectangular top w/three tooled green leather writing insets & a molded & blocked edge, a wide arched kneehole opening below an arched drawer w/thin raised molding panels on each side, each wide side pedestal decorated at the front sides & side corners w/bold carved pilasters headed by a scroll-carved leaf over a lion head above a leaf swag, pilasters on the front & back flanking a single drawer w/a carved leafy swag & fluted band above a large door carved in relief w/a large leaf wreath, matching carving on the end panels, pairs of heavy paw feet on each section flanking a low arched & leaf-carved apron, late 19th - early 20th c., 40 x 72", 31 1/4" h. (ILLUS., top of page) **$4,255**

Fine Cherry Chippendale Desk

Chippendale slant-front desk, cherry, a narrow rectangular top above a wide hinged slant-front opening to an interior fitted w/drawers, including a central one w/an inlaid circle, & open compartments, the case w/four long graduated drawers w/simple bail pulls & brass keyhole escutcheons, molded base on ogee bracket feet, original brasses & surface, New England, late 18th c., 19 1/4 x 39", 42 1/2" h. (ILLUS.) **$4,700**

Chippendale Slant-Front Desk

Chippendale slant-front desk, mahogany, the narrow top above a wide hinged slant-front opening to a three-part fan-carved interior, the case w/pull-out supports flanking a narrow long top drawer over three long graduated drawers all w/brass butterfly pulls, molded base raised on short cabriole legs w/ball-and-claw feet, the apron w/a central shell-carved drop, probably American, late 19th c., restored, crack on side, lip damage, holes in the top for missing gallery, 18 3/4 x 40 1/2", 42" h. (ILLUS.) **$1,438**

Walnut Chippendale Slant-Front Desk

Chippendale slant-front desk, walnut, a narrow rectangular top above a wide hinged slant front opening to an interior w/valanced pigeonholes & drawers flanking a center section enclosing a recessed pigeonhole & drawers, above a pair of slide-out supports & four long graduated drawers w/butterfly brasses & keyhole escutcheons, molded base on scroll-cut bracket feet, replaced hardware, late 18th c., 21 x 38 1/2", 44" h. (ILLUS.)...... **$1,540**

Chippendale Walnut Slant-Front Desk

Chippendale slant-front desk, walnut, a narrow rectangular top above the wide hinged slant top opening to an interior fitted w/12 serpentine-front drawers, four pigeonholes & letter drawers flanking a center door & a variety of concealed drawers, the case w/four long graduated drawers w/butterfly brasses & keyhole escutcheons flanked by narrow fluted colonettes, molded base on scroll-cut ogee bracket feet, old dark finish, some wear & damage on feet, age cracks in slant top, pierced repairs w/some interior replacements, late 18th c., 19 1/2 x 39", 43 3/4" h. (ILLUS.) **$1,323**

Pennsylvania Chippendale Desk

Chippendale slant-front desk, walnut, the narrow rectangular top above a wide hinged slat-front opening to an interior w/a central cupboard door flanked by document drawers, scalloped pigeonholes & serpentine-fronted short drawers, the case w/four long graduated drawers w/butterfly brasses & keyhole escutcheons flanked by fluted quarter-columns, molded base raised on ogee bracket feet, Pennsylvania, late 18th c., 21 x 36 1/2", 43" h. (ILLUS.) **$3,819**

Fine Chippendale-Style Partner's Desk

Chippendale-Style partner's desk, mahogany & mahogany veneer, the large rectangular top w/three tooled green leather inserts, the case fitted on each side w/a stack of two narrow drawers w/simple bail pulls flanking the arched serpentine kneehole opening w/a single drawer, scroll-carved cabriole legs w/claw-and-ball feet, late 19th - early 20th c., 48 x 72", 32" h. (ILLUS., top of page).. **$4,715**

Classical butler's desk, mahogany & mahogany veneer, the thick rectangular top hinged to fold open & form a writing surface, projecting over a case w/three long drawers each w/pairs of turned wood knobs & flanked by free-standing columns, raised on ring-, disk- and knob-turned legs ending in small ball feet, ca. 1830, 18 x 36 1/2", 38" h. (ILLUS., top next column)... **$3,680**

Fine Classical Butler's Desk

Two Views of the Very Rare Stephen Hedges Classical Combination Desk-Chair

Classical desk-chair, mahogany & flame-grained mahogany veneer, the oval top & deep paneled apron hinged to open in the center w/one half forming a desk fitted w/a fold-over writing surface above a single drawer & the other half forming a low barrel-backed chair, raised on four S-scroll legs, by Stephen Hedges, New York, New York, ca. 1854, 26 x 34", 28" h. (ILLUS.) **$16,100**

Rare Early Walnut Classical Plantation Desk

American Classical "Fall-Front" Desk

Classical "fall-front" desk, mahogany & mahogany veneer, the rectangular top above a wide hinged fall-front opening to a writing surface & an arrangement of small drawers & pigeonholes, the lower case fitted w/three long graduated drawers w/round brass pulls flanked by serpentine pilasters, raised on large C-scroll front legs & ring-turned tapering rear legs, some restoration, ca. 1850, 26 3/4 x 43", 48 1/4" h. (ILLUS.) **$1,100**

Classical Plantation desk, walnut, the long top centered by a wide hinged & slightly slanted writing surface opening to a well & flanked on each side by a pair of small arched compartments, bold scroll-cut ends above an apron fitted w/a small drawer w/two turned wood knobs at each end, raised on ring-, knob- and rod-turned legs ending in ball-and-peg feet, ca. 1830-40, 33 x 60 1/2", 37" h. (ILLUS., top of page) **$28,750**

Old Green-Painted School Desk

Country-style school desk, painted pine, the top w/a short three-quarters gallery above a wide hinged lift-top opening to an interior fitted w/six pigeonholes, deep arched aprons on long slender octagonal legs, old green paint w/stenciled flower on central apron & decorative trim on the legs, some wear & stains, mid-19th c., 19 1/4 x 28 1/4", 33 1/2" h. (ILLUS.) **$978**

Empire-Style cylinder-front desk, mahogany & mahogany veneer, a long narrow rectangular white marble top above a row of three short drawers above the cylinder front opening to a pull-out baize-lined writing surface & a variety of drawers & pigeonholes, the lower case w/a long central drawer flanked by pairs of smaller drawers, each side fitted w/a pull-out writing surface, raised on double-baluster- and ring-turned legs w/ormolu paw foot mounts on the front legs, France, mid-19th c., 27 1/2 x 56", 47 3/4" h. (ILLUS., next page) **$2,070**

French Empire-Style Cylinder-front Desk

Nice Federal "Fall-Front" Writing Desk

Federal Child's Slant-Front Desk

Federal country-style child's slant-front desk, cherry, a narrow rectangular top above the hinged slant front opening to five small pigeonholes, the case w/three long graduated drawers w/small brass pulls, ring- and knob-turned legs, paneled ends, original surface, minor chips to beading, early 19th c., 13 x 18 3/4", 21 1/2" h. (ILLUS.) **$6,038**

Federal "fall-front" writing desk, figured mahogany, the upper section w/a narrow rectangular top w/a brass rail above a wide two-panel hinged fall-front opening to an interior fitted w/central letter dividers flanked by six pigeonholes above three small drawers w/ivory pulls, the stepped-out lower section w/a pair of drawers w/lion head & ring brass pulls, raised on slender ring-turned & reeded legs ending in baluster-turned feet on small brass knobs, New York City, descended in the Gardiner Family, 1800-20, 23 1/4 x 33", 61" h. (ILLUS., top next column) **$2,640**

Federal Lady's Mahogany Writing Desk

Federal lady's writing desk, inlaid mahogany & mahogany veneer, two-part construction: the short upper section w/a long rectangular top w/narrow vertical inlaid bird's-eye maple panels flanking the long central section fitted w/tambour doors opening to an interior fitted w/two rows of small drawers above arched compartments; the lower section w/a fold-out writing surface above a case w/three long graduated drawers w/banded inlay trim & round brass pulls all flanked by narrow bird's-eye maple inlaid panels, raised on slender square tapering legs w/further inlaid panels, late 18th - early 19th c., 18 1/2 x 40", 42" h. (ILLUS.) **$1,840**

Federal "Oxbow-Front" Slanted Desk

Federal "oxbow-front" slant-front desk, maple & birch, a narrow top above a wide hinged slant front opening to an interior fitted w/ten small drawers over seven pigeonholes, the case w/a four long graduated serpentine drawers all w/oval brasses & keyhole escutcheons, shallow serpentine apron raised on tall scroll-cut French feet, old replaced brasses, the lid supports, a couple of interior dividers & scalloped decorations are replaced, restorations, refinished, late 18th - early 19th c., 18 x 39 1/2", 47" h. (ILLUS.) **$2,013**

Federal Mahogany Slant-Front Desk

Federal slant-front desk, mahogany, a narrow top above w/ wide hinged fall-front w/pierced brass butterfly keyhole escutcheon opening to an interior fitted w/pigeonholes, small drawers & a prospect door, above the case w/four long graduated drawers w/fancy pierced brass butterfly pulls & keyhole escutcheons, molded base on low block feet, ca. 1800, crazing & loss of finish, repairs & restorations, feet replaced w/blocks, 21 3/4 x 46", 39" h. (ILLUS.) **$1,725**

Fine Inlaid Federal Lady's Writing Desk

Federal "tambour" lady's writing desk, inlaid mahogany, two-part construction: the upper section w/a rectangular top & narrow cornice above a narrow inlaid frieze band above flute-inlaid pilasters flanking a pair of tambour doors opening to fitted interior & centered by a central rectangular door w/banded inlay centered by an oval reserve inlaid w/an American eagle; the stepped-out lower section w/a fold-out writing surface above a case of three long graduated drawers w/inlaid banding & inlaid fans in each corners, oval brasses, inlaid fluted panel heading each side stile continuing into the square tapering legs w/tapering block feet, Northshore, Massachusetts, 1800-10, 19 1/4 x 38 3/4", 46 1/2" h. (ILLUS.) **$12,000**

Fine Federal-Style Tambour Desk

Fine George III-Style Carlton House Desk

Federal-Style tambour desk, inlaid mahogany, two-part construction: the upper section w/a rectangular top w/a narrow molded cornice above mahogany-veneered frieze band & thin molding over two square tambour sliding doors opening to six cubby holes & two small drawers all flanked by narrow band-inlaid side panels & centered by a small door w/banded inlay surrounding a large inlaid flower-filled urn, the door opening to two cubby holes & a drawer; the lower section w/a medial molding above a narrow fold-out writing ledge above a case w/narrow drawer slides flanking the long drawer w/inlaid line banding & oval brass pulls above a deeper long drawer w/matching inlay & pulls, the sides inlaid w/long bellflower swags & line inlay continuing down the square tapering legs, American-made, early 20th c., 18 x 36", overall 45 1/2" h. (ILLUS., previous page)............................ **$805**

George III-Style Carlton House desk, polychromed satinwood, the upper concave stage w/wavy gallery above open compartments, swelled drawers & doors decorated w/festooned garland, portrait medallions & an allegory, the sloped lidded end compartments painted w/musical trophies, the green tooled leather-lined writing surface over three frieze drawers decorated w/floral garlands, the square tapering legs decorated w/classical urns, wreaths & floral pendants, the reverse fully paint-decorated w/matching Adam designs, in the manner of Wright & Mansfield, England, ca. 1875, 23 x 42", 37" h. (ILLUS., top of page) **$8,050**

Fine English George III-Style Mahogany Partner's Desk

Fine English George III-Style Partner's Desk

George III-Style partner's desk, carved mahogany, the wide rectangular top w/three inset red leather writing surfaces above a frieze band fitted on each side w/a pair of small drawers flanking a long drawer over the kneehole opening, each side pedestal bordered by bead-carved stiles flanking a single door decorated w/a raised border panel w/an arched top, three matching panels on each end, on a deep blocked flat plinth base, the base doors opening to shelves or two drawers, England, late 19th - early 20th c., 50 x 78", 31" h. (ILLUS., bottom previous page) **$3,450**

George III-Style partner's desk, walnut, the long rectangular green leather-lined top w/indented center sections on each side, the projecting end sections each w/two drawers w/brass butterfly pulls & a single longer drawer in the center sections, raised on eight cabriole legs ending in pad feet, England, late 19th - early 20th c., 39 x 60", 31" h. (ILLUS., top of page) **$3,565**

Oak Jacobean-Style English Desk

Jacobean-Style desk, carved oak, the rectangular top w/an elaborately carved edge band & molded edges above a deep apron w/a long front drawer elaborately carved w/leafy scrolls centered by a grotesque mask pull, a bold carved grotesque mask at each corner above the bold baluster- and ring-turned legs w/further leafy scroll carving & ending in carved blocks joined by a heavy knob- and rod-turned H-stretcher w/reeding & leaf carving on bun feet, England, ca. 1900, 28 x 42", 30" h. (ILLUS.) **$1,093**

Louis XV Country-style Desk

French Louis XVI-Style Mahogany & Parquetry Desk

Louis XV country-style desk, hardwood, long rectangular two-board top w/framed sides overhanging a case w/a center kneehole opening flanked by single deep drawers w/simple bail pulls, raised on flattened rectangular simple cabriole legs, some repairs & restoration, Europe, probably 19th c., 27 x 68 1/4", 29 1/4" h. (ILLUS., bottom previous page) **$1,150**

Fine Louis XVI-Style Lady's Desk

Louis XVI-Style lady's desk, ebonized wood & boulle, the narrow rectangular top w/a low pierced brass gallery above the slanted hinged front w/a long rectangular inlaid boulle panel & gilt-brass banding opening to drawers, a storage well & a leather-inset writing surface,the serpentine apron & sides w/further ornate inlaid boulle panels, raised on simple cabriole legs w/gilt-brass scrolled knee mounts & ending in gilt-brass foot caps, Napoleon III-era, France, ca. 1870, 25 1/2" w., 36" h. (ILLUS.)..................... **$1,725**
Louis XVI-Style library desk, mahogany & parquetry, the banded rectangular top inset w/a leather writing surface above an apron w/a long central drawer flanked by a deep-

er drawer, all inset w/parquetry-inlaid panels, raised on square tapering inlaid legs ending in brass caps, France, early 20th c., 28 3/4 x 50 1/2", 30" h. (ILLUS., top of page) **$3,220**

Simple Mission Oak Writing Desk

Mission-style (Arts & Crafts movement) desk, oak, rectangular top w/low arched end panels & projecting corner posts continuing down to form the legs, the case w/a pair of flat cupboard doors w/turned wood knobs flanking a long center drawer over an arched apron, early 20th c., 26 x 42 1/2", 27 1/2" h. (ILLUS.) .. **$374**

Simple Mission Oak Fall-front Desk

**Mission-style (Arts & Crafts movement)
fall-front desk,** a narrow rectangular top
above the wide flat hinged fall-front opening to a fitted interior above two long
drawers w/square wood pulls, square
stile legs joined by a rectangular medial
shelf, ca. 1910, 30" w., 40" h. (ILLUS.,
previous page) **$294**

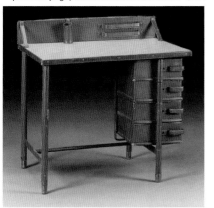

Modern Style Leather & Brass Desk

Modern style desk, leather & brass, the
rectangular yellow laminate top w/a
leather back crestrail attached w/leather
straps & fitted w/a cylindrical leather
pencil holder & double straps for docu-
ments, raised on slender straight round
legs w/the right end fitted w/a stack of
four rectangular leather drawers, brass-
capped feet, designed by Jacques Ad-
net, France, ca. 1950, 23 x 36", 35" h.
(ILLUS.) **$4,183**

Unique & Elaborate North African Desk

North African cylinder-front desk, walnut,
ivory-inlaid & parquetry, the narrow rectangular top above an arched gallery
above the cylinder front decorated overall
w/ornate inlay & reserves of Arabic in-
scriptions, opening to reveal an interior
w/six short drawers centered by a mirrored mihrab above a green felt-covered
writing slide over a long narrow frieze
drawer, supported on a fancy colonnad-
ed trestle base, inlaid overall w/thuya reserves & geometric patterns of various
woods & ivory, late 19th c.,
20 3/4 x 31 3/4", 52 1/2" h. (ILLUS.) **$13,145**

Ornately Carved Indo-Tibetan Walnut Desk

Oriental desk, carved walnut, the top w/an elaborately pierce-carved superstructure w/exotic figures amid
scrolls behind a central open letter slot box & w/surface-carved two-drawer cabinets at each end of the long
rectangular top w/a molded edge overhanging a case w/a pair of ornately carved drawers supported by
figural corner brackets above the kneehole opening, each side section w/wide carved stiles separating
stacks of three curve-fronted carved drawers, raised on seven heavy turned & tapering legs, Indo-
Tibetan, ca. 1900, minor losses, 37 x 84", overall 4' 11" h. (ILLUS.) **$1,150**

Unusual Oriental Slant-front Desk

Oriental slant-front desk, burlwood, a narrow rectangular top above the wide hinged four-panel slant-front opening to an interior fitted w/eight drawers & four pigeonholes around a central drawer, the case w/a row of three deep drawers above two raised panel cupboard doors flanked by a small & paneled door on each side, all atop carved feet joined by an elaborately pierce-carved apron, probably China, mid-19th c. or older, probably original finish, pull on the lid not attached but present, 21 x 40", 48" h. (ILLUS.)............ **$1,725**

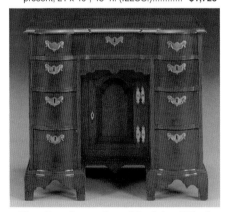

Very Rare Queen Anne "Block-front" Desk

Queen Anne "block-front" kneehole desk, walnut, the rectangular top w/a blocked front w/rounded blocks above a conforming case w/a single long top drawer above two stacks of deep graduated drawers all w/butterfly brasses & flanking the central kneehole w/a scalloped top rail & an inset arched & paneled door w/exposed H-hinges, molded apron on arched, scroll-carved bracket feet, original brasses, Massachusetts, ca. 1740-70, 20 5/8 x 32 1/2", 29 1/4" h. (ILLUS.)...... **$72,000**

Nice Country Queen Anne Desk-on-Frame

Queen Anne country-style desk-on-frame, birch & maple, two-part construction: the upper section w/a narrow top above a wide hinged slant-front opening to three small drawers & six pigeonholes above a single long drawer w/turned wood knob; the lower case w/a wide mid-molding above a single long drawer w/a turned knob, raised on baluster- and ring-turned legs joined by heavy box stretchers, old refinishing & traces of old red wash, old pieced restorations to lid & moldings, one lid support replaced, turned pulls old replacements, 18th c., 17 1/4 x 27 1/4", 39" h. (ILLUS.) **$5,750**

Country Queen Anne Desk-on-Frame

Queen Anne country-style desk-on-frame, painted pine, two-part construction: the top desk section w/a narrow rectangular top above a wide hinged slant top w/wrought-iron staple hinges opening to an interior w/six dovetailed drawers w/brass pulls & a replaced removable board over an open well; the lower section w/a molded rim above an apron w/a single long drawer w/a pierced brass oval keyhole escutcheon & two small turned wood knobs, raised on straight turned & tapering legs ending in pad feet, black repaint over traces of varnish, some wear & damage to hinges, New England, first half 18th c., 26 x 30 1/2", 38 1/4" h. (ILLUS.) **$1,150**

Fine Queen Anne Desk-on-Frame

Queen Anne desk-on-frame, figured maple, a narrow rectangular top above a wide hinged slant-front opening to a fitted interior above a single long drawer w/butterfly pulls & a keyhole escutcheons, raised on a base w/a mid-molding above the deep serpentine apron, raised on straight cabriole legs ending in raised pad feet, original brasses, Connecticut or Rhode Island, ca. 1730-50, 17 x 34", 37 1/2" h. (ILLUS.) **$9,560**

Rare Tiger Maple Queen Anne Desk

Queen Anne desk-on-frame, tiger stripe maple & maple, two-part construction: the upper desk section w/a narrow rectangular top above a wide hinged slant-top opening to an interior fitted w/a central fan-carved drawer flanked by two valanced compartments all above four small drawers, a single long deep drawer below w/butterfly brasses & keyhole escutcheon; the lower case w/a molded rim above a deep valanced apron raised on cabriole legs ending in pad feet, old replaced brasses, probably Massachusetts, mid-18th c., refinished, minor imperfections, 18 3/4 x 34", 40 1/2" h. (ILLUS.).. **$18,800**

Early Queen Anne Slant-front Desk

Queen Anne slant-front desk, tiger stripe maple & maple, a narrow rectangular top above the hinged wide slant front opening to an interior composed of pigeonholes, small drawers & a central shell-carved drawer flanked by small columns, the case w/four long graduated thumb-molded drawers w/butterfly brasses & keyhole escutcheons, molded base w/central drop & short cabriole legs w/pad feet on platforms & scroll-carved returns, refinished, replaced brasses, imperfections, probably Massachusetts, ca. 1740-60, 19 1/4 x 35 1/2", 43 1/4" h. (ILLUS.)....... **$6,463**

English Regency-Style Writing Desk

Ornately Carved European Renaissance-Style Writing Desk

Regency-Style writing desk, mahogany, the kidney-shaped leather-lined top fitted w/a low pierced brass gallery above three frieze drawers, the lyre-form end supports contain brass strings, on outswept legs ending in brass paw feet, simple curved cross-stretcher, England, late 19th c., 20 x 41", 30" h. (ILLUS., previous page).. **$1,265**

Renaissance-Style writing desk, carved mahogany, the large rectangular top inset w/a yellow damask panel, the gadrooned edges overhanging a blocked apron w/a row of three drawers across the top front w/brass pulls above a gadrooned mid-molding above two side stacks of two deep drawers flanking the kneehole opening, each end w/four panels featuring grotesque carved masks, the back featuring ornate floral, fruit & wreath-carved panels, deep flaring & molded base w/gadrooned & egg-and-dart bands, Europe, late 19th c., 40 x 70", 31 1/2" h. (ILLUS., top of page)... **$6,038**

Venetian Painted Rococo-Style Desk

Rococo-Style desk, painted & decorated, the rectangular top w/serpentine edges above a case w/two stacks of concave-front drawers flanking a long bowfront drawer over the kneehole opening, raised on six cabriole legs, painted w/an antiqued green ground decorated on the top, sides & each drawer w/scroll-framed white panels filled w/colorful flowers, Venice, Italy, early 20th c., some paint loss & scuffs, 26 x 48 1/2", 30 1/2" h. (ILLUS.)................ **$863**

Elaborate Rococo-Style Writing Desk

Rococo-Style writing desk, inlaid walnut & marquetry, the upper stepbacked section w/a serpentine top fitted w/a low pierced brass gallery & molded edges above two stacks of three small drawers w/pierced gilt-brass pulls flanking a pair of concave doors decorated w/ornate figural marquetry panels, the lower case w/a rectangular top w/serpentine molded sides above a case w/a single long serpentine drawer w/pierced gilt-brass pulls & gilt-brass corner mounts above two small concave drawers flanking the kneehole opening, raised on simple cabriole legs w/gilt-brass mounts, Europe, late 19th - early 20th c., 23 x 34", 45 1/2" h. (ILLUS.) **$4,140**

Schoolmaster's desk, poplar & pine, the rectangular top w/a short gallery above a hinged slightly slanted top opening to a deep well opening to two small drawers & a letter slot, a single drawer below, raised on simple turned legs, original reddish brown wash, deep brown stenciled named "Michael Sumy, in Zahr, 1853" in a gold panel on the front surrounded by gold & brown tulips, star designs on the drawer front, drawer knob an old replacement, Soap Hollow or Jacob Knagy, mid-19th c., 21 1/2 x 27 1/2", 41 1/2" h. (ILLUS., next page).. **$4,025**

Rare Schoolmaster's Desk

English Victorian "Davenport" Desk

Victorian "Davenport" desk, carved & burl walnut, the top w/a shaped & slanted lift-lid w/tooled leather writing inserts over a fitted interior, the sides installed w/five working & four opposing faux drawers, paneled front w/floral- and leaf-carved cabriole supports, on extended feet on casters, some veneer repairs, England, ca. 1850, 21 5/8 x 23", 31" h. (ILLUS.).......... **$1,150**

Victorian Eastlake style "cylinder-front" desk, walnut & burl walnut veneer, the rectangular top mounted w/a three-quarters gallery w/the back crest carved w/a scalloped crest over line-incised panels & fluted blocks flanked by small squared corner finials, the top above a sawtooth-carved molding over the cylinder front w/two recessed burl-veneered panels & black round knobs opening to a writing surface & fitted interior, the lower case

Fine Victorian Eastlake Cylinder-front Desk

w/a stack of four line-incised drawers w/long angular pulls on one side of the kneehole opening & a single drawer & paneled cupboard door on the other side, paneled back & ends, minor edge damage & wear, ca. 1880-90, 30 1/2 x 52", 56 1/4" h. (ILLUS.) **$3,105**

Early Oak S-Scroll Rolltop Desk

Victorian Golden Oak rolltop desk, a narrow rectangular top above the S-scroll top opening to a wide writing surface & an arrangement of cubbyholes & small drawers, the base w/a stack of four graduated drawers w/wooden grip pulls on one side of the kneehole opening & a small single drawer over a tall paneled cupboard door on the other side, paneled ends, 45" w., 32" h. (ILLUS.)............. **$400-700**

Victorian Golden Oak rolltop desk, a narrow rectangular top w/a low spindled three-quarters gallery above the C-scroll top opening to a wide writing surface & an arrangement of cubbyholes & small drawers, the slide-out writing surface w/a tilting easel, the lower case w/a stack of three graduated drawers w/stamped brass & bail pulls flanking the central kneehole opening, deep molded base on casters, 42" w., 40" h. (ILLUS., next page)... **$588**

Nice Oak C-Scroll Rolltop Desk

Simple Golden Oak Writing Desk

Victorian Golden Oak writing desk, a narrow top w/a high crest w/rounded corners inset w/a mirror above the wide hinged flat fall-front opening to a fitted interior above a long flat drawer & a narrow shaped apron, raised on flat serpentine legs joined by a medial shelf w/incurved sides & a low back crest, w/a shipping tag from the Northwestern Cabinet Co., Burlington, Iowa, ca. 1910, 26" w., 48" h. (ILLUS.)....... **$323**

Victorian Renaissance Revival substyle writing desk, walnut & walnut veneer, a superstructure w/a small pedimented crest above a long narrow shelf raised on four slender spindles above the long rectangular desk top w/a pedimented crest above the wide hinged fall-front writing surface centered by a raised burl veneer panel, supported on a base w/a single

Simple Renaissance Revival Writing Desk

long drawer w/carved leaf pulls raised on four columnar-turned legs atop arched shoe feet on casters joined by a turned cross stretcher, ca. 1870s, 29" w., 5' 1" h. (ILLUS.)... **$382**

William & Mary Slant-Front Maple Desk

William & Mary slant-front desk, figured maple, a narrow rectangular top above a wide hinged slant-top opening to a fitted interior, above a case of four long graduated drawers w/simple turned wood pulls, molded base on shaped bracket feet resting on casters, New England, 1740-60, 17 1/2 x 36", 42 1/4" h. (ILLUS.) **$7,200**

Rare Sornay French Art Deco Dining Room Suite

Rare William & Mary Table-top Desk

William & Mary table-top slant-front desk, maple & pine, a narrow rectangular top above the wide hinged slant front opening to an interior fitted w/a row of arched pigeonholes over a row of five small drawers, the case below w/two long graduated drawers w/batwing brasses & keyhole escutcheons, flaring molded base on turned turnip feet, early 18th c., 14 1/4 x 23", 20" h. (ILLUS.) **$10,200**

Dining Room Suites

Art Deco: dining table & 10 dining chairs; inlaid & inset rosewood, the table w/a long rectangular top composed of large squares of tan travertine, wide corner legs curved at the base w/the central opening fitted at the bottom w/another travertine piece, the chairs w/tall slightly flaring backs w/cream-colored upholstery above half-round upholstered seats, on square tapering legs, chairs stamped "Breveté Sornay France Etranger," Andre Sornay, France, ca. 1935, table 39 x 118", 30" h., chairs 40 7/8" h., the suite (ILLUS., top of page) **$50,190**

Fine French Art Nouveau Dining Room Suite

Baroque Revival Oak Dining Room Suite

Art Nouveau: extension dining table & 12 side chairs; carved mahogany, the table w/a long rectangular top w/molded edges & rounded covers carved w/floral bands & raised on square tapering legs w/block feet, each chair w/a tall back w/a molded & flower-carved frame enclosing an upholstered panel, upholstered seat on slender tapering front legs ending in tiny block feet, & canted square rear legs, designed by Edouard Diot, France, ca. 1905, table w/two leaves, table 47 x 49 1/2", 29" h., chairs 37 3/4" h., the suite (ILLUS., bottom previous page)... **$21,510**

Baroque Revival style: four dining chairs & an extension dining table; carved oak, each chair w/a tall leather-upholstered back w/an arched crestrail carved w/the profile of a man, raised above the leather over-upholstered seat above front legs turned w/large bulbous acorn-form sections w/leaf carving above block- and knob-feet, simple square rear legs & H-stretcher, the rectangular draw-leaf table w/a carved edge above a deep apron decorated at each corner w/two carved lion heads above the legs composed of large bulbous turned acorn-form posts above block & ball feet joined by large incurved stretchers joined by a straight center stretcher, early 20th c., chairs 44" h., table 38 x 62" closed, 32" h., the set (ILLUS., top of page)........................ **$1,380**

Colonial Revival 1920s Dining Suite in the Jacobean Design

Colonial Revival style: dining table, six chairs, a sideboard & a china cabinet; Jacobean design in walnut & burl walnut, the china cabinet w/a tall arched top above a geometrically glazed door above a long deep drawer w/banded carving & burl, the sideboard w/similar details & a case w/two long center drawers flanked by end doors, all the pieces raised on heavy turned legs w/very large central knobs & small bun feet all joined by H-stretchers, ca. 1920s, the set (ILLUS.) **$2,070**

Colonial Revival Dining Suite with Solid Doors

Colonial Revival style: dining table w/two leaves, six chairs, a sideboard, small server & a china cabinet; Jacobean design in walnut & burl walnut, the case pieces w/flat tops over slightly angled fronts, the sideboard & server w/a pair of arched carved central doors w/ring pulls flanked by slightly angled matching doors, the china cabinet w/a large arched carved door above a long carved drawer all flanked by angled side panels, boldly turned knob-, ring- and block-decorated legs on bun feet, the case pieces w/open base shelves w/serpentine fronts, made in Rockford, Illinois, ca. 1920s, table 45 x 66" plus leaves, sideboard 44" l., the set (ILLUS., top of page) **$863**

Federal Revival style: dining table, eight side chairs, sideboard & serving table; inlaid mahogany, the round extension dining table raised on square tapering legs on casters & accompanied by five leaves, each side chair w/an arched crestrail above a tall oblong splat w/a design of pierced slats, slip seat & square tapering legs joined by H-stretcher, the bowfront sideboard w/a high serpentine backsplash above a case w/curved end drawers over curved doors flanking the flat center stack of three long drawers, on square tapering legs, the server w/a high serpentine backsplash above a bowed top over a single long bowed drawer above a medial shelf all raised on square tapering legs, the backsplashes w/inlaid decoration & bellflower inlay on the front legs, ring- and urn-decorated brasses, ca. 1920s, table 54" d., chairs 43 3/4" h., sideboard 25 x 65", 47" h., the set (ILLUS., next column) **$3,220**

Fine Federal Revival Inlaid Mahogany Dining Room Suite

Rare George Nakashima Dining Room Suite

Modern Style: dining table & four "Mira" chairs; walnut, the table w/a square top supported on a simple pedestal on a cross-form foot, each chair w/a wide curved crestrail above seven spindles over a triangular saddle seat, three simple turned & canted legs, by George Nakashima, ca. 1965, table 26 1/4 x 32", 26" h., chairs 27 1/4" h. (ILLUS.) **$14,340**

Heywood-Wakefield 1950s Dining Table & Chair from Set

Modern Style: drop-leaf dining table & six dining chairs; birch w/a champagne finish, the table w/a rectangular top flanked by wide D-form drop leaves & raised on a set of three arched pedestal legs, Model M197G by Heywood-Wakefield, together w/Heywood-Wakefield chairs Model M553A w/a curved back crest above a cross-form splat between the canted stiles above the upholstered seat, squared tapering legs, ca. 1950-53, the set (ILLUS. of part).. **$431**

Dining Table & Chairs from Fine Gothic Revival Dining Suite

Gothic Revival style: dining table, six side chairs, two armchairs, a side cabinet, buffet, side table & wall cabinet; oak, the suite overall richly carved w/Gothic arches & tracery, flowerheads within stepped trefoil surrounds & crocheted finials, the dining table w/a rectangular parquetry inlaid top on pierced trestle-form supports on scrolled feet; each chair w/crocheted finials over an arched crest above rectangular backs each centering a slightly different scrolling foliate & spider web tracery-carved panel over a trapezoidal seat over outswept arms, raised on tapering legs; the side cabinet of court cupboard design, the upper case surmounted by arched crocheted finals over a pair of doors, raised on square supports joined by a platform; the buffet w/a rectangular top over a pair of frieze drawers above a pair of iron-mounted doors on a stepped-out base; the tiered side table w/rectangular top & chamfered edge over a frieze drawers above pierced swagged panels over two shelves ending in an arched base; the wall cabinet w/an arched crest over a single door & arched base, Europe, third quarter 19th c., dining table open 4' 11" x 8' 4", 31" h., court cupboard, 17" x 5', 8' 10" h., the suite (ILLUS. of part).. **$8,225**

Unusual Covered Cherry Drysink

Dry Sinks

Cherry, the rectangular hinged top opens to a well above a pair of paneled cupboard doors w/brass H-hinges & brass latches, simple bracket feet, mid-19th c., sink lining missing & replaced w/a plywood panel, 20 x 36 3/4", 33 3/4" h. (ILLUS., top next column).. **$690**

Painted & decorated poplar, the long arched splashback above a long well above a case w/a pair of large paneled cupboard doors above simple bracket feet, old dark brown graining over an amber-colored ground, evidence of earlier

Painted & Decorated Poplar Dry Sink

red, interior w/two shelves painted light green, wear, door latch missing, 19th c., 17 3/4 x 45", 36" h. (ILLUS.) **$575**

Rare Dated Ohio Dry Sink

Painted pine & poplar, a narrow rectangular shelf atop the raised backboard flanked by shaped sides on the long well above a pair of drawers w/turned wood knobs over a pair of paneled cupboard doors opening to two shelves, simple bracket feet, old yellow paint over earlier colors, signed in pencil in one drawer "Thos. Underwood, Clark Co. Ohio, August 10, 1881," 18 x 42", 41" h. (ILLUS.) **$4,025**

Garden & Lawn

Armchairs, "Laurel" patt., each w/a multi-arched crestrail curving to form end arms all above panels of large fanned leaves, half-round pierced matching seat, canted bar rear legs, figural winged griffin front legs, painted white, pattern registered by the English Coalbrookdale Company in 1875 but was also made in the United States, probably American, late 19th - early 20th c., 27" h., pr. (ILLUS., bottom of page)... **$1,093**

One of a Set of Fern Design Armchairs

Armchairs, the arched crestrail above an openwork large fanned stem of fern leaves & continuing down to rounded arms over ferns, the pierced seat raised on four slender canted legs joined by entwined branch side stretchers, painted white, mid-19th c., set of four (ILLUS. of one)... **$1,093**

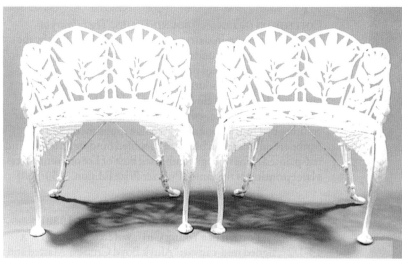

Pair of Laurel Pattern Garden Armchairs

Fine Carved Marble Italian Garden Bench

Bench, carved white marble, the rectangular back w/an arched pediment carved w/griffins flanking an urn, above a fielded panel carved in relief w/scrolling foliage, flanked at the sides by volute-form armrests carved w/a satyr mask & grapevine, on volute supports carved w/acanthus

leaves, Italy, last quarter 19th c., 19 3/4 x 51", 45 3/4" h. (ILLUS.) **$26,290**

Oak & Iron Early Chaise Lounge

Chaise lounge, oak & wrought iron, the adjustable back & long seat tied w/rope webbing & covered w/a pad, half-round & quarter-round oak rod arms flanking the seat, two hard rubber-rimmed wooden spoked wheels at one end, late 19th - early 20th c., 64" l. (ILLUS.) **$2,629**

Italian 20th Century Stone & Iron Garden Suite

Garden suite: table, bench & two armchairs; the long table w/a rectangular Pietra Dura style decorated slate top featuring scrolled ivory-colored acanthus leaves & raised on scrolling wrought-iron end legs topped by pierced spiraling brass balls, the long rectangular bench w/an upholstered top & double-scroll ends legs joined by a long stretcher, each armchair w/a low back w/a long rectangular panel of wide fabric bands, flat serpentine arms above the woven cloth seat supported on slender U-shaped iron frames & wide arched iron bar legs, Italy, mid-20th c., table, 30 x 57", 29" h., the set (ILLUS.)... **$2,415**

Two Matching Oak Leaf & Acorn Garden Settees

Settee, high serpentine long back composed of openwork oak leaves & acorns entwined w/arches, the straight end arms w/alternating ivy & berry & oak leaves & acorns w/figural dog head hand grips, a wooden slat seat above an iron oak leaf & acorn apron above cabriole legs w/paw feet, painted black, mid-19th c., 32 x 59", 37 1/2" h. (ILLUS. right with matching settee, top of page) **$1,495**

Settee, high serpentine long back composed of openwork oak leaves & acorns entwined w/arches, the straight end arms w/alternating ivy & berry & oak leaves & acorns w/figural dog head hand grips, a wooden slat seat above an iron oak leaf & acorn apron above cabriole legs w/paw feet, painted black, mid-19th c., 32 x 59", 37 1/2" h. (ILLUS. left with matching settee, top of page) **$1,265**

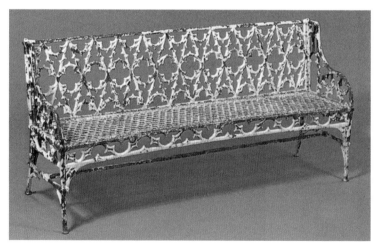

Long Gothic Design Garden Settee

Settee, in the Gothic taste, the long back w/a flat crestrail above a continuous row of Gothic arches & quatrefoils, downswept lacy end arms, grillwork seat w/a narrow Gothic design apron, bar legs, similar to examples by James Yates, Effingham Works, England, second quarter 19th c., white paint w/overall rusting, 19 x 73 1/2", 35" h. (ILLUS.) **$4,370**

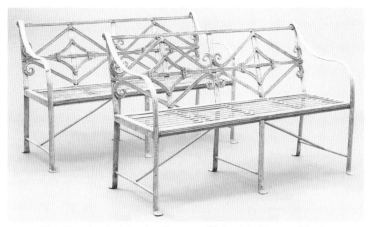

Two Neoclassical Garden Settees with Double-Diamond Backs

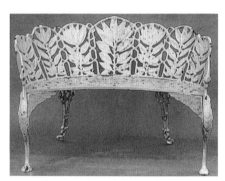

Victorian Laurel Pattern Settee

Victorian Arch-backed Garden Settee

Settee, "Laurel" patt., the curved back & side arms composed of arched panels enclosing fanned leafy branches, half-round openwork seat on figural winged griffin front legs, probably American, mid-19th c., old white paint w/some rusting, 31 x 40", 36" h. (ILLUS.) **$1,265**

Settee, Neoclassical taste, a narrow reeded flat crestrail above the openwork back composed of two large double-diamond panels, serpentine end arms continuing down to form the front legs, long rectangular slat seat, legs joined by stretchers & bar braces, old cream paint, 19th c., 60" l., 38" h. (ILLUS. front with matching settee, top of page) **$2,185**

Settee, Neoclassical taste, a narrow reeded flat crestrail above the openwork back composed of two large double-diamond panels, serpentine end arms continuing down to form the front legs, long rectangular slat seat, legs joined by stretchers & bar braces, old cream paint, 19th c., 60" l., 38" h. (ILLUS. back with matching settee, top of page) **$2,990**

Settee, the leaf-cast serpentine crestrail above the long back composed of rows of small openwork arches, the stepped & canted end arms composed of upright C-

scrolls, pierced-scroll long seat on S-scroll cabriole front legs, old white paint, late 19th c., 44" l. (ILLUS.) **$1,135**

Scrolling Victorian Garden Settee

Settee, the long low back composed of entwined openwork leafy scrolls centered by a large grape clusters, long oblong pierced seat w/a matching pierced scroll apron & floral- and leaf-cast outswept front legs joined by curved bar stretchers to the rear legs, worn white paint, late 19th c., 42 1/2" l. (ILLUS.) **$956**

Three-piece English Garden Set with Gothic Motifs

Settee & armchairs, each w/a back centered by a large round openwork medallion above a back composed of entwined Gothic arches, downswept arms composed of leafy scrolls, planked beadboard seats, Gothic arch-form openwork end legs, dark green paint, England, mid-19th c., the set (ILLUS.) **$1,955**

One of a Pair of Lacy Cast-Iron Victorian Garden Settees

Settees, a long serpentine crest above the ornately pierced back composed of three narrow vertical panels enclosing lacy loops flanking a long central panel filled w/ornately scrolling leafy grapevines, tapering arms & sides enclosing scrolling designs, long slatted seat, old white paint w/minor rusting, mid-19th c., 70 1/2" l., 34" h., pr. (ILLUS., of one) **$805**

Double Gothic Arch Victorian Garden Settees

Late Victorian Laurel Pattern Garden Settees

Settees, double chair-back style w/the back composed of two large open Gothic Arches made of flattened iron straps, simple curved strap end arms above the long rectangular open slat seat raised on six flat bar legs joined by H-stretchers, green paint, 19th c., 42" l., 39" h., pr. (ILLUS., bottom previous page) **$748**

Settees, Laurel patt., the long scallop-topped back composed of openwork panels of large vertical leafy branches curving around to tapering scrolled arms, the long half-round seat composed of leafy scrolls, the front legs in the form a bird head & large wing curving down to a claw foot, old white paint, ca. 1900, 42" l., 29" h., pr. (ILLUS., top of page) **$5,520**

Settees, the back serpentine crestrail above an overall pierced design of scrolling fern leaves continuing to form high arms above the pierced seat,

One of a Pair of Fern Design Victorian Garden Settees

arched end legs, painted white, 19th c., 53 1/2" l., pr. (ILLUS. of one) **$3,450**

One of Two Garden Settees with Vining Backs & a Nymph Plaque

Settees, the long arched back composed of entwining leafy vines w/various birds all centered by a large relief-molded oval plaque showing a seated classical nymph, the cast-iron slatted seat above curved legs ending in hoof feet, painted black, second half 19th c., 24 x 63", 38" h., pr. (ILLUS. of one) **$8,050**

One of Two Arch-backed Settees

Settees, the serpentine crestrail composed of leafy scrolls & florals above a back panel composed of repeating small open arches, the high stepped arms composed of slender C-scrolls, the ornate pierced seat above a scrolling pierced apron & scrolling cabriole legs, white paint w/overall rusting, 19th c., 43" l., pr. (ILLUS. of one) **$1,150**

One of Two Oak Leaf & Acorn Settees

Settees, the serpentine crestrail composed of rings of oak leaves & acorns above a matching back, the flat pierced leaf arms w/figural dog head hand grips, slatted seat w/a long oak leaf & acorn apron, cabriole legs w/paw feet, painted green, minor rusting, mid-19th c., 21 1/2 x 70 1/2", 34" h., pr. (ILLUS. of one)... **$2,415**

Settees, the wide arched back composed of large pierced scrolling fern leaves curving around to form the end arms flanking the wooden slat seat, outswept fern-cast legs, old green paint, England, 19th c., 15 1/2 x 58", 35" h., pr. (ILLUS. of one, top next column).................................. **$1,955**

Table, a rectangular white marble top raised on scrolling lyre-form end legs joined by a pierced leafy scroll stretcher, scroll feet, New York, ca. 1850, 24 x 35 3/4", 28 3/4" h. (ILLUS., middle next column)... **$2,530**

One of a Pair of English Fern Pattern Garden Settees

Victorian Marble & Iron Garden Table

Round Pierced Garden Table

Table, round top pierced overall w/tight leafy scrolls, supported on tall double C-scroll legs headed by pierced lattice panels & joined by a pierced round lower shelf, 39" d., 27" h. (ILLUS.) **$717**

Table & chairs, a round table w/pierced top decorated w/two oval medallions w/raised classical figures above an ornate scrolling apron continuing into four curved cabriole legs, four side chairs each w/an arched tall back w/a bow crest over the wreath-pierced back centered by an oval medallion w/a classical figure, round pierced seat & four scroll-cast cabriole legs ending in hoof feet, painted white w/some rust, second half 19th c., table 24" d., 25" h., the set........................ **$920**

Modern Designer-type Metal Garden Furniture Set

Table & chairs, painted metal, the table w/a round metal meshwork top & curlicue apron raised on a pedestal of tapering & then flaring bar clusters centered by a looped metal ring, each chair w/the tapering back composed of slender bars rolled at the top, armchairs w/matching rolled top arms, round metal mesh seats, simple metal bar chair legs joined by a cross-stretcher, painted white, designed by Mathieu Mategot, ca. 1950, table 39 1/2" d., 29" h., chairs 32" h., the set (ILLUS., top of page)........................... **$14,340**

Victorian Serpentine Wirework Tete-a-Tete

Tete-a-tete, wirework, the S-scroll back composed of slender arched loops of wire above the oblong wire grid seat w/a looped wire apron, S-scroll bar legs joined by an X-stretcher, painted light green, second half 19th c., 21 x 45 1/2", 29" h. (ILLUS.) **$633**

Hall Racks & Trees

Unusual Bamboo-style Hall Rack

Hall rack, Victorian bamboo-style, composed of three tall crossed bamboo-turned legs joined at the bottom w/a triangular metal drip tray & side stretchers, each stick fitted w/coat hooks & topped w/a pointed metal halberd blade, late 19th c., overall 90 1/2" h. (ILLUS.)............ **$230**

Fine Classical-Style Mahogany Hall Tree

Hall tree, Classical-Style, carved mahogany, a tall post ornately decorated w/carved acanthus leaves & ring-turnings & capped by a brass ball & eagle finial, fitted w/serpentine lotus-carved hooks, raised on four scroll-carved heavy paw feet, late 19th c., 88" h. (ILLUS.)............ **$2,990**

Victorian Aesthetic Taste Hall Tree

Hall tree, Victorian Aesthetic Movement style, walnut & burl walnut, the tall crenelated pediment & finials above a molded cornice & geometrically pierced frieze, all above an arched beveled mirror flanked

by projecting line-incised vertical bars fitted w/turned pegs for hats & coats, the rectangular white marble lower top over a drawer & pierced support flanked by rectangular open supports for umbrellas above the plinth base fitted w/metal drip pans above the blocked feet, ca. 1880, 11 x 36", 7' 7" h. (ILLUS.) **$920**

Fine Victorian Bamboo Hall Tree

Hall tree, Victorian bamboo-style, the peaked & arched pediment composed of bamboo rods above a projecting shelf above a pair of lacquered corner panels w/Oriental designs above bamboo rods flanking a tall rectangular mirror, the lower section w/a small stepped-out top above a small drawer over a tall narrow paneled door flanked on each side by racks for umbrellas or walking sticks, ca. 1880s, 12 x 44", 6' 8" h. (ILLUS.)........... **$1,495**

Simple Golden Oak Hall Tree

Hall tree, Victorian Golden Oak style, a large upper octagonal section w/wide flat board sides decorated w/a thin center band flanking a large beveled mirror & mounted w/four double metal coat hooks, the lower paneled back above a hinged-top storage compartment flanked by flat shaped open arms w/the supports forming the front legs, ca. 1900, 27" w., 6' 3" h. (ILLUS., previous page) **$518**

Fancy Victorian Walnut Hall Tree

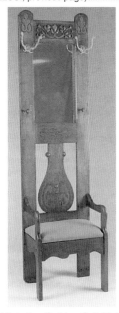

Tall Victorian Golden Oak Hall Tree

Hall tree, Victorian Golden Oak style, the very tall back w/a short leafy scroll-carved flat crest flanked by tall flat side stiles w/arched tops w/leaf carving & flanking a long rectangular mirror above a vasiform-lower splat w/scroll carving, the stile mounted w/two double & two single hat hooks, low shaped open arms flanking the upholstered seat, serpentine apron, flat stile front legs, ca. 1890s, 15 x 21 3/4", 80 1/2" h. (ILLUS.) **$259**

Hall tree, Victorian Renaissance Revival style, walnut, the tall base w/an arched pierced-scroll crest above a frieze band w/notched pegs flanking a small rectangular burl panel & w/hat posts at each side, the main upper section w/stepped & pierce-carved sides w/four hat pegs surrounding an upright rectangular mirror w/rounded corners, the narrower stepped & pierce-carved lower section w/a small candle shelf above an oblong rack w/side openings flanking a small square marble top, two rectangular front uprights to a base shelf fitted w/two cast-iron drip trays, a split in one of the umbrella ring holders, ca. 1890, 11 1/2 x 29", 89" h. (ILLUS., top next column) **$604**

Fancy Renaissance Revival Hall Tree

Hall tree, Victorian Renaissance Revival substyle, walnut & burl walnut, the tall back w/a large shell- and scroll-carved crest centered by a large cabochon above & flanked by a pedimented crest w/a molded cornice above a burled & scroll-cut frieze band continuing down the sides w/narrow raised burl panels all mounted w/six long coat pegs & surrounding a large arched mirror w/a raised molded border, shaped raised burl panels below the mirror & above a narrow rectangular white marble top above a single long narrow drawer w/pear-shaped drop pulls supported on slender columnar supports flanked by C-scroll side bars, the oblong platform base w/round cast metal drip pans at the sides & a wide incurved central apron, ca. 1875, 14 x 48", 7' 8" h. (ILLUS.)...................... **$1,208**

Simple Victorian Radiating Hall Tree

Hall tree, Victorian Renaissance Revival substyle, walnut, the upper section in a sunburst form w/seven radiating arms each fitted w/a peg & centered by a small round mirror, the tall slender double-vase form support also fitted near the top w/a single peg & below w/a C-form bar for umbrellas w/two slender supports above the rectangular base fitted w/a metal drip pan, ca. 1875, 6' 6" h. (ILLUS.)................. **$259**

Highboys & Lowboys

Highboys
Chippendale "bonnet-top" highboy, carved mahogany, two-part construction: the upper section w/a broken swan's-neck pediment terminating in carved rosettes flanked by & centering urn-and-flame finials, above a central shell-carved long drawer w/ornate scrolling tendrils & flanked by two small drawers over a pair of drawers above three long graduated drawers all flanked by engaged quarter columns; the lower section w/a mid-molding over a long drawer over a deep central drawer w/a carved shell flanked by ornate leafy scrolls & flanked by two small drawers, the scalloped apron centered by a carved shell, raised on cabriole legs w/shell-carved knees & ending in claw-and-ball feet, Philadelphia, 1760-80, 25 1/2 x 47", 7' 11 1/4" h. (finials replaced) **$163,500**

Unique Million Dollar Philadelphia Highboy

Chippendale "bonnet-top" highboy, carved mahogany, two-part construction: the upper section w/a very high broken-scroll pediment w/the heavy molded scrolls terminating in large sunflowers flanking a tall cartouche-shaped scroll-pieced finial & mounted w/corner blocks supporting urn-turned & flame finials, the wide upper frieze ornately carved w/bold leafy scrolls centered by a large pierce-carved shell device, the tall case w/quarter-round reeded corner columns flanking a row of three drawers over a pair of drawers above three long graduated drawers, all w/pierced butterfly brasses; the lower section w/a mid-molding above a case w/a single long drawer over a pair of small square drawers flanking a large central drawer w/finely carved leafy scrolls centered by a large shell all flanked by quarter-round reeded columns, the serpentine apron centered by a small carved shell, raised on tall cabriole legs w/scroll- and leaf-carved knees & ending in claw-and-ball feet, attributed to the shop of Henry Clifton & Thomas Carteret, Philadlephia, 1755-65, descended in the family of Benjamin Marshall, unique, 23 5/8 x 45", 94 1/2" h. (ILLUS.).......................... **$1,808,000**

Chippendale "bonnet-top" highboy, carved mahogany, two-part construction: the upper section w/an ornate broken-scroll pediment w/the large molded scrolls ending in a large carved flower head flanking a very tall, large pierced scroll-carved finial, reeded corner blocks supporting urn-turned & flame-carved finials, the wide frieze ornately carved w/leafy scrolls above a row of three drawers over a pair of drawers over a stack of three long graduated drawers, all w/butterfly brasses & keyhole escutcheons,

Exquisite Philadelphia Carved Highboy

fluted slender colonettes down the sides; the lower section w/a mid-molding over a long drawer above a pair of small square drawers flanking a deep, large shell- and scroll-carved center drawer, fluted colonettes down the sides, raised on a scroll-carved apron on cabriole legs w/fancy leaf- and scroll-carved knees & ending in claw-and-ball feet, Philadelphia, ca. 1760-80, descended in the family of Joseph Moulder, 23 7/8 x 42 1/4", 97 1/4" h. (ILLUS.) **$329,600**

Attractive Married Queen Anne Highboy

Queen Anne "bonnet-top" highboy, carved cherry, two-part construction: the

upper section w/a broken-scroll bonnet top centered by a slender fluted post topped by an urn-carved & flame-turned finial, matching corner blocks & flame finials, the case w/a pair of small drawers flanking a deep shell-carved drawer over a stack of four long graduated drawers all w/butterfly brasses & keyhole escutcheons, fluted pilasters down the sides; the lower section w/a mid-molding above a case w/a pair of narrow drawers over a pair of deep drawers flanking a small shell-carved & blocked center drawer above a conforming apron w/two drops, raised on cabriole legs w/scroll-carved returns & ending in raised pad feet, top & base married, Long Island, New York, 18th c., 20 1/2 x 41 1/2", 92" h. (ILLUS.) **$9,000**

Fine Queen Anne "Bonnet-top" Highboy

Queen Anne "bonnet-top" highboy, carved mahogany, two-part construction: the upper section w/a broken-scroll pediment centered by a tall plinth w/an urn- and flame-turned finial & corner plinths w/matching finials above a pair of short drawers flanking a deep center drawer w/a large carved fan above four long graduated drawers w/butterfly pulls & keyhole escutcheons; the lower section w/a molded edge above a long narrow drawer over a row of three drawers, the center one fan-carved, shaped & valanced apron raised on slender cabriole legs ending in pad feet, brasses appear to be original, old refinish, probably Massachusetts, 1786, pencil inscription inside upper case reads "made by Horace Smith, Sept. 9, 1786," minor restoration & imperfections, 22 x 42", 88" h. (ILLUS.) **$23,500**

Cherry Queen Anne "Flat-top" Highboy

Queen Anne "flat-top" highboy, cherry, two-part construction: the upper section w/a rectangular top & widely flaring covered & stepped cornice above a row of three deep drawers each w/a carved fan above four long graduated drawers all w/butterfly brasses; the lower section w/a top molding above a row of three deep drawers w/the center one fan-carved, serpentine apron raised on simple cabriole legs ending in pad feet, old refinishing, drawers w/pieced repairs to top edges, replaced brasses, base has reconstruction, first half 18th c., 21 1/2 x 38 1/2", 66" h. (ILLUS.) **$2,300**

Cherry Queen Anne "Married" Highboy

Queen Anne "flat-top" highboy, cherry, two-part construction: the upper section w/a rectangular flat top w/a deep covered cornice above a case w/a pair of drawers over four long graduated drawers all w/brass butterfly pulls; the lower married section w/a medial rail above a case w/a single long narrow drawer above two deep square drawers flanking a wide center deep drawer w/a fan-carved front, shaped front apron w/two turned drops, cabriole legs ending in raised pad feet, New England, 18th c., restored, top left cornice missing section of back, base 19 1/2 x 38 1/8", overall 78" h. (ILLUS.) **$4,025**

New England Queen Anne Highboy

Queen Anne "flat-top" highboy, maple, two-part construction: the upper section w/a rectangular top above a deep stepped cornice over a stack of four long graduated drawers w/butterfly brasses & keyhole escutcheons; the lower section w/a mid-molding above a single long narrow drawer over a row of three deep drawers, the valanced skirt raised on simple cabriole legs ending raised pad feet, New England, 1740-70, 19 x 38 1/4" h., 69" h. (ILLUS.) **$9,000**

Queen Anne "flat-top" highboy, maple, two-part construction: the upper section w/a rectangular top w/a deep stepped & flaring cornice above a row of three drawers over a stack of four long graduated drawers all w/butterfly brasses & keyhole escutcheons; the lower section w/a mid-molding over two long graduated drawers over a pair of deep square drawers flanking a longer shell-carved drawer all w/butterfly brasses, deep fancy scroll-carved apron, cabriole legs w/scroll-carved returns ending in raised pad feet, old brasses, attributed to the Dunlap family of cabinetmakers, southern New Hampshire, ca. 1780-1800, refinished, minor imperfections, 19 x 38 1/2", 76" h. (ILLUS., next page)............................. **$29,375**

Fine Dunlap Family-style Highboy

Queen Anne Maple Highboy

Queen Anne "flat-top" highboy, maple w/areas of figure, two-part construction: the upper section w/a rectangular top above a flaring stepped cornice over a pair of beaded overlapping drawers w/batwing brasses over a stack of the long graduated drawers w/matching brasses; the lower section w/a medial rail above a long shallow drawer w/three brasses above a row of three deep drawers w/brasses, shaped apron w/two drops w/turned knob drop finials, raised on cabriole legs ending in raised pad

feet, refinished, old replaced leg returns & brasses, minor splits in top case & minor corner chip on cornice, mid-18th c., 19 x 38 3/4", 67" h. (ILLUS.) **$5,175**

Nice "Married" Queen Anne Highboy

Queen Anne "flat-top" highboy, tiger stripe maple & cherry, two-part construction: the top section w/a rectangular top w/a deep flaring stepped cornice above a case w/five long graduated drawers w/brass butterfly pulls & keyhole escutcheons; the married lower section w/a medial molding above a case w/two deep square drawers flanking a short central drawer above a high serpentine apron w/two turned drops, simple cabriole legs ending in pad feet, replaced brasses, New England, late 18th c., base 17 3/4 x 39", overall 76" h. (ILLUS.)....... **$2,300**

English Burl Walnut Queen Anne Highboy

European Jacobean-Style Carved Mahogany Chaise Lounge

Queen Anne "flat-top" highboy, walnut & burl walnut, two-part construction: the upper section w/a flat top w/a narrow cornice above a pair of drawers over three long graduated drawers; the lower section w/a wide flared molding above a narrow center drawer flanked by deep side drawers all w/butterfly pulls & round keyhole escutcheons, arched & serpentine apron raised on cabriole legs ending in raised pointed pad feet, replaced hardware, England, ca. 1720, 40" w., 5' 3" h. (ILLUS., previous page) **$8,050**

Lowboys

Fine Queen Anne Lowboy

Queen Anne lowboy, walnut & mahogany, the rectangular top w/chamfered corners above a case w/a long drawer over a pair of small square drawers flanking a larger, deeper center drawer, all w/butterfly brasses, fluted & canted side stiles, fancy scroll-cut apron, raised on cabriole legs w/leaf- and shell-carved knees & ending in drake feet, ca. 1780, 19 1/4 x 31 1/2", 28 1/4" h. (ILLUS.) **$4,830**

Love Seats, Sofas & Settees

Chaise lounge, Jacobean-Style, carved mahogany, the angled end backrest of square form w/a wide heavily pierce-carved frame of scrolls, leaves & shells centering a caned panel & flanked by spiral- and block-turned stiles, the long rectangular caned seat in a plain frame raised on six spiral- and block-turned legs on ball feet & joined by long flat pierced & scroll-carved side rails, Europe, late 19th c., 22 x 71", 35" h. (ILLUS., top of page)...... **$1,725**

Chaise lounge, Louis XV-Style, carved giltwood, one end w/a caned back w/a gently arched crestrail centered w/shell carving & flanked by scrolling foliage, low curved caned arms w/acanthus leaf grips, on a scroll-carved & molded apron raised on carved cabriole legs ending in scroll feet & joined by U-form stretchers, w/a tapestry cushion, France, late 19th - early 20th c., 30 x 64", 39 1/2" h. (ILLUS., top next page) **$2,990**

Modernist Style Bamboo Chaise Lounge

Chaise lounge, Modernist style, a bent bamboo frame w/long curved back & seatrail flanked by round-fronted arms, bamboo rod framing, ca. 1940s-50s, w/upholstered cushion, 64" l. (ILLUS.)...... **$144**

Fine Louis XV-Style Caned Chaise Lounge

Rare Pair of Early French Art Deco Chaises Lounge

Chaises lounge, Art Deco, giltwood, one end w/a high outswept narrow upholstered back w/a bolster above the long narrow rectangular seat ending in a low outswept upholstered end, flat molded seatrail raised on four reeded & turned tapering legs, from L'Atelier d'Art du Printemps, Paris, France, ca. 1920, 65" l., 35 7/8" h., pr. (ILLUS., middle of page) **$38,240**

Louis XV-Style Upholstered Daybed

Daybed, Louis XV-Style, parcel-giltwood, each end w/an upright scrolling crestrail continuing to scrolling stiles & upholstered sides above a scalloped floral and molded apron continuing to cabriole legs w/scrolling toes, the scalloped siderails also upholstered in a rose & white floral & ribbon velvet fabric, France, late 19th c., 36 x 75", 36" h. (ILLUS.) **$633**

Daybed, Louis XVI style, painted beechwood, the matching head- and footboard w/square molded framing & turned finials enclosing upholstery panels, a long cushion seat above a long molded seatrail, tapering turned & fluted legs, old white paint, first half 19th c., 64 1/2" l., 35 1/2" h. (ILLUS., top next page) **$3,105**

Daybed, Louis XVI-Style, carved mahogany, the gently arched long back w/a narrow molded & floral-carved crestrail above the paneled & caned back, the high arched & caned end arms w/tapering leaf-carved outswept arm supports above the long deep cushion seat, straight molded seatrail centered by a carved floral reserve, carved rounded corner blocks raised on turned & tapering front feet, France, late 19th c., 31 x 81 1/2", 43" h. (ILLUS., middle next page) **$3,220**

Painted Beechwood Louis XVI Daybed

Mahogany & Cane Louis XVI-Style Daybed

Fine Louis XVI-Style Painted Daybed

Daybed, Louis XVI-Style, painted wood, the matching low head- and footboards w/a molded arched crestrail above upholstered panels flanked by reeded columnar stiles w/top & base blocks & topped by acorn-carved finials, raised on turned & tapering carved feet, narrow siderails, old creamy paint, fitted w/mattress & bolsters, France, late 19th c., 39 x 78", 34" h. (ILLUS.).. **$6,325**

Louis XVI-Style Upholstered Beechwood Daybed

Daybed, Louis XVI-Style, upholstered beechwood, the matching head- and footboard w/an arched molded crestrail & sides enclosing upholstered panels, the flat seatrails centered by small carved panels, raised on short tapering fluted legs, France, late 19th c., 39 x 78", 38" h. (ILLUS.) **$1,610**

Duchesse brisée, Louis XV-Style, giltwood, composed of a wing-back armchair w/a rounded crest above the large cushion seat, the serpentine scroll-carved apron & cabriole legs in gilt, w/a matching large rectangular stool w/a large cushion, upholstered in fine claret damask, France, late 19th c., stool 20 1/2" h., chair 37" h., 2 pcs. (ILLUS.) **$2,185**

Fine Louis XV-Style Duchesse Brisée

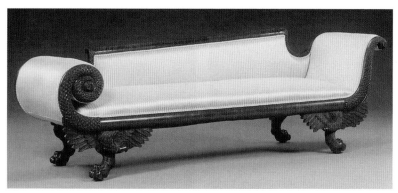

Fine American Classical Carved Mahogany Récamier

Récamier, Classical style, carved mahogany, the long narrow curved back crestrail over a tapering uphol-stered panels, one end of a high out-scrolled upholstered arms w/a diamond point-carved arm support w/scrolled tip & at the other end w//a large in-scrolled low arm w/a carved tightly scroll diamond point-carved supports, the long narrow rounded seatrail supported by large carved spread-winged eagles raised on out-swept carved paw feet, New York City, ca. 1820-30, 25 x 91", 30" h. (ILLUS.)................................. **$4,780**

Fine Quality Classical Philadelphia Récamier

Récamier, Classical style, carved mahogany, the long stepped serpentine backrail carved w/a foliate design & w/a C-scroll above the low upholstered back, one end w/a high S-scroll upholstered arm w/a bolster & a carved reeded & leaf-carved arm support continuing down to the long rounded flat seatrail terminating in a lower outswept S-scroll end arm, raised on ornately carved scrolling figural dolphin front legs, an upholstered cushion seat, possibly by Anthony Quervelle, Philadelphia, ca. 1820-30, 22 x 72", 31" h. (ILLUS.) **$4,183**

Récamier, Empire-Style, ormolu-mounted mahogany, the padded end back w/an outscrolled swan's-neck crest above the long padded seat, the foot slightly raised & scrolled back to carved swans' necks, raised on a griffin- and Bacchus-applied apron raised on winged sphinx legs ending in ormolu paw feet, France, late 19th c., 27 x 70", 36" h. (ILLUS.) **$2,970**

Fine Empire-Style French Récamier

Outstanding American Early Classical Decorated Récamier

Récamier, grain-painted, stenciled & gilded wood, the low upholstered half-back w/the long crestrail ending in a carved lion head & curving up to a gadroon-carved section joining the outward rolled high end back w/a cornucopia-carved front rail continuing into the low seatrail below the upholstered seat & curving up to the low upholstered foot w/a fan- and scroll-carved rail, raised on heavy leaf-carved & ring-turned tapering legs on casters, New York City, ca. 1826-30 (ILLUS.) **$11,950**

Fine English Regency Period Récamier

Louis XV-Style Giltwood Récamier

Récamier, Louis XV-Style, carved giltwood, one end w/a long arched serpentine scroll-carved crestrail tapering into two panels at the back & curving to form the end arms w/an in-scrolled arm support, long padded rectangular seat w/a serpentine front above the conforming seatrail carved w/delicate scrolls & raised on cabriole legs ending in scroll & peg feet, France, late 19th c., 24 x 53", 33" h. (ILLUS.).. **$1,035**

Récamier, Regency style, black lacquered wood, the shaped half-back & outscrolled end above the padded upholstered seat, the long seatrail w/other outswept low arm carved w/an arched palmette, the outswept reeded legs each headed by an ormolu mount & ending in brass caps on casters, England, early 19th c., 31" h. (ILLUS., top of page)... **$7,188**

Rare French Art Deco Macassar Ebony Settee

Settee, Art Deco, upholstered Macassar ebony, the long gently arched wooden crestrail above a tufted back flanked by rolled upholstered arms w/flat heavily grained front supports continuing into simple shaped front legs, the scalloped seatrail connected by four flat front legs, long cushion seat, made by Sue et Mare, France, ca. 1925, 27 x 75", 37 1/2" h. (ILLUS.) **$71,700**

Fine Majorelle Art Nouveau Settee

Settee, Art Nouveau style, mahogany marquetry, the simple narrow crestrail above a three-section back composed of narrow loop stiles alternating w/tapering serpentine splats decorated w/ornate leafy marquetry designs, shaped molded open arms above the long upholstered seat on a flat seatrail & square tapering legs joined by a high slender H-stretcher, designed by Louis Majorelle, France, ca. 1905, 19 x 42 1/2", 38" h. (ILLUS.) **$5,378**

Settee, Chippendale-Style, carved mahogany, the triple chair-back w/scrolling crestrails & pierced vasiform splats flanked by S-curved open arms w/carved bird-head grips, long over-upholstered seat raised on four front cabriole legs w/carved knees & ending in claw-and-ball feet, England, second half 19th c., arm joints slightly loose, 70 1/2" l., 38 3/4" h. (ILLUS., middle of page)........ **$2,185**

Attractive English Chippendale-Style Settee

Fancy Painted & Decorated Country-style Settee

Settee, country-style, painted & decorated pine, the double-back wide crestrail w/serpentine top raised on three wide vasiform splats alternating w/two turned spindles, serpentine open arms raised on a short spindle & canted turned arm support, the long plank seat raised on eight turned & canted legs joined by flat stretchers, original apple green paint w/black, bronze & green stenciled fruit & leafy scroll designs on the crestrail & further leaf designs & banded trim on the splats, spindles & stretchers, arms repaired, ca. 1830-40, 82" l., 36" h. (ILLUS.) **$771**

Finely Painted Early Pennsylvania Settee

Settee, country-style, painted & decorated, the long crest divided into three sections above three wide vasiform splats alternating w/two spindles, scrolled painted arms over two short spindles & a short turned arm support above the long scroll-fronted plank seat raised on four heavy ring-turned front legs joined by flat stretchers & four canted simple turned rear legs joined by flat stretchers, original light green painted w/free-hand decoration of light melon-colored flowers & green leaves accented w/gold & black on the crest, front seatrail & stretchers, mahogany-colored paint arms, Pennsylvania, ca. 1830-40, very minor surface imperfections, 21 3/4 x 77 1/2", 34 1/4" h. (ILLUS., top of page) **$3,408**

Settee, country-style, tiger stripe maple, a wide flat backboard w/rolled top joining the ends, each composed of a short ring-

Victorian Country-style Tiger Maple Settee

and rod-turned front & rear posts topped by a cannonball w/a heavy ring-turned rail joining the balls, the posts raised on blocks above the turned tapering legs w/knob- and peg-feet, round front & back rails pierced w/holes for looping rope, American, mid-19th c., nice alligator finish, 25 x 72 1/2" l., 26" h. (ILLUS.) **$288**

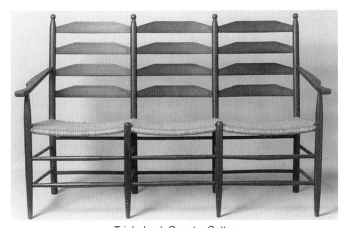

Triple-back Country Settee

Settee, country-style, triple-back, each back section composed of four arched slats between simple turned stiles w/small knob finials, shaped open arms on turned arm supports continuing down to form the front legs, three-section woven rush seat raised on the end legs & four turned inner legs, all joined by double simple-turned rungs, original dark brown wash, original seats, 19th c., 61 1/4" l., 38 1/2" h. (ILLUS.) **$1,380**

Settee, Elizabethan Revival style, carved rosewood, the long back crestrail composed of ornate pierce-carved scrolls above three large upholstered panels flanked by further scroll panels, all flanked by spiral-turned stiles w/ring-turned finials above corner blocks, the shaped open arms w/scrolled hand grips raised on incurved arm supports flanking the long over-upholstered seat w/a narrow seatrail ending in scroll-carved front cabriole legs w/scroll feet on casters, England, mid-19th c., 25 x 60", 47" h. (ILLUS.)
.... **$1,150**

Elizabethan Revival Rosewood Settee

Fine Federal New England Settee

Settee, Federal, carved mahogany, the long flat upholstered back flanked by fluted downswept rails above the closed upholstered arms w/baluster-turned reeded arm supports, cushion seat above a long slightly bowed seatrail raised on four ring-turned & reeded tapering front legs ending in turned tapering feet & four square canted rear legs, New England, 1800-20, 24 x 65", 34 1/2" h. (ILLUS.) **$14,400**

Nice Country Federal Decorated Settee

Settee, Federal country-style, painted & decorated poplar, the long two-section flat crestrail w/rounded corner sections above two lower rails over a row of short turned spindles, the downswept S-shaped open arms on turned spindles & flanking the long plank seat raised on eight turned & canted legs joined by box stretchers, old red & black graining w/the crest stenciled w/baskets of fruit, blue line trim, ca. 1840-50, 23 x 70", 34" h. (ILLUS.) **$633**

Settee, Federal-Style, carved mahogany, double-back style, two shield-shaped openwork panels joined by a pierced central panel, the shaped open arms on incurved arm supports above the over-upholstered bowed seat & seatrail, square tapering legs, minor nicks, late 19th - early 20th c., 44 1/2" l., 36 1/2" h. **$1,115**

Georgian-Style Double Chair-Back Settee

Settee, Georgian-Style, mahogany, a double chair-back with the shield-shaped sections each enclosing a pierced fanned splat & joined by a center scrolled & slatted splat, shaped open arms on incurved arm supports above the spring-upholstered seat, narrow molded seatrail on square tapering legs, minor nicks, England, late 19th - early 20th c., 44 1/2" l., 36 1/2" h. (ILLUS.) **$1,150**

Louis XVI-Style Giltwood Settee

Settee, Louis XVI-Style, giltwood, the long upholstered back w/a long concave giltwood crestrail carved w/a ribbon-wrapped wreath centered by a ribbon & crossed torches crest, downswept padded arm rails above the closed upholstered arms w/a leaf-carved hand grip above a turned & fluted front columnar arm supports, deep upholstered seat w/a gently bowed seatrail, tall slender fluted front legs, peg feet, France, mid-19th c., 47 1/2" l., 37" h. (ILLUS.) **$1,610**

Small Louis XVI-Style Walnut Settee

Settee. Louis XVI-Style, walnut, the long openwork rectangular back w/a leaf-carved frame enclosing three slats composed of four bars centered by three open ovals, narrow padded open arms over an upholstered seat covering the old caning, molded seatrail w/a thin beaded band flanked by rosette blocks above the turned tapering & fluted legs w/peg feet, old refinishing, small chips, Europe, late 19th c. (ILLUS.)............. **$575**

Fine Louis XV-Style Provincial Caned Beech Settee

Settee, Provincial Louis XV-Style, beech, the long rectangular caned back enclosed by an undulating serpentine frame w/a shell-carved center crest, serpentine open arms above the long caned seat above the narrow serpentine leaf-carved apron raised on six simple cabriole legs, France, late 19th c., 62" l., 38" h. (ILLUS.)...................................... **$3,450**

Fine English Queen Anne Revival Settee

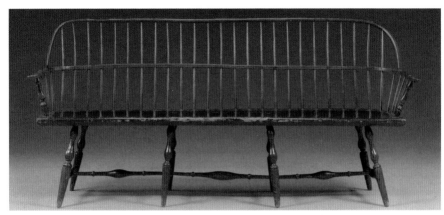

Very Rare Labeled Early Windsor "Sack-Back" Settee

Settee, Queen Anne Revival, mahogany, the high rectangular upholstered back flanked by scrolled upholstered arms & the over-upholstered seat, raised on three front cabriole legs ending in pad feet & joined by simple turned H-stretchers to the square canted rear legs, England, late 19th - early 20th c., 52" l., 41" h. (ILLUS., previous page) **$4,025**

Settee, Windsor "sack-back" style, the very long slender bowed crestrail above numerous slender turned spindles continuing down through the medial rail that curve to form the flat shaped arms on pairs of spindles & baluster- and ring-turned canted arm supports, the long plank seat raised on eight canted baluster- and ring-turned legs joined by three swelled H-stretchers, old finish, label of John DeWitt, New York City, 1797, 22 x 81", 37" h. (ILLUS., top of page) **$31,200**

cherries & gold leaves, the back composed of 12 slender spindles flanked by S-scroll end arms above spindles & a turned & swelled canted arm support, a long shaped plank seat raised on four canted bamboo-turned legs joined by turned side stretchers & a flat rear & front stretcher, the front one decorated w/gold leaves, arm restorations, one support split at the seat, mid-19th c., 15 x 46 1/2", 31 1/2" h. (ILLUS.) **$575**

Fine Windsor-Style "Bow-back" Settee

Settee, Windsor-Style "bow-back" type, mahogany, a long arched crestrail above numerous slender turned spindles continuing through a medial rail curving to form flat shaped arms supported on canted baluster- and ring-turned arm supports, woven rush seat, raised on canted baluster-, ring- and rod-turned legs joined by swelled H-stretcher, early 20th c. reproduction, 20 1/2 x 47", 39" h. (ILLUS.) **$1,093**

Old Painted & Stenciled Windsor Settee

Settee, Windsor style, painted & decorated, painted overall in old black paint, the long narrow rectangular crestrail stenciled w/bowls of fruit flanked by

Nice Early Windsor Settee

Settee, Windsor-style, the long wide flat crestrail above a two-section back composed of fifteen bamboo-turned spindles centered by a heavier turned stile, bamboo-turned open arms on three small spindles & a larger canted arm support, long plank seat raised on six canted bamboo-turned legs joined by box stretchers, nice old worn brown surface, some old repairs, first half 19th c., 44" l., 35 3/4" h. (ILLUS.).. **$2,588**

Painted Pine Paneled Fireside Settle

over traces of dark green, late 18th - early 19th c., wear & minor damage, 56" w., 44" h. (ILLUS.)......................... **$1,265**

One of Two Transitional Settees

Settees, Classical-Victorian transitional style, carved mahogany, a low arched upholstered back centered by a flat rail section fitted w/a pierced scroll-carved crest, the back rail tapering down & curving to form the low upholstered arms above the deep upholstered seat w/a wide serpentine seatrail centered by a large carved shell & continuing into demicabriole front legs w/carved shells at the knees, ca. 1830s-40s, only minor flaws, 43" l., 28 3/4" h., pr. (ILLUS. of one) **$1,840**

Settle, country-style, painted pine, the high back w/panels flanked by shaped open arms on baluster- and knob-turned arm supporting flanking the long lift-seat, a deep paneled apron, short square stile feet, dark brown repaint

Early Painted Pine Fireplace Settle

Settle, country-style, painted pine, the tall back w/arched top composed of wide horizontal board flanked by tall shallow one-board sides continuing down to low curved arms, long hinged seat opening to storage compartment, deep apron, brown repaint, age splits & old repairs, 19th c., 57" l., 60" h. (ILLUS.) **$1,610**

Settle, pine, the high rectangular back composed of four tall panels, shaped open end arms above the long plank seat w/a central removable section to a compartment, deep three-panel front apron, old dark finish, wear, insect damage to feet, England, 19th c., 17 x 54 1/4', 49 1/4" h. **$575**

Unusual Carved Hardwood Spanish Colonial Settle

Settle, Spanish Colonial, carved hardwood, a long scrolling foliate-carved crestrail centering religious cartouche flanked by stiles topped w/tall ring-turned finials, the lower back w/a shaped panel raised on pairs of knob-turned spindles, wide flat serpentine arms above floral-inlaid supports & legs flanking the long plank seat, the six-leg trestle-form base w/a flat floral-carved front stretcher, missing much mother-of-pearl inlay, round burn mark on right side of seat, 18th c., 26 x 81 7/8", 43 1/2" h. (ILLUS., top of page) **$6,325**

Sofa, Baroque-Style, carved oak, a very long & high arched crestrail decorated w/elaborate pierce-carved designs including a large central cartouche flanked by winged lings & scrolling, fruiting vines, all above a long upholstered panel, spiral-twist stiles & padded open arms above spiral-twist arm supports flanking the long over-upholstered seat, raised on eight block-, knob- and ring-turned legs w/knob feet & joined by spiral-twist stretchers, Europe, mid-19th c., old repairs, 72" l., 56" h. (ILLUS.) **$978**

Sofa, Chippendale camel-back style, mahogany, the long serpentine upholstered back flanked by outswept scrolled upholstered arms above the long upholstered seat, raised on eight square legs joined by box stretchers, late 18th c., 88" l. (ILLUS., bottom of page) **$5,019**

Carved Baroque-Style Sofa

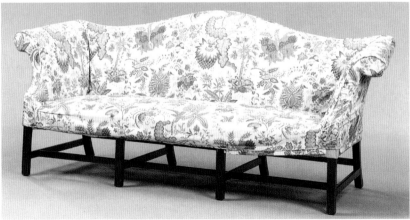

Chippendale Camel-back Style Sofa

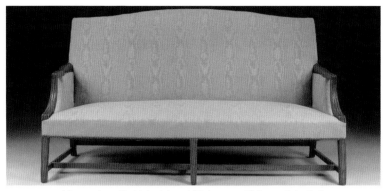

Massachusetts Upholstered Mahogany Chippendale Sofa

Sofa, Chippendale style, mahogany, the long, high upholstered back w/a gently arched crest above shaped arm rails above upholstered panels & w/incurved fluted arm supports, long upholstered seat raised on three square tapering front legs joined by flat stretchers & three square canted rear legs, Massachusetts, 1770-1780, 77 3/4" l., 42 3/4" h. (ILLUS.) **$3,840**

Hickory Chair Co. Chippendale-Style Camel-back Sofa

Sofa, Chippendale-Style, mahogany, the long upholstered camel-back ending in outscrolled upholstered arms above the long upholstered seat, on six square legs joined by flat box stretchers, by Hickory Chair Company, 20th c., some upholstery wear, 76" l. (ILLUS.) **$518**

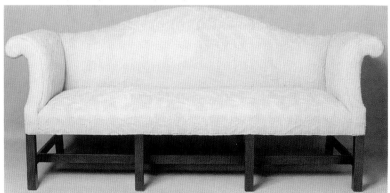

Kittinger Chippendale-Style Camel-back Sofa

Sofa, Chippendale-Style, mahogany, the long upholstered camel-back ending in outscrolled upholstered arms above the long upholstered seat, on eight square legs joined by flat box stretchers, by Kittinger, 20th c., some upholstery stains, 78" l. (ILLUS.) **$978**

Long Classical Country-style Sofa

Sofa Classical country-style, inlaid & veneered mahogany & bird's-eye maple, the wide & long flat round-fronted crestrail & short end stiles above the low upholstered back flanked by heavy low upholstered C-scroll arms flanking the seat w/a long upholstered cushion, the wide strait ogee seatrail raised on long heavy S-scroll legs, some veneer banding missing, attributed to Thomas Day (1801-61), 26 x 93", 30" h. (ILLUS.)
.... **$690**

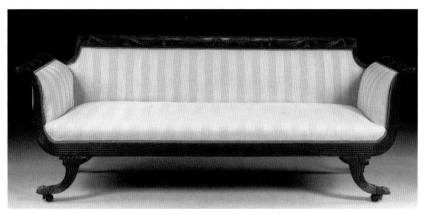

Classical Sofa Attributed to Duncan Phyfe Shop

Sofa, Classical " Grecian" style, carved mahogany, the long flat crestrail carved w/a repeating design swags & tassels w/a pair of addorsed cornucopia issuing grain above the low upholstered back flanked by outswept upholstered arms w/matching carved on the crestrailrails & continuing down into the long fluted seatrail raised on outswept fluted legs w/brass paw caps & raised on casters, attributed to the shop of Duncan Phyfe, New York City, ca. 1810-20, 88" l., 32 3/4"h. (ILLUS.) **$13,200**

Finely Carved New York Classical Sofa

Sofa, Classical style, carved mahogany, a long flat tubular crestrail ending in leaf-carved scrolls above the long, low upholstered back flanked by outward scrolled upholstered arms w/bolsters & a leaf-carved arm support ending in a cornucopia continuing into the flat seatrail, raised on fruit-filled carved cornucopias resting on large paw feet on casters, New York City, ca. 1825, 7' l., 31 1/2" h. (ILLUS.) **$4,600**

Simple Early American Classical Sofa

Sofa, Classical style, mahogany & mahogany veneer, the long serpentine crestrail centered by a slightly wider concave central section above the upholstered back, out-scrolled upholstered end arms w/leaf-carved front rails continuing into the long flat seatrail raised on wide rounded scroll-carved feet on casters, minor flaws, ca. 1830, 82" l. (ILLUS.).. **$717**

Fine American Classical Paw-footed Sofa

Sofa, Classical style, mahogany & mahogany veneer, the long serpentine crestrail centered by a wider concave central section w/carved rosettes above the upholstered back, out-scrolled upholstered end arms w/rosette-carved front rails continuing into the long flat seatrail raised on winged paw feet, minor flaws, ca. 1830, 80 1/2" l. (ILLUS.).. **$1,265**

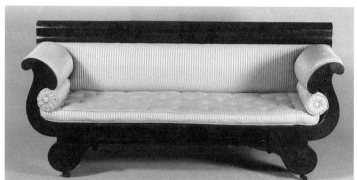

Early Simple Classical Mahogany Sofa

Sofa, Classical style, mahogany & mahogany veneer, the long wide flat-topped ogee crestrail above the long upholstered back flanked by inward-scrolled upholstered arms w/a flat S-scroll support curving down to the long flat seatrail raised on simple heavy scroll-carved front feet on casters, minor veneer wear, ca. 1830, 74 1/2" l. (ILLUS.).. **$575**

Late Victorian Classical-Style Mahogany Sofa

Sofa, Classical-Style, carved mahogany, the long rod-form crestrail w/leaf-carved inward-scrolled ends above a flat rail raised on serpentine ends above the deep out-scrolled upholstered arms w/carved swan's-neck arm supports, the long ogee-molded seatrail w/blocked ends raised on large wings & outswept carved paw feet, old black horsehair upholstery, late 19th c., 64 1/2" l., 35 1/2" h. (ILLUS.)................................ **$2,530**

Classical-Victorian Rococo Transitional Sofa

Sofa, Classical-Victorian Rococo transitional style, mahogany, the long serpentine & arched crestrail centered by a flower- and scroll-carved crest, crestrail curves forward over the deep rolled upholstered arms w/leaf-carved arm supports, long deep serpentine seatrail further carved w/scrolled leaves, raised on leafy scroll-carved front feet on casters, ca. 1840-50, 75 1/2" l., 33" h. (ILLUS.).. **$805**

Fine English Edwardian Brown Leather Sofa

Sofa, Edwardian style, the long back upholstered in brown leather & flanked by outswept leather-upholstered arms above the two-cushion leather-upholstered seat & seatrail w/brass tack trim, short bulbous turned mahogany legs on brass casters, England, early 20th c., 33 1/2" h. (ILLUS.).................................. **$3,450**

New York Inlaid Mahogany Federal Sofa

Sofa, Federal style, inlaid mahogany, the narrow crestrail centered by a low long raised & fluted panel above the upholstered back flanked by stepped & curved reeded arm rails on the closed upholstered arms, long over-upholstered seat, raised on four square tapering front legs w/inlaid bellflower drops & banded ankles on casters, canted square rear legs on casters, New York City, 1790-1810, 75" l., 37 1/2" h. (ILLUS.)
.... **$4,200**

Nice Quality Federal-Style Mahogany Sofa

Sofa, Federal-Style, mahogany & mahogany veneer, the long flat crestrail inlaid w/a light wood band above the upholstered back flanked by downswept upholstered arms w/scrolled hand grips raised on reeded baluster-turned arm supports, a long cushion seat above the flat seatrail w/a light wood band of inlay, raised on four turned, reeded & tapering front legs on ball & peg feet, square canted rear legs, minor veneer damage, 20th c., 66 5/8" l., 32 1/4" h. (ILLUS.).. **$978**

Fine Pair of French Louis-Phillippe-Style Sofas

Fine Regency-Style Mahogany Sofa

Sofa, Louis-Phillipe-Style, ormolu-mounted mahogany, a long gently arched ormolu crestrail centered by a putto flanked by a wave design above a lower wooden rail mounted w/a small ormolu rosette planked by long leaf bands, the high upholstered back flanked by down-swept upholstered arms w/carved hand grips, a long cushion seat above a narrow seatrail mounted w/ormolu rosette & leaf mounts matching the crestrail, on eight square tapering & slightly canted legs, France, late 19th - early 20th c., 68" w., pr. (ILLUS., bottom previous page) **$6,573**

Sofa, Regency-Style, mahogany, the long narrow crestrail above the upholstered back flanked by high upholstered arms w/baluster- and ring-turned reeded front posts, a long cushion seat on an upholstered seatrail, four baluster-turned reeded front legs ending in peg feet, England, early 20th c., 29 x 76", 31" h. (ILLUS., top of page) **$1,495**

Fine French Renaissance-Style Sofa

Sofa, Renaissance-Style, carved oak, the long back w/a very high & ornately pierce-carved crestrail composed of fruit & flowers w/a center oval medallion flanked by griffins, the back frame further carved along the sides & bottom & enclosing a tufted brown leather panel, the back flanked by spiral-turned open stiles w/small turned finials, the padded open

arms raised on short spiral-turned supports flanking the long leather seat raised on eight block-carved legs joined by spiral-carved stretchers, France, late 19th c. (ILLUS.) **$1,380**

Unusual Victorian Renaissance Revival Sofa

Sofa, Victorian Renaissance Revival style, walnut & burl walnut, the long narrow stepped crestrail centered by a high pointed & pierce-carved crest & trimmed w/narrow burl panels & roundels all above the wide upholstered back flanked by large round bolster-style upholstered arms w/round fancy pierce-carved front supports on narrow blocks above the flat molded & burl-inlaid seatrail w/a narrow arched center drop panel, heavy disk- and knob-turned legs, seat fitted w/a long cushion & added pillows, ca. 1875, 75" l., 48 3/4" h. (ILLUS.) **$805**

Small Renaissance Revival Walnut Sofa

Nice Serpetine-backed Victorian Rococo Sofa

Sofa, Victorian Renaissance Revival sub-style, walnut & burl walnut, a double-back style, the double arched & burl-paneled crestrail centered by a tall pointed burl panel cartouche, the two upholstered back panels separated by an openwork shaped flat bar, outswept low upholstered arms w/incurved front rails flanking the upholstered seat w/a gently curved seatrail centered by a burl panel over a low arched drop, ring-turned tapering front legs & canted square rear legs, ca. 1875, 55" l., 41" h. (ILLUS., previous page) **$316**

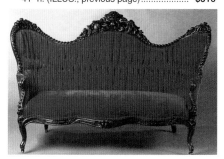

Carved Rosewood Rococo Sofa

Sofa, Victorian Rococo substyle, carved rosewood, the serpentine back w/a long high arched & pierce-carved crest decorated w/a basket of flowers above a cluster of fruit, the rail continuing to arched ends w/carved crests continuing down to the low upholstered arms w/in-scrolled carved arm supports above the long serpentine seat w/a conforming thumbmolded & floral-carved seatrail, demi-cabriole front legs on casters & canted square rear legs, New York City, ca. 1855, 29 x 67", 41" h. (ILLUS.) **$1,610**

Sofa, Victorian Rococo substyle, carved rosewood, the serpentine triple-back mounted w/three high arched floral-carved crests above the long tufted upholstery back, the side rails curving down to low upholstered arms w/ornate scroll-carved arm supports, the long serpentine seatrail ornately carved w/scrolls & floral vines, raised on three heavy carved demi-cabriole front legs

w/scroll feet raised on casters, heavy turned & tapering rear legs on casters, ca. 1860, 30 x 88", 42" h. (ILLUS., top of page) **$1,265**

Triple-back Victorian Rococo Sofa

Sofa, Victorian Rococo substyle, carved rosewood, three-part back, the central shield-shaped panel w/a high arched & ornate scroll-carved crest & tufted upholstered panel flanked by curved upholstered side panels w/wide scroll-carved crestrail curving down the low upholstered arms w/incurved scroll-carved arm supports, the long upholstered seat w/a double-serpentine seatrail w/two carved floral & scroll panels, demi-cabriole front legs w/ornately carved knees, raised on four casters, original cut-plush upholstery, ca. 1860, 28 x 68", 43" h. (ILLUS.) **$1,380**

Victorian Rococo Medallion Back Sofa

Fine Victorian Rococo Triple-Back Mahogany Sofa

Sofa, Victorian Rococo substyle medallion-back design, the back centered by a large oval medallion w/a scroll-carved frame enclosing a tufted upholstery panel flanked by molded & curved crestrails curving down over tufted upholstered arms w/incurved arm supports, the long seat on a serpentine seatrail, demi-cabriole front legs on casters, ca. 1870, 70" l. (ILLUS., previous page) **$460**

Sofa, Victorian Rococo substyle, triple-back design, carved mahogany, the long crestrail w/a long arched center crest pierce-carved w/fancy scrolls & a floral-carved crest, the rail continuing to high arched balloon-form end sections w/matching ornately scroll & flower-carved crests, the rail continuing down to the low upholstered arms w/incurved front supports flanking the long upholstered seat w/a double-serpentine scroll- and leaf-carved seatrail raised on three demi-cabriole front legs on casters, New York City, ca. 1855, 87" l. (ILLUS., top of page) **$3,680**

Simple Victorian Rococo Walnut Sofa

Sofa, Victorian Rococo substyle, walnut, the arched & molded crestrail curving down & around the tufted upholstered back & arms, the long seat w/a simple molded serpentine seatrail raised on demi-cabriole front legs, ca. 1870, 64" l. (ILLUS.) **$300-400**

Victorian Rococo-Style Sofa

Sofa, Victorian Rococo-Style, carved walnut, medallion-back style w/the large central oval tufted upholstery panel topped by a floral-carved crest, the molded & arched side crestrail curving around & down over the tufted upholstered back & long outswept upholstered arms w/scroll-carved arm supports, simple serpentine seatrail continuing into the demi-cabriole front legs, mid-20th c. (ILLUS.) ... **$518**

Fine Country-Style Wagon Seat

Wagon seat, country-style, double-chair design, the two chair backs each w/two arched slats joined to the three ring-turned stiles w/turned ovoid finials, simple turned open arms w/mushroom grips above ring-turned legs & short center legs all joined by double turned stretchers, original woven reed seat w/old red paint, wood w/a reddish brown color & patina, 19th c., 37" l., 32" h. (ILLUS., previous page)... **$2,000+**

Mirrors

English Adams-Style Wall Mirror

Adams-Style wall mirror, carved giltwood, the large oval molded frame w/narrow egg-and-dart rim band topped by a tall carved urn & plume finial flanked by long delicate leafy scrolls continuing down the sides to floral-carved swags, the bottom decorated w/carved fabric swags centered by a leaf- and disk-carved pendant drop, England, early 20th c., restored split in crest, 23 1/2" w., 42" h. (ILLUS.).... **$460**

Baroque-Style pier mirror & console, giltwood, the tall rectangular beveled mirror w/a narrow giltwood border & outer narrow mirror border w/starcut bands, the cushion frame decorated w/bead molding & laurel chains, the high arched ornate crest displaying a classical female mask framed by a cartouche held by griffins, the matching console table w/a marble top above a frieze decorated w/matching decoration, the legs joined by stretchers surmounted by an urn-form finial, France, late 19th c., 47" w., overall 115" h., the set (ILLUS., top next column)
.... **$10,925**

Ornate Baroque-Style Mirror & Console

Flemish Baroque-Style Wall Mirror

Baroque-Style wall mirror, répoussé & tortoiseshell-mounted ebonized wood, the rectangular beveled mirror within a wide frame composed of bands of foliate gilt, tortoiseshell & ebonized wood all surmounted by a scrolling berried foliate crest, Flanders, late 19th c., 24 x 37" (ILLUS.) **$1,410**

Belle Epoque Figural Walnut Mirror

Belle Epoque wall mirror, walnut, the oval mirror within bead & foliate banding & floral swag surmounted by a figural putto above a fringed drapery, the drapery continuing to enfold a lower putto above a floral garland, Europe, late 19th c., 37 x 55" (ILLUS.).................................... **$7,050**

Fancy Black Forest Carved Dressing Mirror

Black Forest style dressing mirror, carved walnut, the oval beveled mirror within an ornate pierced-carved frame composed of oak branches w/acorns & leaves, raised on crossed-branch front legs, one small back chip to mirror, Germany, late 19th c., 11 1/2 x 17 1/2" (ILLUS.) **$1,150**

Chippendale Rococo wall mirror, carved giltwood, in the Chinese taste, the tall rectangular mirror enclosed by a very ornate pierce-carved frame, the wide serpentine crestrail w/carved & pierced wide scrolls centering an openwork pagoda, the crest continuing down into the scrolling openwork sides w/narrow reed-

Chinese Chippendale English Mirror

ed pilasters, the serpentine bottom rail w/further pierced leafy scrolls & a central scrolled panels, in the manner of Thomas Johnson (1714-78), England, late 18th c., 32" w., 56" h. (ILLUS.) **$2,070**

Fine Gilt-Trimmed Chippendale Mirror

Chippendale wall mirror, carved mahogany & parcel-gilt, the high arched & finely scroll-cut crest decorated w/a raised gilt shell above gilt leafy vines, the scroll-carved base drop also trimmed w/gilt leafy vines, tall rectangular mirror w/rounded top corners, American or English, 18th c., 41 1/2" h. (ILLUS.) **$3,840**

Very Fine Gilded Chippendale Mirror

Chippendale wall mirror, inlaid & parcel-gilt mahogany, the high broken-scroll crest trimmed w/gilt, the scrolls ending in large florettes centering a large gilt urn finial issuing delicate leaf & flower vines, the long molded rectangular frame trimmed w/gilt & flanked at the top by pierced gilt flower & leaf pendant swags, a wide arched & finely scroll-cut base drop, probably New York city, 1780-1810, 22 1/4 x 52 1/4" (ILLUS.).............. **$4,800**

Chippendale Mahogany Wall Mirror

mounted w/a giltwood spread-winged phoenix, a narrow molded rectangular frame w/gilt liner enclosing the rectangular mirror, scroll-carved arched bottom crest, American or English, late 18th c., 29" h. (ILLUS.) **$1,673**

Smaller Chippendale Wall Mirror

Chippendale wall mirror, mahogany, the high arched crest flanked by carved scrolls above the rectangular molding enclosing the tall mirror, America or England, 18th c., 17 3/4" h. (ILLUS.) **$1,200**

Chippendale wall mirror, parcel-gilt mahogany, the high arched & pierced scroll-cut crestrail centered by an open circle

Very Fine Chippendale Wall Mirror

Chippendale wall mirror, parcel-gilt mahogany, the high broken scroll swan's neck pediment terminating in applied rosettes & centered by a large spread-winged eagle above a stepped frame w/gilded & molded edge & tendrils, leading to a rounded serpentine bottom edge, all centering a large rectangular mirror, American or English, 1760-80, 25 1/4" w., 51 1/4" h. (ILLUS.) **$5,378**

Fine Chinese Chippendale-Style Mirror

Chippendale-Style overmantel mirror, carved mahogany in the Chinese taste, the long, high serpentine crestrail composed of a large central pierce-carved pagoda flanked by pierced latticework panels topped by scrolls all above the three-part mirror plate w/narrow vertical side panels flanked by stiles carved w/entwining leafy berry vines, the arched base rail also pierce-carved w/long leafy scrolls, England, ca. 1900, 57" w., 76" h. (ILLUS.).. **$3,450**

Large Chippendale-Style Wall Mirror

Chippendale-Style wall mirror, giltwood & mahogany, the high broken-scroll pediment w/a gilt floral border centered by a large spread-winged eagle above narrow rectangular giltwood bands surrounding the tall rectangular mirror & flanked by long openwork bands of laurel leaves down the sides, the serpentine base w/scroll gilt floral bands & rosettes, refinished, restorations & touch-up to eagle & gilding, American, late 19th c., 24 1/4" w., 56 1/2" h. (ILLUS.) **$920**

Fine Chippendale-Style Wall Mirror

Chippendale-Style wall mirror, mahogany, the broken-scroll crest trimmed w/gilt gesso leafy branches & rosettes flanking a large spread-winged eagle crest, long gilt gesso openwork bellflower vines down the sides flanking the frame enclosing the rectangular mirror, scroll-cut bottom frame w/small gesso rosettes, restoration to gesso trim, late 19th - early 20th c., 24 x 45 3/4" (ILLUS.) **$805**

Charming Classical Country-style Mirror

Classical country-style wall mirror, painted & turned wood, the rectangular frame w/a long side rails composed of half-round ring- and rod-turned columns in gold & black, the two & bottom rails w/simple half-round posts in black & gold, the two section w/a rectangular reverse-painted glass pane w/a primitive homestead landscape w/a large two-story house flanked by trees along a road, each corner block w/a small brass rosette, all-original, ca. 1830-40, some paint flecking in landscape, 11 3/4 x 24 1/4" (ILLUS., previous page) ... **$230**

Fine Classical Girandole Wall Mirror

Classical girandole wall mirror, giltwood, a wide round concave frame set w/spheres around the convex mirror, the top mounted w/a large spread-winged eagle & leafy scrolls, a pointed leaf-carved base drop, probably American, 1820-30, 29" h. (ILLUS.) **$3,120**

Eagle-topped American Classical Mirror

Classical overmantel mirror, carved giltwood, a large, wide molded shadowbox frame topped by a large model of a spread-winged American eagle perched on an American shield & flanked by leafy branches & ribbon bands, ca. 1840-60, 54 3/4" w., 74" h. (ILLUS.) **$7,820**

Classical Giltwood Overmantel Mirror with Half-round Columns

Classical overmantel mirror, giltwood & gesso, the long flat narrow cornice w/blocked ends above a frieze band w/florette-decorated corner blocks flanking a bold ring-turned half-round column accented w/bands of delicate floral sprigs, matching shorter half-round side columns resting on plain corner blocks joined by a narrow acanthus leaf-decorated border, three-part mirror, ca. 1825-35, 63" l., 24 3/4" h. (ILLUS.) **$1,880**

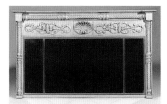

*Fine American Classical Giltwood
Overmantel Mirror*

Classical overmantel mirror, giltwood, the long low flaring crestrail w/blocked ends above corner blocks joined by a three-section spiral-turned columnar rail w/matching two-section columns down the sides, a wide upper frieze band decorated w/long panels of double leafy scrolls flanking a large central mirror all above the three-section mirror plate, a narrow flat bottom rail, ca. 1835, 64" l., 37 1/2" h. (ILLUS.) **$2,875**

*Fine Boston Classical Giltwood
Overmantel Mirror*

Classical overmantel mirror, giltwood, the long wide rectangular frame w/corner blocks decorated w/square florettes joined by half-round leaf tip-trimmed columns, the base resting on small peg feet, Boston, ca. 1825, 64" l, 40 1/2" h. (ILLUS.) **$8,338**

Fine Labeled New York Classical Overmantel Mirror

Classical overmantel mirror, giltwood, the three-section long mirror enclosed by a wide cove-molded frame w/ornate corners decorated w/pairs of cornucopias issuing fruit & leaves, old surface, fragmentary label on back for F. Cainmeyer, New York City, ca. 1825-35, imperfections, 52" l., 28" h. (ILLUS.) **$5,581**

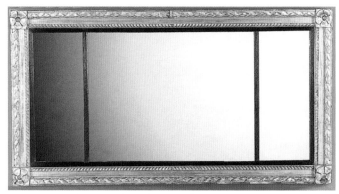

Nice American Classical Overmantel Mirror

Classical overmantel mirror, giltwood, the wide rectangular frame w/a rosette block at each corner joined by sides decorated w/a narrow outer ribbon-and-leaf band & an inner thin gadrooned band enclosing the three-part mirror, ca. 1820, 60" l., 31 1/2" h. (ILLUS.) **$2,300**

Classical pier mirror, gilt gesso & wood, the flat molded & blocked cornice above a row of applied spherules over a two-part mirror plate, the upper section flanked by panels of molded acanthus leaves, flowers & scrolls, the lower sides decorated w/half-round slender reeded columns w/turned capitals & bases, bottom corner blocks molded w/a Grecian mask & joined by a rail decorated w/long leafy sprigs centered by another mask, ca. 1815-20, imperfection & losses, 38" w., 66" h. **$1,880**

Classical Revival Cheval Mirror

Classical Revival cheval mirror, mahogany, a very tall oval beveled mirror within a narrow rounded frame w/a carved crest swiveling between U-form uprights raised on four outswept cabriole legs ending in scroll feet on casters, ca. 1900, 28" w., 5' 10" h. (ILLUS.) **$558**

American Classical Convex Wall Mirror

Classical wall mirror, carved gilded wood, a carved spread-winged eagle perched on scrolls above a round molded frame

w/an inner band of small gilt spherules, convex mirror plate, american, first half 19th c., 27" d. (ILLUS.) **$5,019**

Nice Carved Mahogany Classical Mirror

Classical wall mirror, carved mahogany, the flat-topped stepped narrow cornice w/blocked corners above central panel flanked by lyre-carved blocks above the sides carved w/a long acanthus leaf above a spiral-carved split baluster flanking the mirror plate, the molded & blocked base w/side blocks decorated w/ormolu rosettes flanking a narrow panel decorated w/a thin ormolu leaf mount, one carved lyre w/some damage, probably American, ca. 1815-30, 24 1/2" w., 47 1/2" h. (ILLUS.) **$345**

Rare Round Classical Mirror

Classical wall mirror, ebonized giltwood, a wide round concave frame mounted w/a band of small spheres, the top crest composed of two entwined dolphins & a trident flanked by large leafy clusters of seaweed, the base decoration w/clusters of shorter leaves, ebonized liner, encloses a convex mirror, early 19th c., 53" h. (ILLUS.) **$19,210**

Classical Mirror with Inscribed Banner

Classical wall mirror, giltwood & gesso, the flat pediment w/a flaring cornice & large blocked ends above a wide frieze band w/central leaf cluster flanked by side blocks w/rosettes above an upper reverse-painted glass panel w/a scene of a red-coated Colonial era soldier w/a town & other soldiers in the background as well as a blue banner printed w/"A. Doolittle. N.H. 1788," above the tall rectangular mirror all flanked by half-round ring-turned & fan-carved pilasters ending in bottom corner blocks joined by a smaller ring-turned half-column at the bottom, attributed to Amos Doolittle, ca. 1830, reverse-painting badly flaked, small corner missing & mirror corner cracked, 25 3/4" w., 44 1/2" h. (ILLUS.) **$1,208**

New York City Classical Wall Mirror

Classical wall mirror, giltwood, the flat narrow blocked crest above a conforming frieze band decorated w/molded florettes

& a central shell above tall half-round columns divided into three swelled sections w/the top & bottom section molded w/a long florette & the central section w/a ropetwist design, bottom corner blocks w/florettes joined by half-round double-baluster rail, the tall rectangular mirror plate below a smaller rectangular pane reverse-painted w/a gilt spread-winged American eagle above a shield & crossed flags against a white ground, New York City, 1815-25, plates probably replaced, 28 3/4 x 50" (ILLUS.) **$840**

Classical Wall Mirror with Upper Scene

Classical wall mirror, giltwood, the rectangular frame bordered by half-round ring- and rod-turned columns in gold & black w/florette corner blocks, the upper portion decorated w/a reverse-painted panel showing a mother & child on a recamier w/drapery in the background surrounded by repainted flower & leaf borders, the rectangular mirror plate below, ca. 1830, minor wear, 18 3/4 x 39 3/4" (ILLUS.)....... **$546**

Classical Giltwood Wall Mirror

Classical wall mirror, giltwood, the rectangular frame decorated on each side w/half-round ring-turned & reeded columns w/fleur-de-lis devices at each corner, a small rectangular mirror upper section & a long rectangular mirror lower section, first quarter 19th c., some wear & nicks, 28 x 53" (ILLUS., previous page) .. **$1,150**

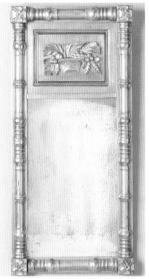

Classical Giltwood Wall Mirror

Classical wall mirror, giltwood, the tall rectangular frame w/florette corner blocks joined by half-round ring- and knob-turned columns, a large rectangular upper panel w/a raised panel enclosed a basket of fruit & leaves in bold relief, mirror streaked & flaking, minor edge flakes, some wear to gilding, ca. 1825-35, 17 x 36 1/4" (ILLUS.)................................ **$345**

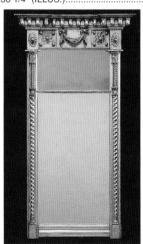

One of Two Rare American Classical Mirrors

Classical wall mirrors, giltwood, the flat flaring blocked pediment decorated w/a row of acorn-shaped drops above a frieze band decorated w/small panels w/a florette & four small balls flanking a central bow & swag design, the sides w/decorated top corner blocks above half-round ropetwist pilasters resting on plain bottom corner blocks joined by a plain molded bottom rail, fitted w/a tall two-part rectangular mirror, ca. 1810-20, 27 1/2" w., 50" h., pr. (ILLUS. of one) **$14,340**

Early Country Hanging Shaving Mirror

Country-style shaving mirror, hanging-type, mahogany, the narrow rectangular top fitted w/an arched back crest w/a hanging hole above a rectangular beaded panel framing the old mirror, projecting shaped lower sides flanking a small shelf over an open compartment, varnish mottling, early 19th c., 7 3/4 x 11 1/8", 22 1/2" h. (ILLUS.) **$764**

Fine Federal Era Girandole Mirror

Federal girandole wall mirror, giltwood, a round deeply molded frame enclosing a ring of gilt balls around the convex mirror, the top centered by a large spread-winged carved gilt eagle looking to the right & flanked by large arched ornate open scrolls, the bottom w/a narrow pleated ribbon band & center drop, England or America, early 19th c., section of gesso missing at bottom, 26 1/2" w., 38" h. (ILLUS., previous page)............... **$2,070**

Small Federal Mahogany Wall Mirror

Tall Federal Pier Mirror and Stand

Federal pier mirror & stand, inlaid & decorated mahogany, the flaring flat & blocked crestrail above a frieze band of gilt leaf stocks above a wide panel w/small rosettes above a black arched panel decorated w/a gilt spread-winged eagle & shield, the long rectangular mirror framed by bands of mahogany veneer outlined in gilt & wide rosette corner blocks, supported by a separate rectangular stand w/the front legs carved w/animal feet, early 19th c., crest w/some missing decoration, stand 30" x., 12 1/2" h., mirror, 28" w., 81" h., the set (ILLUS.)... **$1,208**

Federal wall mirror, carved mahogany, the flat flaring pediment w/blocked sides above a narrow rectangular reverse-painted glass panel decorated w/a primitive landscape w/two houses above the tall rectangular mirror plate, slender reeded pilasters down the sides above the blocked flaring bottom rail, ca. 1820, 18 1/2" w., 33 3/4" h. (ILLUS., top next column) **$374**

Attractive Federal Gilt Gesso Wall Mirror

Federal wall mirror, gilt gesso, the flat flaring crest w/blocked ends above a row of large spheres & a plain frieze over a reverse-painted upper tablet showing a sepia tone rural landscape w/cottage framed by a wide green band within a wide white band decorated w/a brown leafy vine, a long rectangular mirror below, all flanked by half-round spiral-carved columns w/acanthus leaf-carved capitals, blocked bottom corners & a plain rail, probably New England, ca. 1810-15, minor restoration, 17 1/2" w., 30 3/4" h. (ILLUS.) **$499**

Rare Federal Giltwood Wall Mirror

Federal wall mirror, giltwood, the flat covered crestrail w/blocked corners above a suspended row of spheres over a freize band centered by a rectangular panel decorated w/a drapery swag tied w/a bow flanked by panels of molded latticework, all flanked by corner blocks w/rosettes above a wide panel w/a raised Greek key design, the narrow sides molded w/slender reeded & vine-wrapped pilasters resting on small bottom corner blocks, Boston or New York City, ca. 1815-25, 36" w., 61" h. (ILLUS.)......................... **$10,638**

Federal Mirror with Églomisé Panel

Federal wall mirror, giltwood, the flat narrow projecting crest above projecting corner blocks over reeded side columns w/shaped capitals, flanking a top rectangular églomisé panel in black & gold on a white ground, the center w/a rectangular panel showing a woman holding a cornucopia w/raised hand toward a ship sailing away, flanked by delicate squares enclosing a circle around a feathered pinwheel, top & bottom thin leafy vine band above the rectangular mirror plate, molded base band w/projecting corner blocks, early writing on the back indicating a London, England origin, early 19th c., 18" w., 26 1/2" h. (ILLUS.) **$1,610**

Federal Mirror with Naval Battle Scene

Federal wall mirror, giltwood, the low flaring crestrail above a row of suspended spheres above corner blocks over slender beaded sides, narrow bottom corner blocks, the small rectangular upper panel reverse-painted w/a dramatic naval battle scene bordered by a worn salmon-colored band, probably Massachusetts, ca. 1820, some imperfections, 19" w., 32 1/2" h. (ILLUS.) **$1,293**

Fine Labeled Federal Wall Mirror

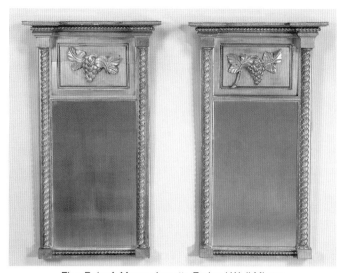

Fine Pair of Massachusetts Federal Wall Mirrors

Federal wall mirror, giltwood, the pedimented crest topped by an eagle w/outstretched wings on a rocky perch above a shaped acanthus leaf plinth above a shaped, molded & beaded frame containing a reverse-painted top tablet decorated w/gilt musical instruments flanked by two smaller tablets joined by a chain w/attached spheres, on a flat cornice molding w/applied spheres & mirror flanked by engaged pilasters w/leaf capitals, old surface, label of Hosea Dugliss, New York City, ca. 1815-20, imperfections (ILLUS., previous page)................ **$5,875**

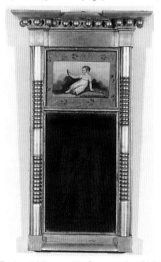

Federal Mirror with Scene of a Child

Federal wall mirror, giltwood, the wide flattened & blocked crestrail above a row of suspended spheres over a plain frieze band, the sides w/half-round ring-turned columns above plain corner blocks, the upper small rectangular panel reverse-painted w/a scene of a young child seated on the ground w/fruit & holding a mirror, long mirror below, ca. 1815, 20" w., 33" h. (ILLUS.) **$1,495**

Federal wall mirrors, giltwood & gesso, the narrow flat blocked cornice w/bands of floral devices above a horizontal spiral band & raised tablets w/a molded grapevine & ropetwist border, spiral-twist side columns on square plinths, rectangular mirror, Massachusetts, ca. 1815-20, old surface, imperfections, 25 x 43", pr. (ILLUS., top of page)........ **$7,050**

Federal-Style Girandole Wall Mirror

Federal-Style girandole wall mirror, giltwood, the wide round concave frame trimmed w/a ring of spheres enclosing a convex round mirror, the crest mounted w/a large spread-winged eagle flanked by arched leafy scrolls, the base w/a curved gadrooned & rayed drop, minor losses to gilt, eagle slightly loose, second half 19th c., 22 1/2" w., 36 1/2" h. (ILLUS.) **$1,495**

Nice Federal-Style Mahogany Mirror

Federal-Style wall mirror, mahogany & gilt gesso, a wide, high broken-scroll crest trimmed w/gilt gesso banding & rosettes centered by a squatty urn finial issuing arching wheat & flower stems, the top block corners w/suspending pierced gilt gesso leaf swags, the large rectangular mirror plate framed w/narrow gilt bands, a wide serpentine-carved bottom rail, restoration to urn, first half 20th c., 26 3/4" w., 55" h. (ILLUS.)........................ **$403**

English George III-Style Pier Mirror

George III-Style pier mirror, giltwood, Neoclassical style, a widely flaring stepped flat cornice w/blocked corners above a narrow band of buttons over a blocked frieze band carved w/a narrow raised rectangular block w/an open book motif flanked by leafy scrolls & wreathes, the molded flat leafy-vine decorated side pilasters decorated w/scroll-carved capitals & urn-shaped bases, the deep flaring plinth base decorated w/a bold scroll band, England, late 19th - early 20th c., 43" w., 55" h. (ILLUS.) **$633**

Nice Victorian Oak Cheval Mirror

Late Victorian cheval mirror, oak, the central upright framework w/an arched & scroll-carved crestrail above the central long swiveling beveled mirror flanked by matching swing-out mirrors, raised on an arched trestle base w/an arched & carved panel cross stretcher, decal label of the Bele Heckey Mfg. Co. Store Outfitters, St. Louis, Missouri, original finish, one finial missing, late 19th c., open 73" w., 6' 7" h. (ILLUS.)......................... **$1,035**

Late Victorian Long Oval Wall Mirror

Late Victorian wall mirror, gilt plaster, long narrow oval frame molded w/a continuous band of laurel leaves & berries, ca. 1900, 30 x 50" (ILLUS.) **$403**

Louis XVI-Style Overmantel Mirror

Louis XVI-Style overmantel mirror, carved giltwood, the tall molded rectangular frame w/rounded top corners centered by a large leafy scroll-carved crest w/two putti flanking a small oval mirror, France, late 19th c., 33" w., 5 6 1/2" h. (ILLUS.).. **$1,840**

Louis XVI-Style Trumeau Mirror

Louis XVI-Style trumeau mirror, painted & decorated, a large rectangular wall panel

w/a gilt flat molded crestrail above a cream-painted ground decorated in the tall narrow side panels w/raised & gilded classical motifs such as ribbons, wreaths & swags, the large upper rectangular panel h.p. w/a colorful romantic scene of three people in 18th c. costume having a picnic in a woodland setting, a shorter, wide mirror panel below, France, ca. 1880, some small missing pieces, minor nicks, 59" w., 83" h. (ILLUS.) **$4,485**

Fine Louis XVI-Style Trumeau Mirror

Louis XVI-Style trumeau mirror, painted & decorated, a tall rectangular panel w/a wide gilt crestrail above a greenish-grey painted panel w/a molded gilt border & a fancy gilt floral swag above an oval reserve enclosing a color-painted romantic scene of a lovelorn damsel pleading w/Eros to assist her, a tall arched & gilded lower molding enclosing the tall mirror, France, late 19th c., 48" w., 84" h. (ILLUS.).. **$11,500**

Rare French Modern Style Wall Mirror

Early Italian Neoclassical Overmantel Mirror

Modern style wall mirror, giltwood 'talosel' style, in the form of an oval sunflower w/a reeded inner frame surrounded by oyster shell-type petals, marked "Line Vautrin France," ca. 1955, 8 1/4" h. (ILLUS., previous page).. **$8,963**

Tall Napoleon III Pier Mirror

Napoleon III pier mirror, giltwood, the tall arched mirror within a bead & ropetwist frame surmounted by an arched swan's-neck pediment over striated acanthus

leaves issuing scrolling foliate garlands, France, third quarter 19th c., 44" w., 8' 4" h. (ILLUS.).. **$881**

Neoclassical overmantel mirror, giltwood, the stepped rectangular plate within gilt ropetwist banding surmounted by an urn-form finial issuing scrolling acanthus leaves above a mask of a beauty flanked at the stepped sides by birds w/elaborately curled tails, Italy, late 18th c., 4' 5" l., 35" h. (ILLUS., top of page) **$3,819**

French First Empire-Style Trumeau Mirror

Neoclassical-Style trumeau mirror, painted & decorated, painted w/a green background, a narrow top panel decorated w/applied & white-painted classical motifs including a rosette & lacy leaves & palmettes above a narrow crestrail above narrow side pilasters w/white-painted tall leafy stems issuing from small urns, a wide upper panel w/raised & white-painted classical designs centered by a round wreath enclosing a Baccante mask above a bold oak leaf swagged garland, a small rectangular mirror in the lower section enclosed by narrow raised molding, France, ca. 1900, 50 x 72" (ILLUS.) **$2,300**

Chinese Carved Teak Dressing Mirror

Oriental dressing mirror, carved teak, table-top style, the oval mirror w/floral-carved frame topped by a figural bird & swiveling between square uprights w/pierce-carved brackets & flanked by openwork carved figural rampant lions, set on a rectangular platform w/gadrooned convex sides & a narrow drawer, resting on carved paw feet, China, late half 19th c., repairs, minor imperfections, 10 x 18 1/2", 26 1/2" h. (ILLUS.) **$999**

Queen Anne country-style wall mirror, painted pine, a wide arched & scalloped top above the ogee-molded frame, old black over red, old but not original backboards, some flaking on mirror silvering, 18th c., 11 1/2" w., 17 1/2" h. **$978**

Queen Anne wall mirror, mahogany, the high arched crest w/scroll-cut details above a shaped arched molding continuing around the sides & enclosing a two-part mirror plate, a flat molded bottom rail, England, first half 18th c., 12 1/2" w., 32" h. (ILLUS., top next column) **$956**

Early English Queen Anne Wall Mirror

Fine Early Queen Anne Wall Mirror

Queen Anne wall mirror, parcel-gilt walnut, the high arched gilded crest decorated w/fancy scrolls & a shell top crest all enclosing a cartouche-shaped urn-etched mirror, the arched borders below enclose a two-part etched & beveled mirror, some chips to gilding, England, 18th c., 25" w., 60" h. (ILLUS.) **$5,290**

European Rococo-Style Overmantel Mirror

Fine Early Queen Anne Wall Mirror

Queen Anne wall mirror, walnut & parcel gilt, the arched & scroll-carved crest above a molded frame w/an incised gilt gesso liner around the rectangular mirror, original condition, England or America, 18th c., minor imperfections, 9 3/4" w., 17 1/4" h. (ILLUS.) **$6,463**

Regency Bull's-eye Wall Mirror

Regency wall mirror, parcel-ebonized gilt-wood, the wide round concave frame carved & ebonized w/thirty-four upright acanthus leaves, the top w/a raised cap-stan mounted w/a large carved spread-winged eagle, the bottom w/a leaf-carved drop, fitted w/a round convex mirror plate, England, early 19th c., 26 3/4 x 40 1/2" (ILLUS.) **$1,150**

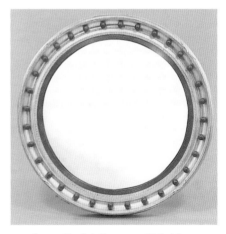

Large English Regency-Style Mirror

Regency-Style wall mirror, partially-ebon-ized carved giltwood, a wide concave-molded round frame mounted w/a ring of ebonized wooden spheres, a narrow inner ebonized molding w/reeding, En-gland, late 19th - early 20th c., 50" d. (ILLUS.) **$2,070**

Rococo-Style overmantel mirror, gilt-wood, a long horizontal rectangular mir-ror enclosed by a wide frame ornately pierce-carved w/large leafy scrolls cen-tering a shell on each side, Europe, late 19th c., 54" l., 42" h. (ILLUS., top of page).. **$1,150**

French Rococo-Style Pier Mirror

Rococo-Style pier mirror, giltwood, tall rectangular mirror in a deep shadowbox frame w/the raised serpentine sides molded w/ornate floral scrolls & shells, France, late 19th c., 39" w., 55" h. (ILLUS.) **$1,093**

Ornate Victorian Rococo-Style Mirror

Rococo-Style wall mirror, giltwood, the wide oval frame elaborately pierce-carved w/a two-headed eagle crest w/draped crossed flags, the sides composed of detailed oak leaf & laurel branches tied at the base w/ribbons, oval beveled mirror, signed w/the conjoined monogram "MP" & the date of 1896, central Europe, 34 1/2" w., 42 1/2" h. (ILLUS.)................................ **$4,370**

Fine Reproduction Rococo-Style Mirror

Rococo-Style wall mirror, giltwood, the high arched crest ornately pierce-carved w/scrolls & leafy vines topped by a spread-winged phoenix finial, the long rectangular frame composed of elaborate openwork scrolls w/a pierced shell at the center of the bottom rail, reproduction marked by the Carver's Guild of West Groton, Massachusetts, a few chips & restorations, 20th c., 32" w., 60" h. (ILLUS.).... **$431**

One of Two Rare Aesthetic Mirrors

Victorian Aesthetic Movement overmantel mirrors, giltwood, the long gently arched crestrail centered by a low pierced rectangular gallery above a low rectangular recessed panel molded w/ornate stylized blossoms, the narrow flaring beaded cornice above an narrow frieze panel decorated w/additional floral designs flanked by blocked top corners above the flattened reeded side pilasters resting on flower-decorated bottom corner blocks joined by a blocked molded & stepped bottom rail, original stenciled label on the back reads "L Uter Dealer in Looking Glasses - N. 17 Royal Street - New Orleans," late 19th c., 60 1/2" w., 79 1/2" h., pr. (ILLUS. of one)...................................... **$7,763**

English Renaissance Revival Mirror

Victorian Renaissance Revival substyle overmantel mirror, carved giltwood, the narrow molded crestrail w/blocked ends mounted in the center by an arched crest composed of floral swags enclosing a blue & white faux-Jasper ware medallion decorated w/a portrait of a Renaissance era lady, the sides composed of slender reeded pilasters above blocked & scroll-carved bottom corners joined by a thin bottom rail, England, late 19th c., 61" w., 71" h. (ILLUS.) **$1,610**

Ornate Rococo Giltwood Overmantel Mirror

Victorian Rococo substyle overmantel mirror, giltwood, the arched crest composed of very ornate entwined leafy scrolls above the molded arched frame enclosing the large mirror, the bottom corners w/further leafy scrolls, ca. 1855, 56" w., 7' h. (ILLUS.) **$6,900**

Fine Victorian Rococo Pier Mirror

Victorian Rococo substyle pier mirror, giltwood, the high arched & ornately scroll-pierced crest above tall molded sides flanked w/S-scrolls at the bottom corners, resting on a half-round serpentine-sided stand w/a conforming white marble top, some old repairs, legs on stand reduced, ca. 1860, 40" w., 104" h. (ILLUS.) **$1,495**

Very Fine Victorian Rococo Pier Mirror

Victorian Rococo substyle pier mirror, carved mahogany, the very high arched

& scroll-carved curved crest topped by a large scallop over a profile of a man & two lion heads & other scroll detail above the very tall arched mirror flanked by sides carved w/simple half-round columns & a leaf-carved central panels, the bottom w/scroll carving above the narrow projecting half-round serpentine shelf w/a pierced scroll-carved apron centered by a cartouche & raised on two short front cabriole legs, ca. 1850s, 12 x 32", overall 102" h. (ILLUS.) **$2,185**

Fine Labeled Rococo Pier Mirror

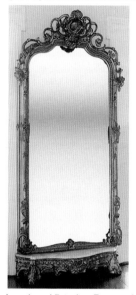

Fine American Victorian Rococo Mirror

Victorian Rococo substyle pier mirror, giltwood, the arched serpentine crestrail centered by a large shell-carved crest framed by large open scrolls continuing down around the top corners to the deep molded sides further decorated w/flowers & leafy scrolls ending in more large pierced corner scrolls at the bottom joining the lower frame rail, all resting on a narrow arched serpentine white marble shelf above a conforming deep apron ornately decorated w/a band of large beads & leafy scrolls, raised on large scroll feet, ca. 1850-60, 50" w., 122 1/2" h. (ILLUS.)...... **$6,900**

Victorian Rococo substyle pier mirror, giltwood, the tall scrolled pediment above a narrow rondel band over a large cabochon flanked by large scrolling corners over the tall rectangular mirror flanked by engaged columns decorated w/clusters of pendent flowers, the later base console w/a serpentine outlined marble top raised upon a conforming frieze on cabriole legs, label on the back for McClees Galleries, Philadelphia, mid-19th c., 33" w., 9' 5 1/2" h. (ILLUS., top next column) **$4,313**

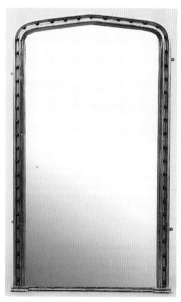

William IV English Overmantel Mirror

William IV overmantel mirror, gilt- and ebonized wood, a tall narrow gently arched concave giltwood frame enclosing fifty small ebonized spheres, England, ca. 1830, 49" w., 82" h. (ILLUS.) **$1,840**

Parlor Suites

Majorelle Art Nouveau Three-Pieced Parlor Suite

Settee from Rare Art Deco Parlor Suite

Art Deco: settee & two armchairs; upholstered giltwood, each w/an arched tufted upholstered back w/a narrow giltwood crestrail continuing down to form the low upholstered arms, deep cushion seat above a curved upholstered seatrail w/a giltwood band, on tapering reeded giltwood feet, designed by Maurice Dufrene, France, ca. 1927, settee, 52 1/2" l., 34 1/2" h., the set (ILLUS. of settee).... **$23,900**

Art Nouveau: settee & two armchairs; carved mahogany & marquetry, the settee w/a gently arched back panel within a molded frame decorated w/a detailed band of poppy-like flowers & stems above a row of numerous slender spindles, the fluted & downswept open arms on further spindles, the upholstered seat raised on slender moled & canted front & rear legs, each armchair w/a molded framework centered by a long wide splat also inlaid w/tall stems of flowers & cattails, downswept arms over spindles, upholstered seat & molded & canted legs, designed by Louis Majorelle, France, ca. 1900, signed, settee 44 1/4" l., chairs 42 1/2" h., the suite (ILLUS., top of page) **$8,963**

French Scrolling Art Nouveau Style Parlor Suite

Art Nouveau style: settee, armchair & side chair; carved giltwood, the settee w/a long serpentine crestrail centered by a pierced scroll-carved crest & w/fanned scroll round corners enclosing the upholstered back, open serpentine arms curving into the narrow serpentine scroll-carved seatrail enclosing the upholstered seat, long C-scroll outswept front legs on scroll & peg feet on casters, the chairs w/matching frames, some rubbing to gilt, fabric worn, France, ca. 1890s, settee 51 1/2" l., 37 1/2" h., 3 pcs. (ILLUS.) **$600**

Outstanding Empire Style Ormolu-mounted Mahogany Parlor Suite

Empire Style: sofa, two open-arm armchairs & two side chairs; ormolu-mounted mahogany, each piece w/a rolled crestrail flanked by molded stiles w/ormolu leaf mounts flanking the raised upholstered back panel, squared open arms w/large figural gilt sphinx armrests above the over-upholstered seats, the flat seatrails w/a slender ormolu leaf band mount w/corner rosettes above front legs formed by winged gilt griffins & ending in a gilt paw foot, square canted rear legs, France, late 19th c., sofa 63" l., the set (ILLUS.)
.... **$26,290**

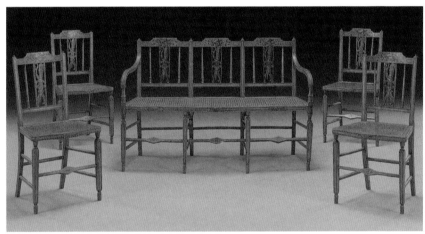

Rare Paint-Decorated Federal Parlor Suite

Federal style: settee & four side chairs; mustard yellow-painted & caned wood, the triple-back settee w/each section of the crestrail w/a raised panel hand-painted above a pierced & painted central splat flanked by slender turned spindles, serpentine opening arms on a turned arm support above the long caned seat raised on four square tapering decorated front legs joined by front stretchers centered by a diamond-shaped panel, square canted rear legs joined by simple stretchers, each side chair of matching design & decoration, stamped "L. Barnes," probably Portsmouth, New Hampshire or New York, 1805-15, settee 53" l., chairs, 34 1/4" h., the suite (ILLUS.) **$21,600**

Very Fine Louis XVI-Style Giltwood Parlor Suite

Chairs from a Louis XVI-Style Parlor Suite

Louis XVI-Style, four open-arm armchairs & eight chaises; Louix XVI-Style, painted wood, each w/an oval upholstered back within a white-painted frame above a pair of open padded arms over incurved arm supports, wide upholstered seat w/a serpentine front seatrail, raised on tapering round fluted legs ending in peg feet, mid-20th c., armchairs 37" h., chaises 35 1/2" l., the suite (ILLUS. of two armchairs)............... **$2,938**

Louis XVI-Style: settee, two armchairs & four side chairs; giltwood, the settee w/an arched crestrail carved w/courting doves & flowerheads above the long oval upholstered back & terminating in ram-headed padded arm supports, the upholstered seat w/gently bowed floral-carved seatrail, raised on fluted columnar legs, the matching chairs w/oval upholstered back panels above the matching seats & legs, France, late 19th c., settee 60" l., the suite (ILLUS., top of page) **$14,400**

Louis XVI-Style: settee, two armchairs & two side chairs; carved walnut, each w/the rectangular-framed upholstered back w/a narrow flat crestrail centered by a small pierced leafy wreath & w/leaf-carved stiles, the rounded over-upholstered seats w/a molded seatrail centered by a carved scroll drop, incurved molded cabriole front legs ending in scroll-and-peg feet, last quarter 19th c., the set **$1,116**

Louis XVI-Style: settee, two armchairs & two side chairs; giltwood, the settee w/a rectangular upholstered back within a beaded & ribbon-carved narrow frame w/ribbon crest raised above the long rectangular seat flanked by squared padded open arms, narrow beaded seatrail, round tapering stop-fluted legs, matching chairs w/square backs, France, late 19th c., settee 52" l., the set.. **$2,300**

Louis XVI-Style: settee & two armchairs; walnut, the settee w/a long oval upholstered back w/a narrow husk-carved frame raised above the long upholstered seat flanked by padded open arms, husk-carved seatrail raised on round tapering stop-fluted legs, matching armchairs w/oval backs, France, early 20th c., settee 51" l., the set **$1,035**

Louis XVI-Style: two open-arm armchairs & a settee; giltwood & tapestry upholstery, the settee w/a long oval back w/tapestry upholstery within a frame w/a ribbon- and bead-carved frame raised above the seat flanked by padded open arms, narrow carved apron raised on tapering cylindrical stop-fluted legs, matching armchairs oval backs, France, late 19th c., armchairs 36" h., settee, 4' 7 1/2" l., the set (ILLUS., top next page).......................... **$2,350**

Fine Louis XVI-Style Three-Piece Parlor Suite

Sofa and Chairs from Fine Louis XVI-Style Parlor Suite

Louis XVI-Style: two sofas, two open-arm armchairs & two side chairs; carved giltwood, the sofa w/a long narrow & gently arched crestrail centered by carved scrolls atop the rectangular frame enclosing a tapestry-upholstered back featuring scenes from "The Fables of Fontaine," padded open arms w/incurved & reeded arm supports above the tapestry-upholstered seat w/a narrow gently arched molded seatrail raised on four turned tapering & reeded front legs ending in knob-and-peg feet, the chairs of matching design, France, late 19th c., 6 pcs. (ILLUS. of one sofa and the chairs) **$6,613**

Marked Heywood-Wakefield Set

Rare Signed Pottier Stymus Victorian Parlor Suite

Modern style: two armchairs & a corner table; bent ashwood w/faux bamboo turnings, each w/a light framework enclosing a square back cushion & seat cushion & supported on a box stretcher base w/U-form front stretchers, the two-tier table w/an incurved upper shelf above the round-cornered top supported on faux bamboo legs joined by curved stretchers & a lower shelf, marked by Heywood-Wakefield, ca. 1955, the set (ILLUS., bottom previous page) **$316**

Victorian Renaissance Revival: sofa & armchair; ormolu-mounted ebonized wood, the sofa w/a raised central tufted back section w/a narrow arched crestrail centered by a carved shell crest all flanked by the lower curved upholstered back sections ending in closed arms w/gilt-bronze & metal putto busts & leaves flanking the long tufted upholstered seat on a gently curved seatrail w/gilt incised trim & a central drop, on tapering front legs ending in hoof-style feet, square canted rear legs all on casters, the matching armchair w/the crestrail centered by a round copper-plated panel flanked by a small recumbent gilt-bronze figural putto, worn original tufted upholstery, signed by Pottier Stymus, New York, New York, ca. 1875, sofa 70" l., 36 1/2" h., two pcs. (ILLUS., top of page) **$4,600**

Fine Renaissance Revival Sofa from Large Parlor Suite

Victorian Renaissance Revival: sofa, two armchairs & four side chairs; walnut & burl walnut, the triple-back sofa w/each upholstered shield-form back panel topped by an arched crestrail w/a carved palmette crest above pierced scroll brackets centering a large rondel, the large center panel w/a classical female face carved in the rondel, each back section separated by an ornately carved urn-form device, upholstered open arms w/the armrests carved as classical female busts, over-upholstered seat on a burl-paneled & line-incised serpentine seatrail w/three drops between the four bulbous turned & tapering front legs on casters, the chairs all w/matching backs & detailing, attributed to John Jelliff, Newark, New Jersey, ca. 1870, sofa 72" l., 46" h., the set (ILLUS. of the sofa) **$4,025**

Rare Victorian Renaissance Revival Parlor Suite

Victorian Renaissance Revival style: sofa & two side chairs; carved & gilt walnut, each piece w/a carved & stepped crestrail centered by a raised panel w/arched crest & enclosing an oval inset porcelain plaque h.p. w/scenes of courting couples & flowers, crestrail ending in leaf & pendant-carved corners above the carved narrow stiles, each piece w/a tufted upholstered back, the sofa w/padded open arms ending in carved sphinx heads above gilt-trimmed carved flutes, the gently curved front seatrails further decorated w/incised carving trimmed in gold, the sofa w/square tapering end legs w/carved paw feet & two knob- and columnar-carved inner legs, all raised on casters, the side chairs w/square tapering legs ending in paw feet on casters, New York City or New Jersey, ca. 1860-1875, sofa 68" l., chairs 38 1/2", the suite (ILLUS., top of page) **$14,400**

Nice French Victorian Renaissance Revival Parlor Suite

Victorian Renaissance Revival substyle: sofa, one armchair & four side chairs; ebonized beechwood, the sofa w/a long

narrow gently arched crestrail centered by carved crossed torches & a quiver tied w/a ribbon & bow, the raised back frame w/rounded lower corners framing the tufted upholstery back, open padded arms w/incurved arm supports above the long gently curved upholstered seat on a conforming three-section seatrail w/a small carved shell centering each, raised on disk-turned and fluted tapering legs, the chairs w/matching shield-shaped backs, France, ca. 1860-70, sofa 70" l., 43" h. (ILLUS. in two photos) **$1,840**

Victorian Rococo Stanton Hall Pattern Sofa & Armchairs

Victorian Rococo: sofa, a pair of armchairs & a pair of side chairs; pierced & carved laminated rosewood, each piece w/a high pierced & scroll-carved crestrail w/a central diamond-shaped scroll-carved medallion flanked by bead-carved rails continuing to curving pierce-carved scrolls

Victorian Rococo Parlor Suite Attributed to John Belter

curving down to the low upholstered or padded arms, incurved carved arm supports & deep over-upholstered seat, serpentine scroll-carved seatrails w/a central medallion, demi-cabriole front legs on casters, Stanton Hall patt. attributed to J. & J.W. Meeks, New York New York, settee 47 1/2" h., the set (ILLUS. of sofa & armchairs) **$16,655**

Victorian Rococo style: settee & armchair: carved rosewood, the settee w/a very ornate pierce-carved serpentine crestrail w/a hign arched central section enclosing floral carving flanked by serpentine pierce-carved sections continuing into rounded scrolled corners curving down around the upholstered back, curved padded open arms w/incurved molded arm supports, long upholstered seat w/serpentine floral & scroll-carved seatrail ending in floral-carved demi-cabriole front legs on casters, matching armchair w/high arched & pierce-carved crestrail, attributed to John H. Belter, New York City, ca. 1850-60, settee 64" l., chair 42 1/4" h., the set (ILLUS., top of page)... **$5,400**

Victorian Rococo style: sofa, two armchairs & four side chairs; carved mahogany, the triple-back sofa w/two large ver-

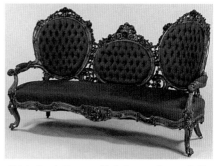

Triple-back Rococo Sofa from a Large Suite

tical oval tufted upholstery back panels flanking a matching horizontal oval panel, each panel w/an arched pierced & floral-carved crest w/scrolling pierce-carved panels between the panels, padded open arms on S-scroll arm supports above the long upholstered seat w/a serpentine seatrail w/undulating molding & a central floral-carved cluster, S-scrolled front legs ending in paw feet, square canted rear legs all on casters, ca. 1860, sofa 85" l., 4' 2" h., the set (ILLUS. of sofa) **$4,600**

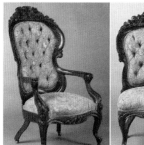

Fine Suite of Carved & Laminated Rosewood Victorian Rococo Chairs

Victorian Rococo substyle: armchair & three side chairs; carved & laminated rosewood, the armchair w/a high arched back w/an ornate flower- and fruit-carved crestrail continuing to scroll-carved waisted sides enclosing a tufted upholstery panel, the curved open arms on incurved molded arm supports above the wide upholstered seat w/a serpentine front above the conforming seatrail carved w/fruits & flowers, demi-cabriole front legs on casters & square canted rear legs on casters, the side chairs of matching design, attributed to John Henry Belter, New York City, ca. 1855, each 45" h., 4 pcs. (ILLUS.)...................................... **$8,625**

Fine & Rare Victorian Rococo Carved & Laminated Rosewood Parlor Suite

Victorian Rococo substyle: sofa, armchair & two side chairs; pierce-carved & laminated rosewood, the long sofa w/double high chair backs flanking a lower long arched central back section, the central section w/a high arched serpentine crestrail ornately pierce-carved w/scrolls & centered by large carved face w/a leaf-form tongue, the high arched chair backs w/higher matching serpentine carved crestrail also centered by carved faces, padded incurved arms on heavy pierced & scroll-carved sides, the long serpentine seat w/a scroll-carved serpentine seatrail centered by a carved face, on demi-cabriole front legs w/leaf-carved feet on casters, canted square reeded legs on casters, each chair w/a high arched back matching the sofa backs, attributed to Charles Boudoine, New York City, ca. 1855, sofa 82" l., 42 1/4" h., the set (ILLUS.)

.... **$29,900**

Sofa & Armchairs from Victorian Rococo Parlor Suite

Victorian Rococo substyle, triple-back sofa, pair of medallion-back armchairs & four medallion-back side chairs; walnut, each piece w/simple finger-molded back frames, padded open arms on incurved arm supports, armchairs & sofa w/a serpentine molded seatrail centered by a ribbed block, demi-cabriole front legs on casters, ca. 1860, sofa 61" l., the set (ILLUS. of sofa & armchairs)... **$2,530**

Wicker: love seat & armchair; each piece w/a wide tightly woven rolled crestrail curving down to form the outswept rolled arms over tightly woven sides, the upper back w/a padded brown leather panel over a tightly woven panel, leather-upholstered seats, deep tightly woven & gently arched aprons, original natural finish, both signed w/a Heywood-Wakefield plaque, early 20th c., love seat 25 x 41 1/2", 36 1/2" h., 2 pcs. (ILLUS.) **$1,380**

Nice Signed Heywood-Wakefield Wicker Set

Screens

Victorian Aesthetic Firescreen

Firescreen, Victorian Aesthetic Movement style, walnut, the wide crestrail w/a narrow central panel flanked by rows of short turned spindles & turned corner posts w/finials, raised on ring- and rod-turned side supports w/ebonized trim flanking a central square panel mounted w/a needlepoint & beaded canvas featuring a classical scene, raised on etched reeded side shoe feet, late 19th c., 32" w., 43" h. (ILLUS.).. **$403**

Late Victorian Tapestry Firescreen

Firescreen, late Victorian, the narrow oak frame w/a row of short turned spindles across the top above the large tapestry insert featuring a romantic couple in a garden setting, raised on short turned shoe feet, losses to tapestry, late 19th - early 20th c., 32" w., 34 1/2" h. (ILLUS.) **$184**

Fancy Walnut & Needlework Firescreen

Firescreen, walnut & needlework, the large upright square walnut frame enclosing a finely detailed colorful needlework panel centered by an ornate scroll-bordered cartouche around a romantic landscape scene all surrounded by an fancy floral border, the framed w/a pierce-cut low crestrail centered by a carved maltese cross, the lower rail w/a pierce-carved scroll drop crest centered by a large diamond, raised on heavy outswept scroll legs, features a/right side pull-out panel to double the size of the screen, late 19th c., 26 3/4" w., 41 1/2" h. (ILLUS.).................................... **$460**

French Rococo-Style Firescreen

Firescreen, Rococo-Style, a slender squared tubular brass frame w/an ornate scrolling crest, enclosing a large h.p. canvas panel featuring a romantic couple in 18th c. costume in a garden setting, raised on scrolled end feet, France, early 20th c., 33" w., 41 1/4" h. (ILLUS.)............ **$690**

Rare Edgar Brandt Iron Firescreen

Firescreen, wrought-iron, Art Deco style, "Les Pins" design, the gently arched flat crestrail above a tall panel composed of alternating pairs of slender rods alternating w/a single wider flat bar, the top half applied w/long branches of pine boughs w/pine cones, supported on gently arched shoe feet, designed by Edgar Brandt, France, ca. 1924, 13 1/2 x 32", 33 1/2" h. (ILLUS.) **$35,850**

Very Rare Art Deco Iron Firescreen

Firescreen, gilded wrought iron, a large upright circle composed of bold openwork scrolls centered by a diamond-shaped lattice panel, raised on a fanned support resting on a narrow oval platform on outswept low scroll legs, designed by Gilbert Poillerat in 1929, manufactured by Baudet, Donon et Roussel, France, ca. 1946, top 26 3/4" d., overall 32 1/4" h. (ILLUS.) **$57,360**

English Jacobean-Style Firescreen

Firescreen, Jacobean-Style, carved walnut, the pierced leafy scroll-carved crestrail centered by a crown & supporting a pierce-carved framework enclosing an armorial needlework panel over a caned lower panel, all supported by spiral-twist side stiles w/upper & lower corner blocks & turned top finials, on a trestle-style base w/arched scrolled legs joined by a small turned stretcher & a long spiral-turned cross stretcher, England, late 19th c., 17 x 31", 44" h. (ILLUS.) **$403**

Louis XV-Style Needlework Firescreen

Firescreen, Louise XV-Style, carved walnut, the rectangular molded frame w/molded sides & rounded corners topped by a central shell-carved crest & top corner scrolls, enclosing a fine needlework panel w/a portrait of a French aristocrat surrounded by ornate florals on a brown ground, trestle base w/inwardly scrolled & leaf-carved feet, France, third quarter 19th c., 27 1/2" w., 46" h. (ILLUS.) **$431**

Napoleon III Era Firescreen

Firescreen, Napoleon III era, ebonized wood, a slender arched crestrail centered by a carved wheat sheaf & tools above a large velvet panel in a framework supported by slender turned side columns w/turned finials, a trestle-form base w/arched & acanthus leaf-carved legs w/scrolled toes, France, third quarter 19th c., 43 1/2" h. (ILLUS.)........................ **$518**

Colorful Victorian Glass Firescreen

Firescreen, Victorian leaded & stained glass, an upright rectangular brass frame w/trestle feet & a row of open spindles across the bottom encloses a large glass panel, the central stained oval decorated w/a bust portrait of a young Victorian maiden holding pale yellow roses, sur-

rounded by a narrow red border & a fleur-de-lis wider band w/four blue half-circles at the top & sides, the triangular corner panels stained w/clusters of whites flowers & golden brown leaves & berries against a pale gold ground, the center section w/a wide border band in black & gold & inset w/leaded glass squares "jewels" in deep red, light & dark blue, ca. 1880s, few small cracks in edge pieces, 20" w., 33" h. (ILLUS.) **$748**

Rare Fornasetti 1950s Floor Screen

Floor screen, four-fold, "Libreria" design, the front of each panel decorated w/a color lithograph design representing tall book shelves also holding various decorative objects, the back decorated w/a design of spears, a cat, a cello & a red cloth, designed by Piero Fornasetti, Italy, 1950s, each panel 19 3/4 x 78 1/2" (ILLUS.) **$14,340**

Louis XV-Style Folding Floor Screen

Floor screen, six-fold, Louis XV-Style, painted fruitwood frame w/each arched panel w/a molded crestrail above fabric panels w/Oriental floral designs, late 19th c., fabric replaced, open 165" l., 62" h. (ILLUS.)....................................... **$1,265**

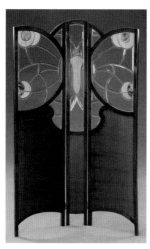

Unusual Art Nouveau Butterfly Screen

Floor screen, three-fold, Art Nouveau style, leaded glass & stained oak, the upper half designed as a clear, blue & white leaded glass butterfly w/the body in the narrow center panel & the wings in the flanking panels, the lower panels in dark blue, attributed to the Wiener Mosaic Werkstatte, Austria, ca. 1905, overall 45 1/2" w., 73" h. (ILLUS.)...................... **$2,151**

Lacquered & Painted Oriental Screen

Folding screen, four-fold, Oriental, lacquered wood & painted canvas, each panel w/a flat rectangular gilt frame enclosing a narrow rectangular upper panel w/a gilt background painted w/a different flowering branch above a tall vertical panel w/a black background decorated in gold & color w/a different garden scene, each outer corner w/an embossed brass bird & leaf mount, China,

early 20th c., some losses, overall 96" w., 69" h. (ILLUS.)...................... **$250-400**

Decorative Spanish Leather Screen

Folding screen, four-fold, parcil-gilt & painted leather, each gently arched panel covered w/three panels of late 17th c. leather h.p. overall w/ornately flowering vines, the back w/floral panels, Spain, late 19th c., overall 96" w., 77 1/2" h. (ILLUS.) **$4,370**

Ornately Carved Chinese Screen

Folding screen, four-fold, pierced & carved hardwood, Oriental style, etched tall panel topped w/an arched & pierce-carved crest above a narrow rectangular lattice-carved panel above a tall central solid panel carved in relief w/a serpentine dragon, a bottom short rectangular panel w/floral carving, the framework carved w/characters & a bamboo-carved edge, scrolled arched base to each panel, China, late 19th c., overall 84" w., 78 1/4" h. (ILLUS.).. **$1,035**

Victorian Screen with Landscape Designs in the Japonesque Taste

Folding screen, four-fold, Victorian Japonesque taste, each tall rectangular panel decorated w/a gold background highlighted w/asymmetrically arranged geometric reserves each painted w/a different landscape & framed w/various flowers & fruits, the largest panels representing the four seasons, English or American, late 19th c., overall 88" w., 70 1/2" h. (ILLUS., top of page) **$1,610**

scape scenes, fish, birds or figure of Immortals, each plaque also w/an overglaze calligraphy poem in black, Kuang Hsu, late 19th c., overall 102" w., 82 1/2" h. (ILLUS.) **$4,600**

Fine Chinese Porcelain Plaque Screen

Folding screen, six-fold, Chinese Export, each narrow panel framed w/burl & ebonized fruitwood forming three rectangular panels & a round bottom panel, each panel mounted w/a different h.p. porcelain plaque decorated w/land-

English Screen with Exotic Landscape

Folding screen, three-fold, Aesthetic taste, the three fabric panels painted w/a large continuous exotic landscape full of birds & leafy trees around a lake, the reverse painted in monochrome claret, scattered small rents & losses, England, ca. 1900, overall 66" w., 65" h. (ILLUS.) **$1,840**

Early 19th Century French Folding Screen

Folding screen, three-fold, Restauration style, striped maple, each simple vertical two-part panel composed of square rails, each panel upholstered in matte silver silk, the back of the panels upholstered in blue & white mattress ticking stripes, France, first quarter 19th c., overall 75" w., 72" h. (ILLUS.)............. **$2,990**

Folding Chinese Wallpaper Screen

Folding screen, three-fold, the panels decorated w/a continuous wallpaper panel decorated in full color w/exotic birds & ducks among flowering trees & shrubs, China, late 19th c., considerable wear, each panel 23 3/4" w., 43 3/4" h. (ILLUS.) **$956**

Fancy Louis XV-Style Two-panel Screen

Folding screen, two-fold, Louis XV-Style, ornate giltwood frame, each panel topped by a large upright oval frame w/scroll crest enclosing color prints of 18th c. courting scenes, the oval supported on large C-scrolls above the scroll-trimmed rectangular panel enclosing gold fabric, France, late 19th - early 20th c., some gesso loss, slight panel warping, each panel 27" w., 82" h. (ILLUS.).. **$2,160**

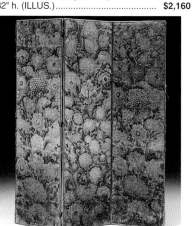

Rare Early French Needlework Screen

Folding screen, three-fold, gross point needlework, each tall rectangular panel completely upholstered w/an overall floral needlework panel w/tack trim, repairs, replaced & rewoven sections, France, 2nd

quarter 18th c., each panel 21 1/4" w., 6'
6 1/2" h. (ILLUS.) **$6,573**

Fancy Louis XVI-Style Folding Screen

Folding screen, three-fold, Louis XVI-Style,
carved parcel-gilt beech, the upper central panel fitted w/a carved hanging basket of flowers against a mirror, carved
leaf swags across the top of the side panels & each upholstered w/a gold damask
fabric, slender molded frame w/slender
molded gilt bands, France, ca. 1900,
overall 58" w., 5' 7 1/4" h. (ILLUS.) **$1,840**

French Screen with Oriental Decoration

Folding screen, four-fold, Napoleon III era,
Oriental taste, colorfully painted overall
w/a continuous Chinese landscape w/fig-
ures & buildings against a black ground,
the reverse w/outlined panels, France,
third quarter 19th c., overall 90" w., 7' h.
(ILLUS.).. **$3,220**

Painted Lacquerware Pole Screen

Pole screen, lacquerware, the arched &
scrolled oblong papier-mâché lacquer
screen h.p. w/a Venetian scene & accented w/inlaid mother-of-pearl, raised
on a brass pole above a ring- and knob-
turned post supported by three pierced
long scroll supports on scroll feet, probably England, ca. 1850, screen 14 x 18",
overall 53 1/2" h. (ILLUS.)........................ **$403**

Pair of English Victorian Pole Screens

Pole screens, inlaid mahogany, each w/a
large oval shield enclosing an embroi-
dered panel of floral design centered by a

cartouche w/a romantic scene, supported & adjusting on a slender square pole
w/a thicker tapering base section above
the stepped square base, banded edge
inlay, wear & losses to embroidery, some
inlay loss, England, late 19th c., 10 1/4"
sq. base, 55 1/2" h., pr. (ILLUS.)............... **$546**

Secretaries

Rhode Island Chippendale Secretary

Chippendale secretary-bookcase, birch &
maple w/some curl, two-part construction:
the upper section w/a rectangular top w/a
flaring stepped cornice above a pair of
raised-panel cupboard doors opening to a
divided interior; the lower section w/a
hinged slant front opening to an interior fitted w/two small drawers & pigeonholes,
the lower case w/four long graduated
drawers w/brass butterfly pulls & keyhole
escutcheons, molded base w/a narrow
serpentine apron & scroll-cut bracket feet,
old replaced brasses, old glued foot restorations, hinged replaced w/pieced restorations, attributed to Rhode Island, old mellow refinishing, late 18th c.,
19 1/2 x 37 1/4", 76 1/2" h. (ILLUS.)........ **$3,738**
Chippendale secretary-bookcase, carved
cherry, two-piece construction: the upper
section w/a rectangular top w/narrow crestrail above a pair of tall geometrically-
glazed cupboard doors opening to wood-
en shelves; the lower section formed by a
slant-front desk w/the wide hinged front
opening to an interior fitted w/a row of pigeonholes centered by a small sunburst-
carved drawer above two rows of small
drawers, the lower case w/four long graduated drawers w/pierced butterfly brasses

Fine Chippendale Secretary-Bookcase

flanked by reeded quarter-round columns,
molded base on scroll-carved ogee bracket feet, Connecticut, late 18th c., replaced
brasses, refinished, alterations,
21 x 39 1/2", 81" h. (ILLUS.) **$6,463**

Rare Chippendale Secretary-Bookcase

Chippendale secretary-bookcase, cherry,
two-part construction: the upper section
w/a rectangular top w/a flaring stepped
cornice above a pair of tall paneled cupboard doors opening to four small drawers; the lower section w/a fold-down slant
front opening to an interior fitted w/a cen-

tral prospect door enclosing four small shelves flanked by pigeonholes, the lower case w/four long graduated drawers w/butterfly brasses & keyhole escutcheons, molded base on scroll-cut ogee bracket feet, some foot restorations, Pennsylvania, 1760-80, 21 1/2 x 39", 84" h. (ILLUS.) **$14,340**

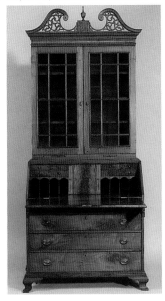

Fine Chippendale Secretary-Bookcase

Chippendale secretary-bookcase, inlaid walnut, two-part construction: the upper section w/a broken-scroll crest pierced w/delicate scrolls & centered by a block w/an urn-turned finial above a deep flaring stepped cornice above a pair of tall geometrically-glazed cupboard doors opening to three shelves above two small pull-out candle shelves; the lower section w/a wide hinged fall-front opening to an interior w/a central prospect door flanked by string-inlaid document boxes, three small drawers & four valanced pigeonholes, the lower case w/four long graduated cockbeaded drawers w/oval brasses, molded base on scroll-cut ogee bracket feet, possibly Maryland, late 18th c., replaced braces, refinished, some restoration, 22 x 40", 95" h. (ILLUS.) **$7,638**

Chippendale secretary-bookcase, mahogany, two-part construction: the upper section w/a rectangular top w/a flaring dentil-carved cornice above a pair of tall geometrically-glazed doors opening to three wooden shelves; the lower stepped-out section w/a hinged fold-down slant front opening to an interior composed of small drawers, pigeonholes & a central door, the lower case w/three long graduated drawers w/simply bail pulls, molded base on scroll-cut bracket feet, underside of interior drawer w/origi-

Rare Chippendale Secretary-Bookcase

nal paper label reading "Elbert Anderson - Makes all knds of - CABINET WARE - on the most Modern & Approved - Methods & on the most reasonable terms - No. 5 or 53 - Maiden Lane in- NEW YORK," one drawer w/a later inscription, New York City, 1786-96, 24 1/4 x 49 3/4", 88 7/8" h. (ILLUS.) **$21,600**

Classical Three-Part Secretary-Bookcase

Classical secretary-bookcase, mahogany & mahogany veneer, three-part construction: the upper section w/a wide gently peaked removable cornice above a pair of tall pointed arch glazed doors opening to wooden shelves above a row of three small drawers; the stepped-out lower section w/a fold-out writing surface above a long narrow round-fronted drawer over a pair of paneled cupboard doors, scroll-cut bracket feet, ca. 1840-50, 83 1/2" h. (ILLUS.)... **$1,668**

American Classical Secretary-Bookcase

Classical secretary-bookcase, mahogany & mahogany veneer, three-part construction: the upper section w/a rectangular top & removable widely flaring stepped cornice above a pair of tall glazed cupboard doors opening to three wooden shelves; the stepped-out lower section w/a fold-down drawer front opening to three small drawers w/bird's-eye maple fronts below eight pigeonholes; the lower case w/a pair of paneled doors opening to two shelves & flanked by pilasters on blocks above the bun feet, ca. 1830, 19 1/4 x 41", 84" h. (ILLUS.) **$2,013**

Classical secretary-bookcase, mahogany & mahogany veneer, two-part construction: the upper section w/a rectangular top w/a deep widely flaring flat cornice above a flat frieze band w/end blocks above a pair of heavy columns flanking a pair of tall Gothic arch paneled cupboard doors opening a two adjustable shelves above a pair of narrow drawers w/turned wood knobs; the lower stepped-out section w/a fold-out writing surface above a long ogee-front drawer over heavy end columns w/carved capitals flanking the set-back long flat drawers w/turned wood knobs, on simple turned legs w/knob feet, probably New England, first-half 19th c., 20 x 42 1/4", 70" h. (ILLUS., top next column) **$805**

Early Classical Two-Part Secretary

Mahogany Classical Secretary-Bookcase

Classical secretary-bookcase, mahogany & mahogany veneer, two-part construction: the upper section w/a wide flattened flaring cornice above a pair of tall 6-pane glazed doors w/the upper panes shaped as Gothic arches, opening to shelves & above a pair of shallow drawers w/wooden knobs; the lower section w/a fold-out writing surface above a long narrow round-fronted drawer projecting above a pair of deep long drawers w/wooden knobs flanked by slender columns, flat base raised on heavy bulbous turned & tapering feet, ca. 1830-40, 22 1/2 x 48", 84" h. (ILLUS.) **$1,265**

Finely Veneered Classical Secretary

Classical secretary-bookcase, mahogany & mahogany veneer, two-part construction: the upper section w/a rectangular top above a deep flaring cornice trimmed w/a thin beaded band above a pair of tall glazed cupboard doors w/beaded banding around the panes & opening to three adjustable wooden shelves above a row of three small drawers w/turned wood knobs; the lower section w/a fold-out writing surface above a case of three long graduated drawers w/turned wood knobs, shaped apron & simple bracket feet, ca. 1840, 21 x 42", 80 1/2" h. (ILLUS.) **$1,380**

Massachusetts Classical Secretary

Classical secretary-bookcase, mahogany & mahogany veneer, two-part construction: the upper section w/a very wide, flaring covered cornice above a pair of tall 9-

pane glazed doors w/the top three panes sharply pointed, opening to two shelves & flanked by tall faceted columns; the stepped-out lower section w/a fold-out writing surface above a projecting convex top drawer over two long lower drawers w/turned wood knobs & flanked by faceted shorter columns, flat base raised on heavy shaped front feet, some pulls original, Massachusetts, ca. 1825, some imperfections, 23 x 52 1/4", 86 1/4" h. (ILLUS.) **$3,819**

Fine Classical Secretary-Bookcase

Classical secretary-bookcase, mahogany & mahogany veneer, two-part construction: the upper section w/a rectangular top w/a deep ogee cornice w/rounded corners above a pair of tall geometrically-glazed cupboard doors opening to three shelves above a row of three narrow drawers; the projecting lower section w/a fold-out writing surface above a long drawer over a pair of paneled cupboard doors, deep base molding raised on scroll-cut bracket feet, ca. 1840, 22 x 42", 87" h. (ILLUS.) **$4,313**

Classical secretary-bookcase, mahogany & mahogany veneer, two-part construction: the upper section w/a rectangular top & low flaring ogee cornice above an arched frieze above a pair of tall set-back geometrically-glazed cupboard doors opening to shelves & flanked by tall turned columns; the lower case w/a hinged fold-out writing surface projecting above a recessed square center door flanked by narrower quarter-round doors all flanked by serpentine front pilasters above the heavy C-scroll front feet, similar to examples produced by Joseph Meeks & Sons, New York, New York, ca. 1830s, 26 x 53", 83" h. (ILLUS., next page).. **$9,200**

Fine New York Classical Secretary

American Signed Rosewood Secretary

Classical secretary-bookcase, rosewood veneer, two-part construction: the upper section w/a rectangular top w/a widely flaring low ogee cornice above a pair of tall glazed cupboard doors w/pierced scroll-cut corner brackets opening to two shelves; the lower section w/a rectangular top above a projecting long fold-down drawer front opening to an interior fitted w/drawers & pigeonholes, two long lower drawers flanked by serpentine pilasters & heavy scroll-form front feet, back signed "J. Alsop, Carlisle, PA," ca. 1830s, 19 1/2 x 43 1/2", 78" h. (ILLUS.) **$1,610**

Classical secretary-bookcase, walnut, two-part construction: the upper section w/a rectangular top w/a deep flaring ogee cornice w/rounded corners above a pair of tall glazed cupboard doors w/pierced

Simple Classical Secretary Bookcase

scrolling brackets in the upper corners opening to wooden shelves above a row of three small drawers each w/beaded molding; the stepped-out lower section w/a hinged fold-over writing surface above small pull-out supports above a slightly projecting long drawer w/turned wood knobs above two long graduated matching drawers, simple front bracket feet, 21 x 43", 6' 11" h. (ILLUS.) **$764**

Classical-Style Secrétaire à Abattant

Classical-Style secrétaire à abattant, walnut & burl walnut, the rectangular top w/a narrow flaring cornice above a frieze band flanked by chamfered blocks above a long narrow drawer w/a raised burl panel & a serpentine brass bail pulls above the wide flat fold-down writing panel opening to an interior fitted w/an arrangement of eleven small inlaid drawers centered by a tall open compartment, the lower case w/three long burl-veneered drawers w/matching brass pulls, the side pilasters w/small carved urns above fluted columns over tall blocks resting on disk-turned front feet, Europe, late 19th c., 23 1/4 x 43 1/4", 64 1/2" h. (ILLUS., previous page) **$1,495**

New Hampshire Federal Secretary-Bookcase

Federal secretary-bookcase, birch & flame birch, two-part construction: the upper short section w/a rectangular top w/a narrow molded cornice above a pair of long rectangular paneled doors opening to an interior w/a shelf above rows of small drawers & pigeonholes, a row of three small drawers w/small round brass pulls below the doors; the lower section w/a gently slanted fold-out writing surface above a single long drawer projecting above two long graduated drawers flanked by ring- and spiral-turned columns, drawers w/oval brasses & keyhole escutcheons, flat base w/blocked ends raised on ring-, knob- and baluster-turned legs ending in peg feet, warm dark refinishing, New Hampshire, ca. 1820-30, old replaced brasses, minor damage & age splits, 40 3/4" w., 56 5/8" h. (ILLUS.) **$2,300**

Federal secretary-bookcase, carved & inlaid mahogany, two-part construction: the upper section w/a high broken-scroll pediment w/scroll-pierced scrolls flanking a central black w/an urn-turned finial above a narrow veneer-paneled frieze band above

Rare Federal Inlaid Secretary-Bookcase

a pair of tall geometrically-glazed doors opening to three wooden shelves; the stepped-out lower section w/a stack of five long graduated drawers w/line-inlaid panels, oval brasses & diamond-shaped inlaid keyhole escutcheons, serpentine apron continuing to tall outswept French feet, Maryland, 1790-1810, 23 1/4 x 42 1/2", 97 1/4" h. (ILLUS.) **$26,400**

Curly Maple Federal Secretary-Bookcase

Federal secretary-bookcase, curly maple & walnut, two-part construction: the upper section w/a rectangular top w/a deep flaring covered cornice above a pair of tall 6-pane glazed doors w/arched top panes opening to two shelves above a low open shelf; the stepped-out lower section w/a hinged slant-top opening to eight nailed small drawers above slide supports flanking a shallow long beaded drawer w/round brass pulls overhanging two long graduated beaded drawers w/matching pulls & flanked by ring-, knob- and baluster-turned columns, raised on swelled ring-turned legs w/ball feet, the top a marriage to earlier base, pieced restoration at hinges, first half 19th c., 20 3/4 x 40 3/4", 78 1/2" h. (ILLUS.) **$2,185**

Fine Figured Maple & Mahogany Secretary

Federal secretary-bookcase, inlaid mahogany & figured maple, two-part construction: the upper section w/a rectangular top w/a low curved front cornice centered by a high rectangular panel topped by an urn-turned finial, matching corner finials, above a mahogany frieze band centered by an inlaid figured maple rectangle above a pair of tall cupboard doors w/eight narrow panes in each above a recessed rectangular lower panel w/inlaid figured maple border; the stepped-out lower section a case of four long drawers w/figured maple veneer banding & two oval brasses, the arched apron centered by an inlaid fan, ring-turned tapering legs ending in knob feet, North Shore Massachusetts, 1790-1810, appear to retain original brasses, 18 x 40", 85 1/2" h. (ILLUS.) **$9,600**

Federal secretary-bookcase, inlaid mahogany & mahogany veneer, three-part construction: the top section w/a low cornice centered by a square block w/banded veneer & topped by a carved spread-winged eagle finial & w/small corner blocks w/small turned wood urn-form finials all above a pair of cupboard doors each w/two arched glazed panels over small blocks & panels; the center section w/a pair of flat cupboard doors centered by a narrow small door; the bottom section w/a narrow fold-out writing surface above a case of four long graduated drawers w/oval brass pulls, serpentine apron on tall French feet, Northshore,

Rare Federal Three-Part Secretary

Massachusetts, ca. 1815, 20 x 41", 81" h. (ILLUS.) **$13,145**

Nice New England Federal Secretary

Federal secretary-bookcase, inlaid mahogany & mahogany veneer; two-part construction: the upper section w/a flat rectangular top over a frieze band & a pair of squared geometrically-glazed cupboard doors over two narrow line-inlaid drawers; the lower section w/a fold-out baize-lined writing surface above a case w/three long graduated drawers w/oval brass pulls, serpentine apron & tall French feet, probably Portsmouth, New Hampshire, late 18th - early 19th c., 17 1/2 x 35", 57" h. (ILLUS.) **$2,760**

New England Mahogany Secretary

Federal secretary-bookcase, inlaid mahogany & mahogany veneer, two-part construction: the upper section w/a low cornice centered by a banded rectangular panel w/a round brass ball finial topped by a small eagle, small corner blocks also w/round brass ball finials above a frieze band over a pair of wide geometrically-glazed cupboard doors opening to two shelves above a narrow row of three drawers; the lower section w/a fold-out writing surface above a case of three long graduated drawers w/period oblong brass pulls, serpentine apron on tall French feet, New England, late 18th c., 17 1/2 x 40", 76" h. (ILLUS.) **$5,750**

Unusual Southern Federal Secretary

Federal secretary-bookcase, inlaid mahogany, two-part construction: the upper section w/a rectangular top above a pair of geometrically-glazed cupboard doors flanking a flat center door opening to a sectioned interior; the stepped-out lower section w/a fold-out writing surface above a case of four long graduated drawers w/oval pulls, narrow shaped skirt & tall splayed feet, Southern U.S., possibly Georgia, ca. 1800, missing some interior dividers, damage to left hinge of writing surface, damage to back of side panels, old repairs, 22 x 44", 57 1/2" h. (ILLUS.) **$2,875**

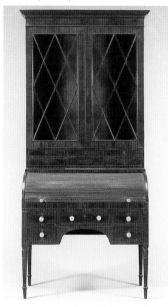

Rare Philadelphia Federal Secretary

Federal secretary-bookcase, mahogany & mahogany veneer, two-part construction: the upper section w/a rectangular top & flaring cornice above a pair of tall diamond-glazed cupboard doors above an arrangement of six small narrow drawers; the stepped-out lower section w/a cylinder tambour front opening to an interior fitted w/eight pigeonholes & twelve small drawers w/figured maple facings over a velvet & mahogany writing surface, the lower case w/a row of three drawers above a pair of drawers flanking an arched knee-hole opening, raised on slender turned & reeded legs w/peg feet, Connelly-Haines School, Philadelphia, ca. 1800-10, 26 x 42", 95" h. (ILLUS.) **$38,240**

George III secretary-bookcase, mahogany, two-part construction: the upper section w/a broken-scroll crest w/carved rosettes above the flaring stepped cornice w/dentil-carved narrow bands above a pair of tall geometrically-glazed cupboard doors opening to three shelves; the lower section w/a wide hinged slant lid opening to an interior fitted w/small drawers & pigeonholes centering a central cupboard

Nice English Georgian Secretary

door above a case w/four long thumb-molded graduated drawers w/simple bail pulls, the molded base on ogee bracket feet, England, late 18th c., 24 1/2 x 48", 103" h. (ILLUS.) **$8,050**

Nice George III-Style Secretary

George III-Style secretary-bookcase, red-lacquered & decorated, two-part con-struction: the upper section w/a low bro-ken-scroll pediment on the rectangular top above a pair of tall solid cupboard doors decorated overall w/gilt Chinese figural & landscape scenes; the lower section w/a hinged fold-out slant front w/Chinese designs opening to an interior

fitted w/pigeonholes above a pair of square paneled cupboard doors w/fur-ther Chinese style decoration, molded base on scroll-cut bracket feet, England, ca. 1900, 16 1/2 x 44", 92" h. (ILLUS.)... **$4,370**

English Queen Anne-Style Secretary

Queen Anne-Style secretary-bookcase, painted & decorated, two-part construc-tion: the upper section w/a double-arched molded crestrail centered by a large scrolled cartouche finial & w/urn-carved corner finials above a pair of tall arched doors fitted w/beveled mirrors separated & flanked by reeded pilasters; the lower case w/a hinged slant front opening to an interior fitted w/a center prospect door flanked by pigeonholes over four small drawers, the lower case w/four thumbmolded long graduated drawers w/butterfly brasses, molded base on large bun feet, the whole deco-rated soft green w/gold trim on the top & gilt Chinese-style figural scenes on the slat front & drawers, cinnabar-colored desk interior, England, late 19th c., 19 1/2 x 36", 81 1/2" h. (ILLUS.).......... **$8,050**
Victorian Golden Oak secretary-book-case, side-by-side type, the tall left side w/a curved glass door opening to four wooden shelves above a conforming top below a wide arched flat crest w/a scroll-carved edge band; the right side w/a large rectangular beveled mirror w/an arched top w/carved crest above a narrow shelf & open compartment above a wide hinged slant front w/a carved panel opening to a fitted interior above graduated stack of three reverse-serpentine drawers w/brass bail pulls, a molded base molding raised on five short cabriole legs w/simple paw

Dark Golden Oak Secretary-Bookcase

feet, original dark finish, late 19th c., 42" w., 6' 1" h. (ILLUS.)............................. **$764**

Simple Oak Side-by-Side Secretary

Victorian Golden Oak secretary-bookcase, side-by-side type, the tall left side w/a slightly curved glazed door opening to four wooden shelves below the small rectangular top w/a pierced scroll-carved crest; the right side topped by a tall pierced & shield-shaped frame enclosing a beveled mirror above a narrow rectangular shelf above the wide hinged slant front opening to a fitted compartment above a single plain drawer over a wide flat lower cupboard doors, raised on flat serpentine front legs, later finish, early 20th c., 36" w., 5' 10" h. (ILLUS.) **$558**

Unusual Oak Secretary-Bookcase

Victorian Golden Oak secretary-bookcase, the top w/a long narrow rectangular shelf supported near the center by two small spindles & rounded sides above a case composed of a pair of small bookcases each w/a single-pane glazed door opening to wooden shelves & centering a wide angled fall-front writing surface decorated w/a delicate ribbon-tied wreath, a long oval mirror above, a single long drawer below the writing surface, all raised on two slender spindles & blocked front legs above a long incurved open lower shelf w/a low scroll-carved back crest w/a central section of small spindles, original finish, ca. 1900, 52" w., 4' 11" h. (ILLUS.) **$823**

Unusual Golden Oak Secretary-Bookcase

Victorian Golden Oak secretary-book-case, the two-part top w/a serpentine scroll crest above a stack of two small drawers at the left & a high squared beveled mirror w/a fancy scroll-carved frame to the right, atop a molding over a long rectangular hinged fall-front w/a carved C-scroll opening to a fitted interior, above a pair of short glazed cupboard doors over a single long drawer at the bottom above the serpentine apron, ca. 1900, 33 1/2" w., 5' 6" h. (ILLUS., previous page) **$558**

Nice Victorian Rococo Secretary

Victorian Rococo secretary-bookcase, mahogany & mahogany veneer, two-part construction: the upper section w/an arched molded cornice above a frieze band centered by a scroll-carved band above a pair of arched glazed doors w/narrow molding & carved scrolls in the top center corners & opening to two shelves; the lower section w/a stepped-back upper section w/a row of three narrow drawers over a single long drawer above a stepped-out fold-out writing surface above a pair of cupboard doors decorated w/raised squared molding forming a panel, serpentine scroll-carved apron & bracket feet, ca. 1850s, 21 x 47", 91 1/2" h. (ILLUS.) **$2,990**

Victorian Rococo secretary-bookcase, walnut, two-part construction: the upper section w/an arched serpentine wide crestrail topped by a high arched pierced & scroll-carved crest w/medallion above a conforming frieze band w/molding above a pair of tall serpentine-topped glazed doors opening to three wooden shelves & flanked by

Nice Victorian Rococo Walnut Secretary

chamfered corners w/applied quarter-round carved drops; the lower section w/a medial molding above the serpentine slant-top opening to a maple & rosewood segmented interior above a pair of narrow drawers projecting above a pair of short paneled base doors flanked by turned drops & base brackets above the flat molded base on casters, ca. 1870, 22 x 45", 101 1/2" h. (ILLUS.) **$3,450**

Shelves

Finely Carved Walnut Magazine Shelf

Magazine shelf, hanging folding-type, carved walnut, the wide pointed backboard w/florets above a finely carved panel of daisy-like flowers among leaves, the fold-out front board held by a side chain & also finely carved w/a design of trumpet flowers, Cincinnati Art Club, ca. 1880s, 16" w., 16" h. (ILLUS.) **$345**

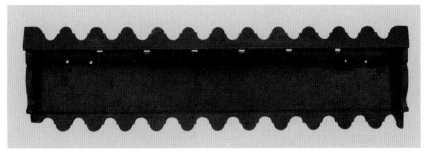

Long Scalloped Pennsylvania Wall Shelf

Blue-painted Plate Shelves

Plate shelves, hanging-type, painted wood, dovetailed construction, three shelves, the narrow rectangular top above graduated sides flanking two upper shelves each w/a front cross rail, a short narrow bottom shelf, old blue paint, some stains, 19th c., 8 1/2" to 4 1/2", 41" w., 32" h. (ILLUS.) **$460**

Wall shelf, country-style, carved & painted, a long narrow shelf w/a deeply scalloped backboard supported on tapering serpentine end brackets flanking a wide lower board w/a deeply scalloped bottom edge, compass-etched decoration, dark grey paint, Pennsylvania, 19th c., 6 3/4 x 69 1/4", 19" h. (ILLUS., top of page) **$3,840**

Very Rare American Figural Eagle Giltwood Wall Shelves

Wall shelves, carved giltwood, each w/a rectangular platform top w/a fruit & floral-carved edge supported atop a large spread-winged eagle w/head slightly bent down & perched on rockwork, probably Boston, ca. 1815, 12 1/2" h., pr. (ILLUS.) **$28,680**

Colorful Wall Shelves with Cabinet Base

Wall shelves, corner-style, painted & decorated, tall tapering backboard w/serpentine edges flanking three quarter-round shelves, painted bright yellow w/Chinese style florals, the bottom shelf above a quarter-round two-door cabinet opening to a shelf, painted deep red w/each door decorated w/a Chinese landscape w/figures, flat base, some wear & paint loss, one shelf w/old repaint & scattered insect holes, probably Europe, 19th c., 18" w., 36" h. (ILLUS.) **$210**

Prince of Wales Plumes Giltwood Shelf

Wall shelves, giltwood, a half-round top shelf w/molded edge supported on tall carved Prince of Wales plumes tied at the base w/a bow & ribbons, England, early 19th c., 8 x 16 1/2", 15" h., pr. (ILLUS. of one) **$431**

Wall shelves, painted & decorated pine, a high top backrail w/a flat center crest & rounded corners above two large hanging holes, decorated w/the original red & black graining & further painted w/a pair of large pink & white blossoms & green leaves, three open graduated shelves each w/slightly canted scallop-cut

Rare Painted & Decorated Wall Shelves

aprons w/further graining & blossoms & supported by scallop-cut bowed supports, gold banding, one side near crest w/minor damage & touch-up, Maine, first half 19th c., 4 1/2 x 15 1/2", 22 1/2" h. (ILLUS.) **$7,130**

Early Shelves with Spoon Rack

Wall shelves, painted maple, the narrow top board carved as a spoon rack above triple-scalloped graduated sides flanking three shelves each w/a narrow front cross rail, yellowish brown finish, 18th c., 21" h. (ILLUS.) **$777**

Country Painted Wall Shelves

Wall shelves, painted walnut & pine, a rectangular top w/a dentil-carved cornice above a single open shelf above the molded base w/dentil band, old mellow brown finish, some empty nail holes on the sides, found in Maine, 19th c., 9 x 20 3/4", 29 1/2" h. (ILLUS.) **$575**

Fancy Four-Shelf Wall Shelf

Wall shelves, walnut, the wide backboard w/a high arched & scroll-carved crest w/shaped finial w/hanging hold above two pierced stars, mounted w/four rectangular open sides each supported at the front corners by slender baluster-turned spindles, arched base rail, old dark surface, two shelf end pieces old replacements, attributed to New Hampshire, 19th c., 6 1/2 x 20 1/4", 40 1/4" h. (ILLUS.) **$805**

Sideboards

Fine French Art Deco Mahogany Sideboard

Art Deco sideboard, gilt-bronze-mounted mahogany, the long rectangular top w/rounded front corners inset w/a long black marble slab above the case w/two large square paneled doors w/round brass hardware, long low pedestal base, France, ca. 1930, 20 1/2 x 67", 40" h. (ILLUS.) **$4,600**

Arts & Crafts sideboard, oak, the long rectangular top backed by a paneled plate rail, the case w/a pair of tall flat doors w/long hammered & riveted copper strap hinges & a rectangular plate pull flanking a central stack of four graduated drawers each w/copper plate & bail pulls, paper label in one drawer for Gustav Stickley, early 20th c., refinished, 24 1/4 x 70", 50" h. (ILLUS., bottom of page) **$8,625**

Gustav Stickley Arts & Crafts Oak Sideboard

Fine Mission Oak Sideboard by Gustav Stickley

Arts & Crafts sideboard, oak, the rectangular top w/a low three-quarters gallery above a case fitted w/a row of three short drawers above a pair of flat cupboard doors flanking a stack of three drawers, a single long drawer across the bottom, each fitted w/a rectangular copper & bail pull, the long arched apron flanked by bootjack ends, original dark finish, Model No. 804, red decal mark of Gustav Stickley, ca. 1904, 22 x 54 1/4", 42 3/8" h. (ILLUS.) **$14,340**

Long Baroque-Style Marble-topped Walnut Server

Baroque-Style server, carved walnut, the long narrow rectangular black marble top above a round-fronted narrow apron w/leaf-carved panels raised on two clusters of four bulbed square tapering legs w/detailed carving & joined by flat serpentine oblong stretchers, each front pair of legs flanking a large half-round pierce-carved drop centered by a large shell, the apron enclosing three silver flatware drawers, some loss to carvings, mark of John Colby & Sons, ca. 1910, 25 x 87", 37" h. (ILLUS.)..................................... **$690**

Finely Carved Mahogany Chippendale-Style Pedestal Sideboard

Rare Philadelphia Classical Server

Chippendale-Style sideboard, carved mahogany, double-pedestal style, each end pedestal w/a gadrooned top edge over a concave drawer above a single flat drawer w/bail pulls over a tall cupboard door decorated w/a large delicately scroll-carved raised rectangular panel, flanking a bowed center drop section w/a flat backboard above a top w/gadrooned edges over a pair of bowed drawers flanking a central swag-carved panel, each pedestal w/a gadroon-carved apron raised on four cabriole legs w/leaf-carved knees & ending in claw-and-ball feet, England, ca. 1870, 89 1/2" l., 46 3/4" h. (ILLUS., bottom previous page) **$2,070**

S-scroll pilasters & raised on heavy C-scroll front legs, dark wood turned knobs, New York State, ca. 1840, 21 1/2 x 47", 59 1/2" h. (ILLUS.) **$2,013**

Classical server, mahogany & mahogany veneer, the rectangular top w/a gadrooned edge above an ogee apron fitted w/two drawers, raised on heavy S-scroll supports w/parcel-gilt leaves, rosettes & stenciling & backed by a pair of mirrored doors, the lower shelf w/a gadrooned edge, resting on heavy gilt paw front feet, Philadelphia, in the manner of A.G. Quervelle, ca. 1830, 23 x 60", 41" h. (ILLUS., top of page) **$16,675**

Southern Classical Mahogany Server

New York State Country Classical Sideboard

Classical country-style sideboard, tiger stripe maple & cherry, the rectangular cherry top w/tall flat back posts & a flat crestrail above a case fitted w/a row of three drawers above two short & deep drawers flanking a deep long drawer, all projecting above a pair of paneled cupboard doors flanking a stack of four small graduated drawers all flanked by heavy

Classical server, mahogany & mahogany veneer, the rectangular top w/a high splashback w/rounded corners above a case w/a pair of drawers w/pairs of turned wood knobs projecting over a row of three paneled cupboard doors flanked by ring-turned columns above beehive-turned front legs, Southern, possibly Beaufort or Charleston, veneer chips, shrinkage cracks, old repairs, ca. 1820, 22 1/2 x 50 3/4", 46 5/8" h. (ILLUS.) **$2,300**

Fine New York City Classical Sideboard

Fine American Classical Server

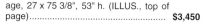

age, 27 x 75 3/8", 53" h. (ILLUS., top of
page).. **$3,450**

Unusual Classical-Style Server

Classical server, mahogany & mahogany
veneer, the rectangular white marble top
above a long ogee-front drawer projecting over a pair of arch-paneled cupboard
doors flanked by free-standing white
marble columns w/ormolu capitals &
bases, the top of each paneled end fitted
w/a pull-out work surface, the front w/bul-
bous squared tapering block feet, ca.
1830s, marble top replaced, 26 x 48 3/4",
41" h. (ILLUS.) **$1,955**

Classical sideboard, mahogany & mahogany veneer, the top backed by a stepped
blacksplash w/a flat center crest of
blocked column ends enclosing three
mirrors, the long white marble top w/an
indented central section above a conforming case w/a long curve-fronted center drawer flanked by projecting flat drawers, all raised on four simple turned
columns framing tall paneled end doors
flanking the deep set-back center opening w/a white marble shelf backed by a
large mirror, flat base w/four blocked supports, New York City, school of Duncan
Phyfe, ca. 1825-30, some veneer dam-

Classical-Style server, mahogany & mahogany veneer, a long half-round top
w/narrow beaded edge above the conforming apron centered by a long drawer
w/two brass lion head & ring pulls, the top
supported at each end by three free-
standing reeded columns flanking an
open serpentine medial shelf & a kidney-
shaped base raised at each end on three
large ball feet on casters, early 20th c.,
18 1/4 x 48", 34" h. (ILLUS.) **$518**

American Classical-Style Sideboard

Classical-Style sideboard, mahogany & mahogany veneer, the rectangular top above a pair long curved-front drawers w/small pulls projecting over four flat cupboard doors above a long, deep bottom drawer, all flanked by free-standing turned columns w/carved capitals & bases raised on heavy carved paw feet, ca. 1890, 24 1/8 x 59 7/8", 40 7/8" h. (ILLUS., previous page) **$500**

French Empire-Style Lacquered Credenza

Empire-Style credenza, gilt-bronze inlaid ebonized lacquer, the long top inset w/white marble w/rounded ends & a blocked front, the conforming case w/a narrow frieze band decorated w/a scroll-inlaid central panel flanked by small gilt-bronze mounts above a large paneled door elaborately decorated w/a large scene of floral baskets & scrolled acanthus in chased bronze & mother-of-pearl, gilt-bronze mounts around the door frame, flanked by narrow vertical panels w/additional inlaid basket & scroll designs, urn- and columnar-turned corner columns w/gilt-bronze capitals, feet & leaf mounts, the curved sides w/further gilt-bronze

mounts, the conforming blocked apron w/further mounts & raised on disk- and peg-turned tapering feet, France, ca. 1950, 18 x 55", 45" h. (ILLUS.) **$2,300**

French Empire-style Sideboard

Empire-Style sideboard, gilt bronze-mounted mahogany, two-part construction: the upper section surmounted by a scrolling palmette & acanthus leaf finial over a rectangular case w/glazed doors flanked by rounded glazed panels above gilt bellflower & acanthus cast supports; the lower section w/a rectangular white marble top over a conforming case w/a pair of frieze drawers above a pair of doors centering a panel mounted w/gilt-bronze ribbon-tied laurel wreath flanked by fluted stiles headed w/gilt-bronze foliate mounts over a stepped apron centering a gilt swagged rocaille mount, raised on toupie feet, France, late 19th c., 22 x 64", 6' 10" h. (ILLUS.) **$4,406**

Rare Early Walnut Southern Huntboard

Very Rare Federal Inlaid Mahogany "Serpentine-Front" Small Sideboard

Federal country-style huntboard, walnut, rectangular top above a deep apron w/a pair of deep raised panel dovetailed drawers flanking a deep matching center drawer, oval brasses, on slender square tapering legs w/small shaped corner brackets, two-board top w/thin piece added to old separation, old refinishing, Southern U.S., late 18th - early 19th c., 24 1/2 x 60 1/4", 41 1/2" h. (ILLUS., bottom previous page) **$20,700**

Federal "serpentine-front" sideboard, inlaid mahogany, diminutive size, the rectangular top w/a serpentine bowed front above a conforming case, a pair of concave-front banded & line-inlaid drawers flanking a long serpentine-front central drawer over a pair of deep concave banded & line-inlaid bottle drawers flanking a pair of banded & line-inlaid serpentine center doors, drawers w/oval brasses, front divided by four line-inlaid stiles that continue down to form the square tapering line-inlaid legs, two square tapering rear legs, Rhode Island or New York City, 1790-1810, 23 x 58 1/4", 42" h. (ILLUS., top of page) **$45,600**

Fine New York Federal Server

Federal server, carved mahogany & mahogany veneer, the rectangular top above a deep apron w/a single long banded drawer w/brass lion head & ring pulls, raised on spiraling leaf-carved supports w/ring- and knob-turned caps above a long medial shelf w/an incurved front, raised on paw-carved front feet, New York City, 1815-25, 19 1/2 x 46 1/2", 41" h. (ILLUS.)............... **$7,200**

Federal sideboard, inlaid mahogany, the long rectangular top w/a bowed central section flanked by concave sections all above a conforming case, the ends w/concave flat-front doors w/inlaid fans in each corner flanking a long bowed top drawer w/rectangular brasses projecting over a slightly bowed pair of smaller doors w/fan inlay flanked by narrow vertical panels each w/an inlaid Liberty Cap, raised on six square tapering legs, the four in front w/bellflower inlay, New York City, ca. 1790-1810, 27 1/2 x 73 1/2", 38" h. (ILLUS., top next page) **$65,725**

Rare Large Federal Inlaid Mahogany Sideboard

Federal sideboard, inlaid mahogany, the rectangular top w/a serpentine front & oval corners above a conforming string-inlaid case a long central drawer flanked by smaller drawers above a central pair of recessed doors & convex panels flanked by curved end doors, all raised on square tapering legs inlaid w/panels, urns & stringing continuing to cuffs & joined lower edge of geometric banding, replaced brasses, refinished, probably New York City, ca. 1795, imperfections, 27 1/2 x 71", 40 3/8" h. (ILLUS.) **$29,375**

Extraordinary New York City Federal Inlaid Mahogany Sideboard

Fine Inlaid Mahogany Federal-Style Sideboard

Federal-Style "bowfront" sideboard, inlaid mahogany & mahogany veneer, the rectangular top w/a slightly stepped-out bowed center section above a conforming case w/a pair of bowed line-inlaid drawers flanking a long center bowed drawer inlaid w/panels to resemble three drawers, all w/oval brasses w/stamped eagles, two bowed & line-inlaid end doors flanking a pair of bowed line-inlaid center drawers flanked by arch-inlaid vertical panels, raised on six square tapering line-inlaid legs, 20th c., minor veneer damage & stains in the top, 73 3/4" l., 39" h. (ILLUS.).. **$1,265**

Victorian Centennial Federal-Style Inlaid Mahogany Sideboard

Federal-Style sideboard, inlaid mahogany & mahogany veneer, the long rectangular top w/a projecting serpentine center section above a conforming case w/a large deep wine drawer at one end & a matching door at the other end, each inlaid w/rectangular border banding & a thin central oval enclosing the oval brass pull, the serpentine center section w/a single long line-inlaid drawer above a long arched inlaid apron, raised on six square tapering legs w/spade feet, ca. 1880, 28 1/4 x 75", 35" h. (ILLUS., bottom previous page).. **$5,865**

Fine Early Federal-Style Sideboard

Federal-Style sideboard, inlaid mahogany, the long rectangular top w/a bowed front decorated w/line-inlay along the edge above the conforming case w/a pair of curved short drawers w/line-inlay flanking a long flat line-inlaid central drawer, all w/oval bail brasses, the lower case w/curved & line-inlaid end doors flanking a pair of flat line-inlaid central doors, the front divided by four line-inlaid stiles continuing down to tapering square line-inlaid legs, branded mark "C. Dodge Furniture Co. - Since 1841 - Manchester, Mass.," late 19th - early 20th c., 22 x 62", 41" h. (ILLUS.) **$1,265**

French Provincial Cherry Buffet

French Provincial buffet, cherry, the rectangular top w/rounded front corners above a case w/a pair of narrow drawers w/small turned wood knobs above a pair of paneled cupboard doors, flat base raised on paneled block feet, France, late 19th c., 19 1/4 x 43 1/4", 39 1/2" h. (ILLUS.) **$546**

French Provincial Sideboard-Cupboard

French Provincial sideboard-cupboard, walnut, two-part construction: the upper cabinet w/a heavy arched cornice centered w/an ornate crest of carved shells & flowers above a frieze molding over a pair of arched 9-pane beveled glass doors opening to two shelves raised on leaf-carved cabriole front supports & a solid back w/two raised panels; the projecting lower sideboard section w/a rectangular top w/molded edges above a case w/two narrow drawers w/serpentine molding & scrolled brass pulls above a pair of large paneled cupboard doors w/serpentine molding, serpentine short apron & bracket feet, France, ca. 1890, some finish faded, feet shortened, 22 1/4 x 57 1/4", 98" h. (ILLUS.) **$1,495**

French Provincial-Style sideboard, carved oak, the long rectangular top w/a stepped-out central section, the back mounted w/a long low & gently arched crestrail centered by a carved fanned scroll crest, the cased fitted at the ends w/a single scroll-carved paneled drawer above a scroll-arched & leafy scroll-carved panel & centered by a pair of matching projecting doors, the serpentine scroll- and lattice-carved apron raised on short cabriole legs, France, early 20th c., 24 x 93 3/4", 50 1/2" h. (ILLUS., top next page).. **$1,150**

Carved Oak French Provincial-Style Long Sideboard

George III sideboard, inlaid mahogany, the rectangular top w/a gently bowed front above a conforming case w/a pair of deep bottle drawers centered by a round inlaid panel w/floral-cast oval brasses flanking a long central drawer w/an inlaid oval panel & two matching pulls above an arch central apron, raised on six square tapering legs, England, late 18th c., 26 1/2 x 65 1/2", 37 1/2" h. (ILLUS.) **$3,680**

Inlaid Mahogany English George III Sideboard

Georgian-Style sideboard, inlaid rose-wood, two-part construction: the tall upper section w/an ornate arrangement of shelves & mirrors topped by a tall project-ing central section w/a broken-scroll crest w/floral inlays above an inlaid frieze band over a tall geometrically-glazed cabinet door above a set-back tapering inlaid pan-el flanked by curved vertical mirror panels, each side of the top w/a half broken-scroll inlaid crest above an arrangement of pro-jecting open shelves supported by slender turned columns & backed by mirrored panels above scroll-inlaid panels, the rect-angular top w/a deep concave central sec-tion above a conforming case, each end fitted w/a narrow flat inlaid drawer above an urn-and-scroll-inlaid cupboard door above a open compartment w/a turned corner spindle & low front gallery, the con-cave section w/a serpentine top shelf above narrow inlaid drawers over a three-part serpentine apron raised on turned spindles & a deep open compartment above three inlaid lower doors, all raised on six ring-turned front legs, some inlay restoration, England, ca. 1880, 18 x 60", 94 1/2" h. (ILLUS.) **$3,450**

Very Ornate Georgian-Style Sideboard

Louis XV-Style Provincial Walnut Sideboard

Italian Baroque-Style Carved Sideboard

Italian Baroque-Style sideboard, carved walnut, a long D-shaped top in multicolored brown marble above a conforming case w/rounded corners flanking two long molded drawers each centered by a carved basket of fruit & trailing vines w/piered brass pulls, velvet lining & silver compartment insert, the beaded apron border above two half-round shell- and flower-carved drops, all raised on seven knob- and ring-turned legs w/bun feet, joined at the front by flat serpentine stretchers, straight side & back stretchers, Italy, late 19th - early 20th c., crack in marble, some damage to feet, 23 1/2 x 84 1/2", 39" h. (ILLUS.) **$633**

Louis XV-Style Provincial sideboard, mahogany, the rectangular top w/molded edges above a case w/a pair of short drawers flanking a long central drawer each w/leafy scroll-carved panels & brass pulls above a pair of narrow tall doors flanking a large square central door each w/arched & scroll-carved panels & long pierced scrolling brass mounts, a deep serpentine front apron centered by a round flower-carved roundel flanked by leafy sprigs, on short front cabriole legs w/scroll feet on casters, France, early 20th c., 22 x 62", 39" h. (ILLUS., top of page) **$6,613**

Early Louis XVI Fruitwood Buffet

Louis XVI buffet, fruitwood, the rectangular molded top w/canted corners above a conforming case w/three short frieze drawers above three paneled cupboard doors divided by scrolling cast-metal mounts, raised on square tapering legs, France, late 18th - early 19th c., 25 x 80", 46" h. (ILLUS.) **$6,463**

Louis XVI-Style Server with Marble Top

Louis XVI-Style server, figured veneers w/h.p. floral designs, red, grey & white shaped marble top over three drawers across the top, two lower drawers w/fronts w/concave arches w/sunburst design & ribbon crest, serpentine doors on either side conceal three drawers each, by "Slack Rassnick & Co., New York," late 19th c., 24 1/2 x 56 1/2", 33 1/2" h. (ILLUS.) **$1,495**

Fine Charles Limbert Mission-style Oak Sideboard

Mission-style (Arts & Crafts movement) sideboard, oak, the long rectangular top backed by a low arched plate rail, the case fitted w/two paneled cupboard doors flanking two small drawers over two long drawers w/hammered copper pulls, a very long drawer w/hammered copper pulls across the bottom, gently arched apron, mortised stile legs, Charles Limbert Furniture Co. branded mark, original finish, water damage to top, small chip to plate rail, early 20th c., 25 x 66", 46" h. (ILLUS.) **$3,450**

Mission-style (Arts & Crafts movement) sideboard, oak, the rectangular top mounted w/a tall superstructure w/a narrow top shelf on curved brackets above a long rectangular mirror, the case w/a pair of tall paneled cupboard doors mounted w/long hammered copper strap hinges flanking a stack of four drawers w/rectangular hammered copper pulls, a long bottom drawer w/hammered copper pulls, paneled ends & square stile legs, new finish, unmarked, L. & J.G. Stickley - Onondaga Shops, early 20th c., 24 1/4 x 53 1/4" l., 62 1/4" h. (ILLUS., top next column).. **$4,600**

Nice L. & J.G. Stickley Mission Sideboard

European Neoclassical Style Server

Neoclassical server, mahogany & marble, the long D-form white marble top w/a low pierced brass gallery above an apron mounted w/long pierced brass mounts, raised on slender fluted & tapering legs & a medial white marble shelf w/brass trim, Europe, second half 19th c., marble sections cracked, some losses to brass & wood trim, 19 3/4 x 58", 37" h. (ILLUS.) **$1,900**

Decorative Queen Anne-Style Server

Queen Anne-Style server, black lacquered & decorated, the long rectangular top w/molded edges mounted at the back w/a long arched & scroll-cut crestrail decorated w/painted Chinese figures & landscape scenes, the case fitted w/a pair of long rectangular paneled doors each decorated w/Chinese-style floral designs within a narrow raised molding, the doors separated & flanked by narrow vertical panels further decorated w/stylized flowers & leaves, a narrow serpentine decorate apron above the cabriole front legs ending in pad feet, square rear legs, shrinkage crack in the top, Europe, ca. 1880, 18 1/8 x 48 1/4", 39 7/8" h. (ILLUS.)................................. **$1,265**

Unique Renaissance-Style Sideboard

Renaissance-Style sideboard, carved oak, two-part contruction: the massive superstructure w/a very large broken-scroll pediment flanking low carved scrolls above the deep flaring, stepped & blocked cornice above a deep frieze w/a long central panel ornately carved w/a large wreath & floral swags flanked by projecting blocks & curved & carved side panels, supported on very heavy scroll-carved brackets centered by a four-panel back; the lower section w/a rectangular

top w/curved ends above a conforming case w/a long carved drawer over a pair of diamond- and scroll-carved cupboard doors flanked by tall carved blocks, the rounded ends w/a single scroll-carved drawer over an open compartment w/two rounded shelves, deep blocked plinth base, Europe, late 19th c., 17 1/2 x 70", 95" h. (ILLUS.) **$1,840**

Italian Renaissance-Style Sideboard

Renaissance-Style sideboard, carved walnut, two-part construction: the upper section w/a long rectangular top w/a widely flaring stepped cornice above a row of three rectangular paneled doors finely carved w/ornate scrolls & medallions & flanked at the side by turned columns, all projecting above a narrow scroll-carved back panel & caryatid-carved supports; the lower section w/a long rectangular top w/a molded edge above a frieze fitted w/three narrow carved drawers over three large paneled cupboard doors w/ornately carved scrolls & medallions all flanked by turned & carved corner columns, the gadroon-carved base raised on carved paw front feet, 16th-century Italian Tuscan-style, Italy, late 19th c., 23 x 81", 81" h. (ILLUS.)...................................... **$1,610**

Very Long Ornately Carved Rococo-Style Server

Rococo-Style server, carved mahogany, the long narrow top w/projecting rounded ends & molded edges above a deep apron decorated w/a very ornately pierce-carved design of Rococo scrolls & leaves, raised on cabriole legs w/floral-carved knees & ending in scroll feet on pegs, dark finish, early 20th c., 25 x 74", 30" h. (ILLUS., bottom previous page).... **$1,150**

American Victorian Baroque-Style Sideboard

Victorian Baroque-Style sideboard, carved oak, the long rectangular top w/a low rectangular back crest ornately carved w/scrolling leaves centered by a cabochon, the apron w/a pair of curved-front drawers ornately carved w/leafy scrolls & flanked at each end by a carved lion head block, raised on heavy scroll- and leaf-carved cabriole front supports resting on a lower shelf w/a serpentine front & backed by a large rectangular mirror, raised on heavy carved paw feet, ca. 1900, 27 x 48 1/2", 36" h. (ILLUS.) **$1,150**

Victorian Elizabethan-Style sideboard, carved oak, two-part construction: the high upper section w/three large carved panels, the raised central horizontal panel topped by an arched scroll- and leaf-carved crest above a heavily chip-carved frame inscribed at the top "I And My House Will Serve The Lord" over the relief-carved panel showing the "Judgment of Christ," all above a projecting narrow shelf w/the narrow apron inscribed "Ye Yeare of Jubilee - 1614" supported on carved seated lions holding a shield flanking a cupboard w/tapering carved panel sides & a small carved panel door, the large vertical side panels each w/a flaring cornice w/a scroll-carved crest above a carved frame, one inscribed at the top "Thomas Machen" & the other "Christian Machen," each panel ornately carved w/an arch & floral pilasters enclosing a large shield & floral scrolls; the lower section w/a long rectangular top above a narrow projecting apron fitted w/a row of narrow drawers carved w/a repeating band of round knobs, rectangular blocks & diamond blocks, supported on five pairs of slender knob-turned & fluted columns supported on blocks along the open bottom shelf backed by large back panels carved w/rosettes, sunbursts, a large diamond & scrolls, raised on five heavy bun feet, England, late 19th c., 22 x 90", 98" h. (ILLUS., bottom of page) **$4,830**

Unique Elizabethan-Style Carved & Inscribed Oak Sideboard

Very Ornate Golden Oak Carved Sideboard

Victorian Golden Oak sideboard, oak, two-part construction: the tall super-structure w/a serpentine low crestrail centered by a large shell-carved crest flanked by griffin heads over a rounded gadroon-carved band & a pair of low arched mirrored panels centered by a carved female head   all flanked by heavy rounded end brackets, a narrow open shelf raised on turned columnar supports over a long rectangular horizontal mirror; the lower section w/a rectangular brown Tennessee marble top above a case w/a long drawer w/two ornate brass pulls beside a small matching drawer all above a pair of small drawers over squared cupboard doors w/a large roundel flanking the very large central door ornately carved w/winged devices above an arched panel carved w/a large shell suspending long leafy scrolls, the side stiles w/curved blocks & ring- and urn-turned columns, a long line-incised apron,   on   casters, ca.   1890s, 26 1/2 x 70 1/2", 92 1/2" h. (ILLUS.) **$3,220**

Victorian Golden Oak sideboard, three-part construction: the long half-round top w/a removable fan-carved crest centered by pair of small carved putti flanking a shield; the upper section w/rounded ends each w/two curved & leaded glass panels flanking a pair of central clear leaded glass doors centered by pink leaded blossoms & raised at the front by large carved C-scrolls each supporting a full-figure winged lady, the

Fantastically Detailed Victorian Golden Oak Sideboard

back panel fitted w/a long beveled mirror; the lower section w/wide rounded corners each composed of a curved & leaded glass end panel & a curved, leaded glass door flanking the center swelled cabinet fitted w/a pair of small drawers w/simple bail pulls above a pair of large flat doors decorated at the center w/delicate scrolls above a single long drawer, the front raised on short cabriole legs w/paw feet, square back legs, ca. 1900, 22 x 61", overall 83" h. (ILLUS.) **$11,213**

Victorian Renaissance Revival credenza, inlaid rosewood, the long rectangular top inset w/white marble w/side concave ends above the conforming case w/a dentil-carved top band above the concave ends each w/a line-inlaid panel above large concave panels w/rectangular molding enclosing a light burl panel centered w/an entwined loop inlay, the flat front section w/two long very shallow drawers w/inlaid bands & small brass teardrop pulls above large cabinet doors w/border molding enclosing delicate inlaid rectangles centered by a large inlaid oval w/a very ornate design of multiple birds among branches, the conforming deep base raised on thin disk front feet, attributed to Herter Brothers, ca. 1880s, 20 x 65", 42" h. (ILLUS., top next page) **$4,830**

Very Ornately Inlaid Victorian Renaissance Revival Credenza

Signed Victorian Renaissance Server

Victorian Renaissance Revival server, ebonized & carved oak, the top back w/an ornately carved crestrail w/a tall center cartouche flanked by ornate scrolls & floral swags connecting at each side to full-figure carved winged putti, the rectangular top w/blocked front corners above a conforming apron w/florette-carved corner blocks flanking a singled long drawer carved w/a wildflower & vines, the front supported by tall caryatid-carved uprights supporting two long open shelves, the lower shelf w/a molded border raised on two front bun feet, by W.B. Moses & Sons, Washington, D.C., marked w/a metal tag on back of the re-movable crest, ca. 1870, 21 x 44", over-all 51 1/2" h. (ILLUS.) **$1,035**

Victorian Renaissance Revival server, gilt-incised & marquetry-inlaid walnut, the very tall superstructure w/a high stepped & arched cornice decorated w/line-incised flower & scrolls & carved drapes flanked by small tapering raised

Rare American Renaissance Server

burl panels, a narrow decorative frieze band above a tall central ebonized panel inlaid w/large ribbon-tied cluster of ob-jects representing the Arts, each tall side section w/a central arched burl panel mounted w/two tiered half-round shelves & flanked by double turned colo-nettes, the rectangular top of tan marble above a case w/a narrow frieze drawer flanked by carved blocks above a large paneled cupboard doors w/ebonized molding enclosing a raised burl panel boldly carved w/drapery swags sus-pending a flower & fruit cluster, raised blocked & narrow raised burl side panels above the deep blocked plinth base, ca. 1870s, 21 x 42", 98" h. (ILLUS.) **$5,750**

Renaissance Revival Game-carved Sideboard

Victorian Renaissance Revival side-board, carved walnut, two-part construction: the tall superstructre w/an arched crestrail above scroll-carved stepped sides centered at the top w/a large boldly carved hanging game cluster flanked by small half-round open shelves all above a narrow rectangular shelf raised on scroll-carved brackets flanking two rectangular molded panels; the lower section w/a rectangular white marble top w/molded edges above a case w/a pair of drawers w/raised rectangular molding & scroll-carved pulls over a medial band & a pair of large paneled cupboard doors w/raised square molding panels centering scroll-carved cartouches, the deep flat apron on thin rounded bracket feet on casters, ca. 1870s, 21 1/2 x 54", 83" h. (ILLUS.)... **$2,990**

Fine Renaissance Revival Sideboard with Carved Scrolls & Fruit

Victorian Renaissance Revival sideboard, carved walnut, two-part construction: the upper superstructure w/an arched & scroll-molded crestrail over a large fruit-carved cluster above the long narrow half-round shelves raised on heavy S-scroll fruit-carved supports, the stepped S-scroll-carved sides also carved w/fruit clusters; the lower section w/a long white marble top w/rounded ends above a conforming case w/a pair of flat paneled drawers w/turned wood knobs over a pair of paneled cupboard doors centered by large carved fruit clusters, the rounded ends each w/a drawer above a curved paneled door, flat molded apron on thick block feet, ca. 1870, 21 x 70 1/2", 73" h. (ILLUS.) **$3,220**

Very Ornate American Victorian Renaissance Revival Sideboard

Very Fine Carved Renaissance Sideboard

Victorian Renaissance Revival sideboard, inlaid walnut & burl walnut, a very tall top backsplash w/an arched & molded cornice centered by a large carved palmette above raised burl panels & trimmed w/carved leafy scrolls, the three-part base w/a higher projecting central section w/a narrow burl panel drawer above a tall paneled cupboard door finely decorated w/an oblong panel featuring an incised gilt center starburst & leaf sprigs all flanked by ornately carved & burl-inlaid pilasters; slightly shorter matching side sections w/a narrow drawer above matching molding & decorative oblong panels, ornate front corner pilasters, deep stepped & blocked flat base, New York City, ca. 1865-70, 22 x 60", 56" h. (ILLUS.) **$4,888**

Victorian Renaissance Revival style sideboard, carved oak, the high super-structure topped by a high arched & ornate pierce-carved crest w/scrolling leaves & flowers centered by a realistic fox head above a tall back w/two narrow graduated open shelves raised on turned spindles & backed by pairs of carved panels centered by a paterae, all resting on the long rectangular top w/angled projecting front corners above a conforming case w/a pair of long narrow ornately carved drawers over a pair of rectangular cupboard doors each carved w/a pair of tall narrow vertical scroll-carved panels flanking a central oval panel carved w/fish & fowl trophies, the angled corners w/turned colonettes, the deep flat base w/projecting corner blocks, ca. 1870, 24 1/2 x 69", overall 88" h. (ILLUS.)....... **$4,225**

Fine Early English Oak Low Welsh Dresser

Welsh dresser, oak, the long rectangular top fitted w/a low four-panel backrail, the flaring molding above a pair of long drawers w/the original engraved brass pulls above a mid-molding over the two-part serpentine apron raised on six simple cabriole legs ending in pad feet, old patina, England, 19th c., 20 x 65 1/2", 33 1/2" h. (ILLUS.) **$4,600**

Stands

Simple Victorian Blanket Stand

Blanket stand, Victorian country-style, mahogany, side turned uprights w/a forked rolled top joined by two bars, three cross bars down the uprights, flared & arched forked feet, second half 19th c., 29 1/2" h. (ILLUS.) **$1,434**

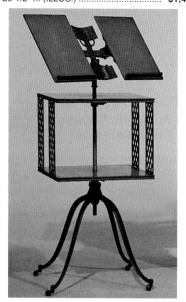

Interesting Revolving Book Stand

Book stand, oak & iron, folding & revolving-type, the top w/oak board racks that fold together & adjust above a slender metal rod that goes through two rectangular oak shelves w/pairs of lattice supports, revolving above a base w/four serpentine outswept slender legs on casters, marked by R.M. Lambie, New York, ca.

1900, missing top slat on central shelf section, some scratches, 16 x 16", 43 1/2" h. (ILLUS.) **$690**

Interesting Chippendale Candlestand

Candlestand, Chippendale, mahogany, a round white marble top enclosed by a pierced brass low gallery above a ring-turned columnar pedestal over the tripod base w/cabriole legs ending in claw-and-ball feet, New York, New York, ca. 1760-80, 17 3/4" d., 27" h. (ILLUS.) **$3,824**

Chippendale Tilt-top Candlestand

Candlestand, Chippendale, mahogany, tilt-top style, the large square top w/serpentine edges tilting above a vase- and ring-turned pedestal on a tripod base w/flattened cabriole legs ending in arris pad feet on platforms, old finish, very minor imperfections, Massachusetts, late 18th c., 28" w., 28 3/4" h. (ILLUS.) **$4,113**

Rare Early Chippendale Candlestand

Candlestand, Chippendale tilt-top style, walnut, the round dished top above a birdcage tilting mechanism above the baluster- and ring-turned pedestal, tripod base w/cabriole legs ending in claw-and-ball feet, Chester County, Pennsylvania, 1750-70, 20" d., 27" h. (ILLUS.) **$14,400**

Federal Country-style Candlestand

Candlestand, Federal country style, stained birch, the two-board square top w/a slight warp raised on an urn-turned pedestal on a tripod base w/spider legs,

original dark red wash, minor hairlines, late 18th - early 19th c., 18" w., 30 1/4" h. (ILLUS.) **$690**

Rare Federal Inlaid Candlestand

Candlestand, Federal, inlaid & carved mahogany, long octagonal top w/banded inlay tilting above a tapering fluted & leaf-carved pedestal on a tripod base w/spider feet ending in tapering blocks, Boston, possibly carved by Thomas Wightman, 1800-10, 19 x 26 1/2", 29 1/4" h. (ILLUS.) **$28,800**

Candlestand, Federal style, butternut & maple, the long octagonal top w/applied molded edges raised on a ring- and knob-turned pedestal above the tripod base w/flattened cabriole legs, New England, 18th c., traces of old red paint, old refinish, imperfections, 17 x 17 1/2", 28" h. (ILLUS. back row right with four other Federal candlestands, top next page) **$1,528**

Candlestand, Federal style, cherry, nearly square top w/serpentine edges & rounded corners raised on a baluster-turned pedestal over a tripod base w/cabriole legs ending in pad feet, New England, ca. 1790, old refinish, imperfections, 16" w., 24 3/4" h. (ILLUS. front row left with four other Federal candlestands, top next page) **$764**

Candlestand, Federal style, cherry, round top above a single double-sided candle drawer raised on baluster- and ring-turned pedestal over a tripod base w/flattened cabriole legs ending in pad feet, old dark stain, New England, late 18th - early 19th c., alterations, repairs, 16 1/2" d., 26 1/4" h. (ILLUS. front row right with four other Federal candlestands, top next page) **$823**

Group of Five Federal Candlestands

Federal Oval-topped Candlestand

Candlestand, Federal style, cherry, the elongated oval top tilting above a slender baluster- and ring-turned pedestal on a tripod base w/flat cabriole legs ending in snake feet, steel reinforcing plate on the bottom, some old repair, slight warp to top, ca. 1800, 27 3/4" h. (ILLUS.).............. **$660**

Candlestand, Federal style, cherry, the nearly square top w/serpentine edges & rounded corners raised on a baluster-turned pedestal over a tripod base w/cabriole legs ending in arris pad feet, Connecticut River Valley, ca. 1790, refinished, minor restoration, 18" w., 26" h. (ILLUS. center back row with four other Federal candlestands, top of page)........ **$2,938**

Candlestand, Federal style, inlaid cherry, rectangular top w/a string-inlaid edge raised on a baluster-turned pedestal above a tripod base w/cabriole legs ending in arris pad feet, probably Connecti-

cut, imperfections, ca. 1790, 13 3/4 x 15", 26 3/4" h. (ILLUS. far left with four other Federal candlestands, top of page).. **$1,116**

Federal Inlaid Cherry Candlestand

Candlestand, Federal style, inlaid cherry, the small square top w/fan-inlaid corners & cloverleaf line inlay above the urn-turned columnar pedestal on a tripod base w/cabriole legs ending in slipper feet, Connecticut, 1790-1810, 13" w., 26 1/4" h. (ILLUS.) **$4,780**

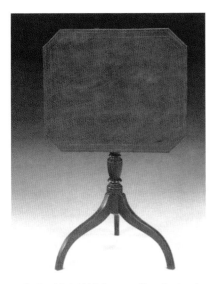

Federal Inlaid Mahogany Candlestand

Candlestand, Federal style, inlaid mahogany, the nearly square top w/chamfered corners decorated w/a band of line-inlay, titled above a columnar-turned pedestal on a tripod base w/spider legs, probably New York, 1790-1810, 22 7/8 x 25 5/8", 29 1/2" h. (ILLUS.) **$4,800**

Fine Queen Anne Candlestand

Candlestand, Queen Anne, cherry & maple, the round top above a turned columnar pedestal w/a knobbed base raised on a tripod base w/cabriole legs ending in snake feet, probably Pennsylvania, late 18th - early 19th c., 17" d., 24 1/2" h. (ILLUS.).................................. **$9,000**

Country Queen Anne Candlestand

Candlestand, Queen Anne country-style, painted, the round top above a slender baluster- and ring-turned pedestal on a tripod base w/flat cabriole legs ending in snake feet, old green paint, New England, 18th c., 17" d., 26" h. (ILLUS.) **$2,640**

Rare Early American Candlestand

Candlestand, William & Mary country-style, painted maple, the central slender screw pole w/a ring-turned two-arm candleholder above a turned platform over a ring- and ball-turned pedestal on a tripod base w/three widely canted rod- and knob-turned legs, old red paint, New England, 1730-50, 43 1/4" h. (ILLUS.) **$3,585**

English Regency-Style Canterbury

Canterbury (music stand), mahogany, Regency-Style, rectangular frame fitted w/four slotted compartments & a carrying handle divided by flat slats & bamboo-turned corner posts w/button finials, the apron w/a single paneled drawer w/round brass pulls, raised on ring- and baluster-turned legs on brass casters, England, late 19th c., 15 x 18 1/2", 23 1/2" h. (ILLUS.).................................... **$345**

Painted Country-style Crock Stand

Crock stand, country style, painted pine & poplar, an arched crest flanked by arched sides on the one-board sides w/arched base cut-outs, two closed-back shelves, square & round head nail construction, old green paint, backboards w/varnished splits, two feet w/added pads, second half 19th c., 13 1/2 x 37 1/4", 44 1/4" h. (ILLUS.).................................... **$403**

Rare Chippendale Mahogany Kettle Stand

Kettle stand, Chippendale, mahogany, square top w/low undulating gallery & candle slide raised on a ring-turned columnar post on a tripod base w/cabriole legs ending in arris pad feet on platforms, old refinish, probably Massachusetts, imperfections, 12 x 12 1/4", 24" h. (ILLUS.) **$11,163**

Marked Stickley Oak Magazine Stand

Magazine stand, Mission-style (Arts & Crafts movement), oak, the rectangular top w/an arched back crest & downswept low sides above three shelves w/a closed back, the bottom shelf w/a narrow arched apron, worn original finish, "The Work of..." mark of L. & J.G. Stickley, early 20th c., 12 x 22", 44 3/4" h. (ILLUS.) **$2,415**

Nice Limbert Mission Magazine Stand

Magazine stand, Mission-style (Arts & Crafts movement), oak, the tall tapering sides w/two squared cut-outs joined by five long graduated open shelves above a narrow apron, branded mark of the Charles Limbert Furniture Company, early 20th c., 13 x 23 1/2", 40" h. (ILLUS.) **$3,450**

George III-Style Mahogany Music Stand

Music stand, George III-Style, carved mahogany, adjustable folio racks w/hinged & slated sides raised on a slender column-turned pedestal above a tripod base w/legs carved to resemble human legs wearing low shoes, England, late 19th - early 20th c., 24" w., 39 3/4" h. (ILLUS.) ... **$489**

Victorian Stick & Ball Music Stand

Music stand, late Victorian, stick-and-ball construction w/four open stick shelves joining the tall stick sides w/the corner posts topped by ball finials & raised on ball feet, late 19th - early 20th c., 18" w., 38" h. (ILLUS.) **$196**

Ornate Rococo Papier-mâché Music Stand

Music stand, Victorian Rococo style, inlaid papier-mâché, tilt-top style, the oblong cartouche-form tilt top w/serpentine sides fitted w/a narrow music rack against a black background ornately inlaid w/mother-of-pearl florals & gilt trim, raised on a heavy spiral-turned pedestal on a tripod base w/flattened scroll-carved legs decorated w/fancy gilt scrolls, in the manner of Jennens & Bettridge, England, ca. 1850, 18 x 18", 43" h. (ILLUS.) **$2,300**

French Renaissance Revival Nightstands

Nighstands, Victorian Renaissance Revival substyle, carved rosewood, a nearly square white marble top w/canted front corners above a conforming case w/a small drawer w/a scroll-carved pull above a cupboard door centered by a tall scroll-carved panel, the bottom of the canted corners mounted w/a scroll-carved bracket above the blocked plinth base on casters, France, ca. 1870s, 16 x 17", 30" h., pr. (ILLUS.) **$2,760**

Unusual Art Nouveau Nightstands

Nightstands, Art Nouveau style, ormolu-mounted carved mahogany, small square pink marble inset tops w/high arched & loop-pierced backsplash above a case w/a small narrow drawer supported by slender flower-carved legs w/forked stems at the top above a tall open compartment above a lower shelf over a small square paneled door, serpentine leaf-carved apron on short canted feet, the lower cabinets lined w/white marble, designed by Louis Majorelle, France, ca. 1905, 13 x 16 1/8", 41" h., pr. (ILLUS.).. **$8,365**

Fine Renaissance Revival Nightstand

Nightstand, Victorian Renaissance Revival substyle, walnut & burl walnut, the rectangular white marble top w/projecting rounded corners above the case w/a single drawer w/pierced brass butterfly pulls above a short door w/a large arched burl panel all flanked by boldly carved caryatids at the canted front corners, paneled sides, deep platform base w/blocked corners, on casters, ca. 1875, 18 3/4 x 24 3/4", 28" h. (ILLUS.) **$1,265**

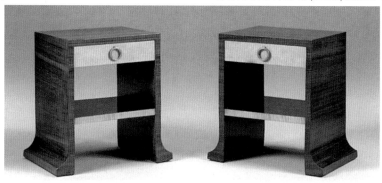

Fine French Art Deco Nightstands

Nightstands, Art Deco style, rosewood & sycamore, the rectangular top above flat sides w/curved-out bases, flanking a narrow sycamore top drawer w/ring pull & a lower medial shelf w/sycamore facing, designed by Jean Pascaud, France, ca. 1933, 13 3/4 x 15 1/2", 19 3/4" h., pr. (ILLUS.) **$5,975**

Fine American Rococo Nightstands

Nightstands, Victorian Rococo style, carved rosewood, rectangular white marble top above a case w/a narrow frieze drawer above a tall paneled door outlined w/a thin gadrooned band & flanked by canted front corners w/bold upper & lower carved scrolls, plinth base raised on disk feet, ca. 1850s, 16 x 20", 32" h., pr. (ILLUS.) **$7,188**

Unusual Reverse-painted Parlor Stand

Parlor stand, Victorian Renaissance Revival substyle, walnut & reverse-painted glass, the tilting round top w/a molded scalloped wood frame enclosing a large round reverse-painted glass panel decorated in the center w/an oval reserve h.p. w/a seascape w/boats & castle surrounded by a wide black border decorated w/large delicate lacy, lattice & swag gilt designs, tilting above the four-section base w/molded S-scroll supports joined to a central post w/an urn-turned

finial & turned drop supports by four molded flat S-scroll legs, some flaking to painted panel, mid-19th c., 23" d., 29 1/2" h. (ILLUS.) **$690**

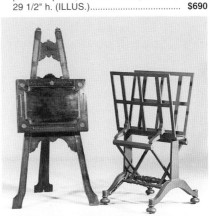

Victorian Picture & Print Stands

Picture stand, carved rosewood, a tapering upright framework w/flattened legs joined by a rectangular raised-panel box backed w/a hinged swing-out back leg, England, ca. 1900, 29 1/2" w., 62 1/2" h. (ILLUS. left with ebonized print stand) **$978**

Oak 17th Century Trestle-base Stand

Pilgrim century stand, oak, a rectangular top w/cut corners raised on a trestle base w/flat scalloped end legs joined just under the top w/a rectangular stretcher & four angled braces, stepped shoe feet, probably England or Europe, 17th c., 18 x 33", 29" h. (ILLUS.) **$978**

Plant stand, Art Deco style, ceramic & wrought iron, the round ceramic top glazed w/a yellow background highlighted w/a bright abstract geometric band in shades of blue, green, yellow & orange, a tall ceramic conical matching base mounted in a wrought-iron stand w/outswept scrolling curl legs, marked "Made in Italy," ca. 1930s (ILLUS., next page)..... **$259**

Unusual Ceramic & Iron Art Deco Stand

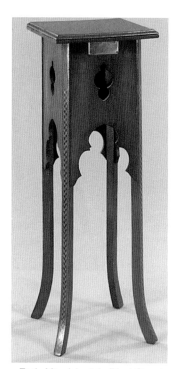

Early Moorish-style Plant Stand

Plant stand, Arts & Crafts style, oak, the small, nearly square top w/a molded edge overhanging a deep apron centered

by a pierced oblong opening above the high Moorish arch edge, the canted corners decorated w/a band of chevron inlay continuing down the slender square & outswept legs, ca. 1900, 11 x 12", 34 1/2" h. (ILLUS.) **$288**

Carved & Inlaid Oriental Plant Stand

Plant stand, carved & inlaid rosewood, Oriental style, the round top inlaid w/pink marble above the deep curved apron pierce carved w/scroll panels alternating w/panels inlaid w/mother-of-pearl vines, raised on notch-carved cabriole legs ending in paw feet & joined by a cross-stretcher, China, early 20th c., 44 1/2" h. (ILLUS.)... **$431**

Fine Late Victorian Oak Plant Stand

Plant stand, carved oak, late Victorian style, a square foot w/a thick ringed base below the tall heavy column w/a spiral-carved lower section below the plain cylindrical upper section w/a scroll-carved capital below the small square top, ca. 1890-1900, 12" sq. top, overall 37" h. (ILLUS.).. **$805**

Early Spiral-twist Turned Plant Stand

Plant stand, late Victorian, carved hardwood, the small round top raised on a bold spiral-twist turned column above a leaf-carved knob above the dished round base on small knob feet, ca. 1900, 12" d., 41 1/2" h. (ILLUS.) **$345**

Victorian Carved & Turned Plant Stand

Plant stand, late Victorian, turned & carved oak, a small round top raised on a tall ornately ring-turned pedestal topped by a full-relief carved classical woman's head, on a round foot w/small knob feet, late 19th - early 20th c., 35 1/2" h. (ILLUS.) **$230**

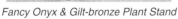

Fancy Onyx & Gilt-bronze Plant Stand

Plant stand, late Victorian, onyx & gilt-bronze, composed of two square inset pieces of white onyx in an ornate metal framework w/onyx columns & finials raised on delicate scrolling & outswept gilt-bronze legs w/dolphin feet, ca. 1900, 16" w., 34 1/2" h. (ILLUS.)........................ **$978**

Late Victorian Turned Plant Stand

Plant stand, late Victorian, turned oak, the thin round top raised on a slender pedestal w/two fluted columns joined by a central knob w/four pointed disks, supported on a domed, stepped round base on small outswept feet, late 19th - early 20th c., 19" d, 33 1/2" h. (ILLUS.)............ **$219**

Rare French Victorian Neo-Grec Stand

Plant stand, parcel-gilt bronze-mounted & ebonized wood, Victorian Neo-Grec style, a round black Belgian marble top framed w/a narrow gadrooned band w/shell drops & raised on a tripod base composed of carved full-body satyr-topped monopodiae joined by a central slender post w/a central disk over scrolls, the outswept legs w/hoof feet resting on a tripartite base, by Charpentier et Cie., Paris, France, ca. 1867, 41 1/2" h. (ILLUS.) **$22,705**

Ornately Carved Walnut Plant Stand

Plant stand, Victorian Aesthetic Movement style, carved walnut, the round top w/a wide band of foliate carving above the three-paneled apron carved w/detailed

leaves & florals, raised on three square & highly carved legs joined by carved flat stretchers joined by a central post w/a carved & domed finial, outswept paw-carved feet, Cincinnati Art Club, Ohio, ca. 1880s, 12" d., 29" h. (ILLUS.) **$1,725**

Victorian Bamboo Planter with Liner

Plant stand, Victorian, bamboo type, a long narrow rectangular well w/a metal liner supported in a geometric bamboo framework centered on each side w/a square plaque painted w/an Oriental figure, bamboo rod trestle base w/bamboo bracket trim, France, mid-19th c., 11 x 37 1/2" l., 30" h. (ILLUS.) **$863**

Plant stands, Regency-Style, mahogany, circular top above molded frieze, three supports w/scrolled mounts, shaped base, stylized paw feet, England, late 19th c., losses & separations to veneer, finish losses & wear, some legs loose, 42" h., pr. **$605**

Print stand, ebonized wood, the top composed of rectangular lattice adjustable panels raised on a trestle-style base w/projecting frames on each side above the arched base on cushion feet joined by a ring- and baluster-turned stretcher, England, early 20th c., 28" w., 44" h. (ILLUS. right with rosewood picture stand, page 285) **$805**

American Classical Walnut Sewing Stand

Sewing stand, Classical style, walnut, the rectangular hinged lid w/a raised center w/a thin hinged lid, the apron w/two long narrow drawers above the arched scroll-cut front apron, raised on tall slender squared serpentine legs joined by a cross-stretcher, drawers w/bird's-eye maple dividers, ca. 1830-40, 16 x 21", 30" h. (ILLUS.) **$460**

Victorian Federal-Style Sewing Stand

Sewing stand, Federal-Style, mahogany, the rectangular top w/rounded ends hinged to open to a divided interior w/pleated upholstered sides & ends, the upholstered panels separated by narrow reeded posts continuing into the very slender ring- and rod-turned legs, New York City or New England, late 19th c., replaced fabric, 13 1/4 x 23 1/2", 28 3/4" h. (ILLUS.) **$1,100**

Fine Gothic Revival Shaving Stand

Shaving stand, Victorian Gothic Revival style, carved rosewood, the top w/a small Gothic arch frame enclosing a mirror swiveling between slender bobbin-turned uprights supported on a pedestal above a rectangular white marble top over a single small drawer supported on a tall paneled column ending in a paneled post supported on a tripod base w/outswept C-scroll legs, marble repaired, second quarter 19th c., 16" w., overall 6' h. (ILLUS.) **$2,760**

Rare Figural Cast-Iron Umbrella Stand

Umbrella/cane stand, cast iron, the upright section cast as a realistic small dog standing on its rear legs & holding a long double-loop whip in its mouth, all painted in naturalistic colors, raised on a cast-iron base w/a blue cylindrical pedestal above the wide fanned & scroll-cast base w/a drip tray cast as large blue leaves, some paint wear, second half 19th c., 12 x 24", 24" h. (ILLUS.) **$3,220**

Washstand, Classical, carved mahogany, a serpentine & scroll-carved high three-quarters gallery on the top surrounding a bowed top centered by a round bowed opening & w/two tiny drawers flanking the central bowed section, raised on ring- and rod-turned back supports & bold carved & molded S-scroll front supports terminating in floral-carved scrolls resting on a medial shelf w/a concave front over a conforming drawer w/round brass pulls, all raised on baluster-, knob- and ring-turned legs, refinished, probably Boston, ca. 1800-25, 16 1/2 x 19 1/2", 38" h. (minor restorations) **$1,880**

Washstand, Classical style, mahogany & mahogany veneer, the rectangular black marble top fitted w/a three-quarters gallery w/a high scroll-carved backsplash & outswept low scrolled sides, the case w/a long ogee-front drawer over a pair of paneled cupboard doors flanked by simple pilasters, C-scroll front feet, ca. 1830s, 18 1/2 x 40 1/2", 43" h. (ILLUS., next page).. **$1,150**

American Classical Mahogany Washstand

Nice Classical Marble Top Washstand

Washstand, Classical style, mahogany & mahogany veneer, the top w/a high scroll-cut three-quarters gallery over the grey marble rectangular top above an apron w/a round-fronted long drawer w/two early pressed glass knobs above a pair of paneled cupboard doors flanked by reeded stiles, on short ring- and knob-turned feet, Philadelphia, ca. 1830, 19 x 28", 36 1/2" h. (ILLUS.) **$2,070**

Classical Washstand with Mirror

Washstand, Classical style, mahogany & mahogany veneer, the rectangular white marble top fitted w/a large oval mirror swiveling in a long U-shaped support raised on a low pedestal base, the case w/a long narrow drawer above a pair of flat cupboard doors, deep plinth base raised on ball-shaped front feet, probably New York City, ca. 1830, 20 x 42", 67" h. (ILLUS.) **$2,185**

Rare Tiger Stripe Maple Classical Washstand

Washstand, Classical style, tiger stripe maple, the rectangular top fitted w/a high rolled three-quarters gallery above a single long drawer w/a small round brass replaced pulls, raised on four simple turned posts joined a rectangular medial shelf w/incurved sides, raised on knob- and ring-turned legs w/knob feet, old refinish, Pennsylvania or Ohio, ca. 1830s, imperfections, 16 x 31", 34" h. (ILLUS.) **$5,875**

Rare New Hampshire Federal Washstand

Washstand, Federal corner-style, inlaid mahogany, the quarter-round top w/a delicate arched backsplash w/a tiny shelf above a top w/a large central hole flanked by smaller holes, the edge of the top w/delicate banded inlay, raised on three slender square supports above a medial shelf above an inlaid apron centered by a small drawer, raised on three slender outswept legs joined by a T-form stretcher, probably Portsmouth, New Hampshire, 1800-10, 16 1/2 x 23", 41" h. (ILLUS.) **$11,400**

Country Federal Cut-out Washstand

Washstand, Federal country style, painted pine, the square top w/a three-quarters gallery above a large cut-out round top

hole w/a smaller cut-out hole beside it, square supports continuing to form the legs & joined by a medial shelf above a drawer w/two small wooden knobs, original dark red paint, first half 19th c., 16 1/2" sq., 31 3/4" h. (ILLUS.) **$460**

Lovely Federal Mahogany Washstand

Washstand, Federal style, inlaid mahogany, the rectangular hinged top w/inlaid edge & attached faux drawer front w/oval crotch mahogany panels bordered by stringing & mitered border opening to a pierced seat above two faux string-inlaid drawers w/ivory diamond escutcheons, all on slightly flaring French feet joined by a shaped skirt w/inlaid crossbanding, original brasses, old refinish, probably Massachusetts, ca. 1805, minor imperfections, 16 1/2 x 23", 27 1/2" h. (ILLUS.) ... **$3,055**

Early New England Federal Washstand

Washstand, Federal style, mahogany & bird's-eye maple veneer, corner-style, the shaped backsplash w/a quarter-round shelf above the pierced top, on square outward-flaring legs joined by a valanced skirt & beaded medial shelf w/conformingly shaped drawer & inlaid edge, shaped stretchers below, possibly Boston, ca. 1800-10, refinished, 15 x 22", 38 1/2" h. (ILLUS.) **$2,820**

Late Victorian Oak Washstand

Washstand, late Victorian style, oak, a rectangular top slightly overhanging a base w/a long drawer w/stamped brass & bail pulls above two deep drawers beside a single paneled door, simple molded base & paneled sides, ca. 1900, missing the towel bar, 31" w., 28" h. (ILLUS.) **$94**

Aesthetic Movement Carved Washstand

Washstand, Victorian Aesthetic Movement substyle, carved walnut, the tall superstructure w/an undulating carved crest

above a molding & foliate-carved frieze band above a large round beveled mirror w/triangular foliate-carved panels at each corner, raised atop a white marble backsplash & rectangular marble top above a case fitted with two long drawers w/incised decoration & pierced brass pulls w/squared bails, a pair of paneled doors at the bottom, each centered by large round panels, plinth base on casters, ca. 1880, 17 x 36", 6' 2" h. (ILLUS.) **$805**

Victorian Aesthetic Style Washstand

Washstand, Victorian Aesthetic Movement substyle, walnut, the rectangular top fitted w/a brass bar gallery above a single narrow drawer w/two rectangular aluminum bail pulls over a single raised panel door w/line-incised floral decoration, slender square reeded stile legs, late 19th c., 16 x 24", 34" h. (ILLUS.) **$185**

Victorian Country Turned Washstand

Washstand, Victorian country style, walnut, the rectangular top w/a high arched & scroll-cut backsplash decorated w/two rondels & flanked by outswept open end towel bars, the carved top edge above a single long drawer w/long wooden bar pull raised on bobbin-turned supports joined by a medial shelf w/incurved front above the bobbin-turned feet, ca. 1870-80, 33" w., 29" h. (ILLUS.)....................... **$127**

Marble-top Renaissance Washstand

Washstand, Victorian Renaissance Revival style, walnut, a low vertical white marble backsplash above the rectangular white marble top over a case w/a long drawer w/raised oval molded & carved pulls above a pair of cupboard doors w/arched molding panels, plinth base on casters, ca. 1875, 16 x 27", 31" h. (ILLUS.)............................ **$374**

Victorian Renaissance Revival Washstand

Washstand, Victorian Renaissance Revival substyle, walnut & burl walnut, the rectangular white marble top w/a rectangular backsplash fitted w/two small half-round shelves, the case w/a long drawer w/a narrow raised burl panel & carved leaf pulls above a pair of cupboard doors centered by raised rectangular burl panels, canted front corners w/scroll-carved mounts, deep plinth base on casters, 16 x 29", 36 1/2" h. (ILLUS.) **$250-450**

Victorian Marble-topped Washstand

Washstand, Victorian Renaissance Revival substyle, walnut, the white marble rectangular top w/a serpentine splash guard above the case w/a single long drawer trimmed w/two raised-molding panels w/leaf-carved pulls & a central round molded circle, the lower cabinet w/a pair of cupboard doors w/arched raised molding panels, deep molded base on casters, ca. 1870, 17 1/2 x 31 1/2", 36" h. (ILLUS.) **$345**

Grain-painted Federal One-drawer Stand

Federal country-style one-drawer stand, painted & decorated, nearly square top overhanging the apron fitted w/a single drawer w/a small turned wood knob, on four tall slender square tapering legs, original black swirling w/red grain painting, first half 19th c., 17 3/4 x 18 3/4", 30 1/2" h. (ILLUS.) **$863**

Federal country-style stand, cherry, nearly square two-board top overhanging a deep apron raised on slender rod-, ring & knob-turned tapering legs w/tall thin peg feet, found in Ohio, glued age split in top, some replaced glue blocks, first half 19th c., 19 1/2 x 19 3/4", 29" h. **$489**

Fine Federal Two-drawer Stand

Federal country-style two-drawer stand, cherry & bird's-eye maple, rectangular top flanked by wide hinged drop leaves above an apron fitted w/two small bird's-eye maple drawers w/large early lacy glass pulls, on ring- and rod-turned legs w/tall peg feet raised on original brass casters, first half 19th c., open 20 x 34 1/2", 27 3/4" h. (ILLUS.) **$1,495**

Federal Country Maple Stand

Federal country-style two-drawer stand, tiger stripe & bird's-eye maple, the nearly square top above a deep apron fitted w/two bird's-eye maple drawers w/small turned wood knobs, on four baluster-, ring- and knob-turned legs w/pointed knob feet, ca. 1830, 19 x 20", 27 1/2" h. (ILLUS.) **$575**

Federal Painted & Decorated Stand

Federal one-drawer stand, painted & decorated, the nearly square top decorated w/a decoupaged design above the decorated apron fitted w/a single drawer w/two round brass pulls, square slender tapering legs, old ebonized background, old paper label inscribed w/the name of the owner/decorator in Worcester, Massachusetts, New England, first half 19th c., 14 x 15 1/2", 26 1/4" h. (ILLUS.) **$2,640**

Simple Federal Walnut One-drawer Stand

Federal one-drawer stand, the nearly square top above an apron fitted w/a single drawer a black knob, square tapering legs, 16" w., 28 1/2" h. (ILLUS.) **$264**

Federal two-drawer stand, mahogany & mahogany veneer, rectangular top flanked by a pair of half-round drop leaves above an apron w/two mahogany veneer drawers each w/two turned wood knobs, raised on slender ropetwist legs w/a knob- and ring-turned top section & ending in cuffed peg feet, old refinishing, veneer restoration on one drawer, first half 19th c., 16 1/4 x 17 1/2", 29" h. **$403**

Stools

Two Classical & a Victorian Organ Stool

French Baroque Style Walnut Stool

Baroque style stool, carved walnut, the rectangular needlepoint-upholstered top raised on four bold S-scroll legs joined by a double-scroll carved H-stretcher, France, late 18th - early 19th c., 18 x 19", 17" h. (ILLUS.) **$1,150**

Chippendale-Style Rosewood Footstool

Chippendale-Style footstool, rosewood, square upholstered top above a wide or-nate pierced scroll-carved apron raised on cabriole legs w/leaf-carved knees & claw-and-ball feet, British Colonial, probably from India, 19th c., 19" w., 18" h. (ILLUS.) ... **$805**
Classical organ stool, rosewood, the square upholstered top adjusting above a

ring- and rod-turned pedestal w/flaring ga-drooned band above the trefoil platform raised on scroll feet, old repair on base, possibly Vose Cabinet Shop, Boston, Massachusetts, ca. 1825, 11" w., 21" h. (ILLUS. left with two other organ stools, top of page) **$316**
Classical organ stool, rosewood, the square upholstered seat w/serpentine edges adjusting above the paneled bal-uster-form heavy pedestal raised on a platform w/four outswept log legs, ca. 1840, 14 1/2" w., 20" h. (ILLUS. right with two other organ stools, top of page) **$316**
Classical piano stool, rosewood veneer, the squared upholstered top above a deep serpentine apron, adjusting above a heavy tapering octagonal column resting on a cross-form base w/tapering feet, ve-neer damages, ca. 1840, 15" w., 20" h. (ILLUS. right with matching stool, below) ... **$690**

Two Classical Rosewood Piano Stools

Classical piano stool, rosewood veneer, the squared upholstered top above a deep serpentine apron, adjusting above a heavy tapering octagonal column rest-ing on a cross-form base w/tapering feet, good condition, ca. 1840, 15" w., 20" h. (ILLUS. left with matching stool) **$805**

French Directoire-Style Decorated Stools

Directoire-Style stools, polychrome-painted wood, the deep square upholstered top above a wide guilloche-carved apron on curved cross-form legs joined by a turned & fluted stetcher & ending in foliate-carved feet, France, late 19th c., 17" w., 19 1/2" h., pr. (ILLUS.).. **$2,990**

Pair of Fine Empire-Style Giltwood Stools

Empire-Style stools, giltwood, upholstered square top above a narrow reeded apron raised on X-form side legs headed by winged lion heads & ending in paw feet, late 19th c., 22" w., 18" h., pr. (ILLUS., middle of page) **$2,760**

Federal piano stool, mahogany, the round seat missing the upholstery adjusting above the round reeded apron raised on slightly canted legs w/ring- and ball-turned upper sections over tapering reed-ed sections on ring-turned feet fitted w/brass ball caps, central wood threaded column w/a slender turned long drop fini-al, New York City, ca. 1800-20, 20 1/2" h. (ILLUS.)... **$3,585**

Rare American Federal Piano Stool

English George II-Style Footstool

English George III-Style Leather-upholstered Stool

George II-Style footstool, carved walnut, rectangular upholstered slip seat above a deep burl apron raised on four cabriole legs w/shell-carved knees & ending in pad feet, late 19th - early 20th c., 16 x 21 1/2", 20" h. (ILLUS., previous page) **$660**

George III-Style stool, the rectangular leather-upholstered tufted seat raised on cabriole legs w/shell-carved knees & ending in hairy paw feet, England, late 19th - early 20th c., 25 x 39", 18" h. (ILLUS., top of page) **$1,840**

Louis XV stool, carved fruitwood, the rectangular tapestry-upholstered seat above a fancy scroll-carved apron raised on cabriole legs ending in scroll feet, France, 18th c., 19 1/2 x 23 1/2", 16" h. (ILLUS., next column)... **$2,415**

Original Louis XV Fruitwood Stool

Pair of Carved Walnut Louis XV-Style Stools

Louis XV-Style stools, parcel-gilt carved walnut, the deep rounded square upholstered seat above a serpentine carved apron raised on slender cabriole legs ending in scroll-and-peg feet, France, late 19th c., 16" w., 19" h., pr. (ILLUS.) **$920**

Nice Tobey Furniture Mission Oak Stool

Mission-style (Arts & Crafts style) footstool, oak & leather, the rectangular curved leather top w/tack trim mounted on a rectangular frame w/square legs joined by box stretchers, medallion mark of the Tobey Furniture Co. on the side of the top rail, replaced leather, early 20th c., 20 x 22", 16" h. (ILLUS.)... **$690**

Fine Gustav Stickley Mission Footstool

Mission-style (Arts & Crafts style) footstool, the rectangular top w/replaced burgundy upholstery w/tack trim along the slightly arched aprons, square corner legs w/slightly tapering feet joined by a flat cross-stretcher, cleaned & waxed original finish, faint signature of Gustav Stickley, early 20th c., 17 x 20", 17" h. (ILLUS.)... **$5,750**

Modernist piano stool, ebonized wood & leather, the low back w/a narrow leather cross strap, turned back stile legs & tall front legs joined by a leather seat, w/blue-stained terminals, designed by Gerrit Thomas Rietveld, ca. 1923, 29 1/2" h. (ILLUS., top next column) **$11,353**

Napoleon III stool, upholstered mahogany, the padded square top above a concave upright base raised on a carved base band & small bun feet, France, late 19th c., 13 1/2" w., 19" h. (ILLUS., middle next column)................................ **$259**

Rare Early Modernist Piano Stool

French Napoloen III Upholstered Stool

Ornately Carved Oriental Footstools

Oriental footstools, carved teak, the square top w/an ornately carved border & edges above an ornately carved curved & serpentine apron continuing into the cabriole legs ending in paw feet, China, late 19th - early 20th c., 20" w., 20" h., pr. (ILLUS.)... **$259**

English Regency Upholstered Long Stool

Regency stool, upholstered mahogany, the long rectangular top w/tufted upholstery raised on bulbous ring-turned & reeded legs on brass casters, England, early 19th c., 27 x 53", 18 1/2" h. (ILLUS.).......... **$1,495**

Fine English Regency-Style Stools

Regency-Style stools, painted & decorated, the rectangular upholstered top w/curved ends above a deep wood-grained apron w/gilt-bordered panels centered by a pierced gilt scroll & leaf cluster, raised on outswept sabre legs w/curved brackets & ending in paw feet, England, mid-19th c., 16 1/2 x 37 1/2", 18" h., pr. (ILLUS.)... **$8,625**

Pair of Victorian Aesthetic Movement Upholstered Stools

Victorian Aesthetic Movement substyle stools, upholstered mahogany, hexagonal upholstered top & side panels alternating w/vertical scroll-incised wood panels, on wooden casters, late 19th c., 15" w., 14" h., pr. (ILLUS.,) **$1,350**

Victorian organ stool, mixed wood, the tall back w/a wide shaped crestrail raised on baluster- and ring-turned canted stiles flanking five matching spindles, above the round adjustable seat above a round platform atop four canted tapering knob- and ring-turned legs ending in metal & glass claw-and-ball feet & joined by short turned spindles to a central post, ca 1900 (ILLUS. center with two Classical organ stools, top of 295) **$1,350**

French Renaissance Revival Stool

Victorian Renaissance Revival substyle stool, polychromed & ebonized beech, the square upholstered top above a pierced apron decorated w/carved pendants, raised on four square tapering legs on outswept feet joined by a turned cross-stretcher joined by a central ball, France, ca. 1865, 13" w., 19" h. (ILLUS.) **$518**

William & Mary-Style Upholstered Stool

William & Mary-Style stool, walnut, the rectangular upholstered top w/tack trim raised on knob- and block-turned legs w/knob feet & joined by baluster- and knob-turned side stretchers & a baluster- and knob-turned H-stretcher, England, late 19th - early 20th c., 17 x 20", 17" h. (ILLUS.) **$633**

Early American Windsor Footstool

Windsor footstool, turned hardwood w/pine top, long oval top raised on four canted knob-, ring- and tapering rod-turned legs joined by a swelled H-stretcher, old worn black or brown-stained sur-

face, top underside branded "B.B. T.," 18th c., 11 1/2 x 19 1/2", 8" h. (ILLUS.) **$633**

Tables

Fine Art Deco Round Coffee Table

Art Deco coffee table, walnut & shagreen, the round top centered by an inset circle of shagreen, molded apron & four thick & gently tapering legs w/scrolled tips, in the style of Sue et Mare, France, ca. 1925, 31 1/2" d., 19 1/4" h. (ILLUS.) **$6,214**

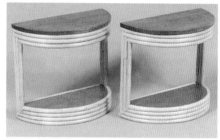

Art Deco Half-round Bamboo End Tables

Art Deco end tables, bent bamboo, a half-round wood top raised on a conforming bamboo rood rail & end upright above a matching lower wood shelf & curved bamboo base, ca. 1930s, 21" h., pr. (ILLUS.) **$431**

Art Deco Bent Bamboo Corner Table

Art Deco lamp table, corner-style, bent
bamboo, the upper triangular wooden
corner shelf on a low bent bamboo rod
frame resting on the squared wooden top
w/rounded corners raised on a deep
openwork bamboo rod apron on short
bamboo feet, ca. 1930s, 26" h. (ILLUS.,
previous page) **$431**

Rare French Art Deco Table

Art Deco side table, fruitwood, "Soleil" design, round top on a flat round apron
w/four low blocks above the square tapering legs capped by turned brass disks
& resting on square brass foot caps, designed by Andre Arubs, France, ca.
1940, 27 1/2" d., 25 3/4" h. (ILLUS.) **$17,925**

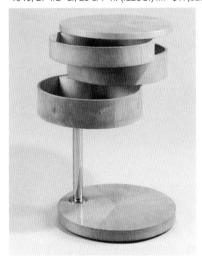

Rare French Art Deco Side Table

Art Deco side table, sycamore & chrome, a
round top above three offset round wood-
en trays raised on a chrome cylindrical
rod mounted at one side of the round

base, France, ca. 1930, 18 1/8" d.,
28 7/8" h. (ILLUS.) **$5,736**

Unique Art Deco "MB 106" Side Table

Art Deco side table, walnut, model "MB
106," fan-shaped extension-type, the
two-tier fanned top supported by a single
straight slender front leg & backed w/two
tiered & curved backboards, designed by
Pierre Chareau, France, ca. 1928, extended 15 x 24", 24" h. (ILLUS. extend-
ed).. **$50,190**

Art Nouveau Dressing Table

Art Nouveau dressing table, mahogany &
mahogany veneer, a superstructure w/a
very tall stylized heart-shaped beveled
mirror swiveling between slender serpentine uprights resting on oval compartments each w/a small curved-front drawer flanking a central drop well, raised on
four simple cabriole legs, 36" w., 5' 6" h.
(ILLUS.)... **$940**

Clematis Art Nouveau Side Table

Art Nouveau side table, carved mahogany, "Clematis" patt., the round top inset w/tan marble, the border carved w/a band of Art Nouveau florals above the shaped apron carved w/clematis blossoms & vines continuing down the three tapering molded legs joined by a triple-arched stretcher, designed by Louis Majorelle, France, ca. 1900, 24 1/4" d., 32" h. (ILLUS.) **$7,170**

Small Hexagonal Art Nouveau Side Table

Art Nouveau side table, stamped oak, the hexagonal top overhanging flat sides each stamped w/an Art Nouveau design of pairs of poppies on leafy vines above Moorish arch legs, ca. 1900 (ILLUS.)........ **$172**

Fine Limbert Arts & Crafts Table

Arts & Crafts center table, oak, chalet-style, the wide octagonal top overhanging wide flat tapering legs w/heart-shaped cut-outs joined to the wide cross-stretcher w/keyed through-tenons, original finish, unmarked Charles Limbert Co., minor chips on feet, Model No. 120, early 20th c., 45" w., 29 1/2" h. (ILLUS.) **$4,313**

Stickley Brothers Arts & Crafts Lamp Table

Arts & Crafts lamp table, oak, the rounded top covered in tacked-on brown leather, on a square apron & four angled slender square legs joined by cross-stretchers w/a small square shelf, new finish & leather, remnant of Stickley Brothers paper label, early 20th c., 26 1/2" d., 30" h. (ILLUS.)... **$1,265**

Signed L. & J.G. Stickley Library Table

Arts & Crafts library table, oak, wide rectangular top overhanging the trestle-form
base w/a pair of wide flat supports at
each end joined to a medial shelf
w/keyed through tenons, shaped shoe
feet, original finish, branded mark of L. &
J.G. Stickley, early 20th c., 30 x 48",
29" h. (ILLUS.) **$1,610**

Arts & Crafts Side Table

Arts & Crafts side table, oak, a narrow
rectangular top raised on slender flaring
flat legs joined by two narrow shelves
w/an X-form back brace & splat side panels, after a design by Rohfs Ross, scuffs
& scratches, original finish, early 20th c.,
13 x 29 1/2", 29 1/2" h. (ILLUS.) **$748**

Asian side table, carved teak, the round
top decorated w/inlaid camels & ele-
phants in ivory circling a central carved
elephant relief w/a border of vine, leaves
& berries, raised on four figural carved elephant head legs w/trunks forming the
legs, each w/inlaid ivory eyes & tusks,
joined by a cross-stretcher w/a dish center, India, first half 20th c., some inlay
missing, 15" d., 19" h. (ILLUS., top next
column) **$201**

Carved Indian Elephant Head Table

1920s Baroque Revival Carved Table

Baroque Revival side table, mahogany,
the half-round shaped top w/six veneered triangular sections, raised on a
scroll carved apron & three serpentine
legs carved at the top w/a stylized lion
head & ending in a flat paw foot, C-
curved flat stretchers joined to a central
turned post, ca. 1920s, 27 1/2" w., 24" h.
(ILLUS.).. **$259**

Chippendale Cherry Pennsylvania Dining Table

Chippendale dining table, cherry, the rectangular top flanked by wide rectangular drop leaves, raised on square tapering legs w/two forming swing-out leaf supports, Pennsylvania, 18th c., open 48 1/2 x 48 3/4", 29 1/2" h. (ILLUS., previous page)... **$7,200**

Pennsylvania Chippendale Dining Table

Chippendale dining table, mahogany, the narrow rectangular top flanked by a pair of very wide drop leaves, the deep apron w/arched ends supports on four cabriole legs ending in claw-and-ball feet, Pennsylvania, 1760-80, open 46 x 56 1/2", 29" h. (ILLUS.) **$4,780**

Extremely Rare Carved Walnut Chippendale Dressing Table from Philadelphia

Chippendale dressing table, carved walnut, the rectangular top w/molded edges & front notched corners overhangs a case w/a long drawer w/butterfly brasses & keyholed escutcheons over a pair of small square drawers flanking a deep drawer finely carved w/a large shell, C-scrolls & scrolling acanthus leaves, fluted front corners, the apron finely pierce- and reverse-carved w/scrolls flanked by cabriole legs w/shell- and scroll-carved knees & ending in high-tongued trifid feet, replaced brasses, attributed to the

shop of Henry Cliffton & Thomas Carteret, the carver, Nicholas Bernard, Philadelphia, 1740s-1750s, minor imperfections, rare, 20 1/2 x 34", 30" h. (ILLUS.) **$171,000**

Fine Walnut Chippendale Dressing Table

Chippendale dressing table, walnut, the rectangular top w/molded edges & notched corners above a deep case w/a long drawer w/bail pulls & a fancy pierced butterfly brass keyhole escutcheon above two deep square drawers flanking a central long drawer all w/matching brasses, the serpentine apron raised on four cabriole legs ending in trifid feet, original brasses, probably Delaware, 1750-80, 20 x 35 1/2", 30 1/2" h. (ILLUS.)............................... **$21,510**

Very Rare Chippendale Card Table

Chippendale game table, carved mahogany, the fold-over top w/serpentined front & incurved sides above a conforming deep apron w/gadrooned edging, five-legged design w/cabriole legs w/leaf-carved knees & ending in claw-and-ball feet, missing small interior drawer, New York City, 1760-90, 16 3/8 x 34 1/4", 27 1/2" h. (ILLUS.) **$42,000**

Fine Chippendale Game Table

Chippendale game table, carved mahogany, the rectangular fold-over hinged top w/serpentine edges & rounded corners overhangs the serpentine skirt w/a scribed edge & a shell-carved center flanked by molded slightly tapering legs w/inside chamfering, Massachusetts, 1760-80, old refinish, minor imperfections, 18 1/4 x 34 1/2", 29" h. (ILLUS.) **$7,050**

Chippendale Tilt-top Tea Table

Chippendale tilt-top tea table, mahogany, the squared top w/serpentine edges tilting on a slender baluster- and ring-turned pedestal raised on a tripod base w/cabriole legs ending in arris pad feet on platforms, Massachusetts, late 18th c., old refinish, minor imperfections, 20 3/4 x 21", 26" h. (ILLUS.) **$5,288**

Chippendale Tilt-Top Tea Table

Chippendale "tilt-top" tea table, carved mahogany, the round top w/a scalloped dished rim tilting above a revolving birdcage supports atop a columnar-turned pedestal on a tripod base w/cabriole legs ending in claw-and-ball feet, some alternations, ca. 1790, 32" d., 27 1/2" h. (ILLUS.) **$3,680**

Nicely Carved Classical Card Table

Classical card table, mahogany & mahogany veneer, the half--round fold-over top above a deep rounded apron, raised on a heavy urn- and disk-turned pedestal w/carved leaves & gadrooning, on a rectangular plinth w/incurved sides raised on four outswept leafy scroll legs ending in large paw feet on casters, refinished, age split in base, ca. 1830, closed 17 1/2 x 35 1/2", 29 1/2" h. (ILLUS.) **$1,265**

Massachusetts Classical Card Tables

Classical card tables, carved mahogany & mahogany veneer, the D-form folding top above a covered apron w/rounded corners, raised on a heavy baluster-turned pedestal w/acanthus leaf carving, on four outswept C-scroll legs w/carved leaves at the top & ending in gilt-brass paw feet, old finish, Massachusetts, ca. 1825, imperfections, closed, 17 5/8 x 36", 29" h., pr. (ILLUS., top of page)......................... **$4,406**

Fine Early Classical Child's Work Table

Classical child's work table, carved mahogany & mahogany veneer, the rectangular top w/oval corners w/inset brass rosettes framed by concentric rings above quarter-engaged corner posts carved w/baskets of fruit against a punchwork ground, flanking the case w/a deep drawer over a shallow drawer, each w/pairs of round brass pulls, a yellow cloth workbag suspended under the case, raised on ring- & spiral-turned tapering legs ending in peg feet on casters, old pulls, probably Massachusetts, ca. 1825, refinished, imperfections, 14 1/2 x 15 3/4", 20 1/4" h. (ILLUS.)... **$8,813**

Classical dining table, carved & veneered rosewood, the veneered round top w/molded edge tilts & overhanging the skirt raised on a ten-panel tapering pedestal ending in shaped rosewood petals on a platform w/rosewood veneered rays ending in a molded edge above three carved paw feet flanked by carved scrolled returns, New York City, ca. 1830, 55" d., 28 1/2" h. (ILLUS., bottom of page)... **$3,408**

Fine Classical Veneered Rosewood Dining Table

Fine Classical Mahogany Extension Dining Table

Classical dining table, mahogany, extension-type, the round top opening to receive nine leaves, raised on a heavy round split column supported on four shaped projecting angled legs w/thin disk feet, New York City, ca. 1840, closed 60" d., 30" h. (ILLUS.).. **$2,875**

Extremely Rare American Classical Mahogany Dining Table

Classical dining table, mahogany, extension-type w/accordion action, the rectangular top w/rounded corners above an accordian-action base w/six baluster- and spiral-turned posts atop flat wide arched rails continuing into downswept square reeded sabre legs ending in brass toes on casters, w/six mahogany leaves stored in their original box, New York City, ca. 1800-1810, open 60 x 167", 30" h. (ILLUS.) **$339,500**

Classical Dressing Table with Mirror

Classical dressing table, mahogany & mahogany veneer, a tall rectangular mirror in a wide ogree frame swiveling between two heavy square posts resting on a narrow rectangular top over a pair of long drawers each w/two small turned wood knobs, resting on a stepped-out rectangular top above a case w/two long graduated drawers w/turned wood knobs, raised on block-, ring- and knob-turned legs ending in ball feet, ca. 1840, 21 x 39", overall 71" h. (ILLUS.).............. **$2,530**

Unusual Classical Dressing Table

Classical dressing table, mahogany & mahogany veneer, the superstructure w/a tall oblong mirror within a Gothic arch frame swiveling within a U-shaped wishbone support raised above a long narrow serpentine top over a conforming row of three small handkerchief drawers, all resting on a rectangular white marble top w/serpentine sides atop a conforming apron, the front edge supported by long S-scroll supports joined by a narrow incurved medial shelf backed by a wide veneered back panel, New York City, ca. 1830, 19 1/2 x 44", 78" h. (ILLUS.) **$2,300**

Classical Carved Mahogany Game Table

Classical game table, carved mahogany & mahogany veneer, the rectangular fold-over top w/rounded front corners above a convex apron raised on a tapering square pedestal w/recessed panels, resting on a concave-shaped platform above scroll-carved feet on casters, old refinish, probably by Isaac Vose, Boston, ca. 1825, imperfections, 18 x 37", 29 1/4" h. (ILLUS.)... **$1,058**

Paw-footed Classical Game Table

Classical game table, mahogany & mahogany veneer, the long D-form hinged fold-over top above a deep conforming apron, raised on four turned columns resting on a quatrepartite platform raised on outswept winged paw feet on casters, New York City, ca. 1825, some veneer damage, 17 1/2 x 36" closed, 30" h. (ILLUS.) **$1,495**

Very Fine Boston Classical Game Table

Classical game table, mahogany & mahogany veneer, the rectangular fold-over top w/rounded corners raised on a heavy turned & acanthus leaf-carved pedestal supported by four arched, molded & outswept legs ending in brass paws on casters, Boston, in the manner of Timothy Hunt, ca. 1825, 17 7/8 x 36", 28" h. (ILLUS.) **$4,380**

Unusual Classical Mixing Table

Classical mixing table, burled elm, the rectangular white marble top w/beveled front corners above a conforming deep covered apron, raised on a wide rectangular pedestal fitted in the front w/a paneled door, resting on a heavy rectangular ogee & covered plinth base raised on scroll feet, probably Philadelphia, ca. 1830, 19 1/2 x 38 1/2", 36" h. (ILLUS.) **$3,450**

Fine Classical Parlor Center Table

Classical parlor center table, carved mahogany, the round black marble top above a plain veneered apron raised on a tapering triangular pedestal carved at the base w/three swans resting on the tripartitie base w/disk feet on casters,

professional restoration to break in marble top, ca. 1830, 38 1/2" d., 29 1/2" h. (ILLUS.) **$2,645**

Rare Classical Marble-topped Center Table

Classical parlor center table, mahogany & mahogany veneer, the large rounded & faceted black & gold marble top above a deep conforming ogee apron raised on a heavy paneled urn-form pedestal atop a cross-form base raised on heavy C-scroll feet on casters, New York City, ca. 1835, 40" w., 31 1/2" h. (ILLUS.) **$7,475**

Fine Boston Classical Parlor Center Table

Classical parlor center table, mahogany & mahogany veneer, the rectangular black & gold marble top w/serpentine molded edges above a deep conforming apron raised on four heavy S-scroll squared legs raised on casters & joined by a cross-form medial shelf, Boston, ca. 1830, 30 x 37", 30 1/4" h. (ILLUS.) **$2,990**

Classical Pier Table Possibly from the Shop of Duncan Phyfe

Classical Marble-topped Parlor Table

Classical parlor center table, mahogany & mahogany veneer, the square white marble top w/serpentine sides above a conforming apron, raised on a square tapering paneled pedestal resting on a crossform platform w/scrolled block feet on casters, ca. 1830, some veneer damage, 31" w., 29" h. (ILLUS.)................................ **$633**

Rare Pier Table Attributed to Quervelle

Classical pier table, gilt-stenciled mahogany & mahogany veneer, the rectangular white marble top above a deep coved apron decorated w/gilt-stenciled palmette corner designs & a central stencil of leafy scrolls, the front supported on heavy acanthus leaf-carved curved supports ending in large paw feet resting on round blocks flanking an tapering serpentine medial shelf backed by a large rectangular mirror, short ring-turned & gadrooned front legs w/small knob feet, attributed to Anthony Quervelle, Philadelphia, ca. 1820, 20 x 42", 38 1/2" h. (ILLUS.) **$54,000**

Classical pier table, mahogany & mahogany veneer, the long rectangular white marble top above a deep coved veneered apron, square S-scroll front supports resting on projecting stretchers flanking the large rectangular back mirror, raised on thick block feet, attributed to the Shop of Duncan Phyfe, New York City, ca. 1825-40, 20 1/4 x 58 1/4", 37 1/2" h. (ILLUS., top of page) **$14,400**

Classical Lyre-based Pier Table

Classical pier table, mahogany & mahogany veneer, the rectangular black & gold marble top w/beveled edges resting on a deep ogee apron raised on a boldly scrolling lyre-form pedestal enclosing a mirror, resting on a wide tapering rectangular platform on ogee bracket feet on casters, ca. 1840, 18 x 35 1/2", 34" h. (ILLUS.).. **$3,110**

Fine New York Classical Pier Table

Fine Philadelphia Classical Pier Table

flanking the central large rectangular mirror, all joined by a shelf w/concave front w/gilt scrolling designs of flowers & cornucopias & applied brass beaded edge all raised on gilt gesso & acanthus leaf-carved front hairy paw feet, New York City, ca. 1825, refinished, restorations & imperfections,   19 1/2 x 50 1/2",   37" h. (ILLUS., top of page).............................. **$7,050**

New York Classical Pier Table

Classical pier table, mahogany & mahogany veneer, the rectangular white marble top above a long ogee-front apron drawer raised on long squared S-scroll supports above a lower shelf backed by a large rectangular mirror, projecting C-scroll front feet, Philadelphia, ca. 1835, 19 x 42", 19" h. (ILLUS.) **$4,370**

Classical pier table, ormolu- and gilt gesso-trimmed rosewood, the rectangular white marble top on a deep apron w/ebonized molding & rosewood veneer w/brass gilt mounts showing Psyche & Cupid in a chariot being drawn by peacocks, flanked by similarly dressed female figures watering flowers, the bottom edge w/a reticulated brass band, raised on columnar front legs w/gilt acanthus leaf capitals, tapering white marble columns on turned gilt plinths, w/corresponding square tapering rear pilasters

Classical pier table, rosewood & gilt stenciling, the rectangular white marble top above a deep apron bordered w/gilt palmettes on an ebonized ground, white alabaster front supports topped by bold Ionic-carved capitals, the lower back fitted w/a rectangular mirror flanked by matching pilasters, the recessed plinth base on parcel-gilt & verde antico melon-ribbed feet ringed w/carved lotus leaves, fine unrestored condition, New York City, ca. 1825, 17 1/2 x 39", 32" h. (ILLUS.) **$6,900**

One of a Pair of Very Rare American Classical Pier Tables

Classical pier table, rosewood, ormolu, gilt gesso & marble, the rectangular white marble top on a conforming base w/applied ebonized molding & rosewood veneer frieze w/gilt-brass mounts showing Psyche & Cupid in a chariot being drawn by peacocks, flanked by similarly dressed female figures watering flowers, the bottom edge w/a brass reticulated band, raised on white columnar front legs w/gilt acanthus leaf capitals & ring-turned bases resting on a rectangular concave-front medial shelf w/matching square rear pilasters flanking a large rectangular mirror, the bottom rail w/gilt scrolling designs of flowers & cornucopias & an applied brass beaded edge, raised on short carved hairy paw feet topped by gilt gesso carved leaves, New York City, ca. 1825, restoration, imperfections, 19 1/2 x 50 1/2", 37" h. **$7,050**

Classical pier tables, mahogany & mahogany veneer, a rectangular white marble top above a flat apron raised on large front column supports w/gilt-brass capitals & bases & joined by a concave shelf backed by a large rectangular mirror, raised on gilt acanthus leaf-carved turned feet, New York City, ca. 1815-30, 17 x 42", 35" h., pr. (ILLUS. of one, top of page)... **$35,850**

Classical side table, mahogany, the round top above a large open lyre-shaped pedestal fitted w/brass rod strings, raised on a small round platform atop three outswept squared legs ending in brass paw feet on casters, old refinish, Middle Atlantic States, ca. 1830, 17 3/4" d., 30" h. (ILLUS., top next column) **$1,528**

Lyre-based Classical Side Table

Classical Tilt-Top Side Table

Classical side table, papier-mâché & ebonized wood, the round papier-mâché
top decorated w/a floral cluster tilting
above a tall slender ring-turned post
above a tripod base w/three flat S-scroll
legs, mid-19th c., 20 1/2" d., 27 1/2" h.
(ILLUS., previous page) **$633**

Interesting Classical Sofa Table

Classical sofa table, carved rosewood, the
rectangular top w/molded edges flanked
by D-form end drop leaves above a
slightly bowed apron fitted w/a pair of
paneled drawers & w/a small turned drop
at each corner, raised on a trestle-form
base w/four ring- and spiral-turned legs
resting on arched long shoe feet joined
by a ring- and spiral-turned stretcher,
New York City, ca. 1840, 25 x 27 1/2"
closed, 29" h. (ILLUS.) **$575**

Unusual Classical "Tilt-Top" Side Table

Classical "tilt-top" side table, walnut, the
large round refinished top tilting above
a heavy ring- and baluster-turned post
raised on a tripod base w/flat serpentine legs ending in scrolled feet, Southern U.S., mid-19th c., 35 1/2" d., 29" h.
(ILLUS.) **$3,910**

Fine New England Classical Work Table

Classical work table, japanned & decorated, the rectangular top decorated w/gilt
Chinoiserie landscape w/buildings &
opening to a fitted interior, the covered
apron fitted w/a single drawer further
decorated w/Chinese motifs, raised on a
trestle-style base w/flattened baluster-
shaped end uprights on arched scroll-
tipped feet joined by a pair of slender
baluster- and knob-turned stretchers,
New England, ca. 1835, 20 x 24", 29" h.
(ILLUS.) **$2,875**

Fine Classical Mahogany Work Table

Classical work table, mahogany & mahogany veneer, the rectangular hinged top
opening to a compartmented shallow interior w/an adjustable writing surface, the
case w/two long drawers w/small round
brasses, raised on a heavy turned &
swag-carved pedestal above four heavy
acanthus-carved outswept legs ending in
paw feet on casters, ca. 1830,
17 1/4 x 22", 32" h. (ILLUS.) **$2,760**

Large Classical-Style Dining Table

Classical-Style dining table, carved mahogany, extension-type, the round divided top w/a foliate-carved edge band above the plain apron, raised on a heavy short pedestal w/a large reeded & flaring bulbous base issuing four outswept acanthus leaf-carved legs ending in paw feet on casters, late 19th c., original fin-

ish, one small cylindrical hole in the top, 54" d. (ILLUS.) **$1,560**

Country Curly Maple Dining Table

Country-style dining table, curly maple, rectangular top flanked by wide hinged D-form drop leaves, the apron fitted w/a drawer at one end, raised on slender ring-turned tapering legs ending in ball & peg feet, good color, minor wear, 20 1/2 x 40" plus 14" w. leaves, 29" h. (ILLUS.).. **$920**

Very Rare Early Louisiana Cypress Kitchen Table

Country-style kitchen table, cypress, the wide rectangular top overhanging an apron fitted w/a long drawer w/a carved wood pull, raised on square legs beveled at the base & joined by an H-stretcher, natural weathered finish, made in Louisiana, mid-19th c., 49 x 64", 31" h. (ILLUS.)... **$14,950**

Fine American Country-style "Sawbuck" Table

Country-style "sawbuck" table, pine the very long rectangular top overhanging heavy X-form end legs joined by angled braces & long slender stretchers, American, late 18th - early 19th c., 34 x 113", 29" h. (ILLUS.) **$6,573**

Early Pennsylvania Country Style Tavern Table

Country-style tavern table, walnut, the wide rectangular two-board top w/original cleats & scrubbed surface widely overhanging the deep apron fitted w/a short & long drawer each w/a brass knob, one w/escutcheon plate & lock, square tapering molded legs, mortise & tenon construction w/pegs, some repairs including drawer runners, Pennsylvania, 18th c., 36 x 60 1/2", 28" h. (ILLUS.) **$1,150**

Early Southern Heart Pine Work Table

Country-style work table, heart pine, the wide square plank top overhanging a deep apron w/a single long drawer w/turned wood knobs, raised on tapering octagonal legs, nicks, scuffs & separations to top, short additions to each leg, Southern U.S., late 18th c., 48" w., 32 1/2" h. (ILLUS.) **$1,093**

Large Old Country Tavern Table

Early American country-style tavern table, painted hardwood, the long rectangular top widely overhanging the deeply scalloped apron, raised on four square slightly tapering legs joined by box stretchers, old reddish finish, found in Maine, late 18th - early 19th c., some repairs & restoration, 28 1/2 x 62", 28 1/4" h. (ILLUS.) **$450**

Very Fine French Empire-Style Ormolu-mounted Pier Table

Decorated Edwardian Pembroke Table

Edwardian Pembroke table, painted & decorated mahogany, in the Adam taste, the rectangular top centered by a round reserve in green decorated w/putti among clouds surrounded by a variety of scrolling floral & foliate designs, each D-form drop leaf w/matching scrolling decoration, the apron fitted w/a drawer at one end & also decorated, raised on slender square tapering legs w/brass caps on casters, England, ca. 1900, 31 1/2 x 42", 29" h. (ILLUS.) **$3,680**

Empire-Style pier table, ormolu-mounted mahogany & mahogany veneer, the rectangular white & grey marble top above a conforming apron applied w/ormolu griffins, anthemia, paterae & lyres, supported on each side by a full-figure seated winged sphinx, the paneled back centered by a ormolu Medusa mask within an ormolu diamond panel, the deep base further decorated on the sides & re-cessed back w/long scroll & florette ormolu mounts & figural ormolu mounts at the front above the leaf-carved gilt knob feet, France, late 19th c., 18 x 51", 39" h. (ILLUS., top of page)........................... **$10,200**

Simple Federal Mahogany Card Table

Federal card table, carved mahogany, the D-shaped fold-over top above a deep ogee apron, raised on a heavy baluster-turned & leaf-carved pedestal supported by four long outswept C-scroll legs ending in brass paw feet on casters, probably New York, first quarter 19th c., 17 3/4 x 36", 28 1/4" h. (ILLUS.) **$805**

Fine Mahogany Federal Console Table

Federal console table, mahogany & mahogany veneer, long demi-lune top decorated w/radiating crotch grain mahogany above the paneled veneer panels separated by for raised panels decorated w/oval inlaid paterae, four square tapering legs ending in stepped square feet, underside of skirt w/a glued piece of a 19th c. Boston newspaper, American-made, possibly Boston or Baltimore, some veneer damage, repairs & loss, top w/section of missing veneers & cracks, 24 1/4 x 51 1/4", 33" h. (ILLUS., previous page) **$2,588**

Federal country-style dining table, birch, the rectangular top flanked by wide hinged drop leaves w/rounded corners, raised on an apron above slender swelled & turned legs w/ring-turned cuffs & peg feet, base w/original chocolate brown paint, scrubbed top, minor chips on rule joints at hinges, early 19th c., 13 7/8 x 36" plus 10" leaves, 27 1/2" h. **$575**

Rare Small Federal Walnut Side Table

Unusual Federal Saddler's Table

Federal country-style saddler's table, painted, the nearly square top w/a molded edge mounted w/an angled two-board saddle support, a single deep drawer w/a turned wood knob below the top, raised on two slender square legs & two slender square legs forming a trestle support at one side, old blue paint, 19th c., 19" w., 31 1/2" h. (ILLUS.) **$720**

Federal country-style side table, walnut, the nearly square top widely overhanging a canted apron fitted w/a single drawer, tall slender tapering splayed square legs, old refinish, probably Pennsylvania, early 19th c. 19 3/4 x 20", 28" h. (ILLUS., top next column).. **$10,575**

Fine Federal Country Work Table

Federal country-style work table, tiger stripe maple, the rectangular top w/covered corners hinged to open above a faux drawer w/a divided interior, a lower working drawer w/round brass pulls & a divided interior, raised on a baluster- and ring-turned pedestal above four outswept legs ending in tiny ball feet, brasses replaced, refinished, New York State, ca. 1820, 15 7/8 x 22 1/2", 32" h. (ILLUS.)............... **$2,820**

Federal dining table, inlaid walnut, extension-type, a center section w/rectangular top flanked by rectangular hinged drop leaves & square tapering legs ending in spade feet, flanked by two D-form end sections on square tapering legs ending in spade feet, skirts & legs inlaid w/stringing & bellflowers, Southern U.S., possibly Georgia, ca. 1825-35, dry & water-stained finish, old repairs, open 44 1/8 x 113 1/4", 29 3/4" h. (ILLUS., top next page)... **$4,140**

Fine Southern Federal Inlaid Walnut Dining Table

Small Federal Mahogany Dining Table

Federal Mahogany Drop-Leaf Dining Table

Federal dining table, mahogany, a rectangular top flanked by two wide half-round & slightly scalloped drop leaves above the apron, raised on four acanthus leaf-carved legs raised on casters, New York City, ca. 1825, 25 x 39 1/2" closed, 29 1/2" h. (ILLUS.) **$2,300**

Federal dining table, mahogany, the rectangular top flanked by wide half-round hinged drop leaves, the deep apron raised on ring-, knob- and spiral-turned legs w/knob feet on casters, a fifth swing-out support leg, ca. 1820s, 44 x 64 1/2" open, 29 1/2" h. (ILLUS.) **$805**

Federal dining table, mahogany, two-part construction, each D-form half w/a hinged rectangular drop leaf supported by a swing-out leg, raised on square tapering legs w/banded inlay at the ankles, ca. 1815-1825, open 80 1/2" l., 29" h. (ILLUS., bottom of page) **$2,300**

Federal Mahogany Two-Part Dining Table

Rare Baltimore Federal Inlaid Game Table

Fine Massachusetts Federal Game Table

Federal game table, inlaid mahogany & bird's-eye maple, the rectangular fold-over top w/serpentine reeded edges & projecting from corners above a conforming apron, the front centered by an inlaid rectangular panel of bird's-eye maple, raised on tall slender reeded legs ending in swelled peg feet, Massachusetts, 1800-10, 16 3/4 x 35 1/2", 29 1/4" h. (ILLUS.)................................. **$4,200**

Federal game table, inlaid mahogany, the fold-over demilune top w/a half-round inlaid panel in the center, above a conforming apron w/two paterae-inlaid panels heading two tall square tapering egs w/long bellflower pendent drops, pairs of square tapering rear legs, Baltimore, Maryland, ca. 1800-10, some veneer damage, 19 x 38", 29 1/2" h. (ILLUS., top of page)... **$24,000**

Fine New York Inlaid Federal Game Table

Federal game table, inlaid mahogany, the hinged half-round top w/a flat projecting center & banded inlay trim above an apron divided by four blocked panels w/oval inlays above the tall slender square tapering line-inlaid legs, a swing-out fifth support legs, New York City, 1780-1810, 18 3/4 x 38", 29 1/2" h. (ILLUS.) **$3,840**

Fine Federal Inlaid Game Table

Extremely Rare New Hampshire Inlaid Federal Game Tables

Federal game table, mahogany w/satin-
wood inlay, the hinged fold-over D-form
top w/notched corners & line inlay
above a deep apron w/rectangular line-
inlaid panels, raised on four square tapering legs w/further line inlay, New
York or New Jersey, late 18th - early
19th c., 16 1/8 x 26 1/8" closed,
32 1/2" h. (ILLUS., previous page) **$2,185**
Federal game tables, inlaid mahogany &
flame birch, the hinged rectangular top
w/serpentine banded inlay edges & oval
corners above a conforming apron
w/wide panels of birch inlay centered by
a large inlaid front oval, raised on slender
ring-turned & reeded legs ending in tall
slender peg feet, probably Portsmouth,
New Hampshire, 1800-10, 18 x 36",
29" h., pr. (ILLUS., top of page) **$54,000**

Federal Mahogany Pembroke Table

Federal Pembroke table, inlaid mahogany,
the rectangular top flanked by hinged
drop leaves w/cut-corners above an
apron w/a single drawer w/an oval brass
pull, square tapering legs w/ankle banding, some restorations, ca. 1800,
20 1/4 x 30 1/4", 29" h. (ILLUS.) **$1,800**

New England Federal Pembroke Table

Federal Pembroke table, inlaid mahogany,
the rectangular top flanked by D-form
hinged drop leaves above an apron
w/one working & one faux drawer above
a banded lower edge w/contrasting inlaid
stringing, raised on faux bamboo-turned
legs w/ebonized turnings ending in casters, New England, ca. 1820, minor imperfections, 21 x 34", 28 3/4" h. (ILLUS.).. **$588**

Rare Rhode Island Federal Pembroke Table

Federal Pembroke table, inlaid mahogany, the rectangular top w/bowed ends flanked by half-round drop leaves, the apron w/a line-inlaid working drawer at one end & a false drawer at the other, raised on square tapering legs headed by inlaid blocks above narrow long inlaid banded triangles, Newport, Rhode Island, ca. 1795, 20 1/2 x 34", 27 1/2" h. (ILLUS., previous page) **$16,730**

Fine New York Federal Pembroke Table

Federal Pembroke table, mahogany, the rectangular top flanked by D-form hinged drop leaves above an apron w/a single end drawer, raised on turned & reeded slender legs ending in tiny brass ball feet, New York City, 1780-1810, 24 x 34", 28 1/2" h. (ILLUS.) **$2,032**

Early New York Federal Pembroke Table

Federal Pembroke table, mahogany, the rectangular top flanked by two D-form hinged drop leaves above a narrow apron w/a single drawer w/a small brass

pull, raised on ring-turned reeded tapering legs ending in brass-cuffed cannon ball feet, attributed to Michale Allison, New York City, ca. 1810, 21 x 36", 29" h. (ILLUS.)... **$2,115**

Nice Federal New York Pembroke Table

Federal Pembroke table, mahogany, the rectangular top flanked by wide D-form notched drop leaves above an apron w/a single drawer at one end, raised on ring- and knob-turned legs raised on casters, New York City, ca 1825, 23 x 36", 29" h. (ILLUS.)... **$2,185**

Rare Salem Inlaid Federal Side Table

Federal side table, inlaid mahogany, the oval top w/an inlaid edge above a deep apron w/a single drawer raised on four line-inlaid square slender tapering legs, Salem, Massachusetts, ca. 1790, 23 1/2" h. (ILLUS.) **$23,900**

Rare Federal Silent Butler Table

Federal silent butler side table, mahogany, the top composed of three round tiers w/reeded edges each supported on a columnar-turned support, the tripod base w/cabriole legs ending in arris pad feet, New England, late 18th - early 19th c., old refinish, minor imperfections, bottom tier 23 1/4" d., overall 43 1/4" h. (ILLUS.) **$7,638**

Fine Federal Inlaid Cherry Work Table

Federal work table, inlaid cherry, the nearly square top above an apron fitted w/two narrow drawers centered by inlaid ovals & fitted w/pairs of small round brass pulls, raised on tall tapering ring-turned & fluted legs ending in peg feet, probably Massachusetts, 1800-15, 16 1/2 x 18", 28 1/2" h. (ILLUS.) **$2,115**

American Federal Sofa Table

Federal sofa table, ebony-inlaid mahogany, rectangular top flanked by wide D-form drop leaves w/reeded edges, the apron fitted w/a pair of drawers w/line & circle inlay, testle base w/end uprights supported on outswept inlaid legs ending in brass paws on casters, flat cross-stretcher, coastal New England, ca. 1800-15, refinished, 25 x 59 1/2" open, 28" h. (ILLUS.) **$3,910**

Fine Astragal-end Federal Work Table

Federal work table, mahogany, astragal-end design, the top w/half-round end w/hinged tops flanking the rectangular central section over a deep case w/a shallow & a deep drawer w/round brass pulls flanking by reeded pilasters ending a tiny ball drops, raised on a baluster- and ring-turned pedestal supported by

four reeded spider legs, old pulls, probably Philadelphia, ca. 1810-15, refinished,
minor imperfections, 14 x 25 3/4", 28" h.
(ILLUS.).. **$2,585**

Rare Inlaid Federal Work Table

Federal work table, mahogany & bird's-eye
maple veneer, the rectangular top of
bird's-eye maple veneer bordered by mahogany crossbanding w/ebonized oval
corners w/concentric rings centering ivory bosses above two cockbeaded graduated bird's-eye maple drawers w/em-
bossed brass pulls & ivory keyhole
escutcheons, the corners w/quarter-en-
gaged ring-turned posts continuing into
slender reeded tapering legs on casters,
probably Massachusetts, ca. 1810-15,
imperfections, 17 x 21 1/2", 28 3/4" h.
(ILLUS.).. **$14,100**

Astragal-End Federal Work Table

Federal work table, mahogany & mahogany veneer, rectangular top w/wide astragal ends, the shaped hinged top
w/reeded edge opening to a compartmented interior & well below on a conforming beaded case & four slender ring-
turned tapering legs on casters, old refinish, possibly Philadelphia, ca. 1805-15,
imperfections, 14 3/4 x 26", 27 3/4" h.
(ILLUS.).. **$1,763**

Massachusetts Federal Work Table

Federal work table, mahogany, the rectangular hinged top w/inset felt writing
surface opening to an interior fitted
w/dividers, the case w/two long graduated drawers w/round brass pulls,
raised on ring-turned fluted tapering
legs ending in cannon ball feet, Massachusetts, early 19th c., 15 1/2 x 21",
30" h. (ILLUS.) **$1,763**

Extremely Rare Early Louisiana Table

French Provincial side table, walnut, rectangular two-board top overhanging a deep apron fitted w/a single drawer above the scalloped apron, raised on simple slender cabriole legs, made in Louisiana, late 18th c., very rare, 20 1/4 x 27 1/2", 27" h. (ILLUS., previous page) **$54,625**

Irish George III Waiter

George III waiter, mahogany, the round banded top joined to a lower shelf by turned brass uprights, raised on a turned & reeded pedestal on a tripod base w/reeded outswept legs ending in brass caps on casters, Ireland, ca. 1800, 24" d., 39 1/2" h. (ILLUS.) **$1,840**

Long George III-Style Side Table

George III-Style side table, mahogany, the long rectangular top raised on cabriole legs w/shell-carved knees & ending in hairy paw feet, England, late 19th c., 20 1/2 x 57", 35" h. (ILLUS.) **$633**

George III-Style Tea Table

George III-Style tea table, mahogany, the large round top above a baluster-turned pedestal on a tripod base w/cabriole legs ending in pad feet, England, late 19th c., 33" d., 30" h. (ILLUS.) **$1,610**

Georgian-Style Oak Dining Table

Georgian-Style dining table, oak, the narrow rectangular top w/rounded ends flanked by wide half-round drop leaves, a scalloped apron raised on straight turned legs ending in pad feet, England, mid-19th c., open 44 x 54", 27 1/2" h. (ILLUS. closed) **$1,265**

Harvest table, country-style, maple & birch, the long rectangular top flanked by long rectangular drop leaves, raised on simple turned legs w/ring-turned ankles & peg feet, old refinishing, attributed to New England, 20 x 60 3/8" plus 10 1/2" drop leaves, 29 1/2" h. (ILLUS., top of next page) **$1,955**

Old New England Harvest Table

Old Painted Harvest Table

Harvest table, country-style, painted, the long wide rectangular two-board top flanked by narrow drop leaves w/rounded corners, raised in simple turned legs on metal casters, old worn red paint, cracks in top, metal supports to top of legs, 19th c., open 28 1/2 x 71 1/2", 28 1/2" h. (ILLUS., middle from top of page) **$805**

Harvest table, Federal-Style country-style, birch & pine, the long narrow rectangular one-board top flanked by long wide hinged leaves, raised on very slender square tapering legs, dark brown finish, apron w/edge staining & some putty-filled holes, early 20th c., 19 1/2 x 72 1/4" w/12" leaves, 29 1/2" h **$403**

Hutch (or chair) table, country-style, pine, the wide three-board top hinged above a single-board cut-out ends flanking a lift-seat opening to a compartment, possibly New England, early 19th c., refinished, 41 x 70", 29 3/4" h. (ILLUS., next column) **$5,581**

Rare Early New England Pine Hutch Table

Fine Country Pine Hutch Table

Hutch (or chair) table, pine, the wide rectangular three-board top tilting above one-board sides w/a curved top above a long lift seat over a deep apron, arched cut-out feet, worn brown stain, early 19th c., wear, stains, minor damage & splits, 29 x 60", 29 1/2" h. (ILLUS.)... **$1,265**

Nice English Jacobean Oak Refrectory Table

Jacobean refrectory table, carved oak, the long narrow top widely overhanging an apron carved w/two narrow scalloped bands on a punchwork ground, heavy ring- and rod-turned legs on block feet joined by wide flat stretchers, England, second half 17th c., some old repairs, 29 1/4 x 91", 31 1/2" h. (ILLUS.)
.... **$3,450**

Nice English Jacobean-Style Oak Refectory Table

Jacobean-Style refectory table, carved oak, the large rectangular plank top above a deep scroll- and leaf-carved apron raised on four large turnip-shaped leaf-carved legs above blocks joined by flat rails, England, ca. 1900, 33 1/2 x 72", 29 1/2"h. (ILLUS., top of page) **$1,265**

Louis XVI-Style Small Oval Table

Louis XV-Style Boullework Game Table

Louis XV-Style game table, ormolu-mounted boullework, the hinged rectangular top w/serpentine edges centered by faux tortoiseshell & brass-inlaid marquetry w/an ormolu border band, the deep serpentine apron w/ornate shaped boullework panels centered by an ormolu classical mask mount, the slender cabriole boullework legs each headed by an ormolu caryatid & ending in ormolu sabots, minor nicks & some brass loss, France, late 19th c., 17 x 34", 29" h. (ILLUS.)...................................... **$2,415**

Louis XVI-Style side table, mahogany, the oval top inset w/brown & white marble & framed w/a low pierced brass gallery, raised on shaped & pierced side uprights joined by two brass-banded oval lower shelves above the trestle base w/shoe feet, France, third quarter 19th c., 10 3/4 x 21 3/4", 29 1/2" h. (ILLUS., top next column)... **$575**

Pair of Louis XVI-Style Marble-topped Side Tables

Louis XVI-Style side tables, giltwood, a rectangular grey & maroon marble top above an apron carved w/a band of florettes centered by a carved maiden head on two sides, raised on turned & tapering fluted legs w/knob feet, France, 19th c., 28 x 56", 38" h., pr. (ILLUS.).................. **$2,990**

Rare Gustav Stickley Director's Table

**Mission-style (Arts & Crafts movement)
director's table,** oak, the large rectangular top overhanging a deep pegged & slightly canted apron raised on heavy square slightly canted legs on thick shoe feet w/beveled ends, refinished, paper label of Gustav Stickley, early 20th c., 42 x 84", 29 1/2" h. (ILLUS., top of page) **$10,925**

Early Gustav Stickley Round Lamp Table

Gustav Stickley Labeled Lamp Table

**Mission-style (Arts & Crafts movement)
lamp table,** oak, round top fitted onto square legs joined by a mortised cross-stretcher, original finish, 1902-03 decal mark of Gustav Stickley, 23 1/2" d., 28" h. (ILLUS.) **$5,750**

**Mission-style (Arts & Crafts movement)
lamp table,** oak, square top w/clipped corners raised on four angled square legs joined by a mortised arched cross-stretcher topped by a large shelf, Crafts-man paper label of Gustav Stickley, early 20th c., 24" w., 29" h. (ILLUS., top next column) **$1,610**

Labeled Stickley Brothers Lamp Table

Mission-style (Arts & Crafts movement) lamp table, oak, the round top covered in original black leather w/embossed tack edging, raised on square legs tapering at the base & joined by a mortised cross-stretcher topped by a square shelf, original condition, stenciled "6729," Model 2505, remnant of paper label of the Stickley Brothers, early 20th c., 26" d., 30" h. (ILLUS., previous page) **$2,645**

Simple Mission Oak Library Table

Mission-style Lifetime Lamp Table

Mission-style (Arts & Crafts movement) lamp table, oak, the round top overhanging four square legs joined by cross-stretchers supporting a small round shelf, unmarked Lifetime Furniture Co., refinished, early 20th c., 30" d., 29 1/4" h. (ILLUS.).................................... **$748**

Mission-style (Arts & Crafts movement) library table, oak, the rectangular top overhanging an apron w/a single drawer w/square wood pulls, square legs joined by side stretchers & a mortised medial shelf, early 20th c., 22 1/2 x 39", 29 1/4" h. (ILLUS., top next column) **$313**

L. & J.G. Stickley Small Oak Side Table

Mission-style (Arts & Crafts movement) side table, oak, the round top resting on flat cross braces & raised on tall slender square legs joined by cross stretchers fitted w/a small round shelf, Model No. 573, red & yellow decal mark of L. & J.G. Stickley, ca. 1912, 17 7/8" d., 27" h. (ILLUS.) **$1,554**

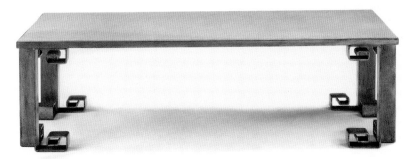

Very Rare French Modern Style Coffee Table

Modern style coffee table, gilt-iron & composite stone, the long rectangular composite stone top set into a narrow gilt-iron frame raised on heavy square gilt-iron legs w/Greek key brackets, designed by Jean Royere, France, ca. 1948, 21 1/4 x 47 1/4", 13 1/2" h. (ILLUS.) **$77,675**

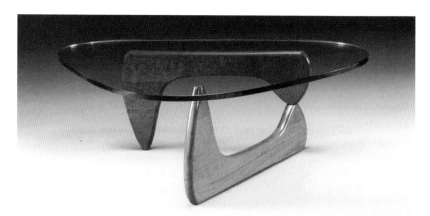

Noguchi-designed Modern Glass & Wood Coffee Table

Modern style coffee table, glass & walnut, "Model in-50" design, the oblong asymmetrical thick glass top raised on two angled shaped long wooden supports, designed by Isamu Noguchi for Herman Miller, designed in 1944, 36 x 50", 15 1/2" h. (ILLUS.) **$4,780**

Rare French Modern Style Coffee Table

Modern style coffee table, palisander, black opaline glass & brass, the long oval glass top framed by a low tapering gallery over a narrow apron raised on four canted turned & tapering legs w/brass foot caps, designed by Louis Sognot for La Maison Rinck, Paris, France, ca. 1950, stamped marks, 25 3/4 x 51 3/8", 19 1/4" h. (ILLUS.) **$23,900**

Pair of Modern Berkey Console Tables

Modern style console tables, black lacquer w/antiqued silver accents, a long narrow rectangular top w/silver edges over a shallow apron fitted w/a long drawer, raised on blocked square tapering legs w/oblong feet, designed by John Widdicomb for Berkey, ca. 1965, 36" l., 29" h., pr. (ILLUS.) **$382**

Extremely Rare Frank Lloyd Wright-designed Side Table

Modern style side table, oak, three-tier 'flower table,' a thick rectangular top overhanging a framework w/a short narrow top shelf raised on four square supports enclosing a medial shelf & joined to four square legs w/outswept feet & joined by a wider bottom shelf, designed by Frank Lloyd Wright in collaboration w/George Mann Niedecken of Niedecken-Walbridge, for the Second Story Hall of the Avery Coonley House, Riverside, Illinois, ca. 1910, 16 x 29 7/8", 25 1/4" h. (ILLUS.)... **$59,750**

Elaborately Inlaid North African Tables

North African side tables, mother-of-pearl & ivory-inlaid mahogany, the octagonal dished top ornately inlaid w/geometric designs & border bands above paneled sides w/delicate lattice-inlaid panels above & below a diamond-inlaid panel, eight legs divided by pointed arches & decorated w/herringbone style inlay, late 19th - early 20th, 16 1/2" w., 24 1/2" h., pr. (ILLUS.) **$1,610**

Napoleon III Rococo Parlor Table

Napoleon III parlor center table, Rococo-style, ebonized wood, the grey marble "turtle top" above a conforming apron w/applied ormolu mounts & beading continuing to cabriole legs joined by a serpentine cross-stretcher centered by a large urn-form post w/ormolu finial, France, third quarter 19th c., 30 x 43", 27" h. (ILLUS.) **$920**

Nutting-made William & Mary Table

Nutting-signed William & Mary-Style side table, wide rectangular top above the trestle base w/block- and knob-turned legs joined by two block-, baluster- and knob-turned cross stretchers, shaped shoe feet, block letter branded signature under the top, 13 x 18 3/4", 26 3/4" h. (ILLUS.) **$518**

Fancy Carved Oriental Side Table

Oriental side table, carved mahogany, the raised pagoda-style square top w/carved edges & incurved sides above the wide curved apron ornately carved w/dragons & scrolls, on tall dragon-carved cabriole legs ending in scroll feet, probably China, first half 20th c., 28" h. (ILLUS.) **$230**

Carved Chinese Side Table

Oriental side table, carved & painted hardwood, a rectangular frame & panel top w/exposed joinery, the case w/a pair of drawers over a long drawer all w/strap metal pulls, flanked by scrolling pierced side brackets, on flat rectangular stile legs, old reddish paint, scorched areas on top, China, late 19th c., 32 x 42 1/2", 34" h. (ILLUS.) **$575**

Oriental side table, carved rosewood, the round top inset w/rose marble & w/a beaded border & an incurved band above the deep apron ornately pierce-carved w/scrolls & bars, raised on four heavy cabriole legs headed by a mask & carved shell & ending in heavy paw feet, joined by a cross stretcher, China, late 19th - early 20th c., top 17" d., 19" h. (ILLUS., top next column) **$316**

Ornately Carved Chinese Rosewood Table

Rare Early Queen Anne Maple Tea Table

Queen Anne country-style tea table, maple, the round top overhanging a deep apron w/a valanced skirt raised on four simple cabriole legs ending in pad feet, probably Massachusetts, ca. 1740-60, refinished, 25 3/4 x 32 1/4", 26 1/4" h. (ILLUS.)... **$21,150**

Country Queen Anne Tea Table

Queen Anne country-style tea table, painted, three-board oval top w/a center cleat above the deep gently arched apron raised on turned & tapering legs ending in small round pad feet, red paint not original, restoration to feet & top, first half 18th c., 26 1/2 x 32", 28" h. (ILLUS.)......... **$920**

Queen Anne Country-Style Tea Table

Queen Anne country-style tea table, painted wood, the oval top widely overhanging the deep apron raised on block-turned legs ending in bulbous feet, original red & brown grained painting, New England, mid-18th c., minor imperfections, 26 1/2 x 37", 27" h. (ILLUS.)......... **$6,463**

Fine Queen Anne Walnut Dining Table

Queen Anne dining table, figured & inlaid walnut, a narrow rectangular top w/rounded ends flanked by wide half-round drop leaves w/molded edges outlined in stringing, the shaped apron raised on slender simple cabriole legs ending in pad feet, old surface, probably Boston area, ca. 1740-50, some imperfections, open 40 3/4 x 42", 28" h. (ILLUS.).. **$11,163**

Scarce Early Queen Anne Dining Table

Queen Anne dining table, maple, the rectangular top w/rounded ends flanked by two wide D-form drop leaves above a deep arched apron, raised on four slender cabriole legs ending in pad feet & two matching swing-out support legs, New England, 1740-60, open 44 x 60", 28" h. (ILLUS.) **$7,200**

Maple Queen Anne Dining Table

Queen Anne dining table, maple, the rectangular top w/rounded ends flanking by a pair of D-form hinged drop leaves above a deep apron, swing-out leg supports, raised on cabriole legs ending in pad feet, New England, late 18th c., open 29 1/2 x 30", 26 3/4" h. (ILLUS.) **$3,231**

Very Rare Queen Anne Dressing Table

Queen Anne dressing table, tiger stripe maple, rectangular thumb-molded top overhanging a case w/two deep drawers w/engraved butterfly brasses flanking a short center drawer above the arched & valanced kneehole opening w/turned drops, raised on cabriole legs ending in pad feet, refinished, probably Massachusetts, 1740-60, minor imperfections, 21 1/2 x 29", 29 1/2" h. (ILLUS.) **$19,975**

Rare Bermuda-made Queen Anne Table

Queen Anne dressing table, cedar, the rectangular tup overhanging an apron fitted w/a pair of deep square drawers flanking a short center drawer all w/butterfly pulls, deeply scalloped apron, straight simple turned legs ending in pad feet, Bermuda, West Indies, 1740-60, 18 1/2 x 26 1/2", 28" h. (ILLUS.) **$12,000**

Fine Early Queen Anne Dressing Table

Queen Anne dressing table, walnut, the rectangular top w/molded edges overhanging a deep apron w/a single long drawer above a row of three deep drawers all w/butterfly brasses, valanced apron & cabriole legs ending in pad feet, Connecticut or Massachusetts, 1740-70, 20 x 34", 29 1/2" h. (ILLUS.) **$6,600**

Very Rare Queen Anne Newport Tray-top Tea Table

Walnut Queen Anne Tea Table

Queen Anne tea table, walnut, the large round revolving & tilting top on a bird-cage mechanism raised on a bulbous baluster-turned pedestal w/a tripod base of three cabriole legs ending in pad feet, dovetail keys installed to stabilize top, dry finish, ca. 1770, 30 3/4" d., 26 3/4" h. (ILLUS.).................................. **$4,370**

Queen Anne "tray-top" tea table, mahogany, the rectangular top w/raised molding above a narrow flat apron raised on four simple cabriole legs ending in slipper feet, Newport, Rhode Island, 1740-60, 21 x 32 3/4", 26 1/2" h. (ILLUS., top of page)... **$66,000**

Renaissance-Style library table, carved mahogany, long rectangular top w/molded edges overhanging a narrow scroll-carved apron raised on a trestle base w/heavy scroll-carved end legs on scroll-carved shoe feet & joined by a medial shelf, ca. 1900, professionally refinished, 24 1/2 x 72", 30 1/2" h. (ILLUS., bottom of page).. **$1,380**

Large Renaissance-Style Carved Library Table

Fine European Renaissance-Style Carved Library Table

Renaissance-Style library table, carved mahogany, the long rectangular top w/a molded edge above a deep rounded leaf-carved apron w/two drawers on one side, raised on wide ornately carved trestle-style end legs w/carved winged griffins at each side flanking a finely carved panel centered by a female mask resting on carved shoe feet joined by a wide ornately carved flat stretcher, the underside of the top center decorated w/two long flat tapering carved drop panels w/turned drop finials, Europe, late 19th c., 30 x 50", 31" h. (ILLUS., top of page) **$2,300**

Pretty Little Rococo-Style Side Table

Rococo-Style side table, inlaid mahogany, the triangular top flanked by three half-round drop leaves opening to form a three-lobe clover-form, each leaf inlaid w/a wreath of sprays of vines & flowers, raised on three simple cabriole legs w/a leaf-carved knee, metal scroll mounts on the feet, Europe, late 19th - early 20th c., top w/open cracks, 20" d. open, 28" h. (ILLUS.)... **$403**

"Sawbuck" table, painted pine, rectangular two-board top w/replaced battens raised on heavy cross-legs w/chamfered edges joined by a square cross-stretcher, scrubbed top, base in old yellow over earlier colors, age splits in the top, 19th c., 53 1/2" l. **$690**

Spanish Colonial table, hardwood, the rectangular long single plank top w/canted corners raised on trestle supports joined by a rectangular stretcher, 19th c., 24 1/2 x 62 3/4", 30" h. (ILLUS., top next page).. **$2,350**

Aesthetic Movement Parlor Table

Long Spanish Colonial Hardwood Table

Victorian Aesthetic Movement parlor center table, carved walnut, the square top w/molded edges & rounded corners above a line-incised apron w/curved corner blocks w/large turned pointed bulbous drops, two sides fitted w/a small central drawer w/a crosshatch-carved front, raised on four brackets above carved bulbous segments & spiral-carved columns, resting on a cross-form platform raised on four angled & scroll-carved legs raised on casters, late 19th c., 30" sq., 30" h. (ILLUS., previous page) **$431**

Victorian Aesthetic Movement side table, carved walnut, the rectangular top w/a narrow carved border & lappet carved edge above a twist-carved apron band & a long narrow drawer w/a carved central diamond flanked by flower & leaf design, the trestle-style base w/wide incurved angular end supports carved w/a tall arched panel filled w/stems of flowers, an open small Gothic arch above the angled & sawtooth-carved shoe feet, the sides joined by a shaped medial shelf on short

Fine Cincinnati Aesthetic Style Table

curved supports above a narrow saw-tooth-carved lower stretcher, made in Cincinnati, late 19th c., 23 1/2 x 34", 30" h. (ILLUS.) **$2,300**

Large Square Baroque Revival Oak Dining Table

Nicely Carved Oak Baroque Library Table

Victorian Baroque Revival dining table, quarter-sawn oak, extension-type, the square top w/a block band-carved deep apron w/florette-carved corners, raised on four serpentine acanthus leaf-carved legs resting on heavy brass caps on casters, joined by a scroll-carved serpentine cross stretcher centered by a raised octagonal platform supporting four bulbous short pedestals, refinished, ca. 1895, w/six leaves, 54" w., 30" h. (ILLUS., bottom previous page) **$3,200**

Victorian Baroque Revival library table, carved quarter-sawn oak, the rectangular top w/a gadrooned edge above a flat apron w/a single drawer w/brass teardrop pulls on one side, rosette-carved corner blocks, raised on heavy S-scroll carved corner supports topped by a short ring-turned column & resting on bun feet, each joined by a wide ornately pierced scroll-carved support joined by a heavy medial shelf, original finish, ca. 1895, 24 x 48", 30" h. (ILLUS., top of page).. **$1,200**

Simple Victorian Eastlake Dining Table

Victorian Eastlake dining table, quarter-sawn oak, extension-type, the divided square top above a reeded apron raised on five heavy square reeded legs

w/curved brackets under the apron, on casters, ca. 1900-1910, w/three 13 3/4" w. leaves, closed 48" sq., 29 1/2" h. (ILLUS.) **$575**

Very Rare Victorian Egyptian Revival Parlor Center Table

Victorian Egyptian Revival style parlor center table, bronze-mounted filt & marquetry-inlaid, the oval top w/a flat gilt border band w/low-relief designs of swans, dolphins & battling centaurs enclosing a large round mirror, the border divided by four projecting panels each above a full-relief carved bust of an ancient Egyptian woman joined by a deep apron centered on each side w/a large oblong floral & cartouche marquetry-inlaid panel above a narrow curved gilt border band, the head issuing long squared inswept S-scroll supports w/narrow mahogany veneer panels each ending in a paneled block on a cross-form platform centered by a round platform supporting a tall tapering urn-turned post & supported by a ring-turned base support, each paneled block issuing an arched outswept leg decorated w/a gilt top band & ending in a gilt hoof-like foot, New York City, ca. 1850, 37 1/4 x 40 5/8", 29 1/2" h. (ILLUS.) ... **$42,000**

Early Victorian Gothic Revival Table

Victorian Gothic Revival card table, mahogany, the fold-over rectangular top w/serpentine edges above a deep apron bordered w/Gothic arches & rounded corners w/small turned drops, raised on four

slender bobbin-turned legs resting on arched trestle feet joined by a bobbin-turned stretcher, ca. 1840-50, closed 16 x 31 1/2", 29" h. (ILLUS.) **$230**

Victorian Jacobean-Style Library Table

Victorian Jacobean-Style library table, oak, the rectangular top w/a faux-painted marbleized insert & gadrooned edge band above the apron w/florette-carved corner blocks flanking two long leaf-carved drawers w/carved lion mask handles, raised on four heavy spiral-turned legs joined by a spiral-turned H-stretcher, carved block & bun feet, dark medium color, ca. 1900, 32 x 48", 29 1/2" h. (ILLUS.) **$748**

Ornately Carved Victorian Renaissance Revival Dining Table

Victorian Renaissance Revival dining table, carved oak, the round extension top w/a drapery-carved edge & deep apron raised on a heavy divided post supported by four large outswept legs each carved as a griffin issuing a cluster of fruit from its mouth, paw feet on casters, one original leaf & three associated leaves, ca. 1870, 55" d. closed, 29" h. (ILLUS.) **$2,875**

Fine Renaissance Revival Parlor Table

Victorian Renaissance Revival parlor center table, carved rosewood, the oval top inset w/white marble above a deep molded apron w/four low arched drops, raised on four incurved S-scroll legs raised on a cross-form base centered by an urn-turned post & resting on four outswept scroll legs on casters, ca. 1870s, 28 x 39 1/2", 31" h. (ILLUS.) **$1,495**

Simple Renaissance Revival Parlor Table

Victorian Renaissance Revival parlor center table, walnut, the oval top above a covered apron w/four low shaped drops, raised on four flattened serpentine legs joined to a turned central post, the outswept lower legs on casters, ca. 1870, 22 x 30", 30" h. (ILLUS.) **$259**

Marble Top Renaissance Parlor Table

Victorian Renaissance Revival parlor center table, walnut, the rectangular white marble top w/molded edges & rounded corners above a conforming apron w/low carved drops, raised on four flattened & curved legs joined to a central turned post above the angular outswept lower legs, ca. 1870s, 21 x 28", 29" h. (ILLUS.).. **$288**

Victorian Renaissance Revival pool table, parcel-gilt marquetry rosewood & walnut, the rectangular top w/molded edge cushions flanking six leather pockets above a molded frieze w/brass roundels above a tapering shaped & molded paneled base inlaid w/stylized flowers within diamond lozenge insets, the corners chamfered & shaped w/similar inlay, raised on four foliate-carved lion head & paw feet, the Monarch model by Brunswick, Balke, Collender, 1880-90, 4' 7" x 8' 5", 34 1/2" h. (ILLUS., bottom of page).. **$18,800**

Outstanding Late Victorian Pool Table

Nice Victorian Renaissance Revival Dining Table

Victorian Renaissance Revival substyle dining table, carved mahogany, extension-type, the oval top over-hanging a deep apron raised on heavy ring-turned & tapering fluted legs w/disk ankles on brass & porcelain casters, w/two leaves, ca. 1870, open 64 x 106", 29 1/2" h. (ILLUS. open) **$1,955**

Rare Victorian Rococo Parlor Center Table Attributed to Meeks

Victorian Rococo substyle parlor center table, carved & laminated rosewood, the shaped "turtle-top" w/a later inset top above a conforming apron w/each deep serpentine side pierced & carved w/or-nate scrolls centering a floral cartouche, raised on four serpentine cabriole legs w/floral-carved knees & ending in scroll feet on casters, legs joined by four arched & pierced scroll-carved stretchers joined by a central post w/a large carved fruit-filled compote, attributed to J. & J.W. Meeks, New York, New York, ca. 1855, 30 x 46", 31 1/2" h. (ILLUS.) **$20,700**

Rococo Marble-topped Parlor Table

Victorian Rococo substyle parlor center table, carved rosewood, the inset tan marble "turtle-top" w/a conforming gadrooned edge above a conforming apron w/ornate scroll-carved serpentine sides, raised on four bold ornately carved S-scroll legs on casters joined by four ornate S-scroll stretchers centered by a short post w/a turned drop finial & a large carved compote-shaped finial, ca. 1860, 32 x 51", 29" h. (ILLUS., previous page) **$8,050**

Victorian Rococo substyle parlor center table, carved walnut, the round white marble top above a deep serpentine apron w/incised ovals & dots & ring-turned drops at the corners, raised on four slender ring- and rod-turned supports joined to a cross-stretcher centered by an open-carved compote & raised on four long outswept double-C-scroll legs ending in casters, ca. 1860, 32" d., 29" h. (ILLUS.).. **$518**

Nice Victorian Rococo Parlor Table

Victorian Rococo substyle parlor center table, walnut, the white marble "turtle-top" above a deep conforming apron carved at the side centers w/bold scrolls & corner blocks w/small turned drops, raised on a very bulbous octagonal pedestal above four long outstretched ornate S-scroll legs on casters, ca. 1855, 27 1/2 x 38", 28" h. (ILLUS.) **$920**

Round Victorian Rococo Parlor Table

Extraordinary Carved Walnut Rococo Parlor Table with Carved Dog

Victorian Rococo "turtle-top" parlor center table, carved walnut, the white marble "turtle-top" above a conforming apron w/wide arched & scroll-carved center sections, raised on elaborately pierce-carved heavy S-scroll legs headed by bold bearded faces & ending in scroll feet on casters, the legs joined by scroll-carved cross-stretchers centered by a small platform mounted w/a carved reclining spaniel dog, attributed to H.N. Wenning & Co., Cincinnati, Ohio, ca. 1850, 29 x 43", 31" h. (ILLUS.) **$3,910**

Rustic Late Victorian Antler Table

Victorian rustic-style occasional table, antler & oak, a large square top raised on pairs of entwined antlers at each corner above a smaller medial shelf raised on additional antlers, late 19th - early 20th c., 20" w., 30 1/2" h. (ILLUS.) **$460**

Rare William & Mary "Butterfly" Table

William & Mary "butterfly" dining table, figured maple, a narrow rectangular top w/rounded ends flanked by wide half-round hinged drop leaves above a splayed apron & baluster- and ring-turned legs ending in turned feet & joined by matching turned stretchers centered by shaped swing-out scalloped & tapering support leaves, New England, early 18th c., refinished, minor height loss, open 40" d., 25" h. (ILLUS.) **$15,275**

Nice Victorian Wicker Side Table

Wicker side table, a rectangular oak top raised on a wide apron composed of wicker spindles & w/corner curlicues, wrapped legs joined by a lower oak shelf w/wicker banding & a low spindle gallery, natural finish, ca. 1890s, 16 x 20", 28" h. (ILLUS.) **$863**

American William & Mary Tavern Table

William & Mary country-style tavern table, maple, the oval top on a rectangular apron raised on four baluster-, ring- and knob-turned legs ending in blocks w/knob feet & joined by flat box stretchers, New England, ca. 1710-35, 27 1/2 x 33 1/2", 26 1/2" h. (ILLUS.) **$4,541**

Extremely Rare Early Bermuda-made William & Mary Dining Table

William & Mary dining table, cedar, the rectangular top w/gently rounded ends flanked by wide D-form hinged drop leaves, raised on fancy bobbin-, baluster- and ring-turned legs w/swing-out gateleg supports, all joined by bobbin-turned stretchers & raised on bobbin-turned peg feet, Bermuda, early 18th c., top replaced, end of one leaf missing, 48 3/4" l., 27 1/4" h. (ILLUS.) **$54,000**

Extremely Rare William & Mary Dining Table from Long Island

William & Mary dining table, maple, a long rectangular top w/slightly rounded ends flanked by wide half-round drop leaves, raised on a shaped apron w/a drawer at one end raised on baluster- and ring-turned legs & a swing-out leg support, all on blocks joined by knob-turned stretchers above compressed feet, Hempstead, Long Island, New York, 1700-20, drawer & one leaf old replacements, closed 20 1/2 x 48", 28" h. (ILLUS.) **$35,850**

William & Mary Maple Dining Table

William & Mary dining table, maple, the narrow rectangular figured maple top w/rounded ends flanked by two wide half-round drop leaves above the apron w/one drawer raised on baluster- and ring-turned legs w/swing-out gateleg support, baluster- and ring-turned stretchers, probably Massachusetts or Connecticut, early 18th c., some old repair & restoration, open 42 x 49", 26 1/2" h. (ILLUS.)................................. **$1,265**

Rare American William & Mary Table

William & Mary dressing table, walnut & burl walnut veneer, the rectangular top w/banded & molded edges above an apron w/two deep square drawers flanking a small shallow drawer all w/brass teardrop pulls, the deeply arched & valanced apron w/two turned drops raised on boldly turned trumpet legs joined by a serpentine X-stretcher & turnip-turned feet, Boston, 1690-1730, 21 x 32 1/2", 30 3/4" h. (ILLUS.) **$7,800**

English William & Mary Side Table

William & Mary side table, walnut & burl walnut, the rectangular top w/molded edges overhanging an apron fitted w/a long burl drawer w/two butterfly brasses, raised on five barley-twist & knob-turned legs joined by flat incurved stretchers resting on five heavy bun feet, England, first half 18th c., old restorations, 26 x 40", 32" h. (ILLUS.) **$9,775**

Wardrobes & Armoires

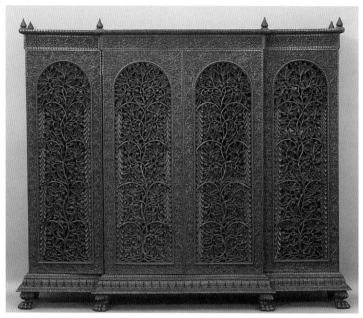

Ornate Anglo-Colonial Carved Rosewood Armoire

Armoire, Anglo-Colonial style, pierced & carved rosewood, the long rectangular breakfront top w/beaded edges & six small turned pointed finials above a conforming fruit & leaf-carved frieze band over four tall doors each w/ornate scroll carving around a large arched panel pierce-carved w/intricate scrolling tree-of-life-style designs, two center doors opening to pull-out shelves & two short drawers over two long drawers, the outer doors opening to pull-out shelves, the deep flaring leaf-carved base raised on carved paw feet, possibly Burma, mid-19th c., 24 x 98", 78 1/2" h. (ILLUS., top of page)... **$6,638**

Armoire, Art Deco style, brass-inlaid walnut veneer, the rectangular top above a pair of tall cupboard doors w/decorative veneering & vertical scalloped veneer bands along the inner edges, an inset plinth base raised on short bulbous stylized cabriole legs, Andre Sornay, France, ca. 1935, 17 1/2 x 39 1/2", 64" h. (ILLUS., next column) **$7,170**

Fine French Art Deco Walnut Armoire

Massive Early Baroque Oak Armoire

Armoire, Baroque style, oak, of massive architectonic proportions, the outstepped arched cornice over a pair of tall doors w/inset oval panels divided & flanked by pilasters headed by ebonized pierced scrolled acanthus leaf capitals above a pair of drawers over a stepped scrolled base, Northern Europe, probably Germany, first quarter 18th c., 29 1/2 x 78", 8' h. (ILLUS.)... **$7,050**

Fancy Baroque-Style Walnut Armoire

Armoire, Baroque-Style, walnut & burl walnut, the long rectangular top w/a widely flaring covered cornice above a pair of tall wide doors decorated w/pairs of patterned burl panels, flanked by narrow vertical side panels w/further burl panels & centered by a narrow paneled stile, the bottom w/a pair of long burl-paneled drawers over the rounded base molding raised on thin bun feet, Europe, mid-19th c., 27 x 78", 77" h. (ILLUS.) **$5,520**

Large Three-part Baroque-Style Armoire

Armoire, Baroque-Style, walnut, the long breakfront-case w/an arched serpentine cornice above a projecting wide arched center section fitted w/a wide arched mirrored door above a long paneled drawer, the tall narrow sides sections w/tall mirrored doors over smaller paneled drawers, plinth base raised on four bun feet, repair to left rear leg, Europe, late 19th - early 20th c., 26 1/2 x 94 1/2", 100" h. (ILLUS.)... **$1,380**

Classical Mahogany Armoire

Armoire, Classical, mahogany & mahogany veneer, the rectangular top w/a deep flared cornice above a pair of tall paneled doors opening to an altered interior of a belt of drawers & shelves to the right & divided open space on the left, on beehive-turned legs w/brass feet, ca. 1830, 23 3/8 x 61", 91 1/2" h. (ILLUS.) **$9,200**

Rare New Orleans Classical Armoire

Armoire, Classical style, mahogany & mahogany veneer, rectangular top w/widely flaring & stepped cornice accented by a beaded band above a single tall mirrored door within a wide molding & flanked by beaded bands down the outside corners, opening to an interior w/original fitted shelves & a drawer belt, a long narrow ogee-front drawer below, raised on a deep flat apron w/low scroll-carved bracket feet, New Orleans, ca. 1840-50, 21 x 50", 99" h. (ILLUS.) **$16,100**

Classical Mahogany Armoire

Armoire, Classical style, mahogany & mahogany veneer, the rectangular top w/a wide projecting stepped cornice above a plain frieze band w/blocked ends above a pair of tall paneled cupboard doors flanked by slender columns opening to an interior w/shelves on one side, deep blocked flat base raised on short turned, tapering & reeded legs w/brass ball feet, restorations, ca. 1820-30, 22 1/2 x 60", 92" h. (ILLUS.) **$7,475**

Small Louisiana Classical Armoire

Armoire, Classical style, mahogany & mahogany veneer, the rectangular top w/a stepped & coved cornice w/chamfered front corners above a pair of tall paneled cupboard doors w/long exposed hinges & pierced scrolling long brass escutcheons, the interior divided & fitted w/shelves & a drawer on the right side, raised on slender turned beehive legs w/ball feet, made in Louisiana, early 19th c., small size (ILLUS.) **$21,850**

Armoire, Classical style, mahogany & mahogany veneer, the wide rectangular top w/a nearly flat overhanging cornice above a long low projecting arch supported on tall slender columns w/carved capitals flanking the set-back pair of tall two-paneled doors w/long pierced brass escutcheons, fitted interior w/open space on the left & shelving & a belt of drawers on the right, raised on heavy turned & gadrooned front legs w/ball feet, attributed to the shop of Duncan Phyfe, New York, New York, ca. 1825, 27 1/2 x 64", 91" h. (ILLUS., next page)............................. **$13,800**

Armoire Attributed to Duncan Phyfe

Rare Simple Louisiana Classical Armoire

Armoire, Classical style, walnut & mahogany, the thin large rectangular top overhanging a deep frieze band above a pair of tall paneled cupboard doors w/a long scrolled brass escutcheon on one door & opening to a fitted interior, deep molded bae raised on heavy bulbous tapering legs ending in brass ball feet, probably made in Louisiana, ca. 1830, 22 x 56 1/2", 93" h. (ILLUS.) **$14,950**

Simple Classical Mahogany Armoire

Armoire, Classical style, mahogany, the rectangular top w/a wide flattened cornice above a cast w/a pair of tall paneled doors opening to a bank of three drawers, raised on bracket feet, restored original finish, ca. 1840, 22 x 60 1/2", 6' 9 1/2" h. (ILLUS.) **$1,840**

Classical Transitional Rosewood Armoire

Armoire, Classical Transitional style, rose-wood, the rectangular top w/a widely projecting stepped cornice above a wide ogee frieze band over the tall rectangular door w/raised molding enclosing a tall mirror & flanked by slender bead-carved corner bands above a single long bottom drawer w/further bead-carved banding, a deep platform base w/a narrow slipper drawer on block feet, possibly made in New Orleans, ca. 1850, 36 x 52", 96" h. (ILLUS., previous page) **$4,600**

Extraordinary Early Louisiana Armoire

Armoire, Colonial Louisiana, inlaid mahogany, the rectangular top w/a deep flaring corner w/rounded front corners above a deep frieze band centered by a finely inlaid design of a drapery swag above an oval inlaid w/the monogram "EM" all flanked by long line-inlaid panels, the pair of tall cupboard doors centered by tall line-inlaid panels w/a short angled band of inlaid bellflowers at each corner, mounted w/long pierced & scrolled brass escutcheons & centered by a long stile delicately inlaid the full length w/delicate entwined flowering vines & urns, the deep serpentine front apron centered by another double-swag drapery, simple cabriole legs, the interior fitted w/cypress shelves, a center belt of three drawers & a lower belt of two drawers, replaced brasses, late 18th - early 19th c., 23 1/2 x 60", 90 1/2" h. (ILLUS.) **$140,000**

Rare Inlaid Louisiana Armoire

Armoire, Federal style, inlaid mahogany, the rectangular top w/a cavetto cornice above a frieze band centering an inlaid octagonal lozenge enclosing a monogram & flanked by inlaid ovals & acanthus leaf inlay, a pair of tall doors w/a false center stile decorated w/a pinwheel boss inlay, unusual door construction w/irregular tapering battens, the case w/chamfered side stiles, short cabriole legs w/restoration, made in Louisiana, early 19th c., 24 x 56", 88" h. (ILLUS.) **$19,550**

Very Rare Inlaid Louisiana Armoire

Armoire, Federal-French Provincial style, inlaid cherry, rectangular top w/a later wide ogee cornice above an inlaid frieze centering an inlaid monogram above a pair tall cupboard doors opening to a replaced well-fitted interior, arched scroll-cut wide apron w/unusual inlaid swag decoration, short front cabriole legs restored, made in Louisiana, early 19th c., 22 x 56", 84" h. (ILLUS., previous page) **$37,375**

Fine Carved French Provincial Armoire

Armoire, French Provincial, carved oak, the rectangular top w/a wide flaring cornice above a leaf- and scroll-carved frieze band above a pair of tall arched three-panel cupboard doors, the top panels carved w/fancy flowers & leaves, the central panel carved w/a paneled cartouche w/more leafy scrolls & the bottom panel decorated w/a plain arched panel framed by leafy scrolls, five-panel sides, a wide flaring & stepped base raised on thin bun feet, France, early 19th c., 22 x 51", 80" h. (ILLUS.) **$2,070**

Armoire, French Provincial-Style, carved walnut, the wide arched crestrail centered by a large scroll-carved crest above a conforming molded frieze band over a pair of tall mirrored cupboard doors flanked by chamfered front corners w/scroll carving, the molded base band above a deep serpentine apron carved in the center w/a large scrolling cartouche, short scroll-carved cabriole front legs, feet cut off, top of large crest missing, France, ca. 1890, 24 x 59", 101" h. (ILLUS., top next column) **$2,530**

Large French Provincial-Style Armoire

English Gothic Revival Armoire

Armoire, Gothic Revival style, mahogany & mahogany veneer, the rectangular top w/a deep flaring stepped cornice above a pair of tall wide doors w/Gothic arch panels flanked by tall spiral-turned corner columns, flat ogee-molded base raised on heavy bun front feet, England, ca. 1840, 21 x 58", 83" h. (ILLUS.) **$2,760**

Early Louis XV Walnut Armoire

Armoire, Louis XV, walnut, the outstepped cornice above a recessed frieze centering a pinwheel over a pair of tall three-panel doors above a scalloped apron, raised on short cabriole legs, France, third quarter 18th c., 22 x 61", 6' 8" h. (ILLUS.) **$4,700**

Fine Louisiana Inlaid Mahogany Armoire

Armoire, Louisiana type, inlaid mahogany, the rectangular top w/a deep flaring cornice w/rounded front corners above a frieze band centered by a large inlaid almond-shaped satinwood device above a pair of tall two-panel doors outlined in satinwood & inlaid in each corner of the panels w/a fan device, the wide central stile centered by another almond-shaped device inlaid w/a classical urn, the deep

arched & serpentine apron also centered by an almond-shaped inlay in slender cabriole legs, early 19th c., 21 x 61", 85" h. (ILLUS.) **$23,000**

Louisiana Louis XV Style Armoire

Armoire, Louisiana-made Louis XV Provincial style, carved walnut, the rectangular top w/a deep coved cornice w/rounded corners above a pair of tall double-panel cupboard doors w/the upper panel slightly arched, exterior long hinges & scrolled brass escutcheons, deep serpentine apron on simple cabriole legs, legs ended-out, late 18th - early 19th c., 21 x 51", 90" h. (ILLUS.) **$23,000**

Fine Neoclassical Inlaid Rosewood Armoire

Armoire, Neoclassical style, marquetry inlaid rosewood, the rectangular top w/a flaring cornice above a narrow frieze band w/a narrow marquetry inlay above a single tall mirrored door w/banded trim & a small rectangular inlaid lower panel, the wide front sides decorated w/tall rectangular upper & lower panels w/marquetry scenes of a standing woman among flowering vines & birds, a round marquetry panel at the center, a narrow base band w/marquetry trim raised on compressed bun feet, interior fitted w/three drawers w/recessed pulls & three shelves, some minor repairs, Europe, 19th c., 18 x 45", 75 1/2" h. (ILLUS., previous page) **$2,013**

Simple English Regency Armoire

Armoire, Regency style, mahogany & mahogany veneer, the rectangular top w/a narrow flaring cornice above a row of three tall doors w/simple Gothic arch panels, flat plinth base, England, early 19th c., 18 x 62 1/2", 77" h. (ILLUS.)...... **$2,070**

Armoire, Victorian faux-bamboo style, maple, the rectangular top fitted w/an elaborate gallery w/short rows of turned spindles centering at the front a large projecting block topped by a ring- and knob-turned finial, matching corner finials, all framed by bamboo-turned banding above a frieze panel w/a long rectangular raised bamboo-turned panel, all above a single tall cupboard door fitted w/a large arched mirror & trimmed w/thin bamboo-turned trim, heavy bamboo-turned posts down the front corners, a single long drawer at the bottom, open interior, disassembles easily for transportation, ca. 1880s, 23 x 45", 102" h. (ILLUS., top next column) **$3,565**

Rare Victorian Faux-Bamboo Armoire

Unique Gothic Revival Armoire

Armoire, Victorian Gothic Revival style, walnut, the pediment composed of two front & two side Gothic arch panels w/scrolling trim & centering raised scrolling burl panels, three tall fluted columns w/tall tapering ring-turned finials dividing the pair of tall paneled doors each decorated w/raised tracery centered by a small cabochon, raised on heavy compressed ring- and knob-turned feet, Mid-Atlantic states, ca. 1855, 26 x 62", 8' 1" h. (ILLUS., previous page) **$4,140**

Nice Renaissance Revival Armoire

Armoire, Victorian Renaissance Revival substyle, rosewood veneer, the rectangular top w/a deep flaring cornice above a frieze band w/a narrow raised burl panel above a pair of tall paneled cupboard doors inset w/tall mirrors & flanked by slender half-round columns over a mid-molding & a pair of bottom drawers w/raised burl panels & round brass bail pulls, flat plinth base on thin blocked feet, ca. 1870, 25 x 67", 97" h. (ILLUS.) **$2,760**

Victorian Renaissance Revival Armoire

Armoire, Victorian Renaissance Revival substyle, carved walnut, the very high arched crest w/a central molded arch panel w/carved scrolls above a medallion cartouche, the quarter-round flanking panels w/raised burl veneer panels, carved umbrella-form corner finials, the arched deep flaring cornice above a conforming frieze band over the wide arched single door w/narrow scroll-trimmed molding around a tall arched mirror opening to the exterior fitted w/bird's-eye maple, the angled narrow front corners w/carved drops & a small raised panel, a lower medial molding above the long paneled drawer w/simple turned wood knobs above the platform base w/rounded front corners on disk feet, on casters, Cincinnati, Ohio, ca. 1875, 24 1/2 x 52 1/2", 112" h. (ILLUS.) **$608**

Victorian Rococo Rosewood Armoire

Armoire, Victorian Rococo style, carved rosewood, the top w/a high arched scroll-carved crestrail w/a large central cabochon above small pierce-carved panels & flanked by pointed knob corner finials, the deep arched & molded cornice above a pair of tall paneled doors opening to a divided interior containing shelves, a single drawer & a half void, the canted front corners decorated w/scrolled pendants at the top corners, the slightly stepped-out lower section enclosing a pair of paneled drawers w/turned wood knobs above the plinth base, probably New York City, ca. 1855, 22 x 64", 9' 2" h. (ILLUS., previous page)...................... **$4,600**

American Rococo Fancy Armoire

Armoire, Victorian Rococo substyle, carved mahogany, the arched flaring cornice topped by a long high arched crestrail pierce-carved w/ornate scrolls flanked by disk-turned corner finials above the arched frieze band carved w/a long scroll band w/fruit & leaves centering a face, the tall arched doors w/large scroll-carved corner panels above the tall inset mirrors, flanked by slender spiral- and baluster-turned quarter-round corner columns, a mid-molding above a pair of bottom drawers w/scroll-carved pulls, the low scroll-carved apron w/rounded front corners, retaining original interior partition & shelving, ca. 1855, 25 x 66", 118 1/2" h. (ILLUS.) **$5,520**

Fine Hudson River Valley Cherry Kas

Kas (a version of the Netherlands kast or wardrobe), cherry, three-part construction: the rectangular top w/a very deep stepped & widely flaring removable cornice above the upper section w/three fluted pilasters w/molded caps & bases flanking a pair of tall raised panel cupboard doors opening to two shelves; the lower section w/a mid-molding above a row of three drawers w/butterfly brasses above a pair of long drawers w/matching brasses, molded base over a narrow scallop-cut apron, raised on cabriole legs ending in pad feet, refinished, repairs, Hudson River Valley, New York, ca. 1740-70, top 18 1/2 x 53", 75 1/2" h. (ILLUS.) **$7,638**

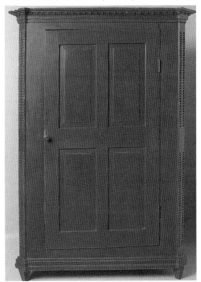

Early Mennonite One-door Kas

Early Hudson River Valley Gumwood Kas

Kas (a version of the Netherlands kast or wardrobe), country-style, maple & walnut, a rectangular top w/angled front corners & a low cornice w/a dentil-carved band above a tall single raised four-panel door decorated w/four star & dot inlays & w/the original brass pull, the canted front corners decorated w/double bands of chip-carving & further star inlays, conforming stepped apron on tapering block front feet, opening to interior side liners & four adjustable shelves, attributed to the Sonnenburg Mennonites, hinges replaced, old red wash, 23 x 53", 6' 4 1/4" h. (ILLUS., previous page).......... **$5,175**

Kas (a version of the Netherlands kast or wardrobe), gumwood, the rectangular top w/a very deep, stepped & widely flaring cornice above a pair of tall paneled doors opening to a shelved interior, centered & flanked by stiles each w/two tall narrow molded panels, set into a base w/a long single narrow drawer w/the face centered by an applied diamond panel flanked by rectangular molded panels w/turned knob pulls, a raised applied diamond at each outside edge, raised on bulbous turned front feet & cut-out rear feet, Hudson River Valley, New York, early 18th c., old refinish, minor imperfections, 22 x 62", 79" h. (ILLUS., top of page)... **$22,325**

Kas (a version of the Netherlands kast or wardrobe), walnut, the rectangular top w/a widely flaring stepped cornice above a dentil-carved frieze band above a narrow molding over the pair of tall cupboard doors each w/tall raised-molding panels

Large Nicely Detailed Flemish Kas

above & below a smaller rectangular center panel, wide side stiles w/narrow raised panels, heavy molded base raised on wide blocked pad feed, Flanders, mid-19th c., 27 x 60", 7' 2" h. (ILLUS.).......... **$5,750**

Fine Chippendale Walnut Schrank

Schrank (massive Germanic wardrobe),
Chippendale style, walnut, two-part construction: the upper section w/a rectangular top & deep covered cornice above a
frieze molding over a pair of tall double
raised-panel doors w/exposed H-hinges
& brass keyhole escutcheons; the lower
section w/a molded top above a pair of
long drawers flanking a small square
center drawer all w/butterfly brasses &
keyhole escutcheons, molded base on
scroll-carved   bracket   feet,
Pennsylvania, ca. 1780-1800, original
brasses, 26 x 60", 82" h. (ILLUS.)........ **$21,600**

Early Canadian Painted Schrank

Schrank (massive Germanic wardrobe),
painted pine, the rectangular top above a
pair of tall three-panel molded doors
w/wrought-iron rat trail hinges opening to
three later shelves above a pair of nailed
drawers w/brass knob pulls on a molded
base, three-paneled sides, old bluish
green paint, worn white paint on the

back, attributed to Canada, 19th c.,
19 x 53", 69 1/4" h. (ILLUS.) **$2,300**

English Chippendale-Style Wardrobe

Wardrobe, Chippendale-Style, mahogany,
the rectangular top w/a narrow flaring
cornice above a pair of tall cupboard
doors each w/three raised panels opening to shelves, flat molded base raised on
high scroll-cut bracket feet, refinished,
restorations w/replacements, England,
late 19th - early 20th c., 24 x 53 3/4",
78" h. (ILLUS.) **$1,495**

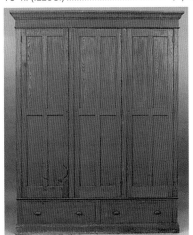

Large Three-door Cypress Wardrobe

Wardrobe, country style, cypress, a rectangular top w/a flaring cornice w/stamped
acanthus designs above three tall four-
paneled doors opening to a blind interior,
the separate lower section composed of
two long drawers w/metal pulls above a
molded plinth base, early 20th c.,
29 x 85", 9' h. (ILLUS.)........................... **$3,163**

Early Painted Breakdown Wardrobe

Wardrobe, country style, painted pine, breakdown type, the rectangular top w/a molded cornice above a deep plain frieze band over a pair of tall double-raised panel doors w/a diamond panel in the top half, cast-iron lift-off hinges, flat molded base, old red paint over earlier green, two removable interior shelves & peg racks, originally had feet, tin patches over old holes, attributed to Ohio or Indiana, 19th c., 22 3/4 x 51 1/2", 6' 2 1/2" h. (ILLUS.)................................. **$1,265**

Colorfully-painted Country Wardrobe

Wardrobe, country-style, blue-painted & decorated, a narrow arched & molded cornice above a pair of tall arched cupboard doors w/two raised panels, the top two painted in color w/figures in landscapes, the lower two painted w/flower-filled vases, each panel framed by ornate gilt scrolls, wide canted front corners w/further painted scrolls, deep plinth base w/further painted scrolls, old woodworm damage, Europe, possibly Portugal, 19th c., 21 x 60", 75" h. (ILLUS.) **$2,645**

Wardrobe, country-style, oak, rectangular top above a narrow molding over a tall arched door set w/a beveled mirror flanked on each side by a molded arched panel above a tall rectangular panel, a single long drawer at the base w/drop pulls, simple bracket feet, early 20th c., 48" w., 7' h. **$374**

European Painted Country Wardrobe

Wardrobe, country-style, painted & decorated, a rectangular top w/a flaring cornice painted w/a blue & white band above a blue frieze band painted w/a row of small white arches above a molding over a pair of tall paneled doors decorated w/a tall central blue diamond framed by white fan carving, a thick blue & white mid-molding above the deep plinth base raised on square legs, Europe, 19th c., 20 7/8 x 47 3/4", 71 1/2" h. (ILLUS.).................................. **$863**

Country Wardrobe with Paneled Doors

Simple Pine Country Wardrobe

Wardrobe, country-style, painted pine, the rectangular top w/a widely flaring stepped cornice above a pair of tall narrow double raised panel doors opening to an interior w/a shelf & five boards w/wooden hooks, some w/added metal hooks, deep serpentine apron & simple bracket feet, original alligatored reddish brown paint, pinned & nailed construction, some edge damage & loss of molding, mid-19th c., 24 1/4 x 50", 76" h. (ILLUS.) **$489**

Wardrobe, country-style, pine, the rectangular top w/a molded cornice above a pair of tall paneled cupboard doors w/brass latches & keyhole escutcheons opening to an interior divided w/replaced shelves, wide molded base on simple bracket feet, pegged mortise joints & square nails, cleaned down to worn red finish, wear, some damage & pieced repairs, replaced latches, mid-19th c., 18 x 49 1/2", 83 1/2" h. (ILLUS., top next column) **$345**

Wardrobe, Victorian country-style, walnut, the rectangular top w/a flaring stepped cornice above a pair of tall double-panel doors, flat molded base on thin block feet, second half 19th c., 21 x 64 1/4", 86" h. (ILLUS., bottom next column) **$1,076**

Simple Victorian Walnut Wardrobe

Rare French Art Nouveau Etagere

Victorian Renaissance Wardrobe

Wardrobe, Victorian Renaissance Revival style, walnut & burl walnut, the rectangular top w/a small arched center crest on the widely flaring stepped cornice above a frieze band w/a pair of long narrow raised burl bands flanking a central rondel, all above a pair of tall arched doors fitted w/mirrors below triangular raised panels in the upper corners, the doors flanked by pairs of long raised burl panels & rondels, the base w/a pair of drawers w/large raised burl panels & turned wood knobs above the plinth base on casters, ca. 1875, 20 x 57", 8' 2" h. (ILLUS.)... **$1,495**

Whatnots & Etageres

Etagere, Art Nouveau style, carved mahogany & marquetry, a high arched back crest w/a marquetry floral band above a top shelf flanked by curved sides above an ornately pierce-carved floral apron curving around the sides of the case & tapering to form a center stile, a large recessed compartment w/original pleated fabric above a lower case composed of a pair of tall tapering cupboard doors w/whiplash marquetry leaves & flowers & opening to a shelf, a flaring & scroll-carved base, designed & signed by Louis Majorelle, ca. 1900, France, 15 x 28 1/2", 5' 5" h. (ILLUS., top next column) **$31,070**

Open Art Nouveau Style Etagere

Etagere, Art Nouveau style, mahogany, the tall back composed of a large oblong beveled mirror in a narrow frame w/a carved crest above a tall vertical rectangular lower mirror, all supported on an arrangement of two curved long front legs & two shorter straight rear legs w/various sized oblong open shelves down the front, ca. 1910 (ILLUS.)............................ **$431**

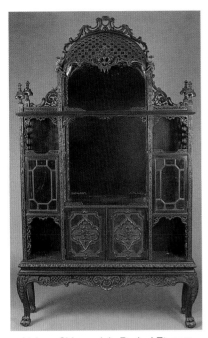

Unique Chippendale Revival Etagere

Etagere, Chippendale Revival style, carved mahogany, the scrolled pediment above a trelliswork half dome fronted by a pierced cartouche, the mirrored back divided by a shelf & over a pair of relief-carved doors, each side w/a shelf surmounted by finials, a glazed center door & two open compartments, on a base w/scroll-carved serpentine apron raised on short cabriole legs w/paw feet, in the manner of Edward and Roberts, London, England, ca. 1900, 13 x 51", 5' 10" h. (ILLUS.) **$5,463**

Etagere, Classical style, mahogany, a rectangular base cabinet w/two cockbeaded drawers above bracket feet on casters, the top supporting four open shelves joined by graduated baluster-turned supports, Boston, ca. 1830, 18 x 23", 5' 2" h. (ILLUS., top next column) **$1,725**

Etagere, Regency Style, mahogany, an arrangement of four open shelves on graduated baluster-turned supports above a bottom shelf over a narrow drawer w/two round brass pulls, on turned peg feet on casters, England, last quarter 19th c., 17 7/8 x 22", 5' 1 3/4" h. (ILLUS., bottom next column) **$2,070**

American Classical Etagere

English Regency Style Etagere

English Regency Four-Tier Etagere

Etagere, Regency style, mahogany, the tall upright design w/a rectangular top w/a low three-quarters gallery above three additional open shelves each supported by ring- and rod-turned supports, the bottom shelf over a single narrow drawer w/two turned wood knobs, simple turned legs on brass casters, England, ca. 1820, 15 x 20", 51" h. (ILLUS.) **$2,070**

Large Marble-topped Rococo Etagere

Etagere, Victorian Rococo style, rosewood-grained hardwood, the tall superstructure w/a high arched & pierce-carved crest w/an acanthus leaf cartouche over a tall arched mirror flanked on each side by four graduated quarter-round open shelves w/S-scroll supports & pierce-carved back brackets, the mirror above a molded rectangular panel flanked by scroll brackets on a half-round marble-topped base w/serpentine molded edges above a conforming apron w/a central drawer & trimmed w/carved scrolls & raised on four cabriole legs ending in scroll feet, ca. 1850s, 52" w., 7' 6" h. (ILLUS.) **$3,450**

Ornate Pierce-carved Rococo Etagere

Etagere, Victorian Rococo style, walnut, the upper section composed of three graduated & shaped open shelves supported by cut-out & molded serpentine brackets, each shelf w/a pierced back crest & gallery, the lower cabinet w/an oblong top above a conforming case w/a pair of cabinet doors w/pierced fretwork panels, serpentine apron above knob-turned feet, ca. 1850-60, 16 x 35", 6' 1" h. (ILLUS.) **$690**

Etagere, Victorian Rococo substyle, carved rosewood, the tall superstructure w/a wide arched scroll-carved & pierced crest above a half-round narrow serpentine top shelf raised on slender S-scroll carved front supports & flanked by S-scroll carved side flanking a mirrored back all above a matching larger lower shelf & mirrored back resting on the half-round serpentine-edged sienna marble top above a conforming cabinet base w/a serpentine-fronted scroll-carved top drawer above a conforming wide door centered by an oval panel, flanked on each side by two open quarter-round shelves w/scroll-carved brackets, the deep conforming apron w/ornate scroll carving, ca. 1850-60, 20 3/4 x 49 1/2", 73 1/2" h. (ILLUS., next page) **$8,050**

Rare Victorian Rococo Rosewood Etagere

Rare Chinese Chippendale-Style Etageres

Etageres, Chinese Chippendale-Style, carved mahogany, in the form of tall pagodas, a top cupola shelf over four graduated open shelves each w/a full pierced gallery, the upright w/blind fret carving, raised on cabriole legs ending in paw feet, late 19th - early 20th c., 20 1/2" sq., 70" h., pr. (ILLUS.) **$4,140**

Late Victorian Whatnot with Desk

Whatnot, Victorian country style, walnut, two narrow rectangular shaped & graduated open shelves joined by pairs of baluster-turned spindles above a rectangular compartment w/a fall front opening to a small writing surface & interior fitted w/small drawers & pigeonholes, raised on two larger matching open shelves supported on matching spindles & turned feet, ca. 1870-80 (ILLUS.).................. **$250-400**

SELECT BIBLIOGRAPHY

Bivins, John, Jr. *The Furniture of Coastal North Carolina, 1700-1820.* Winston-Salem, N.C.: Museum of Early Southern Decorative Arts, 1988.

Butler, Joseph T. *Field Guide to American Antique Furniture.* New York: Facts on File Publications, 1985.

Cathers, David M. *Furniture of the American Arts & Crafts Movement.* New York: New American Library, 1981.

Comstock, Helen. *American Furniture, Seventeenth, Eighteenth, and Nineteenth Century Styles.* New York: The Viking Press, 1962.

Cooper, Wendy A. *Classical Taste in America, 1800-1840.* New York: Abbeville Press, 1993.

Dubrow, Eileen and Richard. *American Furniture of the 19th Century, 1840-1880.* Exton, PA.: Schiffer Publishing, Ltd., 1983.

Dubrow, Eileen and Richard. *Furniture Made in America, 1875-1905.* Exton, PA.: Schiffer Publishing, Ltd., 1982.

Duncan, Alastair. *Art Nouveau Furniture.* New York: Clarkson N. Potter, Inc., 1982.

Fairbanks, Jonathan L. and Elizabeth Bidwell Bates. *American Furniture, 1620 to the Present.* New York: Richard Marek Publishers, 1981.

Fales, Dean A., Jr. *American Painted Furniture, 1660-1880.* New York: Crown Publishers, 1986.

Fitzgerald, Oscar. *Three Centuries of American Furniture.* Englewood Cliffs, N. J.: Prentice-Hall, 1982.

Fredgant, Don. *American Manufactured Furniture.* Atglen, PA: Schiffer Publishing, Ltd., 1988.

Kane, Patricia E. *300 Years of American Seating Furniture.* Boston: New York Graphic Society, 1976.

Kirk, John T. *American Furniture and The British Tradition to 1830.* New York: Alfred A. Knopf, 1982.

Kovel, Ralph and Terry Kovel. *American Country Furniture, 1780-1875.* New York: Crown Publishers, 1965.

Lockwood, Luke Vincent. *Colonial Furniture in America, 2 vols.* New York: Castle Books, 1951, rpt.

Madigan, Mary Jean. *Nineteenth Century Furniture.* New York: Art & Antiques, 1982.

Marsh, Moreton. *The Easy Expert in American Antiques.* Philadelphia: J.B. Lippincott, 1978.

McNerney, Kathryn. *Pine Furniture — Our American Heritage.* Paducah, KY: Collector Books, 1989.

Montgomery, Charles F. *American Furniture, The Federal Period in the Henry Francis du Pont Winterthur Museum.* New York: The Viking Press, 1966.

Morningstar, Connie. *American Furniture Classics.* Des Moines, IA: Wallace-Homestead Book Co., 1976.

Nutting, Wallace. *Furniture Treasury, vols. I, II.* New York: Macmillan, 1928.

Nutting, Wallace. *Furniture Treasury, vol. III.* New York: Macmillan, 1933.

Sack, Albert. *The New Fine Points of Furniture.* New York: Crown Publishing, 1993.

Santore, Charles. *The Windsor Style in America.* Philadelphia: Running Press, 1981.

Santore, Charles. *The Windsor Style in America, Vol. II.* Philadelphia: Running Press, 1987.

Warner, Velma Susanne. *Golden Oak Furniture.* Atglen, PA: Schiffer Publishing, Ltd., 1992.

APPENDIX I
AUCTION SERVICES

The following is a select listing of larger regional auction houses which often feature antique furniture in their sales. There are, of course, many fine local auction services that also feature furniture from time to time.

East Coast:

Christie's
502 Park Ave.
New York, NY 10022
Phone: (212) 546-1000

Douglas Auctioneers
Route 5
South Deerfield, MA 01373
Phone: (413) 665-3530

William Doyle Galleries
175 E. 87th St.
New York, NY 10128
Phone: (212) 427-2730

Willis Henry Auctions
22 Main St.
Marshfield, MA 02059
Phone: (617) 834-7774

Dave Rago
9 So. Main St.
Lambertville, NJ 08530
Phone: (609) 397-9374

Skinner Inc.
357 Main St.
Bolton, MA 01740
Phone: (508) 779-6241

Sotheby's
1334 York Ave.
New York, NY 10021
Phone: (212) 606-7000

Withington, Inc.
R. D. 2, Box 440
Hillsboro, NH 03244
Phone: (603) 464-3232

Midwest:

DuMochelles Galleries
409 East Jefferson Ave.
Detroit, MI 48226
Phone: (313) 963-6255

Garth's Auctions
P.O. Box 369
Delaware, OH 43015
Phone: (614) 362-4771

Gene Harris Antique Auction Center
P.O. Box 476
Marshalltown, IA 50158
Phone: (515) 752-0600

Jackson's Auctioneers & Appraisers
2229 Lincoln St.
Cedar Falls, IA 50613
Phone: (319) 277-2256

Treadway Gallery
P.O. Box 8924
Cincinnati, OH 45208
Phone: (513) 321-6742

Far West:

Butterfield & Butterfield
7601 Sunset Blvd.
Los Angeles, CA 90046
Phone: (213) 850-7500

Pettigrew Auction Company
1645 So. Tejon St.
Colorado Springs, CO 80906
Phone: (719) 633-7963

South:

Neal Auction Company
4038 Magazine St.
New Orleans, LA 70115
Phone: (504) 899-5329

New Orleans Auction Galleries
801 Magazine St.
New Orleans, LA 70130
Phone: (504) 566-1849

APPENDIX II
Stylistic Guidelines: American and English Furniture

AMERICAN

Style: Pilgrim Century
Dating: 1620-1700
Major Wood(s): Oak
General Characteristics:
 Case pieces: rectilinear low-relief carved panels; blocky and bulbous turnings; splint-spindle trim
 Seating pieces: shallow carved panels; spindle turnings

Style: William and Mary
Dating: 1685-1720
Major Wood(s): Maple and walnut
General Characteristics:
 Case pieces: paint decorated chests on ball feet; chests on frames, chests with two-part construction; trumpet-turned legs; slant-front desks
 Seating pieces: molded, carved crestrails; banister backs; cane, rush (leather) seats; baluster, ball and block turnings; ball and Spanish feet

Style: Queen Anne
Dating: 1720-50
Major Wood(s): Walnut
General Characteristics:

    Case pieces: mathematical proportions of elements; use of the cyma or S-curve broken-arch pediments; arched panels, shell carving, star inlay; blocked fronts; cabriole legs and pad feet

    Seating pieces: molded yoke-shaped crestrails; solid vase-shaped splats; rush or upholstered seats; cabriole legs; baluster, ring, ball and block-turned stretchers; pad and slipper feet

Style: Chippendale
Dating: 1750-85
Major Wood(s): Mahogany and walnut
General Characteristics:

    Case pieces: relief-carved broken-arch pediments; foliate, scroll, shell, fretwork carving; straight, bow or serpentine fronts; carved cabriole legs; claw and ball, bracket or ogee feet

    Seating pieces: carved, shaped crestrails with out-turned ears; pierced, shaped splats; ladder (ribbon) backs; upholstered seats; scrolled arms; carved cabriole legs or straight (Marlboro) legs; claw and ball feet

Style: Federal (Hepplewhite)
Dating: 1785-1800
Major Wood(s): Mahogany and light inlays
General Characteristics:
  Case pieces: more delicate rectilinear forms; inlay with eagle and classical motifs; bow, serpentine or tambour fronts; reeded quarter columns at sides; flared bracket feet
  Seating pieces: shield backs; upholstered seats; tapered square legs

Style: Federal (Sheraton)
Dating: 1800-20
Major Wood(s): Mahogany and mahogany veneer and maple
General Characteristics:
  Case pieces: architectural pediments; acanthus carving; outset (cookie or ovolu) corners and reeded columns; paneled sides; tapered, turned, reeded or spiral-turned legs; bow or tambour fronts, mirrors on dressing tables
  Seating pieces: rectangular or square backs; slender carved banisters; tapered, turned or reeded legs

Style: Classical (American Empire)
Dating: 1815-50
Major Wood(s): Mahogany and mahogany veneer and rosewood
General Characteristics:
   Case pieces: increasingly heavy proportions; pillar and scroll construction; lyre, eagle, Greco-Roman and Egyptian motifs; marble tops; projecting top drawer; large ball feet, tapered fluted feet or hairy paw feet; brass, ormolu decoration
   Seating pieces: high-relief carving; curved backs; out-scrolled arms; ring turnings; sabre legs, curule (scrolled-S) legs; brass-capped feet, casters

Style: Victorian – Early Victorian
Dating: 1840-50
Major Wood(s): Mahogany veneer, black walnut and rosewood
General Characteristics:
   Case pieces: Pieces tend to carry over the Classical style with the beginnings of the Rococo substyle, especially in seating pieces.

Style: Victorian – Gothic Revival
Dating: 1840-90
Major Wood(s): Black walnut, mahogany and rosewood
General Characteristics:
    Case pieces: architectural motifs; triangular arched pediments; arched panels; marble tops; paneled or molded drawer fronts; cluster columns; bracket feet, block feet or plinth bases
    Seating pieces: tall backs; pierced arabesque backs with trefoils or quatrefoils; spool turning; drop pendants

Style: Victorian – Rococo (Louis XV)
Dating: 1845-70
Major Wood(s): Black walnut, mahogany and rosewood
General Characteristics:
    Case pieces: arched carved pediments; high-relief carving, S- and C-scrolls, floral, fruit motifs, busts and cartouches; mirror panels; carved slender cabriole legs; scroll feet; bedroom suites (bed, dresser, commode)
    Seating pieces: high-relief carved crestrails; balloon-shaped backs; urn-shaped splats; upholstery (tufting); demi-cabriole legs; laminated, pierced and carved construction (Belter and Meeks); parlor suites (sets of chairs, love seats, sofas)

Style: Victorian – Renaissance Revival
Dating: 1860-85
Major Wood(s): Black walnut, burl veneer, painted and grained pine
General Characteristics:
   Case pieces: rectilinear arched pediments; arched panels, burl veneer; applied moldings; bracket feet, block feet, plinth bases; medium and high-relief carving, floral and fruit, cartouches, masks and animal heads; cyma-curve brackets; Wooton patent desks
   Seating pieces: oval or rectangular backs with floral or figural cresting; upholstery outlined with brass tacks; padded armrests; tapered turned front legs, flared square rear legs

Style: Victorian – Louis XVI
Dating: 1865-75
Major Wood(s): Black walnut and ebonized maple
General Characteristics:
   Case pieces: gilt decoration, marquetry, inlay; egg and dart carving; tapered turned legs, fluted
   Seating pieces: molded, slightly arched crestrails; keystone-shaped backs; circular seats; fluted tapered legs

Style: Victorian – Eastlake
Dating: 1870-95
Major Wood(s): Black walnut, burl veneer, cherry and oak
General Characteristics:
    Case pieces: flat cornices; stile and rail construction; burl veneer panels; low-relief geometric and floral machine-carving; incised horizontal lines
    Seating pieces: rectilinear; spindles; tapered, turned legs, trumpet-shaped legs

Style: Victorian Jacobean and Turkish Revival
Dating: 1870-90
Major Wood(s): Black walnut and maple
General Characteristics:
    Case pieces: A revival of some heavy 17th century forms, most commonly in dining room pieces
    Seating pieces:
    Turkish Revival style features: oversized, low forms; overstuffed upholstery; padded arms; short baluster, vase-turned legs; ottomans, circular sofas
    Jacobean Revival style features: heavy bold carving spool and spiral turnings

Style: Victorian – Aesthetic Movement
Dating: 1880-1900
Major Wood(s): Painted hardwoods, black walnut, ebonized finishes
General Characteristics:
    Case pieces: rectilinear forms; bamboo turnings, spaced ball turnings; incised stylized geometric and floral designs, sometimes highlighted with gilt
    Seating pieces: bamboo turning; rectangular backs; patented folding chairs

Style: Art Nouveau
Dating: 1895-1918
Major Wood(s): Ebonized hardwoods, fruitwoods
General Characteristics:
    Case pieces: curvilinear shapes; floral marquetry; whiplash curves
    Seating pieces: elongated forms; relief-carved floral decoration; spindle backs, pierced floral backs; cabriole legs

Style: Turn-of-the-Century (Early 20th Century)
Dating: 1895-1910
Major Wood(s): Golden (quarter-sawn) oak, mahogany hardwood stained to resemble
     mahogany
General Characteristics:
   Case pieces: rectilinear and bulky forms; applied scroll carving or machine-pressed
   designs; some Colonial and Classical Revival detailing
   Seating pieces: heavy framing or high spindle-trimmed backs; applied carved or
   machine-pressed back designs; heavy scrolled or slender turned legs; often feature some
   Colonial Revival or Classical Revival detailing such as claw and ball feet

Style: Mission (Arts and Crafts movement)
Dating: 1900-1915
Major Wood(s): Oak
General Characteristics:
   Case pieces: rectilinear through-tenon construction; copper decoration, hand-hammered
   hardware; square legs
   Seating pieces: rectangular splats; medial and side stretchers; exposed pegs; corbel
   supports

Style: Wicker
Dating: mid-19th century - 1930
Major Wood(s): Natural woven wicker or synthetic fibers
General Characteristics:
  Case and Seating pieces: Earlier examples feature tall backs with ornate lacy scrolling designs continuing down to the arms and aprons; tables and desks often feature hardwood (often oak) tops; after about 1910 designs were much simpler with plain tightly woven backs, arms and aprons; pieces were often given a natural finish but painted finishes in white or dark green became popular after 1900

Style: Colonial Revival
Dating: 1890-1930
Major Wood(s): Oak, walnut and walnut veneer, mahogany veneer
General Characteristics:
  Case pieces: forms generally following designs of the 17th, 18th and early 19th centuries; details for the styles such as William and Mary, Federal, Queen Anne, Chippendale or early Classical were used but often in a simplified or stylized form; mass-production in the early 20th century flooded the market with pieces which often mixed and matched design details and used a great deal of thin veneering to dress up designs; dining room and bedroom suites were especially popular
  Seating pieces: designs again generally followed early period designs with some mixing of design elements.

Style: Art Deco
Dating: 1925-40
Major Wood(s): Bleached woods, exotic woods, steel and chrome
General Characteristics:
   Case pieces: heavy geometric forms
   Seating pieces: streamlined, attenuated geometric forms; overstuffed upholstery

Style: Modernist or Mid-Century
Dating: 1945-70
Major Wood(s): Plywood, hardwood or metal frames
General Characteristics: Modernistic designers such as the Eames, Vladimir Kagan, George Nelson and Isamu Noguchi lead the way in post-War design. Carrying on the tradition of Modernist designers of the 1920s and 1930s, they focused on designs for the machine age, which could be mass-produced for the popular market. By the late 1950s many of their pieces were used in commercial office spaces and schools as well as in private homes.
   Case pieces: streamlined or curvilinear abstract designs with simple detailing; plain round or flattened legs and arms commonly used; mixed materials including wood, plywood, metal, glass and molded plastics
   Seating pieces: streamlined and abstract curvilinear designs generally using newer materials such as plywood or simple hardwood framing; Fabric and synthetics such as vinyl were widely used for upholstery with finer fabrics and real leather featured on more expensive pieces; seating made of molded plastic shells on metal frames and legs used on many mass-produced designs

Style: Danish Modern
Dating: 1950-70
Major Wood(s): Teak
General Characteristics:

    Case and Seating pieces: This variation of Modernistic post-war design originated in Scandinavia, hence the name; designs were simple and restrained with case pieces often having simple boxy forms with short rounded tapering legs; seating pieces have a simple teak framework with lines coordinating with case pieces; vinyl or natural fabric were most often used for upholstery; in the United States dining room suites were the most popular use for this style although some bedroom suites and general seating pieces were available

ENGLISH

Style: Jacobean
Dating: Mid-17th century
Major Wood(s): Oak, walnut
General Characteristics:

    Case pieces: low-relief carving, geometrics and florals; panel, rail and stile construction; applied split balusters
    Seating pieces: rectangular backs; carved and pierced crests; spiral turnings ball feet

Style: William and Mary
Dating: 1689-1702
Major Wood(s): Walnut, burl walnut veneer
General Characteristics:

    Case pieces: marquetry, veneering; shaped aprons; 6-8 trumpet-form legs; curved flat stretchers

    Seating pieces: carved, pierced crests; tall caned backs and seats; trumpet-form legs; Spanish feet

Style: Queen Anne
Dating: 1702-14
Major Wood(s): Walnut, mahogany, veneers
General Characteristics:

    Case pieces: cyma curves; broken arch pediments and finials; bracket feet
    Seating pieces: carved crestrails; high, rounded backs; solid vase-shaped splats; cabriole legs; pad feet

Style: George I
Dating: 1714-27
Major Wood(s): Walnut, mahogany, veneer and yewwood
General Characteristics:
    Case pieces: broken arch pediments; gilt decoration, japanning; bracket feet
    Seating pieces: curvilinear forms; yoke-shaped crests; shaped solid splats; shell carving; upholstered seats; carved cabriole legs; claw and ball feet, pad feet

Style: George II
Dating: 1727-60
Major Wood(s): Mahogany
General Characteristics:
    Case pieces: broken arch pediments; relief-carved foliate, scroll and shell carving; carved cabriole legs; claw and ball feet, bracket feet, ogee bracket feet
    Seating pieces: carved, shaped crestrails, out-turned ears; pierced shaped splats; ladder (ribbon) backs; upholstered seats; scrolled arms; carved cabriole legs or straight (Marlboro) legs; claw and ball feet

Style: George III
Dating: 1760-1820
Major Wood(s): Mahogany, veneer, satinwood
General Characteristics:
    Case pieces: rectilinear forms; parcel gilt decoration; inlaid ovals, circles, banding or marquetry; carved columns, urns; tambour fronts or bow fronts; plinth bases
    Seating pieces: shield backs; upholstered seats; tapered square legs, square legs

Style: Regency
Dating: 1811-20
Major Wood(s): Mahogany, mahogany veneer, satinwood and rosewood
General Characteristics:
    Case pieces: Greco-Roman and Egyptian motifs; inlay, ormolu mounts; marble tops; round columns, pilasters; mirrored backs; scroll feet
    Seating pieces: straight backs, latticework; caned seats; sabre legs, tapered turned legs, flared turned legs; parcel gilt, ebonizing

Style: George IV
Dating: 1820-30
Major Wood(s): Mahogany, mahogany veneer and rosewood
General Characteristics: Continuation of Regency designs

Style: William IV
Dating: 1830-37
Major Wood(s): Mahogany, mahogany veneer
General Characteristics:
    Case pieces: rectilinear; brass mounts, grillwork; carved moldings; plinth bases
    Seating pieces: rectangular backs; carved straight crestrails; acanthus, animal carving; carved cabriole legs; paw feet

Style: Victorian
Dating: 1837-1901
Major Wood(s): Black walnut, mahogany, veneers and rosewood
General Characteristics:
  Case pieces: applied floral carving; surmounting mirrors, drawers, candle shelves; marble tops
  Seating pieces: high-relief carved crestrails; floral and fruit carving; balloon backs, oval backs; upholstered seats, backs; spool, spiral turnings; cabriole legs, fluted tapered legs; scrolled feet

Style: Edwardian
Dating: 1901-10
Major Wood(s): Mahogany, mahogany veneer and satinwood
General Characteristics: Neo-Classical motifs and revivals of earlier 18th century and early 19th century styles.

Let Krause Satisfy Your Other Collecting Interests

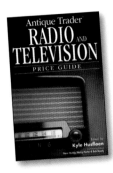